Packaging Sustainability

Tools, Systems, and Strategies for Innovative Package Design

Wendy Jedlička, CPP

With:

Dr. Elise L. Amel, Dr. Dayna Baumeister, Arlene Birt,
Jeremy Faludi, Terry Gips, Fred Haberman,
Dan Halsey, Garth Hickle, Dr. Christie Manning,
Tim McGee, Curt McNamara, Jacquelyn Ottman,
Dennis Salazar, Dr. Pamela Smith, Dion Zuess

Environmental Paper Network, Eureka Recycling,
Package Design Magazine, Packaging Strategies,
Sustainable Packaging Coalition℠

Additional contributions by:
Amelia McNamara, John Moes, Tom Nelson,
Holly Robbins, Sharon Sudman

WILEY

John Wiley & Sons, Inc.

**Library of Congress
Cataloging-in-Publication Data:**

Jedlicka, Wendy

Packaging sustainability : tools, systems and strategies for innovative package design / Wendy Jedlicka.

  p. cm.

Includes bibliographical references and index.

ISBN 978-0-470-24669-6 (pbk.)

1. Packaging. I. Title.

TS158 .J44

688.8—dc22   2008013183

Printed in the United States of America

10 9 8 7 6 5 4 3 2 1

Contents

Introduction   **_vii_**

HOW TO USE THIS BOOK   ix
THE MAKING OF THIS BOOK   x
GIVING THANKS   xi
BIOGRAPHIES   xi

CHAPTER ①
Taking the First Step   **_1_**

Consumption and Renewal   **2**
Choices, Choices, Choices   **2**
  Underconsumption   4
  Overconsumption   5
  Restorative Consumption   6
Nearly All New Products Fail   **8**
What Does Change Look Like?   **9**
  What Is Sustainability?   10
  What Sustainability Is Not   10
  Tearing Down the Tower of Babble   11
  The Next Great Era of Design   12
  How to Avoid Change   14
  It's the Other Guy's Problem   16
Taking Responsibility and Thriving   **17**
  Precautionary Principle   17
  The Hanover Principles   20
  Kyosei   21
  The Caux Round Table   22
  The Triple Bottom Line   24

  Transparency and Honesty   **28**
  Ceres   **28**
A Taste of Things to Come   **32**
Making the Business Case   **32**
Packaging and Sustainability   **34**

CHAPTER ②
The Mechanics of Human Behavior **41**

Chapter Themes   **42**
  Sustainability   42
  Attention   42
  Zone of Acceptability   42
  Expression of Individuality   42
Assumptions vs. Data   **42**
Inside the Consumer   **43**
  What's in Our Hearts
    (Or How We Don't Think)   43
  What's in Our Minds
    (Or How We Do Think)   45
  Other People (Or How Sensitive
    We Are to Social Cues)   50
  Barriers to Action   55
The Nitty Gritty of Collecting Data   **57**
Wrapping It Up   **58**

CHAPTER ③
Marketing and Truth   **61**

The Consumer Relationship   **62**
  Empowering the Consumer   62
  Does the Selling Price Really Tell the Story?   63
  Packaging Can Only Make Them Buy Once   64
  Brand Loyalty   65
Ethics-Based Marketing and Business   **65**
  Social Justice and Marketing   66
  Co-op America's Basics of Fair Trade   70

Package as Bridge or Barrier — 71
  What Is "Good" vs. "Great" Packaging? — 71
  Encouraging Consumer Choice — 72

Thing or Service? — 74

Eco-Labeling and Eco-Marketing Claims — 74
  Nutrition Facts Panel for a Healthier Planet — 75
  Carbon Labeling — 77

Speaking the Truth, and Meaning It — 78
  TerraChoice: Six Sins of Greenwashing — 82
  FTC Green Guides — 83

How to Get It Right — 99
  What Is "Need"? — 99
  Who Are the People Buying? — 99
  Moving Target — 102
  Timing Is Everything — 103

The Package/Product Team — 103

How to Create an Eco-Package in Three Easy Steps — 104

CHAPTER ④
Laws and Economics — 107

The Changing Landscape: Laws and Regulations — 108
  Producer Responsibility — 108
  Why Producer Responsibility for Packaging? — 110
  Producer Responsibility in the European Union — 111

Regulations Around the Globe — 112
  Producer Responsibility in the United States — 112
  Producer Responsibility in Asia — 112
  Producer Responsibility in Canada — 113
  Producer Responsibility in Australia — 114

A Path Forward — 115

Unwrapping Global Packaging: Trade and Policy — 116
  The Scope of Globalization in Packaging — 116
  The Global Magnitude of Packaging — 117
  The Global Supply Chain and Materials Markets — 117
  The Global Purposes of Packaging — 117
  The Global Laws Affecting Packaging — 118

The Scope of Global Trade in Packaging — 119
  Trade in Manufactured Packaging — 119
  Trade in Packaging Materials — 123
  Trade in Waste Materials — 123
  Summary of Facts on Packaging Trade — 125

The Scope of Environmental Impact of Packaging — 126
  The Economics of Environmental Externalities — 126
  The Role of Government Policy — 126
  Optimal Policies — 127

Looking Forward — 129

CHAPTER ⑤
Systems Thinking — 133

The Systems View — 134
  Universal Principles — 135

Bridging the Gap with Systems — 139
  Systems Properties — 140

Systems and Design — 140

Package as a System — 141

Adapt to the Environment — 142

Properties of Systems — 143
  Boundary — 143
  Function — 146
  Feedback and Interchange — 148
  Levels — 149

Taking Advantage of the Systems View — 150
  The Package/Product Team — 151
  Team Learning and Decision Making — 151
  Design Language — 154
  Using Systems Thinking in the Design Process — 157

Biomimicry — 158
  Contain — 158
  Protect — 161
  Communicate — 164
  Mimicking Deep Principles — 166
  Go Outside! — 168

Permaculture Principles in Design 169
    Passive Permaculture Principles 170
    Proactive Measures 172
    Progressive Measures 174

Change Management 177

Technical Approaches 181
    Industrial Ecology 181
    Design Practice 183
    ISO 14000 184
    Life Is Cycles 185
    The Eco-costs Approach 187

Systems Approaches 189
    The Sustainable Packaging Coalition[SM] 189
    The SPC Approach 191
    Definition of Sustainable Packaging 191
    Design Guidelines from the SPC 192
    The Natural Step Framework 197

The Next Level in the Picture 200
    o2's 5Rs of Great Design 201
    The Wal-Mart 7Rs 204
    Cradle to Cradle[SM] 205
    Product Design Perspectives 212

Your Nearest Advantage May Be Behind You 215

Innovation Heuristics 217
    Design Rules 217
    The Basics of Innovation 217
    Ecological Design Principles 218
    Design Mindfulness (Thackara) 219
    Design Approaches 220

CHAPTER ⑥
Materials and Processes 223

Paper or Plastic? Neither! 224

What Are We Trashing? 226

Paper 229
    Wood-Based Paper 229
    Why What's In Your Paper Matters 230

Alternative Papers 232

Plastics 235
    Nonrenewable Plastics 235
    Biobased/Renewable Plastics 237

Metals 243
    Aluminum 243
    Steel 243
    If It Can't Be Grown, It Must Be Mined 244

Glass 251

Energy Changes Everything 252
    Understanding Energy 254
    Carbon Accounting 255

Printing 257

The Wonderful World of Waste 261
    The Economic and Environmental
       Benefits of Recycling 261
    Greenhouse Gas Emissions and Waste 262

CHAPTER ⑦
Innovation Toolbox 267

Eco-Packaging In Three Easy Steps 268

Definition of Sustainable Packaging 268

**Consumer's Shopping List for
    Positive Change** 269

Innovation Heuristics 269

Fair Trade Essentials 275

**Overview of Environmental
    Marketing Claims** 276

Eco Seals, Certifications, and Claims 277

Materials Choices at a Glance 283

Eco-Resources at a Glance 284

Glossary of Basic Packaging Terminology 288

SELECT BIBLIOGRAPHY 320

NOTES BY CHAPTER 324

INDEX 336

Introduction

Wendy Jedlička, CPP

o2 International Network for Sustainable Design

Sustainability isn't hard; it's just not simple.

Approaching problems the same way they always have, companies seem to think they have done their part if they can just locate what could be referred to as the "happy list" of magically green materials. They then pick something off the menu for their project and check "get eco" off their to-do list. Any eco-practitioner worth his or her salt getting a request for such a list, will ask if the inquirer understands systems thinking concepts, or if their company has a training program in place to help the people using the list figure out what will actually *be* eco

Photo: Salazar Packaging, Inc.
Photographer: Don Hinds

for their applications. The answer will almost always be, "No, we don't do any of that; we just want the list."

In theory, picking an eco-material is better than a non-eco one. Very rich lists can be found at packagedesignmag.com and ecopackaging.net. But these are only simple indexes of companies that offer materials, goods, or services with some level of sustainability/eco/green as part of their point of difference. Some of these companies are third-party certified; some are not.

Choosing to be granola for the Minneapolis, MN market. Birchwood Cafe's *Breakfast in Heaven* Granola To-Go.

If one doesn't know why a material is eco, how to apply its use correctly, or even if it actually is eco, taking a typically shallow replacement approach can result in environmental and economic impacts far worse than the thing being replaced.

In addition to applying eco-materials properly, clients are looking to their designers to help them meet new, more restrictive legislation, new initiatives from their own clients (Wal-Mart's scorecard, for example), and a whole host of hot-button issues. These are problems much bigger than picking a recycled paper and calling it good, requiring a careful look at the system of the design, and not just a substrate or two.

The classic request of packaging is only that it protect, inform, and sell. Eco-packaging must do all that but also have minimal eco-impact, be well targeted, be a team player, plan for end of life, and plan for the next life. One might say, "Well, mainstream packaging is supposed to do all that," and you'd be right. But in many markets, the United States in particular, until recently no one's required it to do all that — leaving many of those who do packaging scrambling to figure out how to meet new directives.

One thing that never fails to get eco-practitioners to smile is when very earnest people say, "We want to see pictures of your really cutting edge eco-packaging examples." Most long standing eco-practitioners will reply, "If I've done my job right, you really can't tell the difference, unless that look was the goal." The realities of sustainable packaging are, if a designer chooses to play the granola-look card, that was done completely as a strategic marketing move. In fact, very eco-looking packages may not be eco at all. The real difference between an eco-package and an un-eco one is what the package has embodied, from variables and inputs weighed in the concept phase, through conversion and fulfillment, to the shelf and through the user's hands, and finally through to rebirth — not what it looks like.

As companies adopt sustainability practices for their business model, most quickly find opportunities to leverage whole new profit avenues without changing their packaging at all. When they choose to also visibly change their packaging, that's a strategic decision, with all the marketing benefits that go with communicating that particular message.

To understand sustainable packaging, you must tell an honest story, leverage consumer triggers for the greater good, understand the economic impacts of design choices, and fit how all of that works in a sustainability context. Without that depth of backgrounding, the designer is just decorating another box and calling it "green."

How to Use This Book

One of the author's requirements for doing this book was that the question of sustainable design related to packaging needed to be approached in a completely new way, not only looking at systems thinking in general terms, but looking deeply into the very soul of packaging and its stakeholders. In addition, rather than the outpouring of a single voice, the book needed to be a collection of many voices. This chorus of voices allows people new to sustainable design to experience the broad range of contributions the pioneers of sustainability and today's eco-practitioners draw from. Readers find they can hit the ground running, as they race to catch up with the overwhelming flow of sustainability information coming out daily.

This book is designed to help people clearly see the big picture, what all that means for design, how all the various groups that serve packaging connect and interact — all in a sustainability context.

For those in academia, this book is representative of the core approach of Minneapolis College of Art and Design's (MCAD) Sustainable Design Certificate Program (mcad.edu/sustainable). Most of the key contributors to this book are Sustainable Design Certificate faculty, who welcome the opportunity to open a dialogue about higher education's roll and responsibility in reshaping industry. Taking a holistic approach, MCAD's Sustainable Design Certificate students are taught how to think in sustainability terms, and empower the students to be fellow agents for positive change, fueling true innovation.

Just as one should not pick from a "happy list" of eco-materials and consider the job done, this book is not a complete one-size-fits-all tome. It is a comprehensive guide to sustainability approaches applied to design and business employed by today's sustainability leaders and eco-practitioners using packaging as the industry where examples are drawn from. The goal of this book is to show the reader not only sustainability ideas, but the logic behind them. It is designed to provide the reader with the tools needed to sift through the ever-changing barrage of materials, services, regulations, and mandates that would render any book taking an old-school "replacement approach" out of date.

This book is meant to be used as a portal to works by the original content providers participating, or referred to, as it takes the reader through the process, touching on inputs that make up what packaging is really about. By seeing how those works fit together into the bigger picture, and how they flow together and overlap, identifying quality resources that will address a company's specific needs becomes much easier.

To get an even more detailed picture, it is suggested the reader expand their library to include, *The Wiley Encyclopedia of Packaging Technology,* a great resource partner to *Packaging Sustainability.*

Created as a general industry overview of packaging terms and processes, the book is an essential tool for understanding packaging terms, common materials, structures, processes, technologies, and the related disciplines that serve the packaging industry.

Sustainable packaging options today are growing faster than any one person can keep up with. It is highly recommended that packaging professionals subscribe to one or more of the materials and regulations information update services mentioned throughout this book, and identified through resources like: ecopackaging.net, packstrat.com, and packagedesignmag.com. Additionally, the Sustainable Packaging Coalition^{SM} provides services for members not available through other distribution channels. In collecting cases and examples for this book, it became apparent we would not be able to fit in all of the great work from both past and current production cycles. This in no way is a comment on the value of the work not included. This book is not a portfolio collection of the most eco-packaging ever produced. Examples and cases were selected from companies doing new solutions for their category, and who were willing to offer readers a deeper look at their processes and design logic.

Some of the examples showcased in this book are very good; some are just a solid step in the right direction. But in all cases the companies contributing were willing to talk about the issues they weighed to arrive at their solution. We are still in the early stages of this paradigm shift, and many people are shy about helping to train their competition. Eco-leaders, though, have recognized that the greatest benefits come when ideas and efforts, successes as well as failures, are shared openly. The louder you are they've found, the greater the rewards, and the stronger your market position — leaving competitors scrambling for the me-too slot — which itself creates a positive-shift ripple effect throughout their whole industry.

The Making of This Book

Wiley Publishing is committed to continuous reevaluation of its environmental impacts and partnering with stakeholders to help achieve ever-improving performance. The paper for this book is Rolland Enviro100, manufactured by Cascades Fine Papers Group. It's made from 100 percent post-consumer fiber, and processed chlorine free. Cascades' Rolland Enviro100 is a Chlorine Free Products Association endorsed product.

According to Cascades, for every ton of Rolland Enviro100 Book paper used instead of traditionally processed virgin pulp source paper, the environment is served in the following ways:

— 17 mature trees saved,

— 6.9 lbs. waterborne waste generation avoided,

— 10,196 gal. waterflow saved,

— 2,098 lbs. atmospheric emissions eliminated,

— 1,081 lbs. solid waste reduced,

— 2,478 cu. ft. natural gas use eliminated by using biogas.

Giving Thanks

This book features the work and ideas of many current eco-practitioners. But we all stand on the shoulders of giants — those who walked tirelessly forward in spite of the obstacles set before them. Today we are empowered to make their dreams a reality.

We offer this work as a tribute to the example they set and whose work we are building on. For making our work possible, we would like to extend our deepest gratitude to:

R. Buckminster Fuller, Victor Papanak, David Orr, Sim Van der Ryn, Fritjof Capra, E. F. Schumacher, Karl-Henrik Robèrt, Janine Benyus, Paul Hawken, Hunter Lovins, Amory Lovins, John Thackara, J. I. and Robert Rodale, and of course Rachel Carson.

We are called to be architects of the future, not its victims.

R. Buckminster Fuller

Biographies

Contributing Authors

Wendy Jedlička, CPP
Contributing Editor / Creative Contributor

An IoPP Certified Packaging Professional, Jedlička is president of Jedlička Design Ltd. (jedlicka.com), with over twenty years of packaging and print experience, coupled with eleven years as a retail industry insider. As a design and business strategy vendor, she has served clients such as 3M, Target, Hormel, Anchor Hocking, and Toro. Jedlička writes the regular feature "Sustainability Update" for *Package Design Magazine*, and is regularly tapped to speak on eco-packaging and print design, as well as a variety of sustainable design and business issues.

As part of her professional outreach efforts, Jedlička is the United States co-coordinator for the o2 International Network for Sustainable Design (o2.org) as well as Upper Midwest chapter chair (o2umw.org). Working to change minds in higher education, Jedlička is program development team member and faculty for the groundbreaking Sustainable Design Certificate Program at Minneapolis College of Art and Design (MCAD). (mcad.edu/sustainable)

Attracted to packaging since learning origami at age eight, Jedlička started her formal art training through the Minneapolis Society of Fine Arts experimental youth art program, continuing through high school at Parsons School of Design and the Art Students League of New York. She completed her bachelor's degree in graphic and industrial design at the University of Bridgeport, and her master's degree in international management with a certificate in marketing at the University of St. Thomas.

Dr. Elise L. Amel

Elise L. Amel has a Ph.D. in industrial-organizational psychology from Purdue University and has been teaching at the University of St. Thomas since 1997. She teaches general psychology, research methods, and industrial-organizational psychology. She has consulted for local industry regarding improving job satisfaction, as well as selection, training, and performance appraisal systems. Her current research addresses variables believed to be related to sustainable behavior. Together with Christie Manning and Britain Scott she has worked with governmental (Minnesota Pollution Control Agency), non-profits (e.g., myCV.com), and business organizations (e.g., Peace Coffee) to assess and maximize the attractiveness and likelihood of sustainable behavior. Their work has also been highlighted in the community (e.g., Bell Museum's Café Scientifique) and the media (e.g., The Rake). Dr. Amel has appeared as a featured panelist on the Minnesota Public Radio program, In the Loop, to discuss psychology and sustainability.

Dr. Dayna Baumeister

Dayna Baumeister, Ph.D. is an educator, researcher, design consultant, and co-founder of the Biomimicry Guild (biomimicryguild.com). She holds degrees in marine biology and resource conservation, and a Ph.D. in organismic biology and ecology. Dr. Baumeister has worked in the field of biomimicry since 1998, unifying her lifelong passions for biology, applied natural history, and sharing the wonders of nature. Dr. Baumeister has introduced the idea of biomimicry — nature as model, measure, and mentor — to thousands of designers, business managers, and engineers around the country; she brings her skills as a systems thinker and organic communicator to her dynamic workshops, presentations, seminars, and exhibits.

Dr. Baumeister finds sustenance as a gardener, hunter, yoga instructor, and naturalist. She lives with her family in the foothills of the rugged Rocky Mountain Front in Montana. Dr. Baumeister is also faculty for MCAD's Sustainable Design Certificate Program.

Arlene Birt

Arlene Birt (arlenebirt.com) is a visual storyteller at Haberman & Associates, Modern Storytellers for Media + Marketing, a public relations and marketing agency dedicated to telling the stories of pioneers who change the way business is done or make the world a better place. She created Background Stories, her master's thesis, while studying in the Netherlands on a Fulbright grant. Birt is also faculty for MCAD's Sustainable Design Certificate Program and a member of the o2 International Network for Sustainable Design.

Jeremy Faludi

Jeremy Faludi (faludidesign.com) is a product designer and researcher specializing in eco-design. He has consulted for Rocky Mountain Institute, Janine Benyus, Chorus Motors, ExBiblio, Lawrence Berkeley National Labs, and others. He was a finalist in the 2007 California Cleantech Open competition and is a juror for Dell's ReGeneration contest on green computing. A bicycle he helped design appeared in the Cooper-Hewitt National Design Museum's exhibit *Design for the other 90%*.

In addition to his design work, Faludi is a contributing editor to worldchanging.com and is one of the many authors of *Worldchanging: A User's Guide for the 21st Century.* His articles have appeared in *GreenBiz, Package Design Magazine*, Samsung's *DigitALL* magazine, and the Secretariat of the Commonwealth of Nations's newsletter

Commonwealth Today. He also speaks at conferences, schools, and businesses around the world. Faludi is active in the o2 International Network for Sustainable Design, serving the o2 Bay Area and Cascadia groups. Faludi is also faculty for MCAD's Sustainable Design Certificate Program, and is a lecturer in the product design program at Stanford University.

Terry Gips

Terry Gips is a widely published ecologist, agricultural economist, sustainability consultant, certified independent Natural Step Framework Instructor, speaker, author (*Breaking the Pesticide Habit* and *The Humane Consumer and Producer Guide*), and faculty for MCAD's Sustainable Design Certificate Program.

Gips, president of Sustainability Associates, works with business, government, and organizations to save money, improve performance, and become socially and environmentally responsible. (sustainabilityassoc.com)

Previously, Gips served as Aveda Corporation's director of ecological affairs and sustainability, Cargill grain merchant and assistant to the chief economist, congressional and White House aide, Wall Street brokerage assistant, and co-founder and director of the Cooperative Extension Sacramento Community Garden Program.

Gips volunteers as the co-founder and president of the Alliance for Sustainability (afors.org). As a founding board member of Ceres (ceres.org), he helped develop the *Ceres Principles for Corporate Environmental Responsibility*. He completed his M.S. in agricultural and applied economics at UC Davis and an M.B.A. at the Yale School of Management.

Fred Haberman

As the co-founder and CEO of Haberman & Associates (modernstorytellers.com), Fred Haberman specializes in brand and cause-related storytelling. He has counseled hundreds of companies on how to create emotional connections between their brands and their customers to generate brand awareness, sales, and positive change.

Dan Halsey

Daniel Halsey (Halsey1.com) is a certified permaculture designer, graphic designer, and food photographer. He lives with his wife Ginny in South Woods of Spring Lake, Minnesota, a twenty-five-acre wetland with an edible forest garden installed by the Twin Cities Permaculture Collaborative. He is working on a degree in temperate climate polyculture design at the University of Minnesota, and is faculty for MCAD's Sustainable Design Certificate Program, and his articles have appeared in *Package Design Magazine*.

Garth Hickle

Garth T. Hickle is the product stewardship team leader with the Minnesota Pollution Control Agency (MPCA). He has been with the MPCA since 1996, working on product stewardship for various products including packaging, electronics, and carpet. He has received fellowships from the Bush Foundation and the American-Scandinavian Foundation to study product policy in the European Union. He sits on the board of directors for the Carpet America Recovery Effort (CARE) and the board of advisors for the Electronic Product Environmental Assessment Tool (EPEAT). He has published articles on products policy in *The Environmental Forum, Resource Recycling, Waste Management World, Pollution*

Prevention Review, Environmental Quality Management, and *Package Design Magazine.* Hickle is also faculty for MCAD's Sustainable Design Certificate Program, teaching classes on product policy and sustainable development. He holds a B.A. from the College of Wooster, an M.S.E.L. from Vermont Law School, and an M.P.A. from Hamline University.

Tim McGee

Tim McGee is a trained interdisciplinary biologist with an interest in applying biological know-how to industrial systems. McGee obtained his undergraduate degree in biology from Colby College, where he focused on utilizing the tools of computer science to investigate natural phenomena. McGee's graduate research at the University of California Santa Barbara further refined his interest in sustainable systems by investigating the exciting world of biological molecular materials science, learning how life makes materials.

McGee is a regular contributor to TreeHugger.com, one of the leading media outlets dedicated to driving sustainability mainstream. McGee's wealth of experience in biological research, industry, and design enables him to act as a biologist at the Design Table with the Biomimicry Guild, where he helps clients explore how the natural world can help their company innovate and create a sustainable future.

Curt McNamara, P.E.

Curt McNamara, P.E. (c.mcnamara@ieee.org), is a practicing designer with twenty years experience in commercial and industrial markets. He is a scholar of R. Buckminster Fuller and authored the entry on Fuller in the *UNESCO Encyclopedia of Life Support Systems,* and his articles have appeared in *Package*

Design Magazine. An active Institute of Electrical and Electronic Engineers member, McNamara received the IEEE Millennium Medal in 2000 for his ongoing work in education. McNamara is a board member and serves as the engineering liaison for the o2-USA/Upper Midwest chapter of the o2 International Network for Sustainable Design. McNamara is also faculty and program development team member for MCAD's Sustainable Design Certificate Program.

Dr. Christie Manning

Christie Manning has a Ph.D. in cognitive and biological psychology from the University of Minnesota. She is currently a visiting assistant professor of environmental studies at Macalester College in St. Paul, Minnesota. Her research examines the cognitive and other psychological factors that influence environmentally relevant behavior choices. She is particularly interested in environmental communication and the role of framing in conveying information about environment and sustainability. Together with her colleagues Elise Amel and Britain Scott she is helping local "green" events broaden their impact through well-crafted messages and a better understanding of the barriers that people face in trying to live a more sustainable life.

Jacquelyn Ottman

Since 1989, Jacquelyn Ottman has been helping businesses find competitive advantage through green marketing and eco-innovation. President and founder of J. Ottman Consulting, Inc., she advised clients such as IBM, Interface, DuPont, and the US EPA's Energy Star® label.

A popular speaker at industry conferences around the world, Ottman authored *Green Marketing: Opportunity for Innovation*, 2nd edition, described by the American Marketing Association as the "definitive work on the subject." For seven years, she chaired the special Edison Awards for Environmental Achievement jury.

Her firm is the principal organizer of Design:Green, a pioneering eco-design educational initiative endorsed by the Industrial Designers Society of America. (designgreen.org)

A graduate of Smith College, Ottman also attended the NYU Graduate School of Business. She holds a certificate from the Creative Education Foundation in facilitating the Osborn Parnes Creative Problem Solving Process. Ottman is also faculty for MCAD's Sustainable Design Certificate Program, and a longtime member of the o2 International Network for Sustainable Design.

Dennis Salazar

Dennis Salazar is founder and president of Salazar Packaging (salazarpackaging.com). Salazar has combined passion with over thirty years of industry experience, and has been actively sharing his insight in the area of packaging sustainability through numerous print and internet outlets, including SustainableIsGood.com, GreenBiz.com, TreeHugger.com, *Package Design Magazine*, and *Contract Packaging* magazine.

Dr. Pamela Smith

Pamela J. Smith, Ph.D., is a faculty member in the department of applied economics at the University of Minnesota. Her specializations include international economics and econometrics (statistics). (http://www.apec.umn.edu/Pamela_Smith.html) Dr. Smith is also faculty for MCAD's Sustainable Design Certificate Program, and her articles have appeared in *Package Design Magazine*.

Dion Zuess

With over a decade of design experience in eco-design and visual communications, Dion Zuess is a green advocate who believes designers have a unique opportunity to integrate talent, communication strategies, and social responsibility. Her studio, ecoLingo, is dedicated to green design, blending design ecology, style, and sustainability. The award-winning studio (ecolingo.com) is an approved member of Co-op America's Green Business Network, as well as a member of 1% For The Planet, Design Can Change, The Designers Accord, and the o2 International Network for Sustainable Design.

Her work has been published in a variety of publications, including *Package Design Magazine*, and she is frequently invited to be a guest speaker, guest teacher, mentor, portfolio reviewer, writer, and consultant. In 2006, Zuess received an American Graphic Design Award for excellence in communication from *Graphic Design: USA*. In 2007, she was nominated as a candidate for a Communications Design Award as part of the prestigious Smithsonian Cooper-Hewitt National Design Museum's National Design Awards program. Zuess is also faculty for MCAD's Sustainable Design Certificate Program.

When we heal the earth, we heal ourselves.

David Orr

Contributing Groups

Environmental Paper Network

Environmental Paper Network is a diverse group of over 100 nonprofit social and environmental organizations joined together to achieve the Common Vision for the Transformation of the Pulp and Paper Industry. The EPN provides information, tools, events, and strategic collaboration to advance a more socially and environmentally responsible paper industry.

Eureka Recycling

Eureka Recycling is one of the largest nonprofit recyclers in the United States and an industry leader demonstrating the best waste reduction and recycling practices not only for the Twin Cities metro area, but for the nation. For over fifteen years, Eureka Recycling has been St. Paul's nonprofit recycler. Under a long-term contract with the city, Eureka Recycling provides recycling services to St. Paul's homes and apartments. In addition, Eureka Recycling is a leader in waste reduction education and advocacy. (EurekaRecycling.org)

Package Design Magazine

Package Design Magazine delivers the news and information professionalss need to stay on top of the latest innovations and technology driving industry.

Sustainability is driving changes in industry to protect the earth and find efficient solutions. In addition to their monthly feature column, "Sustainability Update," *Package Design*'s year-end issue is devoted to the latest sustainable materials, initiatives, processes, and advances affecting the packaging industry. (packagedesignmag.com)

Packaging Strategies

Packaging Strategies (packstrat.com) is a leading provider of unbiased insights, analysis, and perspectives on the business and technologies of packaging. Besides producing a twice-monthly newsletter read by top packaging executives in thirty-seven countries. Packaging Strategies also produces world-class conferences, including the Sustainable Packaging Forum, the only event of its kind to earn the official endorsement of the Sustainable Packaging Coalition[SM] and GreenBlue[SM] for four consecutive years. Packaging Strategies directs the content and publishes multi-client reports covering the gamut of packaging business, technology, and trends topics, including the Sustainability & Sustainable Packaging series, authored by Packaging & Technology Integrated Solutions. Packaging Strategies is led by David Luttenberger, CPP, an eighteen-year packaging industry veteran.

Sustainable Packaging Coalition

The Sustainable Packaging Coalition[SM] (SPC) is an industry working group dedicated to creating and implementing sustainable packaging systems. Through informed design practice, supply chain collaboration, education, and innovation, the coalition strives to transform packaging into a system that encourages an economically prosperous and sustainable flow of materials, creating lasting value for present and future generations. (SustainablePackaging.org)

The Sustainable Packaging Coalition is a project of GreenBlue,[SM] a nonprofit, 501(c) 3 tax-exempt institute committed to sustainability by design. (GreenBlue.org)

Creative Contributors

Amelia McNamara
Illustrations

Amelia McNamara is a student at Macalester College in St. Paul, Minnesota. Since leaving a design program in the University of Cincinnati's college of Design, Architecture, Art, and Planning, she has continued to balance her left and right brains with a double major in English and mathematics. She continues to be passionately interested in graphic and lighting design.

Tom Nelson
Product photography

Tom Nelson (tnphoto.com) earned his bachelor's degree in political science from Macalester College in St. Paul, Minnesota. An Upper Midwest native, Nelson has traveled extensively around the world, adding to an already impressive catalog of both captured and created photographic art. Nelson is a board member and serves as the photo industry liaison for o2-USA/Upper Midwest.

Sharon Sudman
Book design

Sharon Sudman (ImageSpigot.com) has been working in graphics and packaging for over thirty years. Her award-winning work has been part of our daily lives. Currently principal of her own firm, Image Spigot, she works with commercial clients as well as nonprofit groups. Her passion is in advocacy work for peace, justice, and sustainability. She is also active with a variety of groups working to effect meaningful change.

Additional Contributions

Holly Robbins

Holly Robbins is currently a creative manager for Target Corporation. She is a graduate of the design program at the University of Wisconsin-Stout. She also studied graphic design and art metals in Hildesheim, Germany at the Fachhochschule Hildesheim/Holzminden. In 1994, Robbins, with partner John Moes, founded Studio Flux, a boutique design firm focused on ecologicall-sustainable design and quality, award-winning work. Her work has appeared in *Print*, *American Corporate Identity*, American Graphic Design Awards, *How*, and AIGA shows, including two AIGA national Greening of Design and five AIGA/Minnesota Green Leaf awards.

Robbins has written articles and lectured on the subject of eco-design and helped develop guidelines for designing more sustainably, including the *GreenBlue SPC Design Guidelines for Sustainable Packaging* and AIGA Green Leaf award criteria. She also is a representative to the Sustainable Packaging Coalition (SPC) on behalf of Target and contributes to themightyodo.com, a collaborative of creatives seeking to reconnect people to nature though design. Robbins is also a program development team member and faculty for Minneapolis College of Art and Design's Sustainable Design Certificate Program.

John Moes

John Moes is a graphic designer and art director specializing in eco-graphic design. He is also a founding member of Organic Design Operatives (ODO), a collaborative of like-minded creatives seeking to reconnect people with Nature via design. His clients include Target Corporation and

Ecoenvelopes. In 1994, Moes, along with partner Holly Robbins, co-founded Studio Flux, one of the first eco-minded graphic design firms. He has written articles on sustainable design, contributed to the AIGA Green Leaf award criteria, and created the ODO Eco-Design Toolkit specifically aimed at graphic designers. (themightyodo.com)

Moes was educated in the design program at the University of Wisconsin-Stout. He also worked an extended stint at the well-known multidisciplinary firm Design Guys, where he designed a vast array of high-visibility projects for the likes of Target, Virgin, Neenah Paper and Apple. Over the years he has received many honors for his work, including recognition from AIGA, *Communication Arts*, *Print*, *How* and IDSA. His work for Target was honored by the Smithsonian Cooper-Hewitt National Design Museum 2003 National Design Awards and 365 AIGA Annual Design Competition: Gold Certificate of Excellence. Moes is most proud of his awards for eco-minded design, which include two AIGA national Greening of Design awards and five AIGA/Minnesota Green Leaf awards. Beyond graphic design, Moes has an appreciation for the amazing design model of Nature, organic architecture and designing and building just about anything.

Eric Edelman: Bottle Whimsy

Also known as a ship in a bottle, this age-old folkcraft shows just how engrained in the culture some packaging forms can become.

Rendered in a variety of motifs, from the familiar ship to a fan carved from a single piece of wood, this modern example does not challenge the viewer to ponder the construction of the piece inside, but just how *did* the artist close that bottle?

"The world we have created is a product of our way of thinking," said Einstein. Nothing will change in the future without fundamentally new ways of thinking. This is the real work

Taking the First Step

Wendy Jedlička, CPP
Minneapolis College of Art and Design
Sustainable Design Certificate Program

With additional contributions from:
Caux Round Table, Ceres, Packaging Strategies,
Sustainable Is Good

The longest journey begins with a single step.

Lao-tzu (c 604–531 bce)

How do market forces shape the way we live, work, and even play? What are the economic lessons that can be drawn from nature? What is natural capital and how is it spent? How can we nurture the green thumb on the invisible hand? Today's eco-leaders understand the interplay between producer and consumer, governments and people, stockholders and stakeholders, humans and the environment, and how all of these things interconnect and direct what and how we create.

Pondering the Great Wall, 1986
Photo: W. Jedlička

1

Consumption and Renewal

The concept of birth > life > death is linear. It has a beginning, a middle, and an end. We view the things we surround ourselves with as having the same linear quality. Things are made, we use them, and then toss them away. But the reality is, there is no "away." Products and their packages have a life after we use them, as garbage (landfill or incineration) or feeder stock for new objects (recycling or reuse reclamation). When objects are reborn (recycled or reclaimed) and put back into the system again, this becomes circular consumption and thus imitates nature: making, using, and remaking without limit. Imagine an upwardly spiraling system where we not only refresh what we take and use, but restore what we've previously destroyed through linear consumption. To get to this level we need to start reexamining not just how we do what we do, but why we do it.

Choices, Choices, Choices

Many examples of human impact on the environment abound in both recent and ancient history. The best-known one is the fate of the Easter Islanders. This group, it has been suggested, drove themselves to extinction by their own excesses and severe lack of planning. As we consider the choices we make each day, think about too what must have been going through the mind of the Easter Islander who cut down the last tree, leaving his people no way to build, repair, or heat their homes, build or repair boats to fish (their main food source), or even get off the island. With a simple strike of his axe he sealed their collective fate.

We must hope in our lifetime, we will not be faced with this dilemma, but every choice we make each day adds or subtracts from the resources available to us tomorrow. Bad choices are accumulating like a death by a thousand cuts. Our salvation will come in much the same way, by regular people making everyday choices.

One of the most powerful avenues for impact we have is what and how we choose to consume. What we buy reveals a lot about how we frame our own impacts. Buying a perfect red apple vs. one that is kind of blemished but just as sweet and free of chemicals needed to attain that perfection, would be a great example.

Heritage Flakes by Nature's Path uses organic grains, and supports sustainable farming practices and biodiversity efforts. They also really understand their buyer.

Not only does the box illustrate an attractive product, plus key into potential buyers looking for more healthful choices and good taste, they also realize they needed to seal the deal by creating and talking about, their packaging reduction efforts. SAME NET WEIGHT, 10% LESS BOX is featured on the front. Finally, someone addressed one of the things that has been a nagging thorn in the consumer's side since boxed cereal came on the scene over 100 years ago: how to fill the box and not leave such a huge space at the top. For most people, this is one of those packaged goods annoyances that just must be endured.

On the product's side panel, Nature's Path continues the discussion of packaging reduction by providing

---

Nature's Path: Right-Sized Cereal Box

Same net product weight, 10% less box. This seemingly small redesign resulted in significant energy, water, and wood resource savings.

Same net weight,
10% less box.

 Global
Sustainability

USDA
ORGANIC

information regarding annual water savings (700,000 gallons), energy savings (500,000 kilowatts), and paperboard savings (about 1300 trees). These are serious and significant impacts all coming from what is in essence just a bit of air space. Now, along with information detailing nutrition and sustainable production practices, not only can the consumer make an educated decision about the food they eat, but about the impact of that choice. By connecting with the consumer on a deeper level, Nature's Path has armed them with the information needed to know they do have a choice — and what instinctively seemed wrong, was indeed very wrong.

As we look at the decisions we make with regard to design, in order to achieve more than simply making things less bad, we have to provide the mechanism for the consumer to participate in the pursuit of good.

Like Nature's Path, we need to consider all of our design choices as part of a greater contract with society. As product producers, we're charged with nothing less than the health and safety of our fellow beings. Nowhere was this contract more brutally illustrated than in the case of the Tylenol murders in the early 1980s, which showed how easily our distribution system can be compromised.

At the time, Johnson & Johnson, the makers of Tylenol, were distributing their product using common and completely legal packaging technology for this product category. To their credit, Johnson & Johnson responded quickly and decisively. They not only pulled all of their products immediately from the store shelves, but became very proactive in the development of tamper-evident packaging — the norm across the pharmaceutical industry today.[1]

> ## As product producers, we're charged with nothing less than the health and safety of our fellow beings.

Underconsumption

It's odd to think of not consuming enough, but this in fact is a very real problem. Malnutrition is a form of underconsumption (not having access to enough nourishment), and so is lack of education (not taking in or being allowed access to knowledge). One might also consider lack of research and the foresight it enables a type of underconsumption (not consuming enough time to make sure what you're going to do will be smart in the long run). There are also systematic imbalances caused by underconsumption.

Deer overpopulation and subsequent overgrazing and habitat destruction are due to too few predators to help keep herds in harmony with the area that sustains them. This is a classic example of an imbalance caused by man's interference. The deer herd's health and their environment's health suffers (too many deer for a given area to support), as the deer are underconsumed because the wolves that helped keep them in healthy balance were overconsumed (hunted to near extinction).

By being aggressive about keeping forests underconsumed by small fires, as had been the standard mode of forest management for the past century, too much underbrush is allowed to build up. What had been taken care of by nature's renewal system, quickly becomes a devastating catastrophe resulting in complete ecosystem collapse. More progressive forest managers have found that working within nature's plan allows their areas to remain healthier, more diverse, and better able to recover after disturbances.

As we begin to look at our products and behavior with an eye to restore what we've been taking out of our natural systems rather than create unstable monocultures for our convenience, looking for balance becomes key. We must look at things as a system and find ways of working to maintain all elements in harmony. Yet to do this, we need to not rush to find "the" solution: one that is convenient for us at the time, but completely ignores long-term impacts.

Overconsumption

Writer Dave Tilford tackled the idea of consumption in a 2000 Sierra Club article, "Sustainable Consumption: Why Consumption Matters":

> Our cars, houses, hamburgers, televisions, sneakers, newspapers and thousands upon thousands of other consumer items come to us via chains of production that stretch around the globe. Along the length of this chain we pull raw materials from the Earth in numbers that are too big, even, to conceptualize. Tremendous volumes of natural resources are displaced and ecosystems disrupted in the uncounted extraction processes that fuel modern human existence. Constructing highways or buildings, mining for gold, drilling for oil, harvesting crops and forest products all involve reshaping natural landscapes. Some of our activities involve minor changes to the landscape. Sometimes entire mountains are moved.[2]

An ecological footprint is defined as the amount of productive land area required to sustain one human being. As most of our planet's surface is either under water or inhospitable, there are only 1.9 hectares (about 4 football fields) of productive area to support each person today (grow food, supply materials, clean our waste, and so on) but our collective ecological footprint is already 2.3 hectares. This means, given the whole of the human population's needs, we would need 1.5 Earths to live sustainably. But this assumes all resources are divided equally. The largest footprint, the biggest consumers, are US citizens, requiring 9.57 hectares each to meet their demands. This means 5 Earths would be needed if everyone in the world consumed at that rate. People in Bangladesh, on the other hand, need just 0.5 hectares, with China for the moment at 1.36 hectares.[3]

What will it look like in just a few decades? As China continues to prosper and grow, what will happen when their new population of 1.5 billion citizens demand their fair share of the pie? If the rest of the world continues to use the United States as the benchmark for success, we would need 25 Earths to meet that level of consumption. Something has to change. (Want to make it personal? Calculate your own footprint: footprintnetwork.org.)

Part of why the United States' footprint is so large has to do with trade access to more than their own account's balance of natural capital. Much of this natural capital comes from countries that have some resources but not much else from which to earn cash. These resources are quickly being sold off regardless of the long-term consequences. With such unbridled access fueling its success, North America (and the United States in particular) hasn't yet developed the deep concern needed to use those resources efficiently. After six months, 99 percent of the resources to make the things we use are converted to waste — disposed of as finished goods, but mostly as process waste.[4]

How did the United States get into this position? After WWII, the chairman of President Eisenhower's Council of Economic Advisors stated that the American economy's ultimate goal was to produce more consumer goods. In 1955 retail analyst Victor Lebow, summed up this strategy that would become the norm for the American economic system: "Our enormously productive economy... demands that we make consumption our way of life, that we convert he buying and use of goods into rituals, that we seek our spiritual satisfaction, our ego satisfaction, in consumption ...We need things consumed, burned-up, replaced and discarded at an ever accelerating rate."[5]

This is in sharp contrast to how resources and goods were viewed in preindustrial times, when moving goods around or even making them in the first place, was a really big deal. In those days, Old Country territories occupied for millennia made residents think hard about resource use. What they had around them was pretty much all there would be, so they had to figure out how to make it work. In contrast the New World was perceived as nothing but space, filled with endless vistas of trees (and a few indigenous people) in the way. Because of this seemingly limitless abundance, the New World's detachment from the realities of resource management and the lingering idea today that resources are limitless and easily obtained, compound the high level of resources demanded per output unit to meet consumption needs. Led by the West, and the United

Too many of today's products, have been allowed to remain market viable simply because they have not had to carry their true weight — their true costs for resource impacts.

States in particular, "Since 1950 alone, the world's people have consumed more goods and services than the combined total of all humans who ever walked the planet before us."[6]

Restorative Consumption

The concept of capital (money) has been understood by civilizations since it was brought into common use thousands of years ago. How much we have and how quickly we earn it has come to be the indicator of successful effort.

As we reexamine why and how we consume — looking for ways to move in a more restorative direction — how we measure our success must also evolve.

In 2003, in the first of a series of annual conferences, Brazilian statisticians got together with the ultimate aim of coming up with a globally applicable Index of "Gross National Happiness," a "Genuine Progress Index" (GPI). This measure was meant to eventually supersede the current global economic indicators embodied by a country's Gross National Product (GNP) and Gross Domestic Product (GDP).[7]

The 2005 conference focused on the topics of "profiling initiatives around the world that integrate sustainable and equitable economic development with environmental conservation, social and cultural cohesion, and good governance." If all developing countries consumed like the West, we would need several Earths to satisfy that "need." The concept of spending every dime you ever made — like using resources until they're gone — must change, or we as a species have no hope of survival.

Author Dave Tilford highlighted some of the problems with our current economic metrics in a 2000 Sierra Club article:

> In 1998, more than $100 billion was spent in the United States dealing with water, air, and noise pollution-and considered growth by the nation's GDP. That same year, criminal activity added $28 billion to the GDP through replacement of stolen goods, purchase of home security systems, increased prison building, and other necessary responses.

> By the curious standard of the GDP ... The happiest event is an earthquake or a hurricane. The most desirable habitat is a multibillion-dollar Superfund site ... It is as if a business kept a balance sheet by merely adding up all "transactions," without distinguishing between income and expenses, or between assets and liabilities.[8]

The originator of the GDP (and GNP) measure, Simon Kuznets, acknowledges these indicators were not a measure of well-being but only economic activity. Expanding on this idea in her booklet *Economic Vitality in a Transition to Sustainability*, Neva Goodwin notes:

> Qualitative improvement of goods as services determines material well-being as much or more than physical quantity of output (especially in the more developed economies).

Goodwin goes on to point out:

> It is not inherent in market systems that they will orient towards social goals. It is a half-truth that market capitalism is the best economic system yet invented. The other half of the truth is that, when markets are allowed to work as though they were self-contained systems, operating within a vacuum, they become increasingly self-destructive, because they degrade the social and environmental contexts in which they exist, and upon which they are entirely dependent.[9]

These ideas have huge implications for packaging, the backbone of today's free market system. Too many of today's packages, and the consumer goods inside, have been allowed to remain market viable simply because they have not had to carry their true weight — their true costs for resource impacts, transportation impacts (greenhouse gas loads, plus fuel extraction and refinement), human health and its economic impacts, and so on.

For an industry that exists on the sheer volume of units produced, how will producers survive when people start to ask fundamental questions like, Can we each be happy without having more and more stuff? Can we create more economic activity without creating stuff (service-based vs. manufacturing-based economy)? Can the activities we value happen without owning stuff at all? Is stuff really the problem, or is it just the way we perceive and produce stuff? And, if we're in the business of making and selling stuff, how can we key into new ways of thinking to help drive true innovation, especially when customer satisfaction is a moving target? (Want to know more? Watch Free Range Studio's *Story of Stuff* at storyofstuff.com.)

Change will come not by just thinking outside the box, but by throwing the box out the window and looking at the space it left behind. Was it needed, will we miss it or some part of it? Was it done well? What impacts did it make? Was making it an investment in our future? Did it add to natural capital (resources each nation naturally possesses) — or was it simply a drawdown of our account? Is it possible to "create more good," as systems thinking pioneer William McDonough is often heard to ask?

With maybe a few exceptions, nobody wakes up in the morning calculating how to trash the planet. Instead, our daily lives are a series of choices, each minuscule in its individual impact. But when multiplied billions of times, day after day and year after year, the impact is enormous.

Your product in its natural environment

So far what we've been doing is "successful" because of, or in spite of, our choices. The funny part about being successful, though, is that it can turn you into a one-trick pony, creating a huge disincentive to change. Capital investment in one production system or reliance on one material type or resource flow, as is common for capital intensive packaging businesses, locks a firm into a narrow operating model. Though the rewards are great when the timing is right, there's no guarantee it can go on forever — be sustainable in the original sense of the word. But in the general scheme of evolution, the species that can adapt quickly are the ones that survive.

Nearly All New Products Fail

The old ways of popping out this week's brilliant ideas and then churning them out by the gazillion despite the consequences still works great. Or does it? The store shelves are bulging with "brilliance," each SKU fighting with their neighbor to be the lucky one to go home with the consumer. Brimming with choice, and competition, there is a generally accepted industry rule of thumb that nearly 70 to 90 percent of all new products fail. Why?

The simplest answer is that the whole selling environment is changing. Or maybe the old products aren't as good as they could be. In addition, consumers are becoming better educated. From nutrition facts, to advocacy groups, to instant information access through the Internet the days of dumping "whatever" out there (at least in the developed world) are over. Finally, there are simply more of us, not only to sell to, but to compete with. As the days of the one-trick pony draw rapidly to a close, products must not only do everything they promise, but must offer more to cut through the noise of the competition.

This concept of offering you more is no better exemplified than in sustainable products. These products are produced to not only meet a need, but depending on the product, are; healthier, more energy efficient (save you run-time dollars), more resource efficient (meaning you can make more selling units per resource unit), and have minimal impact on the waste stream compared to their less conscientious competition — making these products in general better for both the consumer and society at large.

So why aren't all products already sustainable?

As noted before, few people wake up devising ways to trash the planet. Our choices have become a death by a thousand cuts. Manufacturers, their creative service vendors, and the consumer all play a part in this scene, and fear is one of the key factors why change is slow to arrive: fear felt by the consumer that the unfamiliar product isn't as good (or what they're used to) coupled with fear of wasting their ever-stretched dollar, fear felt by the manufacturer that the consumer won't accept the new product, and fear by the manufacturer's creatives of being fired (losing the account) for stepping too far out of the norm.

Yet innovation is about embracing fear and using it to your advantage. Fear is good, and fear is a powerful motivator. In the PricewaterhouseCoopers LLP 2002 Sustainability Survey Report, respondents indicated it was fear that *not* adopting green business practices would have an adverse effect on consumer perception, and so, negatively impact their market share.

In their 2007 Cause Evolution & Environmental Survey, Cone LLC (coneinc.com) a strategy and communications agency, found of the people responding:[10]

— 93% believe companies have a responsibility to help preserve the environment

— 91% have a more positive image of a company when it is environmentally responsible

— 85% would consider switching to another company's products or services because of a company's negative corporate responsibility practices

One of the not so quietly mumbled fears within industry is that if it does not adopt sustainable business practices, they will be legislated into action any way — and certainly not in an advantageous way. The farsighted recognize this and stay ahead of this curve to be best positioned for the inevitable.

What Does Change Look Like?

So if change is inevitable, what will it look like? What is sustainability? To answer that in a packaging context, let's step back and look at the bigger picture in a systems context.

The world is a very complicated place, so it's no surprise the packaging industry is too. Add to that the business of implementing sustainability, which is asking us to literally reexamine at the way we do everything, that covers an even greater mix of industries and disciplines. Naturally, everyone will want their voices heard, and their bottom lines respected. This is such an important question — defining "What is a sustainable package?" — the Sustainable Packaging Coalition (SPC) made it their top-most priority before embarking on further efforts.

The SPC looked to create a set of goals, not mandated rules. Their general idea was that if you define the solution, the problems will take care of themselves.

The SPC criteria for a sustainable package have eight clearly defined points, but really only ask these simple questions:

— Does it make us or the planet sick? Don't do it!

— Can we use renewable resources — energy as well as materials — and then use them again without going back to virgin sources?

— Are we doing it efficiently, considering all true costs (supply chain eco-ness, materials use, loop participation, social impacts, and so on.)?

What Is Sustainability?

Goals and ideas used to define what a sustainable package or product might look like, are not a full definition of what sustainability is. So again we ask what exactly is sustainability?

The simplest answer is one that's been kicking around for some time, but was formalized in 1987 by the World Commission on Environment and Development (the Brundtland Commission):

> Sustainable Development is development that meets the needs of the present without compromising the ability of future generations to meet their own needs.[11]

This most basic idea has been at the core of human society since settled communities began. Ideas like "Don't eat your seed corn" and "Do unto others as you'd have others do unto you" form the core of sustainability thinking, are concepts that have been getting overlooked in our collective push to the future.

"Don't eat your seed corn." Applying these fundamental ideas to today, "Don't eat your seed corn" means do not use-up what you need to keep the system going. With that in mind, one can quickly pull an example from sustainable forestry practices. Traditional clear-cutting is a very efficient and low-cost way to harvest wood, treating wood like annually tilled wheat rather than what it really is, the slow-growing cornerstone of an area's survival system. Sustainable forestry practices using planting, growing, and harvesting methods that mimic nature though, have allowed for healthful and profitable ecosystems, proven over generations.

"Do unto others as you'd have others do unto you." This idea is perfectly illustrated by the new directives companies are pushing back onto their suppliers. In addition to the Wal-Mart scorecard, setting new benchmarks for packaging,[12] making the whole of the packaging industry review what they're doing, Wal-Mart also announced plans to measure the energy use and emissions of the entire supply chain for seven product categories, looking for ways to increase energy efficiency.[13] Eventually this initiative is expected to include other products (if not all) carried by the company. It would be no surprise then that other Big Box retailers as well as Consumer Goods Producers have begun implementing similar benchmarks for their vendors as well.

Put simply, companies are demanding of their suppliers the same criteria for ethics and foresight that consumers and legislators are demanding of them. Rather than simply accepting whatever a company feels like selling, retailers (and other commercial buyers) are now saying to their suppliers, "Do unto us as others would have us do unto them."

What Sustainability Is Not

Sustainability is not a tax on production. It is the end to hidden subsidies, and the beginning of assigning true costs. The best illustration of that in current terms is producer (or user) pays policies. Here, those people who use and benefit from a thing or service, pay the full load for it — from the impacts of collecting the raw materials all the way through processing at end-of-life.

In his article for the Sierra Club, "Sustainable Consumption: Why Consumption Matters" author Dave Tilford points explains:

> Over 2,500 economists, including eight Nobel Prize winners, support the notion of market-based mechanisms for environmental solutions — like carbon taxes and emission auctions, where polluters pay for the right to emit, develop, or use nature's services. In addition, though many economists are hesitant to question our current measurements of economic growth, a small but active number believe only a *true cost accounting* of economic activities will give us an accurate figure of the state of the economy.
>
> These *true cost* economists note that, as the GDP climbed 3.9 percent in 1998, the cost to taxpayers from loss of wetlands and their economic services (like water filtration) climbed 3.7 percent. From 1973 to 1993, the GDP rose by 55 percent, while real wages dropped by 3.4 percent nationally. The emerging field of "ecological economics" is beginning to question these accounting incongruities.[14]

One can easily ask, Is paying the full cost of creating, using, and disposing of a product, a tax or just the end of the free ride? What could be more fair than saying, "If you want it, you must pay?"

Sustainability is also not a trade barrier. Setting standards for health, whether applied to the product itself (e.g. banning lead paint in toys), or for our collective health (e.g. wood certified not from rainforests or old growth forests), sets the stage for eliminating goods globally that don't have our collective long-term interests at heart. Insisting trading partners not create goods in a way (or with materials) — that have been outlawed at home — is hardly an unreasonable request.

Tearing Down the Tower of Babble

Sustainability is quickly becoming the common language for business. Unlike the never ending stream of business fads that get CEOs all excited but leave middle management cringing — now management, marketing, design, engineering, production, procurement, and logistics can all sit down at the conference table and at least start a project on the same page. Though each discipline still has their own language and motivations, the conflicting babble that was the norm of conference rooms everywhere is becoming united in some sort of vision, with shared goals and ethics. Coming now from a similar place of understanding, marketers understand they need to have a clear and verifiable need for demanding oversized package facings. Designers now know, that if they want to specify a given decorative material or technique, the impacts of that choice must have sound reasons — simply being "pretty" or "different" isn't enough. Buyers, along these same lines, understand that if the packaging engineer keeps telling them to ask vendors to avoid certain materials, that guidance has serious implications that must be heeded, no matter how attractive "other stuff" that's "cheaper" may sound.

Another advantage found in using sustainability as part of a company's core ethics has been to increase employee satisfaction, thus reducing turnover. Everyone wants to feel good about the work they do.

What we are seeing the very beginning of one of the most amazing times since the dawn of the industrial revolution. Today, we have the opportunity to do nothing less than completely remake everything we do, but get it right this time, rather than just stumble into it. From the biggest buildings and whole communities, to a simple box — every new project is an opportunity for innovation. Every new innovation is an opportunity for increasing market share, or adding to natural capital (putting back natural resources we've blasted through). Every change we make in the market and how we manage resources is an opportunity to redefine the way we will live over the next hundred years and beyond. Sustainability is hope, it's exciting, and it's a complete paradigm shift. For those willing to get in there and go for it, there has never been a better time to create real, lasting, and positive change.

Even the longest journey starts with one small step. As consumers and lawmakers push for solutions, all eyes are turning to designers for answers. The time for a leisurely stroll has past — now it's time to hit the ground running.

Today, we have the opportunity to do nothing less than completely remake everything we do, but get it right this time, rather than just stumble into it.

The Next Great Era of Design

In the Western world, those at the dawn of the Industrial Revolution (1800s) found themselves coming out of an era where production was the domain of the craftsman. Ordinary objects were artful, durable, and meant to be respected for their function and value as a needed object. Everything was hard to come by, and once a thing outlived its primary function, new uses were found for its elements. Nothing was wasted. As mass-produced goods started to come on the scene, much of the decoration added by craftsman was reproduced in the factory-made product to let the consumer know that even though the thing wasn't handmade, it still had value. This era was the age of Industrial Arts.

As the pace of life accelerated we entered the era of streamlined design, form follows function — Bauhaus, prairie style, mission style, mod, pop, futuristic — smooth elegant lines, bold shapes, fun, playful, sleek, streamlined. All of these ideas made up the palette of choices in the new age of Industrial Design.

But something happened as life raced though the 1900s. As the century screamed to a close, form and function became slaves to price and quantity. Quality, aesthetics, fit and finish — all were abandoned to hit that ever lower price. But that wasn't all that was abandoned. Integrity, fair-play, stewardship — these ideals got tossed by the wayside too as companies leveraged loopholes and backdoor subsidies found in lax environmental regulations, inhuman worker laws, and artificially cheap energy that was openly subsidized or did not carry full environmental and health impact costs. Poverty became ever more entrenched for most, even as living standards improved for many, while whole eco-systems were collapsing and there was nowhere to go but down.

Thankfully, that's not the end of the story. Today we're watching the dawn of a new era. In September 2007 a sustainableday.com blog entry noted:

> The IDSA (Industrial Designers Society of America) has come full circle to openly embrace sustainable design since once supposedly banning environmental design legend Victor Papanek from the society for speaking up against the damage that the industrial design profession has done.
>
> … In this age of mass production when everything must be planned and designed, design has become the most powerful tool with which man shapes his tools and environments (and, by extension, society and himself). This demands high social and moral responsibility from the designer.

As we merged into the new era and the us vs. them ideas from the green vs. mainstream days started to find new direction, a flurry of articles came out titled "Green is Dead." If you paid the slightest bit of attention though, it was pretty obvious they were out to create shock and nothing more. Once you got into the articles, you would come to discover that green as a late twentieth-century "movement" was not dead per se, but was finally maturing from a rabble of unshaven idealism to real and actionable strategies for sustainable living and business. A place to actually be, rather than a place to simply dream about. For the working designer committed to "green" in practice, the image of the radical green proponent made selling the concepts of sustainability nearly impossible in the early days. Afraid to seem too "alternative," too "out there," and too far from the norm, clients instead continued to produce products they knew were not forward thinking simply for fear of losing market share.

Today, the concepts of sustainability — not "greenness" alone — are being integrated into business models and product strategies across the board. Rather than being legislated into action, businesses — not limited to the fringe faithful, but big corporations — are actively looking at their total impact and opportunities (triple bottom line) as triggers for increased competitive advantage, creative levers, profitability, and of course, as a tool to increase positive consumer perception and market share.

Green as we knew it needed to ascend to the next level. It was being perceived as exclusive rather than inclusive, "only for the true believers," limiting the further integration of its actionable principles.

If green were dead, as the articles claim, then its legacy is not only living on, but thriving — and moving closer to the reality green had originally hoped for. Not through calls for the immediate dismantling of capitalism — but through thousands of actions taken every day, by regular people, who recognize opportunities to make positive incremental changes. These changes are made for a variety of reasons — some ethical, some legislated, and some profit driven, but all with an eye on sustaining a positive advantage.

As with any maturing system, there will come a day when we won't have to talk about sustainability. Not because it's dead, but because it's simply just another part of good business. Governments, companies, designers and consumers are waking-up to embrace new products, services and ideas that deliver on the promises they make. Things that aren't just all surface beauty, or brief functionality, but truly innovative and useful. And, most importantly, they were created with all stakeholders in mind — including ones not destined to be born for some time yet.

So though it's not "official," and even the idea of naming a design era is a Western-centric one, plus we certainly have a long way to go before it's done, there are many that are not shy in saying the early twenty first-century is marking the next great era of design — sustainability.

How to Avoid Change

"Those of us who have spent years working towards sustainable prosperity, trying to move investors and corporate leaders to take action to address major environmental and social threats, have often felt like Sisyphus of Greek mythology — destined to spend our lives rolling a huge boulder uphill. Today, it is possible to survey our progress and feel that we have reached a point where that boulder is not going to roll back down the hill," Mindy S. Lubber, president of Ceres notes.[15]

For the change agents out there steeling themselves up for the long haul, pulling those resistant to change into the new era kicking and screaming will be a task with us for some time. Entrenched interests hate change. Ending slavery, women's suffrage, universal equal rights, were all "crazy" ideas that reactionaries swore would doom civil society if they became law. Yet society prospered, becoming better by being able to fully benefit from the talents and contributions of all their citizens. With tongue planted firmly in cheek, Dennis Salazar in a December 2007 sustainableisgood.com piece, asks antisustainability reactionaries and laggards alike to consider these helpful tips as they look for ways to dig in their heels to resist shifting to a world that benefits more than the select few:

1. Refuse to consider thoughts and opinions other than your own. If you are right and everyone else is wrong, why bother?

2. Remain glued to the status quo. After all if what you have been doing works, why take a chance on changing anything?

3. Reject any idea that even remotely sounds like compromise even though sometimes that is the best way to accomplish progress.

4. Resist any new technology unless it is absolutely perfect and supports your position. "See, I told you it wouldn't work" can be so satisfying.

5. Ridicule anyone who appears to be profiting from their work in sustainability, especially if their margin appears to exceed your own.

6. Repel anyone seeking knowledge or help. Everyone knowing as much as you do cannot be a good thing.

7. Resign yourself to the fact that the environmental problem is too large to be fixed. Seek new goals that are easier to achieve!

Glass Plus: Refill Pouches

Glass Plus made a bold step for this category by delivering all of their product's function in a light, slim form. Like a seedpod that "goes away" once its usefulness is at an end, Glass Plus created a dissolving refill pouch for their product. In keeping with their resource reduction effort, these pouches come packaged in a materials-minimal, self-standing, recyclable paperboard sleeve.

When compared to a common refill bottle, and with minimal explanation, the consumer easily understands the advantages gained from reducing materials, volume, and weight. Additional environmental savings are found as well in the reduction in the number of plastic spray bottles needed to serve repeat customers. Retailers find the form attractive too as they can fit more refill-product selling units per shelf and restocking cycle.

It's the Other Guy's Problem

One of the things heard over and over from those slow to embrace change is, "We're not changing until the other guys does, or he'll have an unfair advantage." In their defense, this is absolutely true. As long as the true and full cost of impacts for the things we make and the way we make them are not managed by enforceable law, someone is going to cash in on that hidden subsidy. To the other guy however, you are the "other guy" expected to make the first move.

The problem, of course, is that if everyone is waiting for the other guy to act, no one will. Keeping the whole system stagnant often makes the consequences much worse than if everyone had just done their bit to begin with. In game theory the idea of waiting for the other guy is part of the "prisoner's dilemma."

Two prisoners are arrested for the same crime. Put in separate cells, unable to get their stories in line, the guards try to coax each to implicate the another. If neither goes along with the guards, they will both receive a sentence of just one year. If one accepts the deal and the other keeps quiet, then the squealer goes free while the quiet one gets ten years. But if they both implicate the other, they each get five years.

If one prisoner wants to attempt to get out of responsibility and get off scot-free, he will try and put all the blame on the other guy, even though he risks the other guy doing the same. Even if each conspirator assumes the other would crack, they would still be better off implicating the other, as they would get only five years each rather than maybe get ten years alone for keeping quiet. A rational person acting in their own self-interest would always betray his fellow prisoner. Yet that puts them both in jail for five years, when, in theory, they could have had only a year each if they had both just kept quiet. In other words, if they had taken a chance and done the hard thing rather than try and stick it to the other guy, the outcome would have been better for the two as a community.

In a September 2007, *Economist* article, "Playing Games with the Planet," the author argues that the pessimistic among us would assume that the international response to climate change (and so sustainability in general) will go the way of the prisoner's dilemma. Going on to note, that rational leaders will always neglect the problem, on the grounds that others will either solve it, allowing their country to become a free rider, or let it fester, making it a doomed cause anyway. The author concludes the world would be condemned to a slow roasting even though global impacts could be averted if everyone simply cooperated and took on a share of the load no matter what.[16]

The article goes on to cite a study by Michael Liebreich of New Energy Finance, a research firm. This study draws on game theory to reach the opposite conclusion. The game in general changes dramatically, Liebreich points out, if players know they can play more than once. With this expanded option, players have an incentive to cooperate with their opponent to maintain good favor in later rounds.

Liebreich's paper cites a study by Robert Axelrod and William Hamilton, which highlights three elements for successful repeat play: First, players begin the game cooperating; second, they should deter transgressions by punishing the offender in the next round; and third, rather than hold grudges players should cooperate with misbehaving players again after imposing an appropriate punishment. This strategy made it possible to foster sustained cooperation rather than a collectively destructive cycle of sticking it to the other guy.

With this new insight into game play and its possible implications for negotiating action on sustainability issues, the article notes:

> Mr. Liebreich believes that all this holds lessons for the world's climate negotiators. Treaties on climate change, after all, are not one-offs. Indeed, the United Nations is even now trying to get its members to negotiate a successor to its existing treaty, the Kyoto Protocol, which expires in 2012. Many fear that the effort will collapse unless the laggards can be persuaded to join in. But the paper argues that rational countries will not be deterred by free-riders. They will continue to curb their emissions, while devising sanctions for those who do not.[17]

Due to the complexities involved in sustainability in general and all the details that would need to be covered to mandate specific change, establishing basic codes of ethics is becoming part of the total strategy for holding players accountable for their actions — even if specific laws do not yet exist. Codes of ethics give both players and governing bodies tools by which to judge transgressors, as well as a means to prod those who would try to get a free ride. Covering more turf than any one law, codes of ethics help pull all of the intricate and scattered threads into one more manageable guide. For the more farsighted companies, codes of ethics have become essential tools to get ahead of legislative action, allowing them more time to better manage inevitable change. They also provide benchmarks for improvement to use as a way of maintaining and increasing forward progress, and to promote (and maintain) positive consumer (or investor) perception. Codes of ethics help companies show in a tangible way: "We're not there yet, and we have a way to go, but these are our goals, and this is what we've done so far."

Taking Responsibility and Thriving

Codes of ethics for design have a long history. From ancient Babylon, the Code of Hammurabi is one of the best preserved (ca. 1760 BCE). Enacted by the sixth Babylonian king, Hammurabi, the laws are numbered 1 to 282 and are inscribed in Old Babylonian cuneiform script on the eight-foot stela.[18] Numbers 229 to 233 applying to designers state stiff penalties for compromising production integrity with an *eye for an eye* being the running theme, and *personal guarantee* meaning much more than today's platitude:

> If a builder build a house for some one, and does not construct it properly, and the house which he built fall in and kill its owner, then that builder shall be put to death.

Imagine what products would be like if these laws were applied today. Perhaps we would be a lot less far along progresswise, or maybe we would have positioned ourselves in a much more thoughtful way. Doing things more thoughtfully is the idea behind the precautionary principle.

Precautionary Principle

Many of the concepts that form the foundations of the precautionary principle have been around for some time. Long used aphorisms like "An ounce of prevention is worth a pound of cure," "Better safe than sorry," and "Do no harm," still in today's Hippocratic Oath for doctors, are accepted as part of humankind's collective "common sense."

At a 1998 meeting of scientists, lawyers, policymakers, and environmentalists at Wingspread, headquarters of the Johnson Foundation, the precautionary principle was summarized this way:

When an activity raises threats of harm to the environment or human health, precautionary measures should be taken even if some cause and effect relationships are not fully established scientifically.[19]

This idea is most often applied to impacts on human and environmental health — highly complicated systems with very unpredictable interactions. Release of radiation or toxins, massive deforestation, reduction in biodiversity or wholesale ecosystem collapse, and use of ozone depleting fluorocarbons causing globally borne adverse impacts all imply:

> ... a willingness to take action in advance of scientific proof [or] evidence of the need for the proposed action on the grounds that further delay will prove ultimately most costly to society and nature, and, in the longer term, selfish and unfair to future generations.[20]

The core of this concept embraces man's ethical responsibility to maintain the health of natural systems, and acknowledges the fallibility of humankind. In the absence of perfect understanding, an ounce of prevention (or forethought) is worth a pound of cure.

In 1982 the UN General Assembly adopted the World Charter for Nature, marking the first international endorsement of the precautionary principle.[21]

World Charter for Nature

Reaffirming the fundamental purposes of the United Nations, in particular the maintenance of international peace and security, the development of friendly relations among nations and the achievement of international cooperation in solving international problems of an economic, social, cultural, technical, intellectual or humanitarian character,

Aware that:

(a) Mankind is a part of nature and life depends on the uninterrupted functioning of natural systems which ensure the supply of energy and nutrients,

(b) Civilization is rooted in nature, which has shaped human culture and influenced all artistic and scientific achievement, and living in harmony with nature gives man the best opportunities for the development of his creativity, and for rest and recreation,

Convinced that:

(a) Every form of life is unique, warranting respect regardless of its worth to man, and, to accord other organisms such recognition, man must be guided by a moral code of action,

(b) Man can alter nature and exhaust natural resources by his action or its consequences and, therefore, must fully recognize the urgency of maintaining the stability and quality of nature and of conserving natural resources,

Persuaded that:

(a) Lasting benefits from nature depend upon the maintenance of essential ecological processes and life support systems, and upon the diversity of life forms, which are jeopardized through excessive exploitation and habitat destruction by man,

(b) The degradation of natural systems owing to excessive consumption and misuse of natural resources, as well as to failure to establish an appropriate economic order among peoples and among States, leads to the breakdown of the economic, social and political framework of civilization,

(c) Competition for scarce resources creates conflicts, whereas the conservation of nature and natural resources contributes to justice and the maintenance of peace and cannot be achieved until mankind learns to live in peace and to forsake war and armaments,

Reaffirming that man must acquire the knowledge to maintain and enhance his ability to use natural resources in a manner which ensures the preservation of the species and ecosystems for the benefit of present and future generations,

Firmly convinced of the need for appropriate measures, at the national and international, individual and collective, and private and public levels, to protect nature and promote international co-operation in this field,

Adopts, to these ends, the present World Charter for Nature, which proclaims the following principles of conservation by which all human conduct affecting nature is to be guided and judged,

General Principles

1. Nature shall be respected and its essential processes shall not be impaired.

2. The genetic viability on the earth shall not be compromised; the population levels of all life forms, wild and domesticated, must be at least sufficient for their survival, and to this end necessary habitats shall be safeguarded.

3. All areas of the earth, both land and sea, shall be subject to these principles of conservation; special protection shall be given to unique areas, to representative samples of all the different types of ecosystems, and to the habitats of rare or endangered species.

4. Ecosystems and organisms, as well as the land, marine, and atmospheric resources that are uti-lized by man, shall be managed to achieve and maintain optimum sustainable productivity, but not in such a way as to endanger the integrity of those other ecosystems or species with which they coexist.

5. Nature shall be secured against degradation caused by warfare or other hostile activities.

Over the years, the precautionary principle has been at the heart of many groups' codes of ethics, as well as government's environmental policies, especially in the European Union. The European Commission's new EU regulatory system for chemicals REACH (Registration, Evaluation and Authorisation of CHemicals) explicitly cites these principles as a basis for decision making whenever the scientific data are insufficient. Virtually unknown in the United States for years since its formal inception, it's now gaining ground. In December 2001 the New York Times Magazine listed the principle as one of the most influential ideas of the year, citing the intellectual, ethical, and policy framework the Science and Environmental Health Network (SEHN) had developed around the principle as an example.[22]

Working its way into United States public policy, in 2003 the city of San Francisco passed a precautionary principle purchasing ordinance, with Berkeley following suit in 2006.[23] Encompassing everything from cleaning supplies to computers, this ordinance requires the city to weigh the environmental and health costs of its annual purchases.

Items in the ordinance not only touch on solid sustainability principles and put them into practice, but begin to implement farther-reaching ideas like accounting for true costs (the cost of all impacts along a supply chain, not just direct impacts of a single good or service).[24]

On the corporate side, adoption of the precautionary principle can be seen in the 2006 Chemicals Strategy for The Body Shop International, a UK-based cosmetics and personal care products company:[25]

> The Body Shop is committed to creating desirable, sustainable and safe products, which are inspired by nature. Our products are based on ingredients from natural sources wherever possible, but will contain synthetic chemicals where they are necessary for the quality, safety or efficacy of products and where no suitable natural alternatives exist.
>
> The Body Shop is careful to select chemicals that have a good safety and environmental record. We will also manage the use of chemicals in a responsible manner by applying the precautionary principle. We will continuously review and update our criteria and guidelines for the development of new products, and will implement action plans for the timely and realistic phase-out of relevant chemicals from our formulations. For example, in recent years we have made the decision to move away from using phthalates, even though these ingredients are legal and considered safe for use by our industry and its regulators.
>
> We wish to be responsive to new developments and conduct regular reviews of our use of chemicals against the latest regulatory and environmental research from around the world, and engage with stakeholders and customers to help inform our strategy and action plans.
>
> We believe in open communication and communicate our position to our product suppliers, label our products in accordance with the highest standards and we will produce public annual updates on our position and progress.
>
> We do not believe in double standards. The Body Shop operates in 54 countries, and develops products and packaging to the same high standard regardless of country of sale. If we phase out or ban an ingredient, it will be phased out or banned from all The Body Shop® products in all markets.

The Hanover Principles

As complex as the planet itself, sustainability cannot be approached in a one-size-fits-all way. Different industries have different opportunities, as well as unique obstacles. Ultimately it's not important how we get there, as long as we're all moving in the same direction — and doing it sooner rather than later.

Like the precautionary principle, the Hanover Principles[26] were created to provide a guide for designers, planners, governmental officials, and all involved in setting design priorities for humanity, nature, and technology. Commissioned by the city of Hanover, Germany, as the general principles of sustainability for the 2000 World's Fair, the Hanover Principles, in consort with the Earth Charter and Blue Planet 2020 plan, are intended to serve as the basic tools for the development and improvement of humankind, and as part of a commitment to once again live as part of the earth. The principles ask us to:

1. Insist on the right of humanity and nature to coexist in a healthy, supportive, diverse, and sustainable condition.

2. Recognize interdependence. The elements of human design interact with and depend upon the natural world, with broad and diverse implications at every scale. Expand design considerations to recognize even distant effects.

3. Respect relationships between spirit and matter. Consider all aspects of human settlement including community, dwelling, industry, and trade in terms of existing and evolving connections between spiritual and material consciousness.

4. Accept responsibility for the consequences of design decisions upon human well-being, the viability of natural systems, and their right to coexist.

5. Create safe objects of long-term value. Do not burden future generations with requirements for the maintenance of vigilant administration of potential danger due to the careless creation of products, processes, or standards.

6. Eliminate the concept of waste. Evaluate and optimize the full life cycle of products and processes to approach the state of natural systems, in which there is no waste.

7. Rely on natural energy flows. Human designs should, like the living world, derive their creative force from perpetual solar income. Incorporate the energy efficiently and safely for responsible use.

8. Understand the limitations of design. No human creation lasts forever and design does not solve all problems. Those who create and plan should practice humility in the face of nature. Treat nature as a model and mentor, not an inconvenience to be evaded or controlled.

9. Seek constant improvement by the sharing of knowledge. Encourage direct and open communication between colleagues, patrons, manufacturers, and users to link long-term sustainable consideration with ethical responsibility, and reestablish the integral relationship between natural processes and human activity.

Kyosei

During most of the Edo Period (1603 to 1867) Japan closed itself off to the world, suffering no invasions but also forgoing outside trade. Due to this self-imposed isolation, old skills as well as new ideas for resource management for this island nation became of the utmost importance. Nothing was to be wasted, and everything must have purpose.[27] Over the years, Kyosei, the idea of living and working together for the common good, is a traditional Japanese concept that has been applied to a variety of subjects from biology to business. More recently it has become synonymous with corporate responsibility, ethical decision making, stakeholder involvement, and user and producer responsibility. A specific code of ethics, called the shuchu kiyaku, has direct roots in Confucian writings.[28]

Confucian writings are deep and vast, and were highly influential in the evolution of ethical codes and principles in Japan. The following is a short list of some observations regarding Confucian philosophy:

— Reciprocity should be practiced throughout one's life. In short, one should treat others the way you would like to be treated.

— Virtue, not profit, should be the goal of the superior man.

— There should be a balance between self-interest and altruism.

— We do not exist in isolation; we are part of a larger and more complex family (literally and figuratively) where harmony can be achieved by acting appropriately with one another.

The Caux Round Table

The Caux Round Table (CRT) is an international network of principled business leaders working to promote moral capitalism, where sustainable and socially responsible prosperity can become the foundation for a fair, free, and transparent global society. The CRT was founded in 1986 by Frederick Phillips, former president of Philips Electronics, and Olivier Giscard d'Estaing, former vice-chairman of INSEAD, as a means of reducing escalating trade tensions. At the urging of Ryuzaburo Kaku, then chairman of Canon, Inc., the CRT began focusing attention on global corporate responsibility in reducing social and economic threats to world peace and stability.[29]

Formally launched in 1994 and presented at the UN World Summit on Social Development in 1995, the CRT Principles for Business articulate a comprehensive set of ethical norms for businesses operating internationally or across multiple cultures. The principles emerged from a series of dialogues catalyzed by the Caux Round Table during the late 1980s and early 1990s. They are the product of collaboration among executives from Europe, Japan, and the United States, and were fashioned in part from a document called *The Minnesota Principles*. The principles have been published in twelve languages, reprinted in numerous textbooks and articles, and utilized in business school curricula worldwide. The principles are recognized by many as the most comprehensive statement of responsible business practice ever formulated by business leaders for business leaders.

The Caux Round Table believes that the world business community should play an important role in improving economic and social conditions. Through an extensive and collaborative process in 1994, business leaders developed the CRT Principles for Business to embody the aspiration of principled business leadership. The CRT Principles for Business are a worldwide vision for ethical and responsible corporate behavior and serve as a foundation for action for business leaders worldwide. As a statement of aspirations, the principles aim to express a world standard against which business behavior can be measured. The Caux Round Table has sought to begin a process that identifies shared values, reconciles differing values, and thereby develops a shared perspective on business behavior acceptable to and honored by all.

These principles are rooted in two basic ethical ideals: kyosei and human dignity. The Japanese concept of *kyosei* means living and working together for the common good enabling cooperation and mutual prosperity to coexist with healthy and fair competition. *Human dignity* refers to the sacredness or value of each person as an end, not simply as a means to the fulfillment of others' purposes or even majority prescription.

Following is an excerpt from the *Caux Round Table Principles for Business*. The full document is available at cauxroundtable.org.

Principle 1.
The Responsibilities of Businesses
Beyond Shareholders Toward Stakeholders

The value of a business to society is the wealth and employment it creates and the marketable products and services it provides to consumers at a reasonable price commensurate with quality. To create such value, a business must maintain its own economic health and viability, but survival is not a sufficient goal. Businesses have a role to play in improving the lives of all their customers, employees, and shareholders by sharing with them the wealth they have created. Suppliers and competitors as well should expect businesses to honor their obligations in a spirit of honesty and fairness. As responsible citizens of the local, national, regional and global communities in which they operate, businesses share a part in shaping the future of those communities.

Principle 2.
The Economic and Social Impact of Business
Toward Innovation, Justice, and World Community

Businesses established in foreign countries to develop, produce, or sell should also contribute to the social advancement of those countries by creating productive employment and helping to raise the purchasing power of their citizens. Businesses also should contribute to human rights, education, welfare, and vitalization of the countries in which they operate.

Businesses should contribute to economic and social development not only in the countries in which they operate, but also in the world community at large, through effective and prudent use of resources, free and fair competition, and emphasis upon innovation in technology, production methods, marketing, and communications.

Principle 3.
Business Behavior
Beyond the Letter of Law Toward a Spirit of Trust

While accepting the legitimacy of trade secrets, businesses should recognize that sincerity, candor, truthfulness, the keeping of promises, and transparency contribute not only to their own credibility and stability but also to the smoothness and efficiency of business transactions, particularly on the international level.

Principle 4.
Respect for Rules

To avoid trade frictions and to promote freer trade, equal conditions for competition, and fair and equitable treatment for all participants, businesses should respect international and domestic rules. In addition, they should recognize that some behavior, although legal, may still have adverse consequences.

Principle 5.
Support for Multilateral Trade

Businesses should support the multilateral trade systems of the GATT/World Trade Organization and similar international agreements. They should cooperate in efforts to promote the progressive and judicious liberalization of trade and to relax those domestic measures that unreasonably hinder global commerce, while giving due respect to national policy objectives.

Principle 6.
Respect for the Environment

A business should protect and, where possible, improve the environment, promote sustainable development, and prevent the wasteful use of natural resources.

Principle 7.
Avoidance of Illicit Operations

A business should not participate in or condone bribery, money laundering, or other corrupt practices: Indeed, it should seek cooperation with others to eliminate them. It should not trade in arms or other materials used for terrorist activities, drug traffic or other organized crime.

In industry, Canon first announced its kyosei corporate philosophy in 1988. Their environmental initiatives include a global recycling program for cartridges, and Certification under their ISO 14001 Certification Initiative. Canon's corporate Web site presents their position:[30]

> The world is undergoing a major transformation from a "throwaway" to a "recycling" society. Not satisfied with the progress made to date, Canon is making progressive efforts for the next generation, including the creation of a total cyclical system unifying the development, manufacturing and sales functions, while supplying products that are increasingly friendly to the environment. Canon will continue its quest to become a truly global corporation by fulfilling its environmental responsibilities.

> "Canon is a company devoted to the environment and sustainability. As an organization, we are guided by the corporate philosophy of Kyosei — all people, regardless of race, religion, or culture, harmoniously living and working together into the future," said Joe Adachi, president and chief executive officer, Canon USA, Inc. "With this philosophy at our core and adhering to high-performance standards, such as the ISO standards, we are continuously improving our environmental assurance and performance in all business activities to have the least impact on our environment and burden for future generations."

The Triple Bottom Line

Everyone's heard the complaint "We'd like to go eco, but are afraid our customers won't buy it," or the flat-out "Green doesn't sell." That might have been true once, but not anymore.

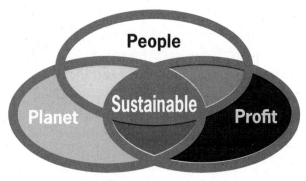

Visualizing the Triple Bottom Line.

Sociologist Paul Ray reported in his groundbreaking study of consumer attitudes — "The Cultural Creatives: How 50 Million People Are Changing the World" — that about a quarter of US adults fit into a segment he tagged "Cultural Creatives." The power of this group to act on personal ethics as a purchase decision making tool, and to be willing to speak-out about product impacts as well, are becoming hot-button issues in today's boardrooms. How those practices are spilling into, and influencing, other consumer groups and society in general is a wave forward-thinking businesses are keen to get ahead of.

Cultural Creatives consider themselves strongly aware of global warming, rainforest destruction, overpopulation, and exploitation of people in poorer countries. They want to see more positive action on these problems, and are more than willing and able to buy and invest according to their values — sustainability values. It's these values, and the devastating effect a tarnished image has on brand equity, that is causing the greatest concern for brand owners. Businesses, take note: Consumer activism works — and conveniently.

In Europe, consumers responding to rate increases for trash removal staged a revolt. Rather than tote home packaging that would need to be disposed of on their dime, they repacked purchased items in reusable containers from home, leaving the original packages piled at the end of the checkout line for the store to deal with.

This quiet revolution was an example of attitude changes that led to the creation of producer responsibility laws there. But rather than simply rolling over and absorbing the new costs, or blindly pushing the problem down the distribution chain, firms started selling their waste to the expanding recycling industry as a valuable resource — turning a disposal liability into a profit center. In addition, more attention was paid to reduce packaging and product needs overall, increasing per-unit profitability.

In the best of all worlds, according to general sustainability models, goods would be produced and consumed locally. In the real world, that's not how it works. We live in a global economy, and not all communities are able to produce all of the goods they need. But the fact that we're transporting goods outside the reach of our own laws doesn't mean manufacturers can, or should want to, produce products and waste with reckless abandon. Even the most conservative study will show there are sound bottom line arguments to be made for achieving profitability and positive image goals through basic sustainable business practices.

Everything we do makes a statement on how we feel about the environment on some level. What are your products saying about you?

The Price Behind the Sticker

Beyond the general view of landfills bursting at the seams, ills related to packaging abound. Consider forests laid bare by clear-cutting to produce packaging that is used only once before being tossed in the bin. Marine animals, starved to death by a plastic six-pack ring binding their mouths wash up on what were once pristine shores, their corpses rotting amid soda bottles and tampon applicators. Not all award-winning design is viewed in a gallery. Is being part of the flotsam and jetsam the place you're introducing your brand to a new audience?

It's estimated it costs as much as five times more to win customers back than it did to attract them in the first place. Even if the actual figure is a fraction of that, it makes good economic sense to take great care with the image you're conveying to your customers, past, present, and future.

Everything we purchase, produce, deliver, and sell makes a statement on how we feel about the environment on some level, and ultimately the consumers served. What is your packaging saying about you?

In a September 1999 *Economist* article, the author notes:

> Companies with an eye on their "triple bottom-line" — economic, environmental and social sustainability — outperformed their less fastidious peers on the stock market, according to a new index from Dow Jones and Sustainable Asset Management.

This Triple Bottom Line is known by many names: TBL, 3BL, People, Planet, Profit (the 3Ps), and Ecology, Economy, Equity (the 3Es). All describe the idea of the major forces of our world that must be served to achieve sustainable balance given our current market models. Formal coining of the phrase Triple Bottom Line has been attributed to John Elkington in 1994, and later expanded on in his 1998 book *Cannibals with Forks: The Triple Bottom Line of 21st Century Business.*[31] The concept of the Triple Bottom Line requires that a company's responsibility be to "stakeholders" (all people involved in or impacted by a venture) rather than shareholders (only those who profit from the venture). According to stakeholder theory, rather than the business of a business being to maximize shareholder (owner) profit — ventures should be looking to benefit all concerned — workers, management, shareholders, and the communities and firms on the supply chain. Triple Bottom Line ideas go much further than those that deal with purely environmental impacts.

After the 2007 ratification of the International Council for Local Environmental Initiatives (ICLEI), Triple Bottom Line criteria for urban and community accounting became the dominant framework for public sector full cost (true cost) accounting. There then developed additional UN standards to focus on natural capital and human capital needs to assist in assigning values for Triple Bottom Line accounting and ecological footprint reporting.

"People + Planet + Profit" is one of the most common Triple Bottom Line heuristics to neatly describe the complex interactions of sustainability and business demands. It doesn't matter how eco a business is, if it's not profitable, it cannot sustain its efforts or its positive impacts in that market sector.

People (*human capital*) refers to equitable and beneficial business practices: how a company treats its workers, their community, and the region in which it operates. A Triple Bottom Line venture tries to benefit the many groups it interacts with and impacts,

and works to not exploit or endanger them. The "People" section of the Triple Bottom Line would see "upstreaming" of a portion of profit from the marketing of finished goods back to the original producer of raw materials. Fair Trade too is a core part of this section. A Triple Bottom Line venture would never knowingly use child labor, would pay fair salaries to its workers, would maintain a safe work environment and tolerable working hours, and would not otherwise exploit a community or its labor force. A Triple Bottom Line venture will often participate in "give back to the community" efforts revolving around health care and education. Quantifying the "People" portion of the Triple Bottom Line is a relatively new effort as it's extremely subjective. The Global Reporting Initiative (GRI) has developed guidelines to enable corporations and NGOs to report on the social impact of a business.

Planet (*natural capital*) refers to a venture's environmental practices. A Triple Bottom Line venture embraces the core concepts from the precautionary principle, "Do no harm" would be the simplest operative phrase. Natural capital is a term closely identified with the Natural Capitalism economic model outlined by Paul Hawken, Amory Lovins, and Hunter Lovins in their 1999 book, *Natural Capitalism: Creating the Next Industrial Revolution* (natcap.org). A Triple Bottom Line venture looks to minimize its ecological footprint by carefully managing its consumption of energy and materials inputs, reducing manufacturing waste, as well as assuring that waste is not (or ever less) toxic before disposing of it not just in a legal manner, but with an eye on next level and long-term impacts as well. Ethical "cradle to grave" planning is the minimum framework for Triple Bottom Line manufacturing businesses. Life cycle assessment of all components to determine true environmental impact and costs is key. This includes looking at impacts from the growth or mining of raw materials, to manufacture, to distribution, to eventual disposal by the end user. Companies going one step further, consider a Cradle to Cradle™ approach, looking at the same cradle to grave impacts, but also consider remanufacture and material afterlife opportunities and impacts.

In today's materials handling model, the cost of disposing of nondegradable or toxic products is borne by the communities the things finally end up in. In a Triple Bottom Line scenario, any venture that produces and markets a product would be responsible for it all the way through to final disposal. As the full costs for impacts are borne by the company ultimately profiting by the venture, Triple Bottom Line companies would avoid ecologically destructive practices such as overfishing or unchecked use of nonrenewable resources. Paying close attention to environmental sustainability is more profitable for a business in the long run, as costs for clean-up or restitution would be paid in inflated dollars. With impact costs far exceeding profits from taking actions with only the short term in sight. Arguments that it costs more to be environmentally sound are usually disproved when time, depth, breadth, and ripple-through of impacts are permitted to be fully accounted for. The first question one must always ask when countering the cost questions is, Are you measuring for the long-term health of the company, or just looking as far as the next quarter? Reporting metrics for sustainability are becoming more standardized internationally and are more tangible than metrics for social impacts. Respected reporting institutes and registries include: The Global Reporting Initiative, Ceres, Institute 4 Sustainability, and others.

Profit (*monetary capital*) is the goal shared by all business, regardless of their ethics. The idea of profit within a sustainability framework, needs to be seen as the economic benefit enjoyed by all stakeholders, not just the company's stockholders. It's the idea that only a healthy company, earning ethically derived profits, can truly be seen as a contributing member of its community, and society at large. A company operating at a loss, or burdened with huge liabilities even if its base operations make money, not only earns no income for its owners, but has no resources to help support anything else (tax dollars, corporate giving, wages, and so on). The company is in essence, simply a drain on resources both economic and environmental.

Which side of the bottom line are you on? In MeadWestvaco's Stewardship & Sustainability Statement, John A. Luke, Jr., chairman and chief executive officer says:

> Stewardship is central to MeadWestvaco's vision for the future. We strive to preserve and enhance our resources through a commitment to sustainability and a steadfast dedication to integrity and innovation in all that we do. At MeadWestvaco, we take seriously this obligation to our environment, to our employees, customers, and shareholders and to the communities in which we live and work. And we feel that we've earned our reputation as a good corporate citizen.

> We're proud to be a global leader in stewardship and sustainability — as recognized by our inclusion in the Dow Jones Sustainability World Index for the past four years. This honor reflects our deep commitment to corporate responsibility, which we believe includes:

Environmental Responsibility

Sustainably managing the forests that supply basic materials for many of our products, minimizing our environmental impact, and respecting the earth, air and water that surround us.

Social Responsibility

Safeguarding our employees' health and safety, ensuring that our products and services are safe and reliable and striving to be a good neighbor in the communities where we operate.

Economic Responsibility

Promoting global prosperity and economic opportunity — for our shareholders, customers, employees and business partners and for every community we touch.

In the end, our commitment to these principles of stewardship and sustainability is more than a set of policies and procedures. It's an indication of our core values — as a company and as individuals — and a key part of our continuing efforts to improve the way we do business.[32]

Transparency and Honesty

Companies at the forefront of sustainability today have a history of commitment to their message. Not resting on their laurels, they continuously address their impacts as part of their operating strategy. The idea that it's cheaper to nip problems in the bud as opportunities and technologies arise, rather than deal with huge calamities later, is a key element in making long-term sustainability sustainable.

For those new to sustainability the simple plan of action should be to use the opportunity for creating trust (and foster brand loyalty) by actually being trustworthy. Although no one can address all issues overnight, everyone can make a genuine pledge to do what they can now, while they continue to address the rest as technology, economics, and opportunity afford.

Ceres

Pledging to do what they can now, and taking verifiable steps to show progress toward a more sustainable future are the member companies of Ceres. Ceres (pronounced "series") is a network of investors, environmental organizations and public interest groups working to address sustainability challenges.[33]

Mission: Integrating sustainability into capital markets for the health of the planet and its people.

In 1989, Ceres introduced a bold vision, where business and capital markets promoted the well-being of society as well as the protection of the earth's systems and resources. Bringing together investors, environmental groups and other stakeholders to encourage companies and markets to incorporate environmental and social challenges into everyday business. By leveraging the collective power of investors and other key stakeholders, Ceres has achieved dramatic results over the years.

Ceres launched the Global Reporting Initiative (GRI), now the de facto international standard used by over 1200 companies for corporate reporting on environmental, social and economic performance.

Ceres member Nike became the first global apparel firm to disclose the names and locations of its contract factories worldwide in 2005. Ceres member Dell Computer agreed in 2006 to support national legislation to require electronic product recycling and "takeback" programs, and Ceres member Bank of America announced a $20 billion initiative in 2007 to support the growth of environmentally sustainable business activity to address global climate change.

Over the years Ceres has brought together Wall Street and corporate leaders along with the United Nations to address growing financial risks and opportunities posed by climate change. These groundbreaking meetings have produced plans seeking stronger analysis, disclosure, and action from companies, investors, and regulators on climate change.

Ceres publishes cutting-edge research reports to help investors better understand the implications of global warming. Among those are *2008 Investor Summit on Climate Risk Final Report, Managing the Risks and Opportunities of Climate Change: A Practical Toolkit for Investors, Mutual Funds and Climate Change: Opposition to Climate Change Begins to Thaw, Investor Progress on Climate Risks and Opportunities, Corporate Governance and Climate Change: The Banking Sector.*

Ceres Principles

In the Fall of 1989, Ceres announced the creation of the Ceres Principles, a ten-point code of corporate environmental conduct to be publicly endorsed by companies as an environmental mission statement or ethic. Embedded in that code of conduct was the mandate to report periodically on environmental management structures and results. In 1993, following lengthy negotiations, Sunoco became the first Fortune 500 company to endorse the Ceres Principles. As sustainability ideas matured and gathered more support, Sunoco has been joined by an ever-growing list including Fortune 500 firms as well as smaller groups that have adopted their own equivalent environmental principles.

By adopting the Ceres Principles or similar code, companies not only formalize their dedication to environmental awareness and accountability, but also actively commit to an ongoing process of improvement, dialogue, and comprehensive, public reporting. Jeffrey Swartz, president and CEO of The Timberland Company, a Ceres member firm, explains in their 2006 CSR Report:

> Publishing a statement of accountability is necessary, but not sufficient. If we write a report and fail to initiate a conversation, we have missed an opportunity. And if our report represents our only venue for engagement, then we have failed. An engaged community — a convening of stakeholders committed to environmental stewardship, community strength, global human dignity, and the quality of life for our workers and those citizens with whom we are privileged to serve — is my intent. Our process of reporting is not "us" to "you." This report is a forum for you. React, respond, challenge, commit. I commit back to you that we will listen and act.

Overview of Ceres Principles

Protection of the Biosphere
We will reduce and make continual progress toward eliminating the release of any substance that may cause environmental damage to the air, water, or the earth or its inhabitants. We will safeguard all habitats affected by our operations and will protect open spaces and wilderness, while preserving biodiversity.

Sustainable Use of Natural Resources
We will make sustainable use of renewable natural resources, such as water, soils, and forests. We will conserve nonrenewable natural resources through efficient use and careful planning.

Reduction and Disposal of Wastes

We will reduce and where possible eliminate waste through source reduction and recycling. All waste will be handled and disposed of through safe and responsible methods.

Energy Conservation

We will conserve energy and improve the energy efficiency of our internal operations and of the goods and services we sell. We will make every effort to use environmentally safe and sustainable energy sources.

Risk Reduction

We will strive to minimize the environmental, health and safety risks to our employees and the communities in which we operate through safe technologies, facilities, and operating procedures, and by being prepared for emergencies.

Safe Products and Services

We will reduce and where possible eliminate the use, manufacture, or sale of products and services that cause environmental damage or health or safety hazards. We will inform our customers of the environmental impacts of our products or services and try to correct unsafe use.

Environmental Restoration

We will promptly and responsibly correct conditions we have caused that endanger health, safety or the environment. To the extent feasible, we will redress injuries we have caused to persons or damage we have caused to the environment and will restore the environment.

Informing the Public

We will inform in a timely manner everyone who may be affected by conditions caused by our company that might endanger health, safety, or the environment. We will regularly seek advice and counsel through dialogue with persons in communities near our facilities. We will not take any action against employees for reporting dangerous incidents or conditions to management or to appropriate authorities.

Management Commitment

We will implement these Principles and sustain a process that ensures that the Board of Directors and Chief Executive Officer are fully informed about pertinent environmental issues and are fully responsible for environmental policy. In selecting our Board of Directors, we will consider demonstrated environmental commitment as a factor.

Audits and Reports

We will conduct an annual self-evaluation of our progress in implementing these Principles. We will support the timely creation of generally accepted environmental audit procedures. We will annually complete the Ceres Report, which will be made available to the public.

For the full content of the Ceres Principles go to: ceres.org.

Aveda: Uruku Lipstick

Ceres member, Aveda, brings together the sustainability concepts of recycled, reuse, natural, and renewable into their Uruku Lipstick packaging system.

Here, their molded pulp outer package is made from 100% recycled newsprint, with a soy-ink printed 100% postconsumer recycled (PCR) content paper sleeve. The accessory case is a blend of 30% flax shives (a crop residue) and 70% polypropylene (containing 90% PCR). The lipstick cartridge is made of up to 65% PCR aluminum.

Internal components are made of recycled polystyrene with 88% PCR content. The system itself is modular, with the idea that the refillable cartridge delivered the consumable and is sold separately from the more durable accessory case.

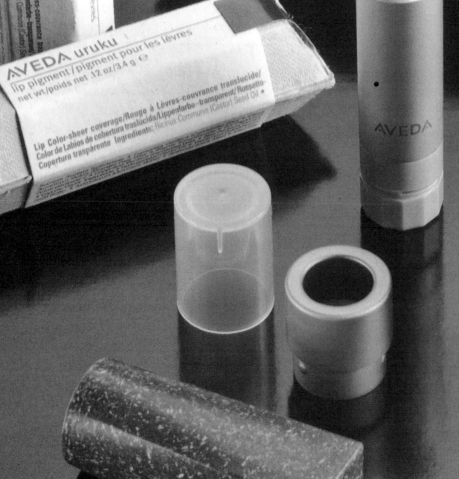

A Taste of Things to Come

Looking ahead at what will be expected for all quality ventures serving the packaging industry, Packaging Strategies, creator of the Sustainable Packaging Forum, one of the first packaging industry events dedicated to applied sustainability, will be taking it up one more level to include "Transparency of Reporting" as a key component for speaker, exhibitor, and host selection. In this, another industry first, the 2008 Sustainable Packaging Forum has established a "certification/reporting" process that then will help ensure the sustainability claims of speakers, expo participants, and even forum hosts and sponsors have been vetted and verified.

The process, which will be monitored by the Sustainable Packaging Forum Advisory Board, will lend objective, third-party credibility to those suppliers who exhibit at the expo and who desire to draw enhanced visibility to their technologies, processes, and services. The reporting criteria for each expo exhibitor and forum host will be published and made available to forum attendees.

Volunteers from top-tier retailers, heads of "Global 100 Most Sustainable" companies, brand owners on the leading edge of sustainable packaging initiatives, respected NGOs, esteemed academics, and highly sought-after sustainability and supply chain consultants make up the forum advisory board. The board helps direct content for the forum and will be an integral part of the speaker, exhibitor, and sponsor certification/reporting process. Packaging Strategies director David Luttenberger notes:

> Up to this point, there has been a well-established and trusted group of eco-professionals to draw from, all with long track records in sustainability.

But in recent years, the market has simply exploded with new technologies, new materials, and new faces. In order to assure these new players are coming from the same place of integrity we've depended on from the pioneers in our industry and to be sure we're providing the best possible quality product for our event attendees, setting "Transparency of Reporting" criteria is the only equitable and reliable way to allow us to maintain our quality standards.

As sustainability relies on quality of information to actually be sustainable, information providers, as well as industry regulators, will be looking ever more closely at all sustainability claims to ensure things are as they are purported to be.

Making the Business Case

In addition to statistics tracking performance showing superior performance by Dow Jones and Sustainable Asset Management, in October 2007, Innovest Strategic Value Advisors released The Carbon Beta and Equity Performance study. The study evaluates the relationship among climate change, companies' ability to manage the associated risks and opportunities, and their financial performance. Innovest notes this is the first study to take this approach, and lays the foundation for further research and investment products. This review of 1,500 companies found that there is a strong, positive, and growing correlation between industrial companies' sustainability in general, and climate change in particular, and their competitiveness and financial performance.[34]

Historically, though many have understood the need for embracing larger sustainability issues, tangible action has been slow to get rolling. Innovest suggests there have been a number of reasons for this, some of which include:

Investment professionals have long believed that company resources devoted to environmental issues are either wasteful or actually injurious to their competitive and financial performance and therefore to both the performance of the companies themselves and investor returns.

Until recently, there has been a dearth of robust, credible research evidence and analytical tools linking companies' environmental performance directly with their financial performance.

Innovest points out that since there is now growing and incontrovertible evidence that superior overall environmental performance can in fact improve profitability, as well as reduce risk levels — with this in mind there is little doubt that these is now sufficient motivation to get companies to address their impacts as part of their long-term strategic plans.

As background for the study, Innovest states:

Few environmental issues pose as real, significant, and widespread a financial threat to investors as climate change. International policy responses aimed at cutting greenhouse gas emissions, together with the direct physical impacts of climate change will require investors and money managers to take a much closer look at how their portfolios might be affected by company "carbon" risks and opportunities.

In their report, Innovest asks investors and other fiduciaries to assess their portfolios for carbon risk for a variety of reasons including:

There is increasing evidence showing that superior performance in managing climate risk is a useful proxy for superior, more strategic corporate management, and therefore for superior financial performance and shareholder value creation.

In the longer term, the outperformance potential will become even greater as the capital markets become more fully sensitized to the financial and competitive consequences of environmental and climate change considerations.

For those in industry these ideas have already started to work into the decision-making process. The Wal-Mart scorecard that has set new benchmarks for packaging is only one criteria-set in one part of their operation. Today, as more and more verifiable data and tools to handle it become available, we're seeing a variety of new initiatives, from carbon footprint metrics to verified resource and supply chain integrity. All are being implemented to help companies better — and more quickly — identify partners willing and able to help them reach their own sustainability goals.

"How companies perform on environmental, social, and strategic governance issues is having a rapidly growing impact on their competitiveness, profitability, and share price performance," said Dr. Matthew Kiernan, founder and CEO of Innovest in a February 02, 2005; *Sustainability Investment News* article from SRI World Group. In the bigger picture, one of the attractive things about adopting sustainability practices as part of a company's larger strategic plan is risk management. It is no surprise then, that some of the companies first to invest serious time and effort in understanding and using sustainability criteria for long-term business strategies were insurance companies and insurance underwriters. As sustainability practices mature and develop, providing tangible historical data to reflect on, the question is bound to come up, Were the companies that resisted change the ones that could only operate with the help of hidden subsidies funded by the well-being of future generations? Companies too now should be asking themselves — "How much more, in inflated future dollars, will it cost us to change if we wait?"

Packaging and Sustainability

In December 2007, *Packaging Digest* and the Sustainable Packaging Coalition (SPC) released the results of a joint survey looking at the state of sustainability and packaging, and to use as a benchmark of current attitudes and practices. The survey showed that "sustainability is a hot button for the industry, and its impact is likely to grow in the coming years."[35] Drawn from the SPC membership, as well as subscribers to *Packaging Digest* and *Converting* magazine, the respondents represented a cross section of today's packaging industry, with the biggest share coming from consumer products goods companies (CPGs), followed by materials manufacturers, converters, machinery manufacturers, packaging services, and retailers.

Looking at the survey data, 73 percent reported that their companies have increased emphasis on packaging sustainability over the year leading up to the survey. This is no surprise given the timing of policy changes by the world's biggest retailer, Wal-Mart, to focus on sustainability in general and packaging in particular in this time frame and the full adoption of the EU Directive on Packaging and Packaging Waste. The data also indicates that while awareness surges packaging businesses have generally been slow to incorporate sustainable business practices, particularly in the United States where sustainability

directives are not as deeply and federally mandated as they are in other countries.

In the December 2007, *Packaging Digest* article announcing the survey, editorial director John Kalkowski comments on the difficult position packaging firms find themselves in: "Modern lifestyles, which demand longer product shelf life and create intense competition among brands, have been major drivers for increased usage of packaging, now seen as a leading contributor to waste streams. Pressure is mounting on the industry to act now."

The article goes on to say

> ... sustainability is reaching new levels of awareness across the industry, especially among companies with more than 1,000 employees and those with formal, written sustainability policies, where 46 percent of respondents rated themselves as "very familiar." Still, only 21 percent of all respondents claimed they were very familiar with the issues of sustainability in packaging. Nearly 40 percent said they were "somewhat familiar," while 10 percent said they were not familiar at all.

Kalkowski notes that unlike typical surveys that take on a classic bell-shaped curve with early adopters forming the foot of the curve, swooping up quickly to mainstream adoption swelling to form the body and peak, with an equally quick slope down to the laggards forming the other foot of the curve, the survey data illustrated a trend toward slower adoption rates spreading out over a much longer period. Kalkowski goes on to note that early adopters are implementing sustainability practices in different areas across the whole of their business, taking a more in-depth systemic approach.

Change in general seems to be a big issue, with about a third of the Packaging Digest/SPC survey respondents expressing concerns about the raise in current raw materials prices as well as how to implement sustainability practices using their existing infrastructure. Moving to sustainability in general sparks similar concern as being forced to change due to purely economic factors. In a capital and process-intensive industry like packaging, these concerns are understandable. But fear of change should not be considered a viable option or as The Economist article discussing implementing sustainability practices and "the prisoner's dilemma" points out, the world will be condemned to a slow roasting, even though global impacts could be averted if everyone simply cooperated and took on a share of the load in the first place.[36]

In his talk at the 2006 Sustainable Packaging Forum, Tyler Elm, at that time sustainability director for Wal-Mart, noted that the move toward a more sustainable business model for Wal-Mart was originally initiated as a defensive strategy — to reduce operations costs, liabilities, and exposure. Wal-Mart is, after all, a very large target. But as they dug deeper into what sustainable business practice really meant, they discovered instead of a defensive tool, it was a powerful *offensive* strategy. Risk and exposure were reduced or eliminated as they got in front of issues before they become problems or additional costs. And systems or operations that were costs under the old way of doing things, were now generating income.

Wal-Mart's online Environmental Overview states:

> Ecologically responsible business practices result in significant gains for our customers, associates, and shareholders. For example, by inventing trucks that get twice the mileage of our current vehicles, we will radically reduce emissions and fossil fuel, but we'll also save millions of dollars at the pump.[37]

Here we can see that rather than just simply demand the lowest cost at any price strictly from the goods they sell, Wal-Mart is looking to leverage a variety of opportunities within their own organization to maintain the price structure their customers expect, while still serving the need to maintain a viable profit structure.

In a February 7, 2008, Reuters article, "*Wal-Mart to Pay More for 'Greener' Goods*," author Nichola Groom details Wal-Mart's policy changes. To incorporate sustainability in both operations and product offerings, and meet aggressive impact reduction and efficiency goals, Wal-Mart is openly saying they are willing to pay more if need be, for products that last longer, hurt the environment less, and better addresses stakeholder issues not reflected in previous pricing structures. The article notes Wal-Mart feels that adding sustainability to the mix does not absolutely need to result in automatic increases in their end retail prices. It quotes Matt Kistler, Wal-Mart's senior vice president of sustainability:

> Bad quality products create waste, and so having tighter standards on the social side, on the environmental side, and on the quality side will reduce waste... We are looking at a very small amount of dollars, and the savings in the supply chain that we are finding because of sustainability in some cases will more than offset the incremental costs of what we are paying for a better quality item.

In 2004, Wal-Mart launched a company-wide, long-term initiative "to unlock" their "potential." Leaders from nearly every part of Wal-Mart formed entrepreneurial teams focusing on areas such as packaging, real estate, energy, raw materials, and electronics waste. These teams partnered with environmental consultants, non-profit organizations, and other groups to help examine Wal-Mart's business practices "through the lens of restoration and sustainability."

Wal-Mart goes on to reflect:

> What we are learning about our footprint on the environment is both shocking and inspiring. Despite our excellence in efficiency, commerce creates a lot of waste. Fortunately, we've identified plenty of opportunities that, if captured, can transform our entire industry. Because we're experimenting in many areas, we expect to make mistakes along the way.

Wal-Mart has established three aggressive goals for their sustainability efforts:

— To be supplied 100 percent by renewable energy;

— To create zero waste; and

— To sell products that sustain our resources and environment.

In the service of their sustainability efforts, Wal-Mart acknowledges:

> What gets measured gets managed. Our teams are developing sets of common sense metrics that hold us accountable for the goals we're setting. We will share these metrics on this Web site once they are established.

It would be fairly easy to dismiss sustainability efforts as only the turf of Wal-Mart sized giants. They are, in any discussion, the elephant in the room that simply cannot be ignored — plus a little action on their part has huge ripple-through impacts. But cost and environmental impact savings, consumer advocacy groups are happy to point out, are accessible to the individual as well as the corporate giant. And it is in fact the actions and ethics of the individual that help drive corporate-level change.

After all, corporations are simply collections of individuals acting as a group. Asking ourselves, "How will history judge us," means understanding what drives individual choices — then using that knowledge to empower individuals to make good decisions — is the first step on this journey. With all eyes turning to industry professionals for answers, we have the opportunity to completely remake everything we do — but get it right this time.

One Laptop per Child:
Cultivating Equality in the Information Age

"One Laptop per Child is about the transformation of education. It's about access, equity, and about giving the next generation of children in the developing world a bright and open future." — Walter Bender, president, Software and Content.

Making laptops accessible to developing nations' children, the OLPC challenge was to create an affordable machine, that was rugged, durable, and child-friendly. This is no child's toy (though it is a lot of fun): it's an opportunity to bridge the information divide for their whole village.

OLPC designers carried the attention to detail all the way through packaging, creating a simple yet highly effective package, sensitive to the end user's community — recyclable, lightweight, resource minimal, and made from renewable resources. Learn more at laptop.org.

Case Study: Winterborne

Winterborne, a Chatsworth, California, based packaging solutions company, has been converting plastics and paperboard into clamshell blister packs, carded blisters, folding cartons, point-of-purchase displays, and a variety of other forms for decades. Their clients are mostly durable consumer goods makers and include well-known brands such as Microsoft, Toshiba, Samsung, LG Electronics, Seiko, Speedo, and Leatherman.

Almost ten years before PVC clamshell issues became part of mainstream buzz with items like CBS News' "Wrap Rage," or the current wave of companies adding PVC to their materials phase-out lists, Winterborne had begun the process of developing a better way to serve their clients' needs. The 2005 introduction of a special bundled version of Microsoft's Xbox 360 entertainment system for Sam's Club stores represented the first appearance of Winterborne's EnviroShell® clamshell packaging alternative.

Designed and developed using solid systems thinking ideas like Cradle to Cradle to help guide the process, Winterborne knew they needed to do more than simple material replacement, or just make the package easy to open. They looked at energy, water usage, greenhouse gas emissions, and recyclability, as well as consumer-related issues like look, feel, and access to product, all while paying attention to theft and stacking issues their clients needed addressed.

The basic form of EnviroShell®, a trapped blister between two layers of paperboard, is not a radically new idea. Converters have been making "foldover" blister cards for decades. Winterborne though, knew how much weight the structure could carry would be the key to addressing head-on, one of PVC clamshell's long-held advantages. They then took their concept one step better by adding levels of recyclablity and recycled content use, that clear clamshells of any kind have yet to achieve.

Using different combinations of mini-flute corrugated and various weights of preprinted liner boards, EnviroShell® integrates a 100-percent postconsumer recycled PET blister sealed between two pieces of recycled corrugated paperboard. Additional advantages over traditional clamshell packaging include glare elimination with beautiful edge-to-edge color and a cleanly finished edge, heat-activated water-based seal (a proprietary feature), size efficiency, and durability. The paperboard component (the bulk of the package) is fully recyclable in most markets, with easy separation for recycling. Visually the EnviroShell® package has a high-quality feel, yet Winterborne notes the package is cost neutral to traditional plastic clamshells. Important to big box retailers, it also passes theft-prevention requirements as well as being capable of withstanding stacking weight loads found in palletized point-of-purchase displays.

In 2007, Winterborne received *Converting* magazine's Innovator Award for Sustainability, as well as the Sustainable Packaging Forum's Sustainable Packaging Leadership award. In 2008, Wal-Mart recognized Winterborne's efforts with a first of its type award for their EnviroShell® packaging. Part of Wal-Mart/Sam's Club preferred packaging provider group, Winterborne was the first packaging supplier to be recognized.

The Mechanics of Human Behavior

Dr. Elise L. Amel
Industrial-Organizational Psychologist, University of St. Thomas

Dr. Christie Manning
Cognitive and Biological Psychologist, Macalester College

Though specific numbers differ from study to study, they all agree: the vast majority of all purchase decisions are made at the store.

With thousands of products competing for the consumer's attention, simply being bigger or louder than the competitor means a product risks either becoming part of the background noise or, worse yet, alienating the potential buyer. Identifying and connecting with the consumer's actual need becomes the key not only to connecting with the buyer, but fostering long-term brand loyalty.

Mother and Child, Beijing 1986
Photo: W. Jedlička

41

Chapter Themes

Nature's distribution model uses a seed pod as the packaging for a plant's reproductive efforts. It protects the genetic information during the distribution process and warehouses it until conditions are favorable for growth. Once its obligation is served, it feeds the young seedling as it breaks down. Where does nature fit into today's market? Understanding the nature of our system to serve, or even change it, becomes the key to creating truly innovative solutions. To do that we must first understand how to identify and service needs, and then connect that service to greater impacts and consumer satisfaction.

Sustainability

The most sustainable packaging is no packaging. However, we live in an industrial age in which we rely on specialization, efficiencies, and exchange. The good news is that there is evidence that packaging can help (or hinder) getting a sustainable product into people's hands, which is important, and that packaging itself can be made more sustainable (improvement imperative).

Attention

Our brains work in some pretty predictable ways. We tend to maximize what we can do while not paying attention, what people commonly refer to as multi tasking: Note the number of people talking on a cell phone while walking, driving, or shopping. But luckily, we can pay attention when circumstances cue us that our behavior is not appropriate or safe. So sustainable packaging needs either to fly under people's radar or force their attention in a way that engages their basic needs and noblest values.

Zone of Acceptability

Since packaging reflects people's identities, it must fall within a "zone of acceptability." Packaging that catches people outside of that zone will either cause consumers to become defensive or write the product off as irrelevant to them.

Expression of Individuality

While people share many common behavioral tendencies, we (especially Americans and those in other individualistic cultures; Schultz & Zelezny, 2003) like to feel special, we have individual preferences, and local needs and customs feel comforting and familiar. Thus there is the opportunity to appeal to uniqueness, the chance to be on the leading edge of trends, and an interest in technological innovation.

Assumptions vs. Data: The Importance of Collecting Information

Research is key to the pre-design understanding of consumers as well as to pilot testing packaging solutions. One of the biggest mistakes we make is assuming we know what motivates others. Not everyone shares the same history, culture, family, friends, education, and work that create our motivations. The only way to confidently understand consumers is to study representative groups. This can be done efficiently through review of the literature, focus groups, observation, and surveys. Literature reviews help identify what is already known in general, focus groups allow for in-depth understanding of a few specific issues, observation can uncover habits people aren't even aware of, and surveys can provide evidence about a broad range of people.

Inside the Consumer

There's a lot going on inside a consumer between seeing a package and making a purchase. A package conjures up memories and directives. They might fall in love with it without realizing it, they may consider what a purchase will do to or for their image, and they'll encounter, and perhaps overcome, barriers to the purchase. When looking at psychological research it quickly becomes apparent that there are endless subtleties to human behavior. These are a function of each person having a unique genetic and experiential background. We can, however, describe some of the most typical patterns of behavior to consider when maximizing the design of a sustainable package.

What's in Our Hearts (or How We Don't Think)

Human beings have needs. Some needs are basic and physiological, and if these needs are not met, we cannot survive. "Sustainable packaging" of basic needs is an oxymoron, for the most basic human needs — air, water, and food — are available in a natural, unprocessed, and unpackaged state, even in our modern industrial age. Other physiological needs include a need for clothing and shelter to provide warmth and protection.

Meeting basic needs is not enough for a fully human life. In fact, we are driven to meet needs that go well beyond the basic and physiological. These are psychological and social needs. Some of the most

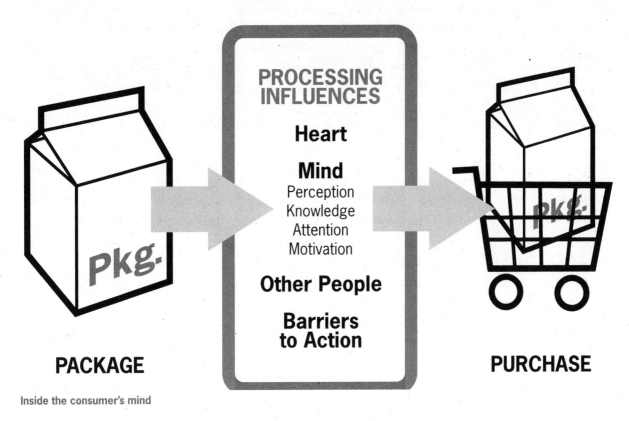

PACKAGE

PROCESSING INFLUENCES

Heart

Mind
Perception
Knowledge
Attention
Motivation

Other People

Barriers to Action

PURCHASE

Inside the consumer's mind

powerful of these are a need for safety and security, a deep need for social connection, a desire for comfort and pleasure, and a yearning toward self-fulfillment and happiness. In almost every situation, these needs influence our behavior; we carry out those actions that we think are most likely to bring us safety, social connection, comfort, and happiness. The influence of these needs is particularly evident in a product-purchasing situation. Why do people buy things? Whether explicitly or implicitly, they buy because they perceive a need and they think that a particular product will meet that need.

Consider, for example, our psychological need for safety and security. People seek homes in safe areas, with security systems. We carry cell phones, and car keys with a red "alert" button. Some people regularly carry things like mace, pepper spray, or even a gun. The need for safety and security leads us to prefer products that come in a "tamperproof" package or layers of plastic that seem to guarantee it is clean, new, and untouched by potential danger or contamination. Furthermore, this need makes us more likely to buy products that are familiar and "safe." We recognize them, we know how they work, and we know they come from a source or company we can trust. Getting people to try something new and different can be difficult in part because of this need for security implied by familiarity.

Also extremely powerful in guiding behavior is our desire for comfort and pleasure. This desire exerts its influence on our behavior every time we purchase something we don't really need, but that makes life a little bit easier or more comfortable: luxury cars, air conditioning, surround-sound stereo, take-out food (just to name a few). We continuously strive for a life of ease and comfort and we seek out things and situations that promise to save us energy and time, decrease physical discomfort, or increase comfort and delight.

An arguably even more powerful influence on human behavior is our need for social connections. We are social creatures and have deep social needs. We are hard-wired to pay attention to the zone of acceptability: What other people around us do (and do not do), and what we do that earns positive feedback. This information is then internalized and these social norms guide our behavior. There are a number of factors that increase the power of a social norm. The actions and opinions of people with perceived high status leave a stronger impression than those of people with perceived lower status (quality). We also pay more attention to the actions and opinions of people who are similar to us (similarity) and whom we are more likely to regularly encounter (proximity). Finally, we are more likely to pay attention to the cues of social acceptability from people we find pleasant, appealing, and admirable (likability). Marketers and salespeople discovered long ago the power of social norms and people's need to be socially connected. Think of the many ads that imply (subtly or not so subtly) a particular product is not only in the "zone of acceptability," but also brings instant popularity and deep, meaningful relationships.

While it is impossible to overstate the influence that social norms and the need for social acceptability have on human behavior, it is important to note that people also like to think of themselves as unique and apart from the crowd. Thus, the ideal marketing message manages to convey that it is within the zone of social acceptability but with a bit of cutting-edge uniqueness or originality. As McDonough and Braungart (2002) point out, products must be adaptable to local tastes and traditions, and they must allow for cultural as well as individual expression. Packaging is an important, and very visible, dimension upon which people judge whether a product's expression is something they feel good about.

Finally, it is interesting to note that in today's consumer (materialistic) society, our drive to acquire stuff in order to increase our comfort and to meet (and even exceed) social acceptability standards has created a conflict with our need for happiness and self-fulfillment. Psychological and sociological studies consistently show that above a certain moderate level of comfort, material wealth does not bring happiness (Kasser, 2002). The more materialistic we are, and the more we consume, the less likely we are to feel happiness and self-fulfillment (even as we increase our comfort and our perception of being socially accepted).

What's in Our Minds (or How We Do Think)

Perception

What do people see in a package? Despite the fact that people encounter packaging almost every time they make a consumer purchase, most people hardly notice packaging or give it much thought. This isn't because they don't perceive the package, it is because they are used to assuming that the packaging is just a throwaway rather than part of the product. Can sustainable packaging bring any benefit if people do not pay the slightest attention to it? From a psychological perspective, sometimes it is the subtle aspects of an object or situation that provoke the most interesting response. So it is with packaging: a chance to present something about a product, or about the package itself, without having to be explicit.

People are amazing at figuring out meaning. Our brains are constantly working on understanding our environment. This need to constantly make sense of things even has us seeing things that are not really there, but only alluded to. To make a package stand out against a background of products competing for our attention, consider some basic perceptual principles. Eye-catching objects tend to be smaller as well as higher in contrast and symmetry, and have smooth form (Palmer, 2003; cited in Weiten, 2007).

Simple is better. The more complex the new packaging, or the message implied by the new packaging, the less people are likely to pay attention, especially in situations that are stressful or exciting (Hunt and Ellis, 2004). For example, the benefits of a new package that requires a one-step process for disposal or reuse (e.g., throw in the garden) will grab more attention than a more complex option (e.g., tear off and recycle the metal bottom, tear off and throw away the plastic top, then use the middle to make a paper airplane). You know which instruction set most people will stop reading.

Packages that are dissimilar to the other objects in the surrounding space can take advantage of the contrast effect. Specifically, when comparing two items, we tend to see the second object as more extreme than it really is (Cialdini, 2001). For instance, if we first see a conventional package, then we see a recycled and recyclable package, this will enhance the sustainable image of the recycled and recyclable package.

Despite a brilliant design, however, many people will skip over a product due to inattentional blindness, which is when a person does not see or hear what is right in front of them, because their attention is focused on something else. For instance, when shopping with children who are asking questions, needing to go to the bathroom, and attempting to persuade an adult to make certain purchases, there is little additional attention available for the shopper to discern from the variety of shampoo options available.

Consistency between product and package can help us accurately recognize a product we are searching for (Davenport and Potter, 2004; cited in Weiten, 2007). If we are looking for an all-natural product, eco-packaging will be more likely to trigger our attention than traditional packaging. The "sustainable" versions of daily products such as cotton balls, cotton swabs, and muffin cups are packaged in brown paperboard-like stiff paper. It stands out because it looks like it must be more green, yet it is still an attractive package.

Connecting with the consumer with eco-aware impacts. Seasonal packaging by Celery Design.

Some natural cosmetic products, such as those created and sold by Aveda, use unbleached paperboard packaging. Product and packaging are consistent.

Packaging can be an asset or a liability in terms of getting eco-friendly products into people's hands. McDonough and Braungart (C2C™ 2002, pp. 172–3) mention how:

> A small but significant number of consumers chose to buy [a] lotion in a highly unattractive "eco" package shelved next to the identical product in its regular package, but the number who chose the "eco" package skyrocketed when it was placed next to an over-the-top "luxury" package for the very same product. People like the idea of buying something that makes them feel special and smart, and they recoil from products that make them feel crass and unintelligent.

Neither ugly nor outrageous will do. Packaging needs to fall within the zone of acceptability.

For example, the company IF YOU CARE which makes baking and other kitchen paper products, uses very standard geometric shapes for their plain brown packages. These brown packages tend to have a neutral connotation; we are used to receiving such packages in the mail. The packaging implies, and their purchasers get that the packaging is secondary to the product, and that less packaging means both saving the environment and saving money.

Knowledge

What should a purchaser learn from the packaging? Packaging is the first contact a person has with a product. Packaging thus offers a chance to tell people something that they don't already know. In some cases, the message on the packaging might be something that only becomes important to the purchasers when they see it there in print on the store shelf. Until they see it and process it, they don't realize that it is something they care about. Presenting information about the greenness of the packaging, and the product contained within it, is an important role that packaging must play. What should the message be, and how can it be conveyed? Some elements to consider:

Message Feature A. How does this product help people be "green"? For many people, green has already become, or is becoming, synonymous with "good." There are two ways that "green" = "good." First, green is good because green products are usually better for personal health and for the planet. And for the growing number of people who express values in line with environmental sustainability, "green" is also good because it implies "the right thing to do." By providing a green rationale on the product packaging, you are giving a significant number of people who are concerned about the environment (between 83 and 93 percent in a poll by Yale University, 2007) an even better reason to make a purchase they already want to make: It is in line with their values, it is the right thing to do. The purchase allows people to display consistency between their values and their behavior.

Message Feature B. How does the packaging enhance the greenness of the product? Does the packaging of the product significantly enhance its green credibility? If it does (as of course it should), then it is important to make people aware of this. People who are concerned about the environment are sensitive to waste, and in many cases will forego an environmentally benign purchase if it is wrapped in layers of non-reusable or recyclable packaging. Even people who are just beginning to be aware of the environmental impacts of their actions and purchases are more likely to be sensitive to things like packaging waste because

they get the immediate feedback of dealing with a pile of nonrecyclable "garbage."

Message Feature C. How does the (sustainable) packaging fit into the bigger picture of an "eco" lifestyle? People's behavior is heavily influenced by their need to be within the "zone of acceptability." Fortunately for the planet, many aspects of a sustainable lifestyle are entering this zone. Not only are well-known personalities extolling the virtues of being green (e.g., the Queen of England, Leonardo DiCaprio), but everyday people such as our friends, neighbors, co-workers, and family members, are showing a sometimes surprising level of interest in things like corn-based plastics or hybrid cars. Now, more than ever before, trying to live sustainably is viewed as socially acceptable. Thus products that help people live sustainably have also acquired an aura of acceptability. Whereas in the past a label like COMPOSTABLE PACKAGING may have elicited a "yuck!" Response, today, the response is different. Anything associated with a green (or sustainable) lifestyle is likely to be viewed as neutral at worst and more often positive, even if people don't know exactly what it is. An important caveat is that people may distrust the truth of green claims. Savvy (and even the not so savvy) consumers know that greenwashing (making false green claims for the purpose of selling more product) is alive and well. It is best to avoid exaggerating or making misleading statements.

The fact that sustainable products are entering the "zone of social acceptability" means more people will consider buying them. Pointing out how the product and packaging are unique may be the key to getting people to move beyond just considering the product to actually purchasing it. People appreciate creativity, cleverness, and good design. They also like the opportunity to set themselves just a little bit apart from the crowd (yet still be within the zone of social acceptability). Consider how IKEA continues to delight people with their products and geometric puzzle like packaging. They are clearly within the zone of social acceptability, and they also maintain a cache of uniqueness by finding new ways to present fairly standard products.

Consumers know greenwashing is alive and well. Is your message one they will trust, or view with skepticism?

Message Feature D. Caveat/opportunity: Packaging messages must bring cognitive closure. It seems that claims of green are everywhere these days, whether they are billboards for automakers, magazine ads for investment brokers, or radio ads for garden products. Clearly, green claims work (Gross, 2007). As the number of products making green claims rises, it is becoming clear that producers make their claims based on wildly varying standards, some resort to pure greenwashing. How does the average consumer know which claims to trust and which to approach with a healthy dose of skepticism? When only one product on the shelf is claiming to be green, then the green-leaning customer has an easy task: Choose that product immediately, or choose to investigate that one product's claims further. However, as the number of similar products making competing green claims increases, so does the complexity of the consumer's decision. Most people have neither the time nor the desire to inform themselves about the differ-

ing health and environmental impacts of "totally chlorine free" vs. "processed chlorine free" or "made of recycled materials" vs. "made of post-consumer waste materials." People want cognitive closure; they want a definitive answer without doubt or ambiguity: Product/package X is definitely a better environmental choice than product/package Y. Consumers will be drawn to package messages that fulfill this desire for definitiveness. They want to know that they are making the right choice, a choice they will not have to regret later.

Attention

Eliciting an automatic response. It is not just the competing green claims on different products that create an overly complex cognitive scenario for people. Complexity surrounds us — we live in an era of information overload. One estimate claims we are bombarded daily by over 3000 product advertisement messages alone. How many of these make it into our consciousness? Despite the amazing abilities of the human brain, we are in fact very limited in the amount of information we can accurately and effortfully process all at once. Thus, of the 3000 product messages, we notice 80 of them, and truly process only about 8 to the extent that we have any sort of reaction (Twitchell, 1996, cited in Corbett, 2006). Because our brains do not have the capacity to process all the information available to us (particularly in our modern information age), we have evolved the ability to overlearn things to the point that we can do them automatically, without much mental effort. An obvious example of this is driving. For most of us, driving has become so overlearned that we carry out almost all the actions needed completely automatically. We use our attention and cognitive effort to daydream, find a good radio station, or carry on a conversation (often on a cell phone). The minute our attention is needed for some tricky maneuver on the road, our cognitive effort focuses on driving but then switches off again once the danger is past. Automaticity obviously has many benefits: It allows us to do things faster, to multitask, and to save precious cognitive processing capacity for things that are really important. However, the downside is that when we do things automatically, we are making less effort to truly understand and evaluate whatever information or choices are in front of us.

Our culture places such great value on productivity and busyness that people frequently find themselves with too little time and too much to do. Multitasking becomes a necessity and some jobs are relegated to automatic mode. Shopping is a case in point. People navigate crowded grocery store aisles with their cell phone or BlackBerry in their hand, checking e-mail, talking to a colleague or family member on the phone, avoiding collisions with other shoppers, all while looking for items to put in their shopping cart. Add a couple of unruly children to the mix, and you have a typical American shopping experience. How much mental attention are people giving to their choices under these circumstances? Chances are, not much. They are very likely selecting items without processing or evaluating any information about what they're purchasing. This type of behavior is often referred to as mindless responding or mindless behavior.

Mindless behavior most often occurs when people are under conditions of stress or divided attention, such as while multitasking in a grocery store. Some salient feature of a product, the package, or the environment causes a person to pick up that item, which might not occur if the person were really thinking.

The salient feature could be due to familiarity (they've heard a jingle about the product over and over), habit (it is what they've always bought), availability (eye-level or end-of-aisle displays), or eye-catching design that forces them to pay attention (color, shape, uniqueness, a sign that reads SALE!). Whatever it is, this feature persuades a person to buy the product without thinking deeply about it.

Eliciting a mindless response, perhaps through packaging, is one way to persuade people to pick up a particular item. The question is whether the mindless response works more than once? It can, if the salient feature that elicited the response the first time continues to be attention grabbing and appealing. However, it can also be a onetime deal, if there is a shift in what draws people's attention.

Motivation

What gives a product/package that extra appeal? Needs alone tend to influence people's automatic, nonthinking responses. However, we have the capacity to think in more complex ways about our choices. When we are attentive, we think about how likely it is that our expectations are going to come true. We are more likely to act the more confident we are about the results. To understand these more complex thoughts we can ask ourselves several questions: Does packaging have value for the consumer? How difficult is it for the consumer to achieve this valued benefit? How certain is the valued benefit?

Question A: Does packaging have value for consumers? What can they expect from it? (Plant it in garden and watch it grow? Less garbage? Less hassle?) This draws from the idea of needs and desires adding layers of beliefs, values, and cultural traditions. Here it is especially important to research and align packaging so it demonstrates value or benefit to the consumer. People want to be good and to behave consistently with their values. However, what people say and what they do are often based on two different value systems (Farrell, 2007). Core values people claim include family, freedom, fairness, equality, justice, conservation, quality, independence, and innovation. On the other hand, values that tend to drive actual purchasing behavior include fun, novelty, trendiness, efficiency, comfort, convenience, conformity, image, quantity, and whether it's a bargain. Many of the proclaimed core values tend to be more in line with sustainability, while consumer values are not necessarily so. Packaging should be designed so that it is "easy to be good" (Cornell, 2007). In other words, create packaging that appeals to people's core values rather than consumer values. This has the added benefit of creating consistency between consumers' thoughts and actions, which relieves their angst (see the discussion of cognitive dissonance in Weiten, 2007).

Question B: How difficult is it to achieve this benefit?

Is it a matter of simply planting the biopack in the back yard? Well, "simply planting" has two features: the action itself and a person's sense of whether they can handle it. Scratching a hole in the yard may or may not be easy (not to mention irrelevant to those who don't have a yard). Then comes the question about efficacy — can I count on myself to plant this? Maybe I can get my kids to help, but I don't know where I put my gardening stuff...darn it, I have a boatload of other activities that supersede this one. When confronted with having to "do something," minimal or no packaging used by a producer may have an advantage — the benefit is automatic — the consumer has no further (or little) remaining obligations in the product consumption process.

Question C: How certain is the benefit?

These are considerations about aspects (e.g., reliability, accuracy) that are out of the consumer's control. Does the consumer trust the source of this information or the company or manufacturer? For instance, have they really tested this product to ensure its safety? Or, when I send back the packaging, are they really reusing it?

We can think of the likelihood that someone will mindfully select a certain package by combining these questions through multiplication, motivation to buy = value x difficulty x certainty. (Note: Difficulty is discussed in depth later in this chapter under "Barriers to Action.") If any one of the responses is low, it brings down the likelihood they will select the package (Vroom, 1964). The consumer reasons: *So, even if I see the value in a particular package, if I don't believe there's a chance I'll follow through with the necessary actions, or I don't trust the manufacturer or recyclers, then that diminishes the probability that I will make that purchase.*

Other People
(or How Sensitive We Are to Social Cues)

Social Comparisons

How do we know when an action is worthwhile? People are motivated to maximize their sense of fairness. People want to believe they are putting in and getting out as much as others. For instance, if they pay more, they ought to be getting more than others who are paying less (Adams, 1965). If there is less packaging, what are they missing out on? On the other hand, what might they be gaining for that "sacrifice?" Sometimes it may be worth explicitly pointing out the trade-offs so people don't just focus on the costs, but also include the benefits in their calculations.

Social Influence Below the Radar

Why does what others do affects us? To get through our busy lives we tend to use heuristics or shortcuts based on our experience. People embrace a single feature of an object or situation and use it to formulate an automatic response. These shortcuts work well enough, or we wouldn't use them. However, these same shortcuts can be exploited by others to influence us (Cialdini, 2001). While these are largely strategies used for marketing, packaging can embody them as well.

Material self-interest. People want the biggest bang for their buck. One approach that takes advantage of this is creating packaging that allows for more product due to space or money saved on packaging, e.g., buying bulk with reusable containers.

Reciprocation. This is an incredibly strong and ubiquitous influence tactic. If someone does us a favor or gives us something we feel obligated to reciprocate.

Consistency. People feel uncomfortable when what they say doesn't match what they do, whether it is an internal voice or somebody calling it out. So, once a person commits to an idea or product, they tend to stand by it, even fiercely so, pointing to whatever evidence is available to justify it. This is the fertile ground of brand loyalty.

Social proof. The more people engaging in a behavior, the more we sense that it is the right thing to do, and we often receive social approval for complying. In packaging terms, this means giving consumers some indication that "everybody's doing it." Using the shape of a popular animated character that kids see on lunch boxes, and other products they use daily, will provide support that this product is okay.

Liking. We tend to choose people and things we like. There are some very predictable ways to enhance liking. Specifically, we like attractive things; note the presence of buxom women in all kinds of ads. People like others who are similar or objects that reflect their identity, such as boyish or girlish colors. People feel good about compliments (smart shoppers buy recycled) and cooperation (together we can save the rainforests). They also respond well to familiarity and association with other things they like. One way to take advantage of this is to connect new packaging to a product that is already very popular (New, improved package!). Leveraging what is comfortable allows innovation introduction without creating fear of the unknown. In this kind of iterative approach a product and package initially look and feel the same. Then the product changes, but the packaging looks familiar. Then finally, the package can change. Without realizing it, people are buying a whole new paradigm.

Authority. In ambiguous or novel situations, people rely on other's opinions to know what is good, especially those who they think are powerful. We gather information about authorities through their titles (e.g., Dr.) and jobs (e.g., chef), what they wear (e.g., a judge's robe), and status symbols such as rare or expensive automobiles. Effective strategies for building credibility use shapes, images, expert opinions, and associations that elicit perceptions of authority.

Scarcity. Most likely due to its evolutionary value, we tend to want to "act now" if we think there are limited numbers (limited edition holiday decanter!) of a product or a limited time to acquire it ("Wheaties champions" or "10th anniversary package"). Also, we tend to act fast and irrationally if an item has been censored or its availability has been decreased in some way, especially if it is due to popular demand.

Case Study: Peace Coffee

Peace Coffee, based in Minneapolis, Minnesota, defines itself as a "A cultural, social and consumable revolution with grounds firmly fixed in a farmer friendly, fair trade reality."

Since its inception in 1996, Peace Coffee has believed sustainable business is vital to local communities, both where it's products are sold, as well as where their coffee is grown. All Peace Coffees are 100 percent fair trade, certified organic and shade grown, and purchased directly from the growers.

Taking a holistic as well as realistic approach, Peace Coffee understands that some things may cost more up-front, but will yield economic and environmental benefits, as well as help maintain brand loyalty.

Addressing supply chain issues, Peace Coffee co-founded Cooperative Coffees, a co-op of roasters who import 100 percent fair trade coffee direct from the growers. This has allowed them to develop equitable and sustainable relationships that positively affect the farmers, their families, their community, and the consumer.

For their bulk bean bag, Peace Coffee wanted a bag that could transport the beans, and then act as collection vessel for the used grounds, then be thrown — grounds and all — into a backyard composter to fully decompose. Rather than settling for what was available, Peace Coffee worked with suppliers to develop a solution that would be true to their mission and message.

Peace Coffee found people really connected with the compostable bags vs. the plastic bag coffee commonly comes in (as their market's awareness of plastic's impact is high). But Peace Coffee wanted to look past the bag on the store shelf to the whole of their distribution impacts. A distribution mainstay around the world, bicycle delivery seemed like a low-impact solution, but questions were raised about reliability in their car-reliant and often snowbound and frigid home market of Minnesota. Being realistic, as well as holistic, Peace Coffee added a biodiesel van to their bicycle delivery fleet to expand their service area into the suburbs and neighboring states. The biodiesel option has helped them stay true to their mission, and has given them the chance to show other businesses that there can be a wide variety of viable solutions when you are willing to explore new ideas.

In 2008, Peace Coffee, and their innovative distribution system, were honored as part of the exhibit — *Minnovation: 150 Years of Ingenuity* — celebrating Minnesota's Sesquicentennial.

In general, Peace Coffee has found their design and distribution choices have been well received and have helped to set them apart not only as a fair trade coffee company, but one willing to assess all of their impacts to find viable solutions. There is always room for improvement, Peace Coffee points out, and so they would like to get away from using plastic bags for their retail prepackaged coffees, currently one of the few shelf-stable choices that preserve the freshness and integrity of the beans. Their goal is to find an alternative solution that will be completely renewable and reusable.

Social Influence Above the Radar

Another way to get people to consider a product is to try to engage them at a more mindful level. Effortful processing and evaluation of information tends to lead to long-lasting understanding and even behavior change. However, in order to get people to process and evaluate your message, you first have to get them to break out of their mindless, automatic mode. One way to accomplish this is to provide some sort of cue on the product packaging or near the point of purchase. Studies suggest that just a simple reminder to pay attention spurs people to be more mindful of their choices (Langer, 1989). Pictures can be very powerful, and subtle, cues. The appropriate cue and how best to display it, must be determined through research and testing.

Avoiding Propaganda

Information/education on packaging has an important caveat: There is a fine line between information that persuades and educates and information perceived as propaganda. The difference is not in the message, but the audience who receives it. People respond positively to information they can accommodate within their already held beliefs. Information that lies outside of their zone of acceptability will be dismissed, or might even make them angry. Thus, messages touting the green benefits of a product or package will most likely elicit a negative reaction in people who are not yet convinced that environmental issues are for real, and that sustainability is important.

Message Framing

The best way to avoid this negative reaction is to know your audience/customer and tailor your message to them; this is often called message framing.

Using message framing you can convey the same basic information but pitch it slightly differently depending on whom it is intended for. When it comes to messages of sustainability, there tend to be three groups for whom you should design a unique message. These groups are the clueless, the open-minded, and the converted (Amel and Manning, 2007).

The Clueless. The clueless are the relatively small group of people who are either completely unaware of sustainability issues, or in denial that these issues are real. The types of framing that might appeal to this group are messages that appeal to their concern for their own and their family's health. For example "this container is made with no PVC." Messages emphasizing personal benefits such as health, convenience, or a sense of novelty are also effective.

The Open-Minded. There is a growing market segment of people who are aware of and sympathetic to the idea of sustainability. This group often intentionally buys green products, but they also often let other product features take precedence over sustainability. Very often the packaging sustainability is not even on the radar for this group. Consequently, these people have a higher impact on the environment than they realize, in part because they don't consider packaging part of the "product." However, because

Creating clear instructions.

If consumers should do something other than throw the packaging away, make sure:

— Instructions are available, short, and clear.

— The action is easy to spot on the package.

— Systems for next step are readily available.

this group actually does want to do the sustainable thing, they tend to respond to messages that emphasize effectiveness.

The Converted. A smaller but rapidly growing group of consumers do pay close attention to packaging sustainability. Their goal is to minimize their ecological footprint; it is part of their identity and important to their personal standards. For people like this the best message demonstrates that there is consistency among values and product and packaging. Here, clearly identifying packaging benefits is critical.

Barriers to Action

Knowledge Is Not Enough

A well-framed message will go a long way to convince your audience of the benefits of your product and packaging. However, even if they are fully convinced and truly intend to buy your product as part of a sustainable lifestyle, there is still a good chance they won't make the purchase as they intend. Or, if they do make the purchase, they won't use it or dispose of it in the way that maximizes its sustainability. For instance, The Body Shop had to give up its comprehensive refill program a few years ago because people were throwing out the heavy, expensive, refillable bottles. These bottles were much more expensive to transport than the lighter, nonrefillable ones. It was costing the company money and creating more pollution to transport the heavier, refillable bottles that never got refilled (Gander, 2007). People often do not act in line with their values or their intentions. Psychological research is full of examples of this well-known "attitude/behavior gap." Fortunately, there are ways to reduce the attitude-behavior gap and make it easier for people to act on their sustainability intentions.

Lessons from Social Marketing

A professor of social psychology from Canada, Doug McKenzie-Mohr, has developed a method to encourage people to be more sustainable. His approach, based on social marketing and psychological research is called Community-Based Social Marketing. Using this approach, one can design a sustainability campaign that makes a particular sustainable action the easiest, most obvious, and more socially acceptable than the alternative, nonsustainable action. Dr. McKenzie-Mohr points out that even the most dedicated environmentalists sometimes do things they know to be bad for the environment, such as drive a car or throw their recycling in the garbage, because they encounter barriers that prevent them from taking the more sustainable action. If barriers prevent even ardent environmentalists from acting sustainably, they have an even stronger effect on less committed people.

The lesson, according to McKenzie-Mohr, is that sustainable actions will be carried out in direct proportion to how easy, convenient, and rewarding they are. His book and online resource guide (cbsm.com) offer a number of tools that help make a particular sustainable action, such as buying milk in reusable containers, more likely to occur at a small-community level. Some ideas from his work are relevant to packaging design.

Lesson A: Convenience. If packaging is reusable, make sure people have to make very little effort to return it for reuse; otherwise they won't do it. Many companies, such as The Body Shop, have learned the hard way that a refilling scheme is usually not adhered to even by the most loyal customers. People also do not reuse packaging for the simple reason that they forget to bring it every time they head to the store. Reminders and incentives are useful tools to overcome the barrier of forgetting.

People are also unlikely to recycle properly, or do anything other than throwing the packaging into the garbage unless the process is made as easy and clear as possible. Case in point: Curbside recycling has increased recycling rates dramatically in communities where it is available.

Lesson B: Clarity. Consider the current plethora of "degradable" plastic bags. Some of these are made of plant products like cornstarch and are designed to be composted. Other "biodegradable" bags are made with petroleum products and must be exposed to heat, moisture, and/or UV light in order to break down. Putting some bags on the compost heap or in the garbage halts the breakdown process and creates more plastic waste. Yet most consumers have no idea about the differences in degradability types and assume that a bag called biodegradable will break down wherever it ends up: compost, recycling, or garbage. The problem here is complexity. One part of the solution is clarity of instructions.

Lesson C: Creating social norms. People aren't likely to do things they don't see others doing. One way to create a sense of normality is encouraging people to display that they like and use your product/packaging. For example, a reusable bag or some other useful container people can carry in the store, displays the product logo, and shows others that the product is popular, and thus within the zone of acceptability.

Lessons from Human Factors Design/Engineering Psychology

Even the most knowledgeable and committed consumer might not take the most sustainable action with the product once he has purchased it. Take, for example, plastic water bottles in the recycling bin.

To most efficiently transport these bottles to the recycling facility, they should be flattened so as many as possible fit in the truck. However, most people do not do this. Perhaps they would, if the bottles were designed so they could more easily be flattened once empty. Human factors engineers can help overcome a problem like this. Their advice is: Design your product so it "affords" sustainability (Norman, 2002). "Affordance" is a term that refers to what a product invites a person to do. All objects have affordances. An example of a misleading affordance that we've all encountered is a door with the metal plate that clearly "affords" that you push it. However, as you try to push the door you realize somewhat sheepishly that you're pushing on the sign that says PULL. Human factors experts would place the blame for this clearly on the designer of the door, rather than on your inability to read a sign. If you want people to carry out a specific action with a product or its packaging, do not rely on instructions, however clear and obvious they might be. Design the product and packaging so that it invites whatever action is most sustainable and appropriate. An example of a type of packaging with a clear and sustainable affordance is the marmalade (and mustard) jars that are the perfect size and shape to be used as drinking glasses.

Barriers preventing even ardent environmentalists from acting sustainably, have an even stronger effect on the less committed.

The Nitty Gritty of Collecting Data

This chapter begins and ends with notes about collecting data systematically. We began this way to emphasize the role that research can, and should, play in maximizing sustainable packaging design. Each data collection method has its own charms and pitfalls, so ideally should use several different methods in the research process. Literature reviews are a good place to start — don't reinvent the wheel. Observation allows you to understand behaviors and contextual factors that people sometimes don't notice. Focus groups allow for in-depth exploration of specific issues. Surveys have the benefit of accessing large groups of diverse people. While the methods sound straightforward, there are best practices for each. If you don't have the background yourself it is worth familiarizing yourself with the details or even hiring experts.

Literature Reviews

Technology makes literature reviews easy as many library databases (accessing thousands of psychological, marketing, communication, and sociological journals and books) can be searched quickly for relevant information. While the accuracy of such publications is not guaranteed, most have been peer-reviewed to maximize quality. Web sites (e.g., cbsm.com) are another good source, but caveat emptor as anyone can post their opinions.

Observation

Sometimes people cannot articulate what they do because their behavior is often habitual and, thus, automatic. When we do things, even highly complex things, out of habit, description can elude our verbal skills. A trained observer can identify how often a certain behavior occurs, under what conditions it occurs, and important attributes of the behavior itself. The beauty of observation is that it does not rely on people remembering what they do or when. A hidden or well-integrated observer limits the tendency for people to act unnaturally or in a socially desirable way when they are being watched.

Focus Groups

Focus groups are small face-to-face gatherings that encourage a dynamic exploration of questions by a small group of consumers. Because it is face-to-face, structuring the makeup of the focus groups becomes critical. Power imbalances (say, between men and women) may stifle the participation of some members, thus losing important information. Depending on your circumstances, you might separate focus groups by gender, self-report position on consuming, or relevant issues such as where they typically shop (e.g., big box retailer, co-op, mom & pop, discounters, and so on). Because people are meeting in groups, the psychological risks (e.g., embarrassment, guilt) for any one participant increases as does the moderator's responsibility for setting boundaries and attending to basic privacy issues (Morgan, 1998).

Surveys

Once your product idea's key principles are identified, survey a larger group representing a variety of constituents (e.g., green, neutral, antigreen) to see if your hunches generalize or not.

When you are surveying a large group of people you will want to ask closed-ended questions because organizing and interpreting open-ended responses become extremely time consuming. Closed-ended responses include yes/no, check boxes, and scales ranging in value from STRONGLY AGREE to STRONGLY DISAGREE, for example. Good survey design avoids questions that are leading (Is it important for you to avoid contributing to the injustices of corporate agriculture?), double-barreled (Do you find wooden handles convenient and attractive?), or jargonish (Are you worried about polyethylene terephthalate?).

Other survey basics are to make sure questions are free of errors, printed in an easily read font, use appropriate vocabulary, and are culturally sensitive (Litwin, 2003). People's estimates of their own behavior tend to be inaccurate due to the basic human desire to seem like a good person. However, the link between people's attitudes and what they do is even weaker. So, you might want to stick with mostly behavior-oriented questions.

Finally, people have limited time and attention. After you have put together your questions, try them out on a few people and make sure it takes them no more than ten minutes. After that, people tend to either think less about the questions and their answers, or quit altogether. Often the biggest problem with surveys is a low return rate. This is problematic in that the people who return the surveys may be unique in critical ways from the people who don't. The return rate can be improved with reminders and incentives.

Wrapping It Up

The mechanics of human behavior are many and complex. However, they are critical to ensuring the effectiveness of the sustainable packaging movement. With people, one size does not fit all. Do you know your customer? Sometimes people pay attention, sometimes not. Does your package need to accommodate both scenarios? People like being comfortable yet consider themselves unique. Does your package ride this fine line?

"Packaging can serve its purpose without harming the earth. Make people notice sustainable packaging — and be awed by its innovation. The key is to consider what people are (or are not) thinking" (Amel and Manning, 2007).

Preserve® Tableware

Helping the consumer "close the loop." Preserve® Tableware is dishwasher safe and reusable, made from 100% recycled plastic, which includes recycled yogurt cups. The tableware is again recyclable in communities where #5 plastics are recycled.

The primary package is made from renewable cellulose film. The handy, resealable container encourages reuse.

To see the entire line of innovative Preserve® products or to learn about their earth efforts, visit their Web site at preserveproducts.com

preserve
CUTLERY

8 FORKS, 8 KNIVES, 8 SPOONS

REUSABLE, dishwasher safe
RECYCLED, 100% recycled plastic
RECYCLABLE, #5 plastic

by Recycline.

Preserve™ Cutlery
Preserve™ Cutlery is the environment-friendly
disposable cutlery. We make it from 100% rec
including recycled yogurt cups, and it is re
communities with #5 plastics recycling. It is
on low-heat cycles and packaged in a reusable
All helping you to conserve resources and

by Recycline. The makers of the Preserve™
and the Preserve™-Reusa

www.recycline.com • 888-354-7

Canister - #7 (made from) renewable
wood sources), Label - PP #5 (plastic
label facilitates canister recycling),
Cap - HDPE #2.

3 Marketing and Truth

Wendy Jedlička, CPP
Jedlička Design Ltd.

Jacquelyn Ottman
J. Ottman Consulting

With additional contributions from:
*Dr. Paul H. Ray, Arlene Birt, Fred Haberman, Jeremy Faludi,
TerraChoice Environmental Marketing, Co-op America,
US Federal Trade Commission*

People today are looking for products or services that not only whiten and brighten, but deliver an intangible extra: ethical values.

From production methods, business practices, and stakeholder relationships to corporate giving and vendor associations, people are paying attention to who serves their needs as much as what they are selling. Successful firms are developing deeper relationships with their target audience, in spite of tightening markets, by learning how to create that extra something to nurture healthy, long-term, stakeholder relationships.

Pike Place Market, Seattle 2002
Photo: W. Jedlička

The Consumer Relationship

In the earliest days of humankind, people made or gathered goods and traded them for things they hadn't gathered, or couldn't make — and the barter economy was born. People needed stuff, other people developed the skills to make stuff, and each contributed their skills for the betterment of the whole community. You knew the producer of your goods, and they knew you and your needs. Marketing was all by word of mouth, and goods carried the personal guarantee of the maker, making the whole affair a fairly straightforward process. It's in this simple space that the idea of the market's guiding hand as a benevolent force works well, with localized checks and balances keeping the system in line. Eventually, as mass production and the use of currency, rather than trading for completed local goods became the norm, producers far removed from markets where their goods would be consumed began to decide what would be made, assuming a posture of *If we make it, they will buy* regardless of the impacts, or how well it fit with the end market, or even if it really needed to be made in the first place. In the beginning years of the Industrial Revolution the net inflight of people to population centers making demand outpace supply, meant that people bought what was available, not what they really wanted, or even what was best for them or their community.

Empowering the Consumer

Zip forward a few hundred years of technological improvements and we find markets becoming more competitive and supply chains more global, opening markets to even more competitors. In contrast to the days of yore, consumers today are learning they not only have a choice, but these choices have deeper impacts than sales volumes for the producing company. Taking back some of the power they once had in a barter economy, consumers are redefining "needs" and "wants." Through each buying decision, they're molding the market, dictating what goods will be produced. And, more importantly, they're shaping how these goods are produced and delivered. This choice of how an item is produced breaks down to: made with no regard for the product's impacts, focusing only on the final piece (price, excessive resources used) or with very close attention to the product, and its production and afterlife impacts.

As populations grow and competition increases, producers now find themselves held hostage to the demands of the market rather than dictating its shape from a more convenient stance. By signaling their approval or disapproval with their purchases, consumers could be telling producers they couldn't care less and are simply living for the moment. Or they could indicate that they're tired of bad products that foul their neighborhoods, make them sick, or don't deliver on promises. For producers trying to better position themselves and their products, the realization that markets maybe don't know best makes current economic trends so dynamic. The importance of connecting with the buyer as a stakeholder in the production process becomes key to the firm's long-term success.

How can we connect with consumers and empower them to help industry make better decisions that will lessen the impacts both products and packaging have on our world?

Every second of every day, a barrage of advertising reminds us we live in a market economy, that works in a framework where buyer and seller are far removed from each other. Though we don't think about it each day, our buying choices do have a direct impact on how industry shapes our world. All of these choices together decide our collective fate. "Hold on there," says the consumer. "I'm just buying a soda, not driving an oil tanker into a wildlife sanctuary!" Being so far removed from the production process, the consumer naturally fails to make the connection that their soda requires petroleum to make the bottle, as wells as fuels the trucks to move their water from spring to store — their purchase is partly why the tanker was there. Getting exposed to the deeper supply chain issues by eco-advocates, the consumer starts to feel bad about their choices, and yet feels helpless to make an impact: "I'm only one person. What can I do?"

A market-based economy's demands don't always fit neatly within the boundaries of sustainable production models. To be sustainable, goods should be produced, sold, used, and disposed of by and for local consumers. The technologies we've come to enjoy consume resources from all around the world, making production today anything but a local affair. Does that mean that to be sustainable we need to turn the clock back before the Industrial Revolution to the ancient days of barter? It's a fairly safe to say, the genie won't go quietly back in the bottle. So it's unreasonable to expect all regions to produce all goods for their local consumers. Buying choices then become the driving force in determining how green a local market will be, its ripple effect on a global scale, and ultimately how successfully we can shift from being blind consumption machines to being agents of positive change.

Connect with consumers and empower them to help industry make better decisions that will lessen the impacts both products and packaging have on our world.

Does the Selling Price Really Tell the Story?

Paper packaging is made from trees, a renewable and carbon-sequestering resource. But from where? A plantation, an old growth sanctuary, or a sustainably managed forest? Even when a tree is planted for commercial use, trees produce less pulp per acre than higher yield annual pulp crops like kenaf and hemp, and do nothing to help close an ecological and economic loop like agripulp (field residue). Doing something as basic as buying a box of tissues now becomes a test of your forestry practices and supply chain integrity knowledge. What on the surface seemed an easy choice (lotion dipped or extra strong?) becomes a much harder decision with far reaching impacts. Eco-advocates are working to make complex decisions tangible, and are asking consumers targeted questions like, "Do you really need to cut down a virgin forest to feel clean?"

Glass packaging comes from fairly abundant resources, though not all glass-using regions have all of them. Metal packaging resources like steel and aluminum have high eco-impacts to collect and refine from virgin ore. "Well, that's easy then, I'll just buy stuff in glass" — if only it were that simple. Glass packaging is heavier to transport in all phases of its life cycle than steel for the same uses (prepared/

Shopping List for Positive Change

The following are ideas consumer advocates use to help buyers better align their purchases with their ethics.

— Choose products/packaging that use sustainably renewable or recycled materials first.

— Encourage manufacturers to do the right thing. Help make those eco-choices part of their competitive advantage.

— Buy locally to help cut down on fuel for transportation And keep jobs in local communities.

— Choose products currently recycled in YOUR area, plus look for those that close the loop.

— Stay familiar with the recycling rules for your curbside program. Not all areas take all materials. Give preference to products that allow you to close the loop.

— Use common sense.

Concentrates are more cost effective than ready to use. Do you really need cheese in individually wrapped slices? If the package is plastic, is it adding a positive user feature, like shampoo in a shatterproof bottle for safety? If it looks wasteful, it is.

If you regularly buy a product that's overall really good, but has un-eco packaging, drop the company a letter. Be an eco-purchasing activist. Tell them you'd like to keep buying their product but their un-eco packaging is making it hard for you. If there's a competing product packaged in a more responsible way, point that out too. Support manufacturers who are proud of their eco efforts (usually printed right on their packaging with more details on their Web site).

At home:

— Encourage family and friends to use eco-alternatives.

— Teach your kids why good buying choices and recycling are important. There are many Web sites to help them get involved.

At the office:

— Give your company's purchasing department alternatives for more eco-friendly products. Most people will pick a more eco product if given the option, make it easy for them.[1]

preserved foods). Heavier transport weight means burning more oil. Oil is not renewable, an eco-hazard waiting to happen, and when burned as fuel, adds to global warming. Plastic packaging is used today in place of glass because of its light weight (less transport costs), durability, and clarity. But it's made from oil, and does not recycle as universally (or continuously, Cradle to Cradle) as versions in steel or aluminum, which are also lighter than glass in the same applications.

As the true cost of impacts are not yet directly (and universally) attached to the goods we buy, allowing price to make the decision for us, it's been left up to consumers to pay attention (or not) to the goods they buy. This unbridled choice means that every purchase we make, and everything we create, becomes a statement about how we really feel about the environment. Whether we mean to or not. Did we care enough to research our purchases (look for certifications printed on the package), or did we just shop and go?

Packaging Can Only Make Them Buy Once

The Pet Rock from the 1970s is a good example of packaging that sells the product. In fact it is the product, and part of the pantheon of icons representing any useless but wildly successful product. Unless you really had a lot of friends you wanted to push this joke on, it was a onetime sale.

Package designers employ a variety of tricks to make the sale. Appealing photography, expert use of color signals, layout harmony, typography, humor or glamour, visual/structural/tactile excitement — all play a part in moving the product off the store shelf and into the consumer's hands.

Packaging can make shoppers buy a product, but it can only make them do it once. The product itself must do all it claims to do, and the company must work to connect with its customer base on a deeper level — developing brand loyalty. In a very competitive market, brand loyalty becomes a very precious asset.

Brand Loyalty

There was a time when people passed down their shopping habits and favored brands like family traditions. Today competition is fierce, and brands compete in their home markets with competitors from all over the globe. For the consumer these are heady times. Products are diverse, abundant, and — as many producers do not attach the true cost of production to the cost of the product — prices are disproportionately cheap relative to their actual cost to produce (and distribute, market, and dispose of!). It's easy to make cheap goods when you take advantage of lax environment and labor laws in another country. And it's easy to leverage that advantage as long as the true cost (for instance, the cost to society for pollution) is not applied to the goods being shipped.

Because there are so many ways to avoid paying the true cost of producing a good, almost no product is safe from a competitor introducing a cheaper version that has cashed in on its environmental health or taken undue advantage of its citizens. Selling on price alone then seems like a fool's game, because with each new competitor, firms find themselves pushing their profits (and production centers) to the point where they can no longer afford to make the products at all.

Developing and maintaining brand loyalty becomes critical. It's easy to understand that big ticket items, like cars, where a manufacturer may only sell a few units to a consumer over the course of their lifetime, must cultivate a positive user experience and brand loyalty as part of the company's long-term strategy. But small, frequently purchased goods like toiletries and packaged food, where price is often the main purchase driver, have found developing and sustaining brand loyalty through quality of product and integrity of message allows them a greater range of strategic positioning, and pricing options, if they approach the task with the same attention to marketing basics as mainstream products, and don't rely on the old idea of "If we make it, they will buy."

Ethics-Based Marketing and Business

As connecting with the consumer on a deeper level becomes part of a product manufacturer's long-term strategy, in crowded markets like food and personal care, innovators like Ben & Jerry's and Aveda have changed the whole complexion of the industry by using ethics as part of their products' point of difference.

Our mission at Aveda is to care for the world we live in, from the products we make to the ways in which we give back to society. At Aveda, we strive to set an example for environmental leadership and responsibility, not just in the world of beauty, but around the world.

Since its inception, working with and giving back to nature have been the cornerstones of Aveda's mission. Taking a systems approach, they partner with their supplier communities to assure not only consistent supply of raw materials, but also work to keep in balance the area's social, as well as environmental health.

Extending this philosophy further, Aveda partners not only with their immediate suppliers, but their suppliers' suppliers, working up and down their supply chain, checking the integrity of all materials and processes undertaken in the creation of their products.

Aveda was one of the first companies in the United States to openly disclose recycled content for their plastics packaging, as well as the recycled content and ink composition of their paper packaging. Not stopping with simply improving existing materials, Aveda looks for new approaches and opportunities to further their goals through design and production innovation.

Empowered by its unique Mission, Aveda believes that authentic beauty is one that works in harmony with the greater web of life. It does not qualify as beauty if it hurts any of the diverse life forms that the best beauty artist of all, Nature, created. Authentic Beauty cares for the environment which we inherited from elders and will leave to generations that follow us. Beauty cares for the society in which we live, enhancing harmony in the way we live and interact with one another as human beings. In order to be Beauty, it also needs to be Good. Beauty is the result, but also the process followed in pursuing that result. Said simply, *Beauty Is As Beauty Does.* — Dominique Conseil, President.[2]

Due to their unflinching attention to quality, healthful, products, Aveda enjoys some of the best brand loyalty in their industry. Their customers feel they are getting the best quality possible, and are willing to pay a premium for the level of quality assurance Aveda delivers.

Today, one is hard pressed to find a personal care competitor that doesn't work the nature angle somehow, from corporate giving to basic ingredients. There are few companies in today's beauty market that will openly highlight unnatural ingredients as they did in the past. Imagine a label reading NOW WITH MORE LYE! as hair products once boasted.

Ethics is only one part of a total product driving team. Clever packaging relying on ethics alone to sell a product only works in the short term. The product, its package, and the company behind it must all deliver on the promise they make to the consumer.

Social Justice and Marketing

One of the cornerstones of the Natural Step method of systems thinking is the concept that there can be no eco-justice without social justice (System Condition 4).

A farmer scratching out a living on the edge of a rainforest has more pressing needs than the fate of a few trees. His family is hungry and his land is becoming unable to sustain crops. He doesn't care that the area he lives in is really only suited to being a rainforest: All he knows is farming — what he can get cash for right now. So each year he clears a little more forestland to help feed his family. But what if the forest itself became valuable if left intact? And what if that farmer were given the tools to help develop the forest's earning potential for what it really is in economic terms — a stable and yet dynamic, millennia-old production facility?

From *The Economist* (07/22/04):

> If conservation of tropical forest offers global benefits, ways must be found to charge beneficiaries globally. These are beginning to emerge. There is a fledgling market for payments for

"environmental services," such as sequestering carbon and preserving biodiversity. Peru, for example, offers "conservation concessions" to groups with the means and know-how to manage forest. A proposal for "compensated reduction" of carbon emissions would discourage deforestation and give developing countries, which have few commitments under the Kyoto Protocol, a bigger role in reducing greenhouse gases.

So how does all this far-off thinking impact product marketing? We can use the Home Depot Old Growth and Nike Sweatshop lessons as examples.

Home Depot unduly exposed themselves to public criticism by not taking a more watchful stance on the products they sold. From 1997 to 1999, protests against the company were mounted by environmental groups in an effort to get the world's biggest buyer of wood to assure it was not selling wood from endangered forests. Over this period, Home Depot stores were picketed, banners were hung at its corporate headquarters in Atlanta, and activists demonstrated at shareholder meetings. Home Depot became increasingly afraid the negative publicity would result in consumer backlash and sliding sales, so they took steps to change.

Today Home Depot is part of a growing effort by corporations to work with global activists toward positive change. In this example, Home Depot began by lobbying governments and loggers to stop over-cutting forests from their lumber supplying regions. In Chile, they helped broker a pact to deter landowners from converting native forests into the very kind of tree farms the retailer depends on.

To meet environmentalists' demands, Home Depot agreed to change its buying practices to preference wood logged in environmentally preferable ways.

The first guidelines used were from the Forest Stewardship Council, a group that certifies sustainably harvested wood. But going a step further, as certified supplies would not be enough to meet their demand and they needed to better assure the integrity of their supply chain, Home Depot worked to identify endangered forests around the world and persuaded their suppliers not to log there.[3]

Many retailers find that working with green groups is a fairly inexpensive way to better connect with customers and end negative publicity. Home Depot notes the cost of the new initiatives is small relative to their total sales. Many companies that have been forced into change due to citizen action, and then put pressure on their supply chain to help meet those new goals, have created a ripple effect throughout their entire industry.

Though Nike and Home Depot both found themselves in trouble due to lack of supply chain vigilance, Nike's brand was tied to basic sustainability concepts. When it came to light that Nike was using sweatshop labor to manufacture their goods, the integrity of their marketing message, in fact their entire corporate brand, was immediately called into question. This is a serious thing for a company. There are many numbers tossed around, but the general rule of thumb in marketing is: It takes much more money to win a customer back than to get them in the first place.

In an effort to realign its supply chain with its core ethics, Nike now encourages third-party verification of factory conditions by trade unions and NGOs. Beginning with its second Corporate Responsibility Report (2004), Nike publicly released a list of the factories it contracts with. This level of transparency is a first in the apparel and footwear industries.

Case Study: Distant Village

A member of Co-op America, Organic Trade Association (OTA), and the Fair Trade Federation, Distant Village is a producer of alternative pulp and specialty packaging. They believe that central to sustainability is compassion, honesty, and social service. Rich Cohen, the driving force behind Distant Village, explains:

> Sustainability should not be misconstrued as primarily "eco-friendly," which might be the case with marketing-driven sustainability initiatives. Sustainability must be complete in its scope, and is most successful when the core company values, and fundamental mission, are supporting and cohesive with sustainability.

At the heart of their operations Distant Village uses a systems model it developed in 2000, called Complete Sustainability. One aspect of this model — economic inclusion of economically dislocated communities — is often overlooked in materials-focused eco-friendly models.

Environmental: Cradle to Cradle perspective of sourcing, extracting, and processing of raw materials used in creating packaging, as well as the utility, reusability, and long-term environmental impact of eco-reintegration of the packaging.

Distant Village uses materials such as: tree-free paper made from wild grass, which is abundant and renewable; 100% banana fiber waste collected from banana plantations/processing plants; and mulberry papers from abundant troublesome weed trees.

These materials produce beautiful new hand-crafted packaging from waste or abundant natural materials, instead of using and extracting valuable resources.

Distant Village often uses sun and natural heat to dry papers. Other heat needs are often fueled with rice hull waste instead of fossil fuels — all part of current solar income balance, a key element in controlling global warming. Though their shipping methods are conventional, Cohen notes they are quite skilled at consolidating multiple shipments for multiple customers and bringing them to the United States as one large shipment. "Of course this just makes good business sense," Cohen points out.

Social: Contribution, inclusion, and advancement of artisans, families, and communities that develop packaging in distant villages. This includes a scholarship program, which customers fund and participate in as part of a holistic approach to positive perception.

Economic: Fair trade, fair wages, and infusion of economic fuel (jobs, money, commerce) in distant villages. This provides an outlet for skilled craftspeople and opportunities for learning new skills.

Innovation and development are central to Distant Village's mission, with industry firsts like tree-free chipboard, tree-free labels (with eco-adhesive, and recycled release paper), and agro-forest packaging (made up of forest floor scraps). Distant Village delivers sustainable, but also highly differentiated packaging designed to meet the branding and marketing needs of companies. "Our secret, is just great packaging," says Cohen.

The general rule of thumb in marketing is: It takes much more money to win a customer back than to get them in the first place.

"While we cannot say with certainty what greater levels of factory disclosure will unleash, we know the current system of addressing factory compliance has to be fundamentally transformed to create sustainable change," said Hannah Jones, Nike's vice president of corporate responsibility. "We believe disclosure of supply chains is a step toward greater efficiencies in monitoring and remediation and shared knowledge in capacity building that will elevate overall conditions in the industry. No one company can solve these issues that are endemic to our industry. We know the future demands more collaboration among stakeholders, not less."[4]

Co-op America's Basics of Fair Trade

Packaging and product are not just about materials alone. Fair Trade is one of the key elements employed by today's sustainability leaders. Ethics-based companies need to be sure their talk is walked. Part of a company's vertical supply chain management system would use fair trade practices to help assure the integrity of a company's message is carried through — from the growers in the field and sewers at the factory to the product on the store shelf. Aligning a company's supply chain on more than a simple materials level can seem like a daunting task at first, but finding ethical suppliers (or helping established sup-

pliers realign their priorities) is getting easier every day, and there are a variety of groups serving various industries to help make the job easier still. Co-op America is one of the oldest and most respected groups working with both businesses and consumers. Founded in 1982, Co-op America is a nonprofit membership organization working to harness economic power — the strength of consumers, investors, businesses, and the marketplace — to create a socially just and environmentally sustainable society. For a free download of the full version of Co-op America's Guide to Fair Trade go to fairtradeaction.org.

To get started understanding what fair trade is, below is a basic overview of fair trade principles and practices from *Co-op America's Guide to Fair Trade.*

A Fair Price

Fair Trade Certified™ product prices are set by the Fair Trade Labeling Organization. Prices set not only cover the cost of goods, but strive to provide a fair living wage for the people involved in the production process.

Investment in People and Communities

Often Fair Trade producer cooperatives and artisan collectives reinvest their revenues back into their communities — strengthening local businesses, building health clinics and schools, supporting scholarship funds, building housing and providing leadership training and women's programs. All work to build stronger, healthier communities.

Environmental Sustainability

Fair Trade producers respect their natural habitat and are encouraged to use sustainable production methods. Example: Nearly 85 percent of Fair Trade Certified™ coffee is also organic.

Empowering Stakeholders

Fair Trade promotes producer empowerment in their communities and in the global marketplace. For Fair Trade coffee producers, their cooperatives or associations are transparent and democratically controlled by their members. For estate grown products like tea and bananas, Fair Trade provides revenue that is invested in a fund, managed and controlled by the farmers, and used for the interests of the community — providing education, access to health care, and so on.

Empowering Women

Recognizing the untapped potential of all stakeholders in a community, Fair Trade encourages participation by women in local cooperatives and in leadership roles. Fair Trade revenue is also often used to support or promote women's programs.

Direct, Long-Term Relationships

Those who import Fair Trade Certified™ products and other fairly traded goods contribute to the endeavor to establish long-term stable relationships with producer groups. Not only helping to create healthier communities, but providing a more stable, and sustainable economic base allowing entire regions to benefit.

Package as Bridge or Barrier

A generally accepted industry statistic is that about 70 percent of all purchase decisions are made in the store, and 70 to 90 percent of new products fail each year. These are sobering numbers. Combine this with the eighth of a second you get to catch a poten-

tial buyer's eye, and you've got to wonder why anyone would want to sell products at all.

The simple answer is, we have to. Most of us are unable to make all of the goods we need to survive on our own, so we must participate in an integrated and cooperative economic system. Moving product then becomes not just an intellectual exercise — but an act of survival.

Given the huge weight involved with in-store decision making, finely tuned and effective packaging becomes one of the single most important elements a company can engineer to guarantee a product's success — and their survival.

This is pretty intense. Because so many people making so many of their purchase decisions at the store, packaging can either be the bridge — uniting the customer to a product — or a barrier, keeping the product unsold on the shelf.

What Is "Good" vs. "Great" Packaging?

A "good" package is one that does what it's supposed to with a minimum of expense and hassle for everyone involved. "Great" packaging, on the other hand, takes that even further by delivering maximum sales per market segment with maximum middle and end buyer satisfaction.

Oddly, in spite of all the economic, environmental, and actual weight a package must carry, today's packaging decisions are still too often driven by people with little or no training in engineering and design, buyer motivation science, or even an understanding of the real "need" the package must serve. With millions of dollars at stake, why do companies continue to do that? At least in the United States the answer is because they still can. Very few states have enacted the strict producer responsibility laws that are being enacted in markets best positioned to afford US goods: the EU, Japan, Australia, and Canada.

Also, the United States has not experienced a direct consumer revolt, forcing producers to take responsibility for their products. By contrast, in the 1980s Germany had a garbage crisis. In an effort to better attach costs to consumption, lawmakers increased all trash hauling fees. The increase was so high, consumers began emptying their purchase contents into containers from home, leaving the empty packages at the end of the checkout line. Not wanting to be left "holding the bag," retailers in turn demanded less (or more efficient) packaging solutions from their suppliers, pulling the whole system into line in short order.

Today, while enjoying a comparable standard of living, "Europeans on average use 47.2% fewer resources per person (in oil energy equivalent units) as their North American counterparts."[5]

Packaging does not require those involved in making key decisions to be experts in every point of minutia, but it does demand that they have a solid enough background to know which questions to ask, who to seek out for answers, and what to do with the answers once they get them.

A universal lament among designers is: You're only as good as your clients let you be. Yet innovation can only happen when people lose their fear of asking questions. Often a simple "Why do we do it this way?" or "Do we really need it (or this part)?" can spark real and positive change.

Encouraging Consumer Choice

With the world's increased focus on green living, companies are clamoring to tell their customers what they're doing to benefit the environment.

And, consumers are demanding transparent and truthful communication about all aspects of the products they use.

They both know consumer choice is one of capitalism's most powerful tools — and the environment's trump card. How do products communicate to the consumer to encourage good choices?

Communicating a Product's Story

Traditionally, eco-labels or similar "stamps of approval" produced by a plethora of certifiers have helped conscientious consumers make purchasing decisions that benefit the environment. But as applied sustainability gains momentum, both companies and consumers need a more effective tool to demystify how products impact the planet.

Growing segmentation within the sustainability market has brought an array of green-marketing claims (organic, local, fair trade, zero emissions, carbon neutral), causing confusion among consumers. We've all heard examples of something sustainable in one context and environmentally damaging in another.

Background Stories: Connecting the consumer to their supply chain

No product fits a cookie-cutter definition of sustainability. Communicating sustainability requires big-picture connections between the product in your hand and the outside world. The need is greater than an eco-label can possibly address.

Background Stories

One way to arm consumers with the information they need to gauge the eco-worthiness of a product is through visual storytelling.

Born of a master's thesis project, Background Stories is a prototype of a tool that reveals a product's social and environmental impact by visually describing the life cycle of a product —from the production line to the store shelf — with graphics and fact-based captions in a storyline.

Just as nutrition labels provide consistent information (calories, total fat, sodium, and the like), Background Stories can note a product's carbon footprint and other Life Cycle Analysis (LCA) indicators in a framework that also supports existing product labels that certify elements of sustainability, like organic and fair trade.

A product's Background Story continues on the company's Web site, where consumers are offered the opportunity to dig deeper into the manufacturer's business practices.

Consumers can choose to explore the information at their own pace, or not at all. Just as some consumers are avid readers of Nutrition Facts and others only occasionally glance at sodium levels, Background Stories allows consumers to adapt to their own way of navigating a product's social and environmental information.

The system can be customized for any product and speaks to the consumer in a positive way. No scolding fingers are wagged. Consumers do not get told what is right or wrong. They are simply presented with facts through storytelling — a familiar, engaging form of communication.

Why It Works

Background Stories present a win-win situation for the environment, consumers, and business. Consumers are armed with information about a product's environmental impact before purchasing, driving healthy choices for people and the planet. Companies can present their products' sustainability stories — typically buried in sustainability and corporate social responsibility reports — at the point-of-sale.

Longer-Term Impact Is Even More Promising

Companies with Background Stories on their products will innovate toward manufacturing, transportation, and production practices that reduce negative environmental impact.

Consequently, the bar will be raised in sustainability reporting and action. Background Stories can help drive consumers' demand for simpler and more accessible information from companies on packaging, enabling companies to evaluate their approach to preserving the planet and how they share preservation practices.

Learning from Background Stories on select products, consumers will be better educated on the processes behind products and inclined to explore the impacts of products without Background Stories.

Compared to other information sources, Background Stories gets stuff right into the consumers hands, allowing companies to put substantive information, not just marketing hype, about their sustainability practices on the back of a box, a hang tag on a garment, or the side panel of a toy package. Where eco-labels mark single attributes, Background Stories put them in context.

Article by Arlene Birt and Fred Haberman. Visit backgroundstories.com for more information.

Thing or Service?

We can't really begin to understand what the problem is until we step way back and look at things from a new perspective. We buy things, but is it the thing we want or the service of the thing? When we buy a car are we interested in the ownership of the car (status symbol) or the function of the car (moving people and stuff around)? When we buy a cup of coffee, are we really interested in the physicality of the coffee (water, beans, heat) — or what the coffee provides (refreshment, warmth)?

These are some fundamental questions that lie at the heart of circular and restorative consumption and, by extension sustainable design. In the case of packaging, our bird's-eye view tells us unless some secondary use is built into the thing (Tazo Tea Infuser [refill from bulk tea]), we're not really interested in the package but the function the package provides (safety assurance, convenience, information).

One company that looks at what packaging does from a service standpoint is Minnesota-based Restore Products. Restore Products' mission is to serve customers by making it fun, easy, and cost effective to clean and maintain their investments (clothes, dishes, homes, businesses) without harm to the planet or its people. All Restore cleaning prod-

ucts are designed with performance, user safety, and the environment in mind.

Restore's products are made from renewable, plant-based ingredients, and use no petroleum solvents, chlorine, ammonia, alcohol, or hazardous ingredients. They don't give off toxic fumes or irritate the skin if used correctly, contain no known carcinogens, and are readily biodegradable.

Building on the idea that people are really looking to buy a product's service, not necessarily the physical product (and the packaging that goes with it), the Restore Products system was born.

Restore's products are purchased in a specially sized and labeled package, created to key into their refill stations. By making it so only their packages trigger the refill stations' mechanism, Restore allows the consumer to maintain the advantages of the package (use information and product safety warnings — critical for cleaning products), while still helping to keep thousands of tons of plastic out of area landfills and incinerators. See restoreproducts.com for more information.

Eco-Labeling and Eco-Marketing Claims

Many in industry today are talking about a "life cycle facts" label for packaging/products. Similar to nutrition facts this label would allow consumers to make important comparisons when choosing which product to buy. To get beyond wild claims and greenwashing, a labeling program of this depth would require standards that do not yet exist (including measurements along the whole of the product's supply chain). This level of detail though is currently in the works by many governments and

NGOs around the world. It may not be in place now, but like the Nutrition Facts panel of the 1990s, we will be seeing this information as standard packaging fare in one form or another very soon.

Nutrition Facts Panel for a Healthier Planet

How do you know what's good to buy? In an age of marketing spin and greenwashing, how can consumers trust a label saying eco-friendly, Organic or Energy Star? Simple yes or no systems get trapped by either low standards or excluding good but not great contenders. Even multilevel systems can seem opaque and arbitrary. Customers need objectivity, not just an opinion about quality. You get objectivity by showing the numbers.

Marketers usually try to avoid numbers because they worry consumers get scared by them, and the numbers won't make sense to them. (Is 75kg of carbon emission for a cell phone good or bad?) But nutrition labels are full of numbers, with ingredients lists full of unpronounceable chemical names, and consumers want them. First, they make people feel safer because, even if they don't understand the data, they feel reassured by the level of transparency between them and the producer. Second, if consumers are educated about certain things (e.g. fat, calories, or sodium), the labels are a tool for decision making. Third, even if people are uninformed, the labels educate them about nutrition, just by seeing what is important to list. Curious consumers may then compare products side by side in the store, and after some experience they know a "good" number of calories for a certain kind of food, without needing to compare. Nutrition labels not only aid consumer decision making, but also increase the general public's nutritional awareness.

Nutrition Facts for a healthier planet

A Hypothetical Full Life Cycle Label

Shown on page 75 is a hypothetical Environmental Facts label, modeled after the Nutrition Facts label. The text portion gives quantitative details of production and ingredients — it is the product's life cycle analysis in a nutshell. The graphic portion gives qualitative information at a glance, summarizing the product's impacts in four categories: resource use and waste, energy, water, and toxics.

Resource use, energy use, water use, waste, and labor practices are the main things you need to know to decide how sustainable a product is. Energy use (including production, transport, and usage) is usually one of the biggest impacts, with consequences for climate change, peak oil, and air pollution. Resource use has long been known to be an environmental problem, causing deforestation and other habitat loss, as well as pollution and landfills. In addition to listing the resources used, the label would note how to dispose of the product after use (recycling, takeback, compost, and so on). Toxins could be a separate section, calling out chemicals known to have human or environmental health impacts, so you can see how healthy the product is to have in your home, and how safe it is to produce. Water is becoming an increasingly serious issue in the world as population pressures cause scarcity. The amount of water used to make a product can be surprising. (A pound of US beef requires between 440 and 2500 gallons of water to produce.) Finally, exploitative trade and labor conditions are unsustainable, while good practices should be rewarded, as should transparency (organizational accountability and openness).

The data listed in the text would include all material ingredients and wastes (with toxic and nonrenewable materials and wastes labeled as such), as well as all embodied energy and water, transportation averages (or countries of origin), and social/labor factors. Measuring all this is not simple. Some items do not inherently have numbers (like labor practices) and would be assigned a score based on either internal company metrics (which Nike, Starbucks, and many other companies already have) or a third-party standard such as the Human Rights Campaign's Corporate Equality Index. The ingredients, waste, and other numbers would require an agreed-upon depth of life cycle measurement: Do you measure the product's assembly stage, or also include vendors' subassemblies, and their vendors' sub-subassemblies, or go all the way back to mining the raw materials?

While it is difficult to make this data perfect, it is not difficult to get a decent estimate of a product's impacts using life cycle analysis (LCA). Many LCA software tools already exist, and dozens of major companies already practice it (such as 3M, HP, and Toyota). As with anything, more standards will develop as more companies do it. As we saw with nutrition labels around the world, government may create standards that are mandatory. Already, the Federal Trade Commission has guidelines for what product labels may legally claim is recyclable, biodegradable, compostable, and so on. The European Commission's new EU regulatory system for chemicals REACH (Registration, Evaluation and Authorization of CHemicals) is already pushing companies to investigate and report the materials they use throughout their entire supply chain. Given the complexity of the information, the EU might eventually require a label similar to a nutrition facts label be on all products.

A label's graphic elements are designed to make the label more accessible. Six-year-olds should be able to read it and get decision-making value from it, even if they don't understand any of the numbers or big words in the text. The graphic's color scale of good to bad would be relative by product type, grading products on a curve so that computers would be colored on a different scale from sofas, for instance. The colors could also be renormalized every few years, so that the best products continue to stand out even when industries as a whole improve.

A Driver for Change

On a single company's packaging, an eco-nutrition label would be a green marketing rocket engine, propelling them far ahead of the competition. On a single industry's packaging, such labels would be a boon to consumer choice. On all products everywhere, quantitative eco-labels would embed sustainable thinking into the mental landscape of consumers and industrial purchasers. One of the main barriers to green purchasing today is simple lack of information.

No system is perfect, and any system can be "gamed," but even a slightly flawed system is vastly better than consumer ignorance. Shoppers, manufacturers, and investors are already clamoring for measurement systems in many markets, because there is a strong correlation between environmentally and socially responsible companies and companies who make quality products. In the coming decades labels will become much more ubiquitous and informational.

Article by Jeremy Faludi. Article concept first appeared in "Worldchanging: A User's Guide for the 21st Century," by Alex Steffen, Al Gore, and Bruce Sterling.

Carbon Labeling

In addition to the carbon footprint created by the production process, one of the larger impacts a product can have is in transport to the store. The carbon footprint of fruit shipped from southern climates to northern ones via air, is often much greater than fruit grown in the north during their appropriate season. A 2001 Iowa State University study showed that using conventional food supply chains, the average piece of produce travels 1,494 miles to get to the Iowa consumer. Compared to purely locally supplied foods, the conventional system used much more fuel, resulting in the release of 5 to 17 times more carbon dioxide into the atmosphere.[6]

With this impact in mind, the British grocery giant Tesco announced plans to label products with their carbon footprint. Using an airplane icon on products, customers can recognize and then purchase goods based on the amount of CO_2 embodied in their goods and produce, as well as the nutrition information they already use to weigh their choices. Combining with other emission reduction schemes, Tesco's goal by 2020 is to reduce emissions from existing stores worldwide by at least 50 percent, and will restrict air transport to less than 1 percent of its products.

Transportation is only one part of the equation. Produce grown in the south and imported by air may have a lower carbon footprint than those grown in heated greenhouses in the north, according to experts developing carbon labeling in Britain. Ministers are working with the Carbon Trust and BSI British Standards to develop a benchmark for measurements, allowing businesses to calculate the overall carbon load of their goods and label them accordingly.

Ian Pearson, Britain's environment minister said, "More and more, businesses are looking for ways to reduce their impact on the environment. To help them achieve that we need a reliable, consistent way to measure these impacts that businesses recognize, trust, and understand."[7]

Speaking the Truth, and Meaning It

Attitudes are beginning to change. The idea of taking one's global impact personally — that "being part of the global village" is more than a platitude — is starting to become part of our shared psyche. In the more eco-forward countries, strict regulations governing the sustainability (eco-ness) of what you sell and how you sell it have been a normal part of doing business for years. For US companies, this means getting their arms around the idea that living off of loopholes and workarounds, does not fly in other markets. In fact, companies have found if they want to sell on foreign turf, or even maintain positive consumer perception at home against foreign brand "invaders," they need to approach their products with the same concern as competitors from more contentious markets. How profitable is it really to stick to the (lax) letter of the law at home, when their hometown buyer begins to find the foreign brand more attractive? The United States has already seen this in the auto industry — with Japanese auto makers selling "features" to the US market, things that are mandated in their home market (higher gas mileage, tougher emissions requirements, and so on).

On the federal level in the United States, current guidelines governing the use of eco-marketing claims are voluntary. The ideas these guidelines cover are becoming mandatory in the more aggressively green states (like California), as well as becoming verifiable benchmarks for eco-goals set by large goods buyers and distributors in the United States (Wal-Mart score-card for example). In addition to realigning efforts to meet domestic buyers' demands, firms selling in major trading markets that can afford US goods have already begun to adopt, or in some cases exceed the demands of, the FTC Green Guides. This not only better positions them for selling abroad, but is also a sound defensive strategy against foreign competitors selling in their home markets. Who wants to be shown up in front of their hometown crowd?

Issued in 1992 and last updated in 1998, the US Federal Trade Commissions's (FTC) *Environmental Marketing Claims Guidelines (Green Guides)* have been around for quite some time. Consumers, and eco-advocacy groups that serve them, have begun to express concern (and confusion) over the new flood of products touting "green-ness" but with producers and buyers alike having no real understanding of what that means. In an effort to make the guides more effective, in 2008, the FTC initiated an overhaul of their guide, starting with hot-button terms like *carbon offsets*, *renewable*, and *sustainable* that have no definitions under the 1998 guidelines.[8] In addition to defining new terms, they will be going on to better define a variety of labels and terms already in the guide.

Relating directly to packaging, the FTC workshop *Green Guides and Packaging* addressed topics such as:

1. trends in packaging and the resulting environmental packaging claims;

2. packaging terms currently covered by the *Green Guides* and whether the perception of these terms has changed over the past decade;

3. new green packaging terms not currently addressed in the *Green Guides*;

4. claims based on third-party certification and consumer perception of such claims;

5. the impact of scientific and technological changes, including the use of new packaging materials and their impact on the environment;

6. the current state of substantiation for green packaging claims; and

7. the need for new or updated FTC guidance in these areas.[9]

Commitment to their ethic and message has been the common thread all of today's eco-leaders share. Not only do they make sure they understand the impacts of their current efforts as part of their core ethic, but they understand no one can do it all perfectly right from the start. With this in mind, they continuously look for ways to improve on what they are already doing right, as well as staying on top of things they need to work on. But most importantly, they talk openly about those efforts to maintain transparency, a key element of sustainable business practice.

For companies just beginning their journey, the easy answer is: Go for the low-hanging fruit, but really mean it. Then make a serious, and public, commitment to working on the rest. As noted, this last part is key. There have been many companies that have been the subject of very public advocacy action for being seemingly inactive (or indifferent) on sustainability issues — taking hits to their brand equity in the process —when in reality, they were working hard on the problem for years before the eco-campaign, but did not want to talk about it until they got it "just right."

In contrast to companies actually trying to do well, but not talking about it, are companies that have no problem "talking." These companies in fact, are doing almost nothing but talking, treating the shift toward sustainability like just another fad, just more romance copy fodder to fill up blank space on a box or ad.[10] Because the United States is such a huge market, and its directives on the use of eco-marketing claims are still voluntary, being all talk but no walk (greenwashing) is easy, and becoming epidemic. According to a 2007 report by TerraChoice Environmental Marketing, an overwhelming majority of environmental marketing claims in North America are inaccurate, inappropriate, or unsubstantiated. Using metrics from the FTC and the Environmental Protection Agency (EPA), of the over 1000 products reviewed, TerraChoice concluded that "all but one made claims that are either demonstrably false or that risk misleading intended audiences."[11]

Six types of common labeling problems surfaced from the study. These issues included false claims, true but unverified claims, nonspecific claims, claims that could be true of any product, true claims that are used to mask problems, and claims that exceed third-party certification limits. Embracing new members to the "Club" has been a difficult task for longtime eco-practitioners for these very reasons. "If not forced by regulation" they argue, "what's to stop any competitor from just donning a green suit and exclaiming — We're here! — taking away some of our hard-earned market share?" The reality is, very little. But this is not the Dark Ages, and news about bad behavior can be around the world in seconds. Consumers, bloggers, eco-advocacy groups are all just waiting to pounce on companies just in it for the "green" — and not following through on what that actually means. Greenwashing does work, but only for a little while. As new scrutiny avenues expand, stakeholders at all levels are taking another look at the people they do business with, asking, "If they're not taking things that impact the long-term health of my brand (and company) seriously, what else are they doing that needs looking harder at?"

Case Study: Knoend

Begun in 2006, Knoend is an eco-design focused company dedicated to bringing accessible, affordable, environmentally friendly products to consumer markets. By using materials that are biodegradable, recycled or recyclable, salvaged or reusable, Knoend's designs not only allow the consumer to participate in closing the loop, but get materials out of the waste stream altogether.

Knoend's goal is to change the consumer product culture in a proactive way and provide sustainable solutions that extend the traditional dead-end product life cycle. Living their talk, Knoend's people are members of the o2 Sustainable Design Network, and the company endorses the Designers Accord (designersaccord.org).

Knoend's designs are Cradle to Cradle centric, but incorporate the R's as well as believing strongly in the triple bottom line. The term Knoend uses is econnovation = ecologic + economic + innovation.

Knoend looks at existing projects and zeros in on areas for potential improvement or creative flare. Their first product to rethink was a household lamp. Knoend approached the process with the general question "How to make light, lighter?" Knoend's answer: Pick lightweight materials, lessen components, and shed excess packaging.

Material selection is the biggest challenge in any project. They considered bioplastics right from the start, as they are part of current solar income, a key feature in Cradle to Cradle design thinking, but heat resistance over time for these relatively new materials was an unknown for this application. Knoend also knew that a lamp is something that should not degrade, so this aspect of bioplastics was not a plus. By selecting a petroleum-based product they knew they would open themselves to criticism, but it was the best solution for their lite2go product.

Introduced in April 2007, Knoend's lite2go is a new lighting concept that eliminates packaging waste. While traditional packaging functions only for display and protection and is then discarded, lite2go's packaging actually becomes part of the lampshade, with all other components either biodegradable or recyclable. The product is free from staples, peanuts, foam, or adhesives. In addition to packaging impact savings, the compact fluorescent lightbulb (CFL) Knoend currently supplies as part of the product will potentially save 317,196W of energy over its lifetime compared to traditional lamps. Knoend's instruction manual is 100 percent recycled content paper to help save trees, and is printed with soy inks.

Shipped mostly from Asia, lite2go's materials are shipped flat to their California warehouse to make the most of the resources used. For bulk shipments, Knoend utilizes kraft paper and recycled content paperboard boxes.

With the full extent of impacts in mind, Knoend calculates their products' carbon emission loads to be able to offset each lamp sold, and vows to reclaim any unwanted products, taking responsibility for the life cycle of their products. To read more about their design principles, go to knoend.com.

TerraChoice: Six Sins of Greenwashing

Making the FTC *Guides for the Use of Environmental Marketing Claims* easier to understand, TerraChoice Environmental Marketing's Six Sins of Greenwashing is a handy heuristic to keep in mind.

Green-wash (green'wash', -wôsh') — verb: the act of misleading consumers regarding the environmental practices of a company or the environmental benefits of a product or service.

Sin of the Hidden Trade-off

E.g., paper (including household tissue, paper towel and copy paper): "Okay, this product comes from a sustainably harvested forest, but what are the impacts of its milling and transportation? Is the manufacturer also trying to reduce those impacts?"

Emphasizing one environmental issue isn't a problem (indeed, it often makes for better communications). The problem arises when hiding a trade-off between environmental issues.

Sin of No Proof

E.g., personal care products (such as shampoos and conditioners) that claim not to have been tested on animals, but offer no evidence or certification of this claim.

Company Web sites, third-party certifiers, and toll-free phone numbers are easy and effective means of delivering proof.

Sin of Vagueness

E.g., garden insecticides promoted as "chemical-free." In fact, nothing is free of chemicals.

Water is a chemical. All plants, animals, and humans are made of chemicals as are all of our products. If the marketing claim doesn't explain itself ("here's what we mean by 'eco' ..."), the claim is vague and meaningless. Similarly, watch for other popular vague green terms: "nontoxic," "all-natural," "environmentally friendly," and "earth friendly."

Sin of Irrelevance

E.g., CFC-free oven cleaners, CFC free shaving gels, CFC-free window cleaners, CFC-free disinfectants.

Could all of the other products in this category make the same claim? The most common example is easy to detect: Don't be impressed by CFC-free! Ask if the claim is important and relevant to the product. (If a lightbulb claimed water efficiency benefits you should be suspicious.) Comparison shop (and ask the competitive vendors).

Sin of Fibbing

E.g., shampoos that claim to be "certified organic" but for which our research could find no such certification.

When we check up on it, is the claim true? The most frequent examples in this study were false uses of third-party certifications. Thankfully, these are easy to confirm. Legitimate third-party certifiers — EcoLogo™, Chlorine Free Products Association (CFPA), Forest Stewardship Council (FSC), Green Guard, Green Seal, for example — all maintain publicly available lists of certified products. Some even maintain fraud advisories for products falsely claiming certification.

Sin of the Lesser of Two Evils

E.g., organic tobacco, "green" insecticides and herbicides.

Is the claim trying to make consumers feel "green" about a product category of questionable environmental benefit? Consumers concerned about the pollution associated with cigarettes would be better served by quitting smoking than by buying organic cigarettes. Similarly, consumers concerned about the human health and environmental risks of excessive use of lawn chemicals might create a bigger environmental benefit by reducing their use than by looking for greener alternatives.

"Six Sins of Greenwashing," by TerraChoice Environmental Marketing Inc. To read more go to terrachoice.com.[12]

"Greenwashing: A Dirty Job?" Article concept by Wendy Jedlička, first appeared on BrandChannel.com, Feb 4, 2008.

Businesses are asking, "If my vendors are not taking seriously things that affect the long-term health of my brand, what else are they doing that needs looking harder at?"

FTC Green Guides

The United States Federal Trade Commission (FTC) began public comment to update their *Environmental Marketing Guidelines* in January of 2008. The FTC Guidelines have been out for over a decade, available both online, and in the appendices of countless books — but the TerraChoice study showed, people were still totally unaware the Guides existed, didn't bother reading them, or were intentionally ignoring them. The most current guidelines (1998) are supplied here as a learning tool for better understanding the details and backgrounding for making marketing claims disclosures for any market, and to prepare people for the eventual updating and strengthening of the Guidelines now in progress.[13]

Statement of purpose (260.1)

These guides represent administrative interpretations of laws administered by the Federal Trade Commission for the guidance of the public in conducting its affairs in conformity with legal requirements. These guides specifically address the application of Section 5 of the FTC Act to environmental advertising and marketing practices. They provide the basis for voluntary compliance with such laws by members of industry. Conduct inconsistent with the positions articulated in these guides may result in corrective action by the Commission under Section 5 if, after investigation, the Commission has reason to believe that the behavior falls within the scope of conduct declared unlawful by the statute.

Scope of guides (260.2)

These guides apply to environmental claims included in labeling, advertising, promotional materials and all other forms of marketing, whether asserted directly or by implication, through words, symbols, emblems, logos, depictions, product brand names, or through any other means, including marketing through digital or electronic means, such as the Internet or electronic mail. The guides apply to any claim about the environmental attributes of a product, package or service in connection with the sale, offering for sale, or marketing of such product, package or service for personal, family or household use, or for commercial, institutional or industrial use.

Because the guides are not legislative rules under Section 18 of the FTC Act, they are not themselves enforceable regulations, nor do they have the force and effect of law. The guides themselves do not preempt regulation of other federal agencies or of state and local bodies governing the use of environmental marketing claims. Compliance with federal, state or local law and regulations concerning such claims, however, will not necessarily preclude Commission law enforcement action under Section 5.

Structure of the guides (260.3)

The guides are composed of general principles and specific guidance on the use of environmental claims. These general principles and specific guidance are followed by examples that generally address a single deception concern. A given claim may raise issues that are addressed under more than one example and in more than one section of the guides.

In many of the examples, one or more options are presented for qualifying a claim. These options are intended to provide a "safe harbor" for marketers who want certainty about how to make environmental claims. They do not represent the only permissible approaches to qualifying a claim. The examples do not illustrate all possible acceptable claims or disclosures that would be permissible under Section 5. In addition, some of the illustrative disclosures may be appropriate for use on labels but not in print or broadcast advertisements and vice versa. In some instances, the guides indicate within the example in what context or contexts a particular type of disclosure should be considered.

Review procedure (260.4)

The Commission will review the guides as part of its general program of reviewing all industry guides on an ongoing basis. Parties may petition the Commission to alter or amend these guides in light of substantial new evidence regarding consumer interpretation of a claim or regarding substantiation of a claim. Following review of such a petition, the Commission will take such action as it deems appropriate.

Interpretation and substantiation of environmental marketing claims (260.5)

Section 5 of the FTC Act makes unlawful deceptive acts and practices in or affecting commerce. The Commission's criteria for determining whether an express or implied claim has been made are enunciated in the Commission's Policy Statement on Deception.(1) In addition, any party making an express or implied claim that presents an objective assertion about the environmental attribute of a product, package or service must, at the time the claim is made, possess and rely upon a reasonable basis substantiating the claim. A reasonable basis consists of competent and reliable evidence. In the context of environmental marketing claims, such substantiation will often require competent and reliable scientific evidence, defined as tests, analyses, research, studies or other evidence based on the expertise of professionals in the relevant area, conducted and evaluated in an objective manner by persons qualified to do so, using procedures generally accepted in the profession to yield accurate and reliable results. Further guidance on the reasonable basis standard is set forth in the Commission's 1983 Policy Statement on the Advertising Substantiation Doctrine. 49 Fed. Reg. 30999 (1984); appended to Thompson Medical Co., 104 F.T.C. 648 (1984). The Commission has also taken action in a number of cases involving alleged deceptive or unsubstantiated environmental advertising claims. A current list of environmental marketing cases and/or copies of individual cases can be obtained by calling the FTC Consumer Response Center at (202) 326-2222.

> **Qualifications or disclosures such as those described in these guides should be sufficiently clear, prominent, and understandable to prevent deception.**

General principles (260.6)

The following general principles apply to all environmental marketing claims, including, but not limited to, those described in 260.7. In addition, 260.7 contains specific guidance applicable to certain environmental marketing claims. Claims should comport with all relevant provisions of these guides, not simply the provision that seems most directly applicable.

(a) Qualifications and disclosures

The Commission traditionally has held that in order to be effective, any qualifications or disclosures such as those described in these guides should be sufficiently clear, prominent and understandable to prevent deception. Clarity of language, relative type size and proximity to the claim being qualified, and an absence of contrary claims that could undercut effectiveness, will maximize the likelihood that the qualifications and disclosures are appropriately clear and prominent.

(b) Distinction between benefits of product, package and service

An environmental marketing claim should be presented in a way that makes clear whether the environmental attribute or benefit being asserted refers to the product, the product's packaging, a service or to a portion or component of the product, package or service. In general, if the environmental attribute or benefit applies to all but minor, incidental components of a product or package, the claim need not be qualified to identify that fact. There may be exceptions to this general principle. For example, if an unqualified "recyclable" claim is made and the presence of the incidental component significantly limits the ability to recycle the product, then the claim would be deceptive.

Example 1: A box of aluminum foil is labeled with the claim "recyclable," without further elaboration. Unless the type of product, surrounding language, or other context of the phrase establishes whether the claim refers to the foil or the box, the claim is deceptive if any part of either the box or the foil, other than minor, incidental components, cannot be recycled.

Example 2: A soft drink bottle is labeled "recycled." The bottle is made entirely from recycled materials, but the bottle cap is not. Because reasonable consumers are likely to consider the bottle cap to be a minor, incidental component of the package, the claim is not deceptive. Similarly, it would not be deceptive to label a shopping bag "recycled" where the bag is made entirely of recycled material but the easily detachable handle, an incidental component, is not.

(c) Overstatement of environmental attribute

An environmental marketing claim should not be presented in a manner that overstates the environmental attribute or benefit, expressly or by implication. Marketers should avoid implications of significant environmental benefits if the benefit is in fact negligible.

Example 1: A package is labeled, "50% more recycled content than before." The manufacturer increased the recycled content of its package from 2 percent recycled material to 3 percent recycled material. Although the claim is technically true, it is likely to convey the false impression that the advertiser has increased significantly the use of recycled material.

Example 2: A trash bag is labeled "recyclable" without qualification. Because trash bags will ordinarily not be separated out from other trash at the landfill or incinerator for recycling, they are highly unlikely to be used again for any purpose. Even if the bag is technically capable of being recycled, the claim is deceptive since it asserts an environmental benefit where no significant or meaningful benefit exists.

Example 3: A paper grocery sack is labeled "reusable." The sack can be brought back to the store and reused for carrying groceries but will fall apart after two or three reuses, on average. Because reasonable consumers are unlikely to assume that a paper grocery sack is durable, the unqualified claim does not overstate the environmental benefit conveyed to consumers. The claim is not deceptive and does not need to be qualified to indicate the limited reuse of the sack.

Example 4: A package of paper coffee filters is labeled "These filters were made with a chlorine-free bleaching process." The filters are bleached with a process that releases into the environment a reduced, but still significant, amount of the same harmful byproducts associated with chlorine bleaching. The claim is likely to overstate the product's benefits because it is likely to be interpreted by consumers to mean that the product's manufacture does not cause any of the environmental risks posed by chlorine bleaching. A claim, however, that the filters were "bleached with a process that substantially reduces, but does not eliminate, harmful substances associated with chlorine bleaching" would not, if substantiated, overstate the product's benefits and is unlikely to be deceptive.

(d) Comparative claims

Environmental marketing claims that include a comparative statement should be presented in a manner that makes the basis for the comparison sufficiently clear to avoid consumer deception. In addition, the advertiser should be able to substantiate the comparison.

Example 1: An advertiser notes that its shampoo bottle contains "20% more recycled content." The claim in its context is ambiguous. Depending on contextual factors, it could be a comparison either to the advertiser's immediately preceding product or to a competitor's product. The advertiser should clarify the claim to make the basis for comparison clear, for example, by saying "20% more recycled content than our previous package." Otherwise, the advertiser should be prepared to substantiate whatever comparison is conveyed to reasonable consumers.

Example 2: An advertiser claims that "our plastic diaper liner has the most recycled content." The advertised diaper does have more recycled content, calculated as a percentage of weight, than any other on the market, although it is still well under 100% recycled. Provided the recycled content and the comparative difference between the product and those of competitors are significant and provided the specific comparison can be substantiated, the claim is not deceptive.

Example 3: An ad claims that the advertiser's packaging creates "less waste than the leading national brand." The advertiser's source reduction was implemented sometime ago and is supported by a calculation comparing the relative solid waste contributions of the two packages. The advertiser should be able to substantiate that the comparison remains accurate.

Unqualified general claims of environmental benefit are difficult to interpret, and depending on their context, may convey a wide range of meanings to consumers.

Environmental marketing claims (260.7)

Guidance about the use of environmental marketing claims is set forth below. Each guide is followed by several examples that illustrate, but do not provide an exhaustive list of, claims that do and do not comport with the guides. In each case, the general principles set forth in 260.6 should also be followed.

(a) General environmental benefit claims

It is deceptive to misrepresent, directly or by implication, that a product, package or service offers a general environmental benefit. Unqualified general claims of environmental benefit are difficult to interpret, and depending on their context, may convey a wide range of meanings to consumers. In many cases, such claims may convey that the product, package or service has specific and far-reaching environmental benefits. As explained in the Commission's Advertising Substantiation Statement, every express and material implied claim that the general assertion conveys to reasonable consumers about an objective quality, feature or attribute of a product or service must be substantiated. Unless this substantiation duty can be met, broad environmental claims should either be avoided or qualified, as necessary, to prevent deception about the specific nature of the environmental benefit being asserted.

Example 1: A brand name like "Eco-Safe" would be deceptive if, in the context of the product so named, it leads consumers to believe that the product has environmental benefits which cannot be substantiated by the manufacturer. The claim would not be deceptive if "Eco-Safe" were followed by clear and prominent qualifying language limiting the safety representation to a particular product attribute for which it could be substantiated, and provided that no other deceptive implications were created by the context.

Example 2: A product wrapper is printed with the claim "Environmentally Friendly." Textual comments on the wrapper explain that the wrapper is "Environmentally Friendly because it was not chlorine bleached, a process that has been shown to create harmful substances." The wrapper was, in fact, not bleached with chlorine. However, the production of the wrapper now creates and releases to the environment significant quantities of other harmful substances. Since consumers are likely to interpret the "Environmentally Friendly" claim, in combination with the textual explanation, to mean that no significant harmful substances are currently released to the environment, the "Environmentally Friendly" claim would be deceptive.

Example 3: A pump spray product is labeled "environmentally safe." Most of the product's active ingredients consist of volatile organic compounds (VOCs) that may cause smog by contributing to ground-level ozone formation. The claim is deceptive because, absent further qualification, it is likely to convey to consumers that use of the product will not result in air pollution or other harm to the environment.

Example 4: A lawn care pesticide is advertised as "essentially non-toxic" and "practically non-toxic." Consumers would likely interpret these claims in the context of such a product as applying not only to human health effects but also to the product's environmental effects. Since the claims would likely convey to consumers that the product does not pose any risk to humans or the environment, if the pesticide in fact poses a significant risk to humans or environment, the claims would be deceptive.

Example 5: A product label contains an environmental seal, either in the form of a globe icon, or a globe icon with only the text "Earth Smart" around it. Either label is likely to convey to consumers that the product is environmentally superior to other products. If the manufacturer cannot substantiate this broad claim, the claim would be deceptive. The claims would not be deceptive if they were accompanied by clear and prominent qualifying language limiting the environmental superiority representation to the particular product attribute or attributes for which they could be substantiated, provided that no other deceptive implications were created by the context.

Example 6: A product is advertised as "environmentally preferable." This claim is likely to convey to consumers that this product is environmentally superior to other products. If the manufacturer cannot substantiate this broad claim, the claim would be deceptive. The claim would not be deceptive if it were accompanied by clear and prominent qualifying language limiting the environmental superiority representation to the particular product attribute or attributes for which it could be substantiated, provided that no other deceptive implications were created by the context.

(b) Degradable/biodegradable/photodegradable

It is deceptive to misrepresent, directly or by implication, that a product or package is degradable, biodegradable or photodegradable. An unqualified claim that a product or package is degradable, biodegradable or photodegradable should be substantiated by competent and reliable scientific evidence that the entire product or package will completely break down and return to nature, i.e., decompose into elements found in nature within a reasonably short period of time after customary disposal.

Claims of degradability, biodegradability or photo-degradability should be qualified to the extent necessary to avoid consumer deception about: (1) the product or package's ability to degrade in the environment where it is customarily disposed; and (2) the rate and extent of degradation.

Example 1: A trash bag is marketed as "degradable," with no qualification or other disclosure. The marketer relies on soil burial tests to show that the product will decompose in the presence of water and oxygen. The trash bags are customarily disposed of in incineration facilities or at sanitary landfills that are managed in a way that inhibits degradation by minimizing moisture and oxygen. Degradation will be irrelevant for those trash bags that are incinerated and, for those disposed of in landfills, the marketer does not possess adequate substantiation that the bags will degrade in a reasonably short period of time in a landfill. The claim is therefore deceptive.

Example 2: A commercial agricultural plastic mulch film is advertised as "Photodegradable" and qualified with the phrase, "Will break down into small pieces if left uncovered in sunlight." The claim is supported by competent and reliable scientific evidence that the product will break down in a reasonably short period of time after being exposed to sunlight and into sufficiently small pieces to become part of the soil. The qualified claim is not deceptive. Because the claim is qualified to indicate the limited extent of breakdown, the advertiser need not meet the elements for an unqualified photodegradable claim, i.e., that the product will not only break down, but also will decompose into elements found in nature.

Example 3: A soap or shampoo product is advertised as "biodegradable," with no qualification or other disclosure. The manufacturer has competent and

reliable scientific evidence demonstrating that the product, which is customarily disposed of in sewage systems, will break down and decompose into elements found in nature in a short period of time. The claim is not deceptive.

Example 4: A plastic six-pack ring carrier is marked with a small diamond. Many state laws require that plastic six-pack ring carriers degrade if littered, and several state laws also require that the carriers be marked with a small diamond symbol to indicate that they meet performance standards for degradability. The use of the diamond, by itself, does not constitute a claim of degradability.

(c) Compostable

It is deceptive to misrepresent, directly or by implication, that a product or package is compostable. A claim that a product or package is compostable should be substantiated by competent and reliable scientific evidence that all the materials in the product or package will break down into, or otherwise become part of, usable compost (e.g., soil-conditioning material, mulch) in a safe and timely manner in an appropriate composting program or facility, or in a home compost pile or device. Claims of compostability should be qualified to the extent necessary to avoid consumer deception. An unqualified claim may be deceptive if: (1) the package cannot be safely composted in a home compost pile or device; or (2) the claim misleads consumers about the environmental benefit provided when the product is disposed of in a landfill. A claim that a product is compostable in a municipal or institutional composting facility may need to be qualified to the extent necessary to avoid deception about the limited availability of such composting facilities.

Example 1: A manufacturer indicates that its unbleached coffee filter is compostable. The unqualified claim is not deceptive provided the manufacturer can substantiate that the filter can be converted safely to usable compost in a timely manner in a home compost pile or device. If this is the case, it is not relevant that no local municipal or institutional composting facilities exist.

Example 2: A lawn and leaf bag is labeled as "Compostable in California Municipal Yard Trimmings Composting Facilities." The bag contains toxic ingredients that are released into the compost material as the bag breaks down. The claim is deceptive if the presence of these toxic ingredients prevents the compost from being usable.

Example 3: A manufacturer makes an unqualified claim that its package is compostable. Although municipal or institutional composting facilities exist where the product is sold, the package will not break down into usable compost in a home compost pile or device. To avoid deception, the manufacturer should disclose that the package is not suitable for home composting.

Example 4: A nationally marketed lawn and leaf bag is labeled "compostable." Also printed on the bag is a disclosure that the bag is not designed for use in home compost piles. The bags are in fact composted in yard trimmings composting programs in many communities around the country, but such programs are not available to a substantial majority of consumers or communities where the bag is sold. The claim is deceptive because reasonable consumers living in areas not served by yard trimmings programs may understand the reference to mean that composting facilities accepting the bags are available in their area.

To avoid deception, the claim should be qualified to indicate the limited availability of such programs, for example, by stating, "Appropriate facilities may not exist in your area." Other examples of adequate qualification of the claim include providing the approximate percentage of communities or the population for which such programs are available.

Example 5: A manufacturer sells a disposable diaper that bears the legend, "This diaper can be composted where solid waste composting facilities exist. There are currently [X number of] solid waste composting facilities across the country." The claim is not deceptive, assuming that composting facilities are available as claimed and the manufacturer can substantiate that the diaper can be converted safely to usable compost in solid waste composting facilities.

Example 6: A manufacturer markets yard trimmings bags only to consumers residing in particular geographic areas served by county yard trimmings composting programs. The bags meet specifications for these programs and are labeled, "Compostable Yard Trimmings Bag for County Composting Programs." The claim is not deceptive. Because the bags are compostable where they are sold, no qualification is required to indicate the limited availability of composting facilities.

(d) Recyclable

It is deceptive to misrepresent, directly or by implication, that a product or package is recyclable. A product or package should not be marketed as recyclable unless it can be collected, separated or otherwise recovered from the solid waste stream for reuse, or in the manufacture or assembly of another package or product, through an established recycling program. Unqualified claims of recyclability for a product or package may be made if the entire product or package, excluding minor incidental components, is recyclable. For products or packages that are made of both recyclable and non-recyclable components, the recyclable claim should be adequately qualified to avoid consumer deception about which portions or components of the product or package are recyclable. Claims of recyclability should be qualified to the extent necessary to avoid consumer deception about any limited availability of recycling programs and collection sites. If an incidental component significantly limits the ability to recycle a product or package, a claim of recyclability would be deceptive. A product or package that is made from recyclable material, but, because of its shape, size or some other attribute, is not accepted in recycling programs for such material, should not be marketed as recyclable.

Example 1: A packaged product is labeled with an unqualified claim, "recyclable." It is unclear from the type of product and other context whether the claim refers to the product or its package. The unqualified claim is likely to convey to reasonable consumers that all of both the product and its packaging that remain after normal use of the product, except for minor, incidental components, can be recycled. Unless each such message can be substantiated, the claim should be qualified to indicate what portions are recyclable.

Example 2: A nationally marketed 8 oz. plastic cottage-cheese container displays the Society of the Plastics Industry (SPI) code (which consists of a design of arrows in a triangular shape containing a number and abbreviation identifying the component plastic resin) on the front label of the container, in close proximity to the product name and logo. The manufacturer's conspicuous use of the SPI code

in this manner constitutes a recyclability claim. Unless recycling facilities for this container are available to a substantial majority of consumers or communities, the claim should be qualified to disclose the limited availability of recycling programs for the container. If the SPI code, without more, had been placed in an inconspicuous location on the container (e.g., embedded in the bottom of the container) it would not constitute a claim of recyclability.

Example 3: A container can be burned in incinerator facilities to produce heat and power. It cannot, however, be recycled into another product or package. Any claim that the container is recyclable would be deceptive.

Example 4: A nationally marketed bottle bears the unqualified statement that it is "recyclable." Collection sites for recycling the material in question are not available to a substantial majority of consumers or communities, although collection sites are established in a significant percentage of communities or available to a significant percentage of the population. The unqualified claim is deceptive because, unless evidence shows otherwise, reasonable consumers living in communities not served by programs may conclude that recycling programs for the material are available in their area. To avoid deception, the claim should be qualified to indicate the limited availability of programs, for example, by stating "This bottle may not be recyclable in your area," or "Recycling programs for this bottle may not exist in your area." Other examples of adequate qualifications of the claim include providing the approximate percentage of communities or the population to whom programs are available.

Example 5: A paperboard package is marketed nationally and labeled, "Recyclable where facilities exist." Recycling programs for this package are available in a significant percentage of communities or to a significant percentage of the population, but are not available to a substantial majority of consumers. The claim is deceptive because, unless evidence shows otherwise, reasonable consumers living in communities not served by programs that recycle paperboard packaging may understand this phrase to mean that such programs are available in their area. To avoid deception, the claim should be further qualified to indicate the limited availability of programs, for example, by using any of the approaches set forth in Example 4 above.

Example 6: A foam polystyrene cup is marketed as follows: "Recyclable in the few communities with facilities for foam polystyrene cups." Collection sites for recycling the cup have been established in a half-dozen major metropolitan areas. This disclosure illustrates one approach to qualifying a claim adequately to prevent deception about the limited availability of recycling programs where collection facilities are not established in a significant percentage of communities or available to a significant percentage of the population. Other examples of adequate qualification of the claim include providing the number of communities with programs, or the percentage of communities or the population to which programs are available.

Example 7: A label claims that the package "includes some recyclable material." The package is composed of four layers of different materials, bonded together. One of the layers is made from the recyclable material, but the others are not. While programs for recycling this type of material are available to a substantial majority of consumers, only a few of those

programs have the capability to separate the recyclable layer from the non-recyclable layers. Even though it is technologically possible to separate the layers, the claim is not adequately qualified to avoid consumer deception. An appropriately qualified claim would be, "includes material recyclable in the few communities that collect multi-layer products." Other examples of adequate qualification of the claim include providing the number of communities with programs, or the percentage of communities or the population to which programs are available.

Example 8: A product is marketed as having a "recyclable" container. The product is distributed and advertised only in Missouri. Collection sites for recycling the container are available to a substantial majority of Missouri residents, but are not yet available nationally. Because programs are generally available where the product is marketed, the unqualified claim does not deceive consumers about the limited availability of recycling programs.

Example 9: A manufacturer of one-time use photographic cameras, with dealers in a substantial majority of communities, collects those cameras through all of its dealers. After the exposed film is removed for processing, the manufacturer reconditions the cameras for resale and labels them as follows: "Recyclable through our dealership network." This claim is not deceptive, even though the cameras are not recyclable through conventional curbside or drop off recycling programs.

Example 10: A manufacturer of toner cartridges for laser printers has established a recycling program to recover its cartridges exclusively through its nationwide dealership network. The company advertises its cartridges nationally as "Recyclable. Contact your local dealer for details." The company's dealers participating in the recovery program are located in a significant number — but not a substantial majority — of communities. The "recyclable" claim is deceptive unless it contains one of the qualifiers set forth in Example 4. If participating dealers are located in only a few communities, the claim should be qualified as indicated in Example 6.

Example 11: An aluminum beverage can bears the statement "Please Recycle." This statement is likely to convey to consumers that the package is recyclable. Because collection sites for recycling aluminum beverage cans are available to a substantial majority of consumers or communities, the claim does not need to be qualified to indicate the limited availability of recycling programs.

(e) Recycled content

A recycled content claim may be made only for materials that have been recovered or otherwise diverted from the solid waste stream, either during the manufacturing process (pre-consumer), or after consumer use (post-consumer). To the extent the source of recycled content includes pre-consumer material, the manufacturer or advertiser must have substantiation for concluding that the pre-consumer material would otherwise have entered the solid waste stream. In asserting a recycled content claim, distinctions may be made between pre-consumer and post-consumer materials. Where such distinctions are asserted, any express or implied claim about the specific pre-consumer or post-consumer content of a product or package must be substantiated.

It is deceptive to misrepresent, directly or by implication, that a product or package is made of recycled material, which includes recycled raw material, as well as used, (5) reconditioned and remanufactured components. Unqualified claims of recycled content

may be made if the entire product or package, excluding minor, incidental components, is made from recycled material. For products or packages that are only partially made of recycled material, a recycled claim should be adequately qualified to avoid consumer deception about the amount, by weight, of recycled content in the finished product or package. Additionally, for products that contain used, reconditioned or remanufactured components, a recycled claim should be adequately qualified to avoid consumer deception about the nature of such components. No such qualification would be necessary in cases where it would be clear to consumers from the context that a product's recycled content consists of used, reconditioned or remanufactured components.

Example 1: A manufacturer routinely collects spilled raw material and scraps left over from the original manufacturing process. After a minimal amount of reprocessing, the manufacturer combines the spills and scraps with virgin material for use in further production of the same product. A claim that the product contains recycled material is deceptive since the spills and scraps to which the claim refers are normally reused by industry within the original manufacturing process, and would not normally have entered the waste stream.

Example 2: A manufacturer purchases material from a firm that collects discarded material from other manufacturers and resells it. All of the material was diverted from the solid waste stream and is not normally reused by industry within the original manufacturing process. The manufacturer includes the weight of this material in its calculations of the recycled content of its products. A claim of recycled content based on this calculation is not deceptive because, absent the purchase and reuse of this material, it would have entered the waste stream.

Example 3: A greeting card is composed 30% by fiber weight of paper collected from consumers after use of a paper product, and 20% by fiber weight of paper that was generated after completion of the paper-making process, diverted from the solid waste stream, and otherwise would not normally have been reused in the original manufacturing process. The marketer of the card may claim either that the product "contains 50% recycled fiber," or may identify the specific pre-consumer and/or post-consumer content by stating, for example, that the product "contains 50% total recycled fiber, including 30% post-consumer."

Example 4: A paperboard package with 20% recycled fiber by weight is labeled as containing "20% recycled fiber." Some of the recycled content was composed of material collected from consumers after use of the original product. The rest was composed of overrun newspaper stock never sold to customers. The claim is not deceptive.

Example 5: A product in a multi-component package, such as a paperboard box in a shrink-wrapped plastic cover, indicates that it has recycled packaging. The paperboard box is made entirely of recycled material, but the plastic cover is not. The claim is deceptive since, without qualification, it suggests that both components are recycled. A claim limited to the paperboard box would not be deceptive.

Example 6: A package is made from layers of foil, plastic, and paper laminated together, although the layers are indistinguishable to consumers. The label claims that "one of the three layers of this package is made of recycled plastic." The plastic layer is made entirely of recycled plastic. The claim is not deceptive provided the recycled plastic layer constitutes a significant component of the entire package.

Example 7: A paper product is labeled as containing "100% recycled fiber." The claim is not deceptive if the advertiser can substantiate the conclusion that 100% by weight of the fiber in the finished product is recycled.

Example 8: A frozen dinner is marketed in a package composed of a cardboard box over a plastic tray. The package bears the legend, "package made from 30% recycled material." Each packaging component amounts to one-half the weight of the total package. The box is 20% recycled content by weight, while the plastic tray is 40% recycled content by weight. The claim is not deceptive, since the average amount of recycled material is 30%.

Example 9: A paper greeting card is labeled as containing 50% recycled fiber. The seller purchases paper stock from several sources and the amount of recycled fiber in the stock provided by each source varies. Because the 50% figure is based on the annual weighted average of recycled material purchased from the sources after accounting for fiber loss during the production process, the claim is permissible.

Example 10: A packaged food product is labeled with a three-chasing-arrows symbol without any further explanatory text as to its meaning. By itself, the symbol is likely to convey that the packaging is both "recyclable" and is made entirely from recycled material. Unless both messages can be substantiated, the claim should be qualified as to whether it refers to the package's recyclability and/or its recycled content. If a "recyclable claim" is being made, the label may need to disclose the limited availability of recycling programs for the package. If a recycled content claim is being made and the packaging is not made entirely from recycled material, the label should disclose the percentage of recycled content.

Example 11: A laser printer toner cartridge containing 25% recycled raw materials and 40% reconditioned parts is labeled "65% recycled content; 40% from reconditioned parts." This claim is not deceptive.

Example 12: A store sells both new and used sporting goods. One of the items for sale in the store is a baseball helmet that, although used, is no different in appearance than a brand new item. The helmet bears an unqualified "Recycled" label. This claim is deceptive because, unless evidence shows otherwise, consumers could reasonably believe that the helmet is made of recycled raw materials, when it is in fact a used item. An acceptable claim would bear a disclosure clearly stating that the helmet is used.

Example 13: A manufacturer of home electronics labels its video cassette recorders ("VCRs") as "40% recycled." In fact, each VCR contains 40% reconditioned parts. This claim is deceptive because consumers are unlikely to know that the VCR's recycled content consists of reconditioned parts.

Example 14: A dealer of used automotive parts recovers a serviceable engine from a vehicle that has been totaled. Without repairing, rebuilding, remanufacturing, or in any way altering the engine or its components, the dealer attaches a "Recycled" label to the engine, and offers it for resale in its used auto parts store. In this situation, an unqualified recycled content claim is not likely to be deceptive because consumers are likely to understand that the engine is used and has not undergone any rebuilding.

Example 15: An automobile parts dealer purchases a transmission that has been recovered from a

junked vehicle. Eighty-five percent by weight of the transmission was rebuilt and 15% constitutes new materials. After rebuilding(6) the transmission in accordance with industry practices, the dealer packages it for resale in a box labeled "Rebuilt Transmission," or "Rebuilt Transmission (85% recycled content from rebuilt parts)," or "Recycled Transmission (85% recycled content from rebuilt parts)." These claims are not likely to be deceptive.

(f) Source reduction

It is deceptive to misrepresent, directly or by implication, that a product or package has been reduced or is lower in weight, volume or toxicity. Source reduction claims should be qualified to the extent necessary to avoid consumer deception about the amount of the source reduction and about the basis for any comparison asserted.

Example 1: An ad claims that solid waste created by disposal of the advertiser's packaging is "now 10% less than our previous package." The claim is not deceptive if the advertiser has substantiation that shows that disposal of the current package contributes 10% less waste by weight or volume to the solid waste stream when compared with the immediately preceding version of the package.

Example 2: An advertiser notes that disposal of its product generates "10% less waste." The claim is ambiguous. Depending on contextual factors, it could be a comparison either to the immediately preceding product or to a competitor's product. The "10% less waste" reference is deceptive unless the seller clarifies which comparison is intended and substantiates that comparison, or substantiates both possible interpretations of the claim.

(g) Refillable

It is deceptive to misrepresent, directly or by implication, that a package is refillable. An unqualified refillable claim should not be asserted unless a system is provided for: (1) the collection and return of the package for refill; or (2) the later refill of the package by consumers with product subsequently sold in another package. A package should not be marketed with an unqualified refillable claim, if it is up to the consumer to find new ways to refill the package.

Example 1: A container is labeled "refillable x times." The manufacturer has the capability to refill returned containers and can show that the container will withstand being refilled at least x times. The manufacturer, however, has established no collection program. The unqualified claim is deceptive because there is no means for collection and return of the container to the manufacturer for refill.

Example 2: A bottle of fabric softener states that it is in a "handy refillable container." The manufacturer also sells a large-sized container that indicates that the consumer is expected to use it to refill the smaller container. The manufacturer sells the large-sized container in the same market areas where it sells the small container. The claim is not deceptive because there is a means for consumers to refill the smaller container from larger containers of the same product.

(h) Ozone safe and ozone friendly

It is deceptive to misrepresent, directly or by implication, that a product is safe for or "friendly" to the ozone layer or the atmosphere.

For example, a claim that a product does not harm the ozone layer is deceptive if the product contains an ozone-depleting substance.

Example 1: A product is labeled "ozone friendly." The claim is deceptive if the product contains any ozone-depleting substance, including those substances listed as Class I or Class II chemicals in Title VI of the Clean Air Act Amendments of 1990, Pub. L. No. 101-549, and others subsequently designated by EPA as ozone-depleting substances. Chemicals that have been listed or designated as Class I are chlorofluorocarbons (CFCs), halons, carbon tetrachloride, 1,1,1-trichloroethane, methyl bromide and hydrobromofluorocarbons (HBFCs). Chemicals that have been listed as Class II are hydrochlorofluorocarbons (HCFCs).

Example 2: An aerosol air freshener is labeled "ozone friendly." Some of the product's ingredients are volatile organic compounds (VOCs) that may cause smog by contributing to ground-level ozone formation. The claim is likely to convey to consumers that the product is safe for the atmosphere as a whole, and is therefore, deceptive.

Example 3: The seller of an aerosol product makes an unqualified claim that its product "Contains no CFCs." Although the product does not contain CFCs, it does contain HCFC-22, another ozone depleting ingredient. Because the claim "Contains no CFCs" may imply to reasonable consumers that the product does not harm the ozone layer, the claim is deceptive.

Example 4: A product is labeled "This product is 95% less damaging to the ozone layer than past formulations that contained CFCs." The manufacturer has substituted HCFCs for CFC-12, and can substantiate that this substitution will result in 95% less ozone depletion. The qualified comparative claim is not likely to be deceptive.

260.8 Environmental assessment

NATIONAL ENVIRONMENTAL POLICY ACT: In accordance with section 1.83 of the FTC's Procedures and Rules of Practice(7) and section 1501.3 of the Council on Environmental Quality's regulations for implementing the procedural provisions of National Environmental Policy Act, 42 U.S.C. 4321 et seq. (1969),(8) the Commission prepared an environmental assessment when the guides were issued in July 1992 for purposes of providing sufficient evidence and analysis to determine whether issuing the Guides for the Use of Environmental Marketing Claims required preparation of an environmental impact statement or a finding of no significant impact. After careful study, the Commission concluded that issuance of the Guides would not have a significant impact on the environment and that any such impact "would be so uncertain that environmental analysis would be based on speculation." (9) The Commission concluded that an environmental impact statement was therefore not required. The Commission based its conclusions on the findings in the environmental assessment that issuance of the guides would have no quantifiable environmental impact because the guides are voluntary in nature, do not preempt inconsistent state laws, are based on the FTC's deception policy, and, when used in conjunction with the Commission's policy of case-by-case enforcement, are intended to aid compliance with section 5(a) of the FTC Act as that Act applies to environmental marketing claims.

The Commission has concluded that the modifications to the guides in this Notice will not have a significant effect on the environment, for the same reasons that the issuance of the original guides in 1992 and the modifications to the guides in 1996 were deemed not to have a significant effect on the environment. Therefore, the Commission concludes that an environmental impact statement is not required in conjunction with the issuance of the 1998 modifications to the Guides for the Use of Environmental Marketing Claims.

Environmental Marketing Claims Guidelines Notes

1. Cliffdale Associates, Inc., 103 F.T.C. 110, at 176, 176 n.7, n.8, Appendix, reprinting letter dated Oct. 14, 1983, from the Commission to The Honorable John D. Dingell, Chairman, Committee on Energy and Commerce, U.S. House of Representatives (1984) ("Deception Statement").

2. These guides do not currently address claims based on a "lifecycle" theory of environmental benefit. The Commission lacks sufficient information on which to base guidance on such claims.

3. The guides' treatment of unqualified degradable claims is intended to help prevent consumer deception and is not intended to establish performance standards for laws intended to ensure the degradability of products when littered.

4. The Mercury-Containing and Rechargeable Battery Management Act establishes uniform national labeling requirements regarding certain types of nickel-cadmium rechargeable and small lead-acid rechargeable batteries to aid in battery collection and recycling. The Battery Act requires, in general, that the batteries must be labeled with the three-chasing-arrows symbol or a comparable recycling symbol, and the statement "Battery Must Be Recycled Or Disposed Of Properly." 42 U.S.C. 14322(b). Batteries labeled in accordance with this

federal statute are deemed to be in compliance with these guides.

5. The term "used" refers to parts that are not new and that have not undergone any type of remanufacturing and/or reconditioning.

6. The term "rebuilding" means that the dealer dismantled and reconstructed the transmission as necessary, cleaned all of its internal and external parts and eliminated rust and corrosion, restored all impaired, defective or substantially worn parts to a sound condition (or replaced them if necessary), and performed any operations required to put the transmission in sound working condition.

7. 16 CFR 1.83 (revised as of Jan. 1, 1991).
8. 40 CFR 1501.3 (1991).
9. 16 CFR 1.83(a).

Distant Village: Wild Grass Box

Distant Village packages have helped their clients set themselves apart from the crowd. What goes into creating the box becomes as much a part of the story as the product that goes into the box, making packaging composition disclosure an important part of the product selling experience.

This package is made of 100% postconsumer recycled (PCR) content paperboard, covered in woven, wild grass paper.

How to Get It Right

What Is "Need"?

Much of what manufacturers offer is in response to a "need" they perceive in the market. But what is need? The reality is, as a species we really only need things that provide health: warmth, an environment in equilibrium, nourishing food, clean water, sleep, companionship, replications of ourselves to keep the species going, and a way to occupy our day. Everything else is a want. It's wants, not "needs," that are the bulk of what drives our current economy. Targeting wants and pushing them to a level of desire so as to create "need" is how successful products gain market share, and how companies serving the market can begin to change end buyer behavior, by only supplying choices that keep societal and environmental impacts in mind.

Who Are the People Buying?

To successfully reshape "need," one of the most fundamental questions we ask when we begin to design is: Who is the thing supposed to serve and what do "they" want/need? A pretty basic concept, but one that gets overlooked (or grossly compromised) constantly in the push-pull dynamic that makes up this thing we call — the market.

What people want, what they're willing to pay, and what the producer is able to do (time/cost), plus what producers perceive their competitors are doing (or getting away with) are all seemingly at odds with each other. Yet, successful products manage to find the sweet spot, riding that wave all the way to the bank.

As we begin to examine the things that make up highly successful or catastrophically bad packaging, defining who the thing will serve (and so how to define the fulfillment of their need/want) is essential.

Demographics

Demographics is the statistical characteristics of human populations (such as age or income) used especially to identify markets.

There are a variety of ways to zero in on who potential buyers might be. One is to do the sort of cold calling that has been the bane of civilized dining since telemarketing was invented. Another is to pay people to offer their time and opinions (focus groups, secret shoppers). Focus groups, it must be noted, though a mainstay of today's strategic marketing mix, is only a sketch of what a potential buyer thinks, and at worst is an expensive catastrophe in the making. The conviction that the focus group "knows all" has been the downfall of many otherwise well intentioned products. Finding the right combination of questions and moderator is key to getting good information. And in all cases, Focus Group conclusions need to be backed up by other research methods.

As markets began their slow green shift, a demographic committed to sustainability in practice emerged. The LOHAS group (Lifestyles of Health and Sustainability) is a consumer often also referred to as a Cultural Creative, a term coined by Paul H. Ray and Sherry Ruth Anderson in their book *The Cultural Creatives: How 50 Million People are Changing the World*. This group cares deeply about ecology, the planet, relationships, peace, and social justice. The size of the market ranges from 15 to 30 percent of the adult population in the United States, but is much higher in markets the United States exports to.

Though already established in US trading partner countries, the emergence of the LOHAS consumer as a market driving group in the United States has been unparalleled in its history. These consumers care a great deal about all aspects of the products they buy, and are becoming ever more active in using their dollars to push for progressive social, environmental, and economic change.

Going past using their ethics as a product decision-making tool, the LOHAS consumer takes a holistic worldview, believing global economies, cultures, environments, and political systems are all interconnected, so that failure in one area ripples through the whole of society. So too, mind, body, and spirit within individuals are recognized as inter-connected, with personal development, spirituality, and personal ethics as their fundamental belief.

With the interconnectedness of all humankind at the core of their ideals, it's no surprise that LOHAS consumers come from all ages, races, religions, and economic classes, making them a difficult group to reach using broad brush mainstream marketing tactics. Truth and transparency become key tools to making inroads into this highly motivated market. One of the distinguishing characteristics of this group is that it is not an organized movement or "club," individuals become LOHAS by feeling strongly about something, making up their own minds, and using their personal ethics as their guide to action.

The Natural Marketing Institute breaks US consumers into the following categories.[14]

The LOHAS Consumer

63 million adults. Attitudes, behaviors, and usage of goods and services are affected by concern for health — the health of their families, the sustainability of the planet, their personal development, and the future of society.

Nomadics

79 million adults. "A conglomeration of consumers who are in search of their true sense of well-being. As such, they tend to move from place to place with regard to personal ideals, environmental platforms, and the overall relevance of sustainability."

Centrists

52 million adults. "A middle-of-the-road assemblage who congregates toward the central ground when it comes to dealing with health and sustainability. They are more steadfast in their attitudes, behavior, and usage of specific products and services, regard-less of their impact on the planet and self."

Indifferents

15 million adults. "A consumer group that sees no need nor recognizes any connection between their consumption patterns and the effect they have on resources. They are caught up in the day-to-day challenges, not necessarily looking out for tomorrow."

Like any demographic breakdown, there are people who fit into several groups at once. As demonstrated by the SUVs in an organic grocer's parking lot, not all people who participate in LOHAS behavior, fit wholly into the LOHAS mold.

Marketing to the LOHAS consumer though, has multiple rewards. Ideas such as fairness, health (for people and planet), and ethical practices — as well as transparency and honest quality — are all ideas that have a long track record of building brand loyalty in all consumer sectors.

Differing from other groups, the LOHAS consumer is willing to pay up to 20 percent more for products that fit their ethics. LOHAS consumers are more driven by product honesty than price. Products and services that truly deliver real benefits and solutions, allowing them to act on their ethics, are not as subject to the spiraling drive to the bottom many consumer goods manufacturers find themselves caught in.

Ethnographics

Unlike demographics that paint a portrait of a population with broad strokes, ethnographics is the fine brushwork that brings out detail. Doing just a few focus groups can't paint a complete picture, especially when dealing with a socially charged issue. Who will admit they're not for sustainability on some level?

An ethnographic study, though still more subjective than actual purchase data, can work with each subject in a place with no distractions or outside influences, or observe each shopper in their natural environment. Investigators too can key into unspoken communication: Is the shopper hurried or relaxed, what items do they look at before buying, do they shop alone or are they wrestling with toddlers? All of these are important factors that can color the data.

A bigger problem with understanding market greening is how to interpret the gap between how eco people say they are, and how they ultimately act at the checkout line. Everybody wants to save the planet — but only if it's convenient — has been the trend for many years. As markets change and choices (and competition) increase, learning to target your

product well is key to leveraging an increasing variety of materials, structural options, distribution schemes, and supply chain opportunities.

In gathering data for *The Cultural Creatives* Paul H. Ray, Ph.D. and Sherry Ruth Anderson, Ph.D., amassed an immense amount of survey data from over 100,000 people over 13 years. This work included 500 focus groups, and 60 in-depth interviews to reveal personal stories of how people's lives are changing. The authors note that this is the first book on social transformation to offer extensive hard data to back up their conclusions, proving that change is happening right now and what's going on is much bigger than they expected.[15]

The authors ask, "Are you a Cultural Creative? This list can give you an idea. Choose the statements that you agree with."

You are likely to be a Cultural Creative if you

1. love Nature and are deeply concerned about its destruction;

2. are strongly aware of the problems of the whole planet (global warming, destruction of rainforests, overpopulation, lack of ecological sustainability, exploitation of people in poorer countries) and want to see more action on them, such as limiting economic growth;

3. would pay more taxes or pay more for consumer goods if you could know the money would go to clean up the environment and to stop global warming;

4. place a great deal of importance on developing and maintaining your relationships;

5. place a lot of value on helping other people and bringing out their unique gifts;

6. do volunteering for one or more good causes;

7. care intensely about both psychological and spiritual development;

8. see spirituality or religion as important in your life, but are concerned about the role of the Religious Right in politics;

9. want more equality for women at work, and more women leaders in business and politics;

10. are concerned about violence and abuse of women and children around the world;

11. want our politics and government spending to put more emphasis on children's education and well-being, on rebuilding our neighborhoods and communities, and on creating an ecologically sustainable future;

12. are unhappy with both the Left and the Right in politics, and want a to find a new way that is not in the mushy middle;

13. tend to be somewhat optimistic about our future, and distrust the cynical and pessimistic view that is given by the media;

14. want to be involved in creating a new and better way of life in our country;

15. are concerned about what the big corporations are doing in the name of making more profits: downsizing, creating environmental problems, and exploiting poorer countries;

16. have your finances and spending under control, and are not concerned about overspending;

17. dislike all the emphasis in modern culture on success and "making it," on getting and spending, on wealth and luxury goods;

18. and, like people and places that are exotic and foreign, and like experiencing and learning about other ways of life.

If you agreed with ten or more, you probably are a Cultural Creative.[16]

For more information on Cultural Creatives, a huge breakout of data from the book, other work by Paul H. Ray, Ph.D., as well as new research in Europe and the United States, visit culturalcreatives.org.

Moving Target

As eco/green/sustainable products make their way out of dusty corners and niche eco-stores and into mainstream supermarkets and big box retailers, the cold realities of marketing and packaging need to be given special attention. Products that could limp along in the rarefied atmosphere of a dedicated eco-store, now have to compete in the real world.

In the past it didn't mater so much. People predisposed to eco-consumption were exclusively shopping in natural/eco niche stores. No matter what the package looked like, if the eco-product fit the need well enough, the eco-consumer would buy it, period. Today though, sustainable products, and natural/organic foods in particular, are outgrowing their mainstream counterparts. Annual growth rates for this segment are staying solidly in the 20 to 25 percent range. Where is this growth coming from?

Natural/eco products are no longer just selling to a few fanatical diehards, but to the mainstream shopper looking to include healthier products as part of a shift to a lifestyle. Expansion of organic and natural product offerings in mainstream stores has had the largest impact on the growth of the eco-products segment. Nearly half of eco-product sales today are moving through mainstream retailers.[17]

To cater to their needs, mainstream retailers have integrated natural/eco products into their regular product lineups. To help the eco-shopper find the natural products now mixed in with regular stock, and to help the new to eco shopper spot the natural products, stores are developing in-store ID systems to feature their eco-selections.[18]

Shifts in consumer awareness aren't just coming from a newfound desire to pursue a more healthful life. Developed countries are becoming even more melting-pot-like: Ethnic shoppers, as well as mainstream shoppers looking for more variety, are finding common ground in natural products. Products seeming exotic to the mainstream shopper, are comfort food to the ethnic shopper. Only about a sixth of the world even has access to the highly processed packaged goods of the West. Natural and unprocessed foods are simply normal fare to newcomers.

As mainstream stores add eco-products to keep from losing market share, producers who can both express a natural point of difference, and their corporate ethics, are finding a new audience to share their products with, creating a more diverse and interesting shopping experience.

Minnesota's Byerly's shows off their natural products.

Timing Is Everything

Why a person chooses one product over another can change with time. Age, income, family status, and personal values all color what we do. These variables also change as we get older.

Social values also change with time. Cosmetics made of whale oil, common in the past, would have a tough time in the market today, even though whaling is still active in many parts of the world. Today plant and pure mineral-based products, versus complex chemical mixes, are becoming much more common for cosmetics.

What we expect from products also changes. Today, as competition increases, people feel free to move from one product to another if they perceive they're not getting value for their dollar. Advances in communication from broadcast media to the Internet, means news about products moves quicker than a company might like. Timing for introduction or removal of a product becomes critical, as any miscalculation can seriously damage the market share of not only that product, but the whole brand.

The Package/Product Team

For the most part, manufacturers devise a product, then figure out how to get it to market. Successful products, on the other hand, bring all stakeholders to the table before the product even hits the drawing board.

Here's a great example of what happens when you ignore this most basic strategy:

Brought in at the end of the project to supply the shipping box for a new stereo system, a team of engineers found themselves with a baffling problem.

With no visible signs of stress, the stereo was arriving at the stores damaged and nonfunctional. With failure rates alarmingly high and stores ready to drop the line altogether, the team began adding more and more packaging to cushion the unit better. But the units still arrived damaged and unsellable.

Finally, they took a step way back, and really looked at the stereo itself rather than just the box they were shipping it in. Apparently, on the trip to the store, a circuit board inside the unit was free to vibrate, and did so with such vigor that the components became seriously damaged. Now, instead of adding layers of unrecyclable foam, corrugated supports, and packaging, a simple rubber stop costing only pennies was fitted inside the unit and the vibrations were eliminated. With the addition of this simple part, making the unit more durable, they were able to reduce packaging to a minimum and saved the company hundreds of thousands of dollars — not just in damaged returns and lost customers, but transport fuel, packaging costs, and warehousing costs for the larger, bulkier, boxes.

This example illustrates the advantages of systems thinking, and resulted in a huge win for the company (minimal packaging costs), the consumer (increased product durability), and of course the environment (reduced energy use, reduced materials use, reduced materials disposal).

Symbolizing the very essence of an unnecessary fad item, the Pet Rock of the 1970s is a great example of packaging as product. The entirety of the presentation, from box form to look like a pet carrier, to loose fill inside simulating animal bedding, to the *Care and Feeding* book that came with the thing — every element exquisitely thought through — is a good example of systems thinking with tongue planted firmly in cheek.

Do we really need the shelves filled with useless products like the Pet Rock? Of course not, but looking at product and package as one selling team will make the most positive impact. In fact, it's the most cost-effective, and eco-effective, way of increasing market share and profitability.

How to Create an Eco-Package in Three Easy Steps

1. Know what the market expects your package to do, then exceed those expectations.

    What is your package (and product) saying about how you feel about the consumer, and the environment?

    Is it well researched, do you really understand your end user as well as competitive market?

2. Know what the package actually needs to do, the Package/Product Team.

    Is it well researched, do you really understand your supply chain as well as end-of-life and rebirth possibilities?

3. Connect with the consumer and foster brand loyalty with the true quality and deep integrity of your product and message. Empower the consumer to make good decisions that ultimately benefit us all.

Distant Village: Handmade Box

A small box with a lot of impact. This box makes the most of materials using recycled and tree-free papers and boards, as well as inviting reuse by the end user.

Laws and Economics

④

Garth Hickle
Minneapolis College of Art and Design
Sustainable Design Certificate Program

Dr. Pamela J. Smith
University of Minnesota
Department of Applied Economics

Regulation is a failure of design.

William McDonough

Laws, and the economic issues they are often used to address, have strong impacts on packaging decision-making processes. Reducing risk by understanding the political climate of trading and manufacturing partners' countries, maximizing recycling (and cost management) potential by understanding materials flows and markets, and creating better positioned long-term strategic plans to address probable changes all require at least a basic understanding of how regulations get formed, and how economic changes impact product profitability.

A Ponderance of Minds, Florence, 1997
Photo: W. Jedlička

The Changing Landscape: Laws and Regulations

by Garth Hickle

Producer Responsibility: The Next Step in Materials Management

Producer responsibility or product stewardship, a term more commonly used in North America, means that all parties involved in designing, manufacturing, selling, and using products take responsibility for the environmental impacts at every stage of a product's life. In particular, producer responsibility asks manufacturers to share in the financial and physical responsibility for recovering and recycling products when they have reached the end of their useful life. While debate exists as to the differences between product stewardship and producer responsibility, particularly surrounding the role of manufacturers vis a vis other actors along the product chain, for the purposes of this analysis, both terms will be used interchangeably. When manufacturers share in the costs and responsibility for collecting and recycling products, they have an incentive to design products differently, to reduce toxic constituents, and to increase the use of recycled materials.

While producer responsibility is often recognized as an end-of-life management strategy, Thomas Lindqvist of Lund University and other advocates argue that it is a policy principle that extends up and down the product chain.[1] The Organization for Economic Cooperation and Development (OECD) defines extended producer responsibility as an environmental policy approach in which a producer's physical and/or financial responsibility for a product is extended to the postconsumer stage of a product's life cycle.[2]

A key thematic element of producer responsibility is the internalization of the environmental costs of the product so they are not borne by parties other than producers and consumers (aka User Pays). Not only does this internalization promote a more economically efficient model for managing the environmental impacts of products, but it may result in expanded economic development opportunities due to the increased collection and recycling activity. As expected, local governments, who have traditionally assumed much of the financing responsibility for municipal waste management, are key advocates for producer responsibility since it reduces their costs and liability.

As a result of the internalization of costs, manufacturers have an incentive to redesign products to promote the disassembly, reuse, and/or recycling of their products, to reduce or eliminate the use of toxic constituents and other strategies to lessen the environmental impact of their products. As an illustration of potential design for environment activities driven by end-of-life management responsibilities, packaging manufacturers may opt for more readily recyclable or biodegradable packaging.

The following analysis explores the fundamental themes of producer responsibility and offers a synopsis of selected global stewardship programs for packaging. It is not intended as a comprehensive cataloguing of laws and regulations but reveals the breadth and distinction of global packaging policy.

Emerging sustainability themes are motivating companies to examine their supply chains.

Principal Themes

When constructing a producer responsibility framework, several key themes are paramount for consideration but their application is often dependent upon circumstances particular to that product or industry.

Of central importance for producer responsibility is articulation of the funding mechanism to implement the program and the subsequent collection and recycling infrastructure. While not a comprehensive menu of financing options, the financing of producer responsibility programs is either internalized in the cost of the product or a fee is assessed for products placed on the market. In the case of the packaging stewardship programs, fee-based financing mechanisms are predominant with the fees generally determined by the weight and material type of the packaging. To achieve the desired outcomes, including incentives for product redesign, the fee should be assessed as far up the product chain as possible.

Another fundamental consideration is whether the program is structured to encourage or even allow, individual producer responsibility. Some argue in favor of programs emphasizing individual producer responsibility to more effectively support product redesign. Here manufacturers either directly take back or finance collection and recycling programs themselves rather than participate in joint efforts. Maintaining direct knowledge of what is and isn't working well in the systems they've set up for their products, helps manufactures fine-tune both product and supply chain more quickly.

Alternatively, collective responsibility programs promote a cooperative model for producers with little brand differentiation. Collective (cooperative) programs, the predominant method of implementation for fulfilling packaging responsibilities, are

marked by the presence of Producer Responsibility Organizations (PROs). PROs are established to manage stewardship programs with the producers assuming the financial burden which is typically determined by a company's market share. Collective responsibility programs are often instituted due to the potential for enhanced program efficiencies and the ability to compel participation of producers.

Another significant element of a producer responsibility policy is the assurance that a level playing field will exist for participating producers. Addressing free-riders, or those companies that benefit from the stewardship program but do not participate, is of particular necessity for products with many manufacturers and little history of collaboration. The failure to ensure broad-based participation by all producers is a primary stumbling block for the viability of voluntary approaches for implementing producer responsibility mechanisms.

Implementation Mechanisms

Producer responsibility programs are implemented through a variety of mechanisms ranging from individual company initiatives to industrywide voluntary programs and finally, programs resulting from legislative or regulatory action.

While each of the implementation mechanisms has advantages and drawbacks, the product chain, the number of entities within a product sector, the existing framework for cross-industry collaboration and, of course, the overall political context determine the appropriate approach.

In the absence of an established national regulatory footprint for the United States, individual states have assumed the primary role for instituting producer responsibility measures with the federal government. This lack of defined federal role is in part due to historically localized responsibility for solid waste management.

While Congress has yet to carve out a defined federal role for mandatory product policy compliance, several products have been addressed through national voluntary agreements. For example, the 2002 National Carpet Recycling Agreement was put together by the US EPA, environmental agencies at the state level, and carpet manufacturers, to establish national recycling goals for discarded carpet.[3] Similarly, the National Mercury Auto Switch Agreement implements a collection program for old mercury switches found in automobiles.[4]

Why Producer Responsibility for Packaging?

Advocates support the argument for selecting producer responsibility as the appropriate policy measure for packaging for several reasons. First, the overall growth in waste generation globally, and packaging's contribution to that growth, has sharpened awareness regarding waste management and recycling. The Organization for Economic Cooperation and Development (OECD) estimates that municipal solid waste generation increased 40 percent between 1980 and 1997 in OECD member countries.[5] Resource conservation, a concept that embraces a reduction in the use of materials, energy, and water, thus creating a reduced environmental footprint for the production and consumption of goods and services, continues to gain traction as a desired goal.

A second factor that supports producer responsibility is the growth of complex packaging such as

aseptic packaging and other multimaterial options. Changing consumption patterns also influence recycling rates, such as the proliferation of single-serve containers. This is further compounded by the growth of "away from home" consumption patterns. For instance, in the United States, the per capita consumption of bottled water has risen to eighteen half-liter bottles per month.[6]

It's important to recognize it's most often financial limits that hinder the ability of traditional government programs to achieve broad-based, significant levels of recovery of packaging, even though momentum has accelerated to examine alternative options, including adoption of stewardship requirements.

Lastly, the emerging themes of corporate environmental management and sustainability are motivating companies to examine their supply chains, material selections, and ultimately, how their products are managed at the end of their useful lives, thus fostering a greater acceptance of producer responsibility.

> **Motivated to realign the waste management responsibilities of business and government, the EU has enacted producer responsibility requirements for several products, most notably automobiles, electronics, and packaging.**

Producer Responsibility in the European Union

Motivated by a desire to realign the waste management responsibilities of business and government, the European Union has enacted producer responsibility requirements for several products, most notably automobiles, electronics, and packaging. The concept of producer responsibility was enshrined in EU waste policy with its inclusion in the 1996 Community Waste Strategy.[7]

Packaging Policy Development

The focus on packaging waste was greatly accelerated by the German Packaging ordinance, which became effective in 1991. The German Ministry of the Environment was motivated by diminishing landfill capacity and the growing volume of waste generated by households. Through the Ordinance and the subsequent creation of Duals System Deutschland (DSD) and the "Green Dot," the German government sought to discourage the use of unnecessary packaging, promote the use of reusable and recyclable packaging, and engage manufacturers in a closed loop system for packaging.

The EU Packaging Directive

Following the example in Germany, the European Union first took steps to address packaging waste in the member countries in 1994 with the enactment of the Packaging Directive.[8] The directive requires member states to enact programs to reduce packaging waste. The directive established recovery and recycling rates for waste packaging, required reductions in the heavy metal content of packaging, and obligated member states to implement recycling education campaigns among other provisions.

This legislation wanted to promote environmental protection, resource conservation, and spur manufacturers to develop more environmentally preferable packaging while ensuring the functioning of the EU market and striving for consistency.

As an illustration of the recovery and recycling rates, member states were required to introduce systems for the return and/or collection of waste packaging to achieve goals as defined in the directive. The following targets were established by a revised directive adopted in 2004:

— Recovery of at least 60% and recycling of between 55 and 80% by weight of the packaging waste by December 2008.

— Material-specific minimum recycling rate starting at 15% for wood and climbing to 60% for glass and paper by December 2008.

The European parliament and the council, acting on a proposal from the commission, is establishing targets for 2009 to 2014.

Harmonization Among the Member States

One key aspect of the packaging directives outcomes is to establish consistency as to how the member states would address packaging waste.

The success of the harmonization is debatable, in part due to the often significant role played by municipalities, but each program has similar components.

Each country has a functioning third-party organization, often referred to as a producer responsibility organization, to implement industry obligations.

These organizations participate in PRO Europe an overarching entity to promote consistency among packaging programs in Europe.

Regulations Around the Globe

Following enactment of the EU Packaging Directive, producer responsibility for packaging has gained prominence globally as a key strategy for addressing packaging waste. However, each jurisdiction has implemented policy and programs in a very diverse fashion, with varying financing mechanisms and differing degrees of responsibility apportioned between government and industry.

Producer Responsibility in the United States

Comprehensive packaging management programs with significant participation by industry have yet to be implemented in the United States. Producer responsibility advocates have maintained a much greater focus on products exhibiting toxic or hazardous characteristics, such as mercury containing products and electronics, carpet being an exception, but it is expected that the tide of stewardship programs will spill over to other products and materials in the near future. While states remain at the vanguard of product policy in the United States, Senator Jim Jeffords of Vermont did introduce the National Beverage Producer Responsibility Act of 2003 that, while implementing a ten-cent deposit on containers, provided beverage manufacturers with significant latitude in designing the system to meet the 80-percent recycling rate.[9]

Container Deposit

While not exhibiting many of the features of the stewardship programs implemented for the broad array of packaging, the container deposit approach is the most recognizable product-specific funding mechanism in the United States. Eleven states have adopted container deposit programs, albeit with varying programmatic elements.

Container deposit, while resulting in higher collection and recycling rates than other container recycling approaches, faces intense opposition from a wide spectrum of impacted stakeholders.

Recycled Content Laws and Other Tools

Recycled content mandates for several packaging types were promoted as one policy option for closing the loop. Both California and Oregon adopted laws in the early 1990s requiring rigid plastic containers to meet one of several conditions:

— Contain a minimum of 25% post-consumer content level.

— Achieve a certain recycling rate.

— Be reusable or refillable.

California has since eliminated the recycling rate performance as a compliance option in part due to the perception that this option served as a disincentive to source reduction efforts.[10]

Based on model legislation drafted by the Council of Northeastern Governors (CONEG) in 1989, nineteen states have toxics in packaging regulations that restrict intentionally added heavy metals such as lead, mercury, hexavalent chromium, and cadmium in packaging. The Toxics in Packaging Clearinghouse was established in 1992 to provide compliance assistance and conduct evaluation of packaging.

Producer Responsibility in Asia

While the European Union has garnered much of the policy spotlight for producer responsibility, several Asian nations are implementing measures requiring manufacturers to assume physical or financial responsibility for discarded packaging.

Japan

In 1995 the Japanese Diet adopted the Containers and Packaging Recycling Law. Under the law, the following are considered "specified business entities":

1. business entities that use "containers" or "wrapping" for merchandise they manufacture or sell;

2. business entities that manufacture "containers";

3. business entities that import and sell "containers" or merchandise in "containers" or "wrapping."[11]

The manufacturers and importers of packaging are assigned the responsibility to recycle packaging based on the volume that they manufacture or sell. To assist with compliance, businesses may fulfill their obligations by paying a recycling fee to the Japan Containers and Packaging Recycling Association, a government-designated organization.

Taiwan

The Taiwanese government enacted the Resources Recycling and Reuse Act (2002), introducing recycling and reuse measures.[12] The act stipulates that the Taiwanese EPA take action to ensure that packing is in compliance with several objectives in the law:

1. Companies are to reduce the footprint of their packaging with a specific emphasis on space ratio, layers, materials, and weight. The EPA is empowered to take regulatory action for companies that fail to do so voluntarily.

2. Companies that package products are to utilize materials that facilitate recycling, use refillable containers for a percentage of their products, and reuse an amount of recycled material.

Following the regulatory lead of Australia and Korea among others to promote packaging source reduction, Taiwan implemented the Regulation on Excessive Packaging in 2006.[13] The regulation targets the packaging volume ratio for designated products, such as software disk covers, gift boxes containing pastries, cosmetics, alcoholic products, and processed foods. The regulation also takes aim at multimaterial packaging for designated products by restricting them to three permitted layers.

Producer Responsibility in Canada

The Canadian Provinces have emerged as global leaders in product stewardship during the past decade, with several products ranging from waste electronics to paint falling under provincial stewardship programs. The federal government in Canada does not have the legal authority to enact producer responsibility measures, but the Canadian Council of Environmental Ministers (CCME) promotes harmonization of provincial stewardship programs. In an effort to promote packaging reduction and recycling, the CCME developed the National Packaging Protocol (NaPP) in 1990, a voluntary agreement with industry.[14]

For packaging, seven provinces have implemented container deposit programs for beverage containers with two other provinces with modified systems. However, the locus of policy activity for packaging has been the development of multimaterial programs with a shared responsibility funding model.

Ontario

In 2002, the parliament in Ontario passed the Waste Diversion Act, which empowers the minister to designate a material for which a waste diversion program is to be established.[15] The first product category designated under the act was "blue box" packaging materials collected in curbside recycling programs: glass, metal, paper, plastic, and textiles.

The Waste Diversion Act creates a shared responsibility model for managing "blue box" materials with a 50-50 cost-sharing arrangement between industry and the municipalities. The act established a 50-percent recycling target for 2006 curbside collection.

The act created a nonprofit organization, Waste Diversion Ontario, that serves as the implementation entity for the act and oversees the development of the industry funding organizations to fulfill the stewardship obligations.

For traditional recyclables generated from households, Stewardship Ontario was established in 2003 as the industry organization to fulfill responsibility for "Designated Blue Box Waste." Stewardship Ontario initiated the collection of fees from stewards in February 2004 with measurable annual increases in fees remitted. For the 2007 program year, Stewardship Ontario collected $59 million from the approximately 1,400 stewards. Stewardship Ontario has contributed to an average annual recycling rate increase of 6.5 percent.

Quebec

Quebec has adopted a similar approach to Ontario for the management of household packaging waste. RECYC-Quebec is an organization established to fulfill the recycling goals established by the 1998–2008 Quebec Residual Materials Management Policy.[16] The policy stipulates a provincial recovery and recycling rate of 65 percent by the end of 2008.

Since 2005, a regulation has been in effect that obligates manufacturers to partially fund curbside recycling programs. Similar to Stewardship Ontario, an industry organization, Eco Enterprises Quebec, serves as the voice for printed material, container, and packaging manufacturers with local government and collects fees.

Manitoba

In 1995, the Province of Manitoba instituted a levy on beverage containers that is remitted to the Manitoba Product Stewardship Council (MPSC), a stewardship organization that funds the provincial recycling programs. Building on the MPSC model as well as capturing elements from the Ontario and Quebec stewardship programs, the provincial government issued a draft regulation for printed paper and packaging in late 2006. However, the provincial government in Manitoba is seeking a more robust financial commitment from industry with an 80-percent share, and local government responsible for the remaining 20 percent.

Producer Responsibility in Australia

Australia has implemented a unique program for managing consumer packaging waste that features voluntary industry responsibility measures with a regulatory support mechanism. The National Packaging Covenant (NPC) was created in 1999 and reviewed in 2004.[17] Following the review and revisions to the covenant, the covenant was renewed as a more robust program in 2005 and extended for a five-year period. The covenant is to undergo an extensive midterm evaluation in 2008.

The covenant contains specific recycling goals for weight-based material, and an overall national goal of 65 percent to be achieved by January 1, 2011.

Often referred to a "co-regulatory" measure, the NPC is buttressed by the National Environmental Protection Measure, a regulatory tool to address free riders.

Signatories to the covenant (approximately 541 as of July 2007) are required to prepare action plans that articulate steps to meet the targets of the covenant.

A Path Forward

Producer responsibility represents the emerging standard for waste management globally and the debate is transitioning from why manufacturers should be engaged in stewardship programs to the most effective implementation mechanisms. The next vista for international producer responsibility for packaging is to recognize the burgeoning global trade of goods and services and integrate it into producer responsibility measures through a harmonization initiative.

For packaging, as well as other high-volume components of municipal solid waste, emerging climate change regulations offer an opportunity to increase recycling rates if recycling can be effectively integrated into the prevailing cap and trade mechanisms.

Finally, the growing prominence of retailers in the sales chain, as evidenced by in-house brands and the ability to dictate packaging as well as other features of products, needs to be recognized by policymakers and effectively addressed within stewardship programs.

US Postal Service: Round-trip Packaging

Bins for "hold" mail are light, durable, and a time-tested component of the US Post Office's resource savings strategy. More and more companies keep their packaging in-house as part of a service system, rather than continuously buying new.

Unwrapping Global Packaging: Trade and Policy

by Dr. Pamela J. Smith

Imagine that you are in the grocery store selecting a carton of milk. Perhaps you check the origin of the milk or read the nutrition label. But, have you ever considered the origin of the packaging? Where did the paperboard and the plastic cap come from? Where did the materials that comprise the paperboard and the plastic cap come from? Perhaps you decide to purchase the milk in a particular carton because your community recycles these cartons. But, have you considered where do the waste materials go? Are they traded to other countries? What is the environmental impact of that packaging once you've put it out on the curb for recycling? What is the role of governments in addressing the environmental impact? How might governments choose among alternative policies to address the environmental impact? These are just a few questions that this section will tackle.

This section contributes a snapshot of the scope of the global packaging industry. First, we'll consider the scope of globalization in packaging, for example, how the markets along the supply chain are linked. Next, we'll look at the scope of world trade in packaging and the geographic distribution of the packaging market and its impact. Here we show that while the packaging industry is geographically concentrated, its impact is diffuse across both developed and developing countries. We also show how the markets for materials, manufactured packaging, and waste are linked through trade. Finally, we'll explore the scope of the environmental impact of packaging. We discuss how to think "economically" about environmental impacts and about policies designed to mitigate these impacts.

The goal of this section is to demonstrate the complexity of these issues of global scope. Understanding this complexity is a prerequisite to designing effective policy. The central point of the section follows from a fundamental economic insight: If the scope of the policy to remedy a market problem is not the same as the scope of the problem, the policy is inefficient and will create new economic distortions. Thus, the global aspects of packaging require global coordination. But, such coordination is currently lacking. Current efforts to address packaging issues are piecemeal or partial. Even so, such efforts can create "building blocks" to broader and more global initiatives.

So, let's unwrap global packaging and see what's inside. What are the global issues? Which countries are involved? How can policy address the global environmental effects?

The Scope of Globalization in Packaging

To understand packaging in this larger context, we first must consider the magnitude of trade in packaging, then the supply chain and materials markets for packaging, looking then at the global purposes of packaging, and finally how international laws affect the packaging market.

Have you ever considered the origin of the packaging? Where does the waste go? Is it traded to other countries?

The Global Magnitude of Packaging

The packaging market today is global. The annual value of world trade in packaging was 60.2 billion dollars in 2005. To give some perspective, this packaging trade is 4.4 percent of the value of trade in all manufactures, 19 percent of the value of world trade in refined petroleum products, and only slightly smaller than world trade in medicinal and pharmaceutical products. Furthermore, this packaging trade is more than four times the value of world trade in coffee. Indeed, the next time you order a cup of java, consider that the value of global trade in packaging (including your coffee cup and lid) far exceeds the value of trade in coffee beans.

The Global Supply Chain and Materials Markets

Trade in packaging is only one slice of the larger industry pie. Indeed, the packaging market comprises a supply chain that includes five types of suppliers:

1. Firms that produce packaging materials.

2. Firms that manufacture packaging.

3. Firms that use packaging.

4. Firms that distribute and retail packaged goods.

5. Firms that recover or dispose of packaging materials.

Trade in packaging (step 2) represents only one step in this supply chain. Thus, the 60.2 billion dollars of trade in packaging is one slice of trade along this supply chain. A broader estimate of the value of the global packaging industry would capture the value across the whole supply chain. Indeed, the World Packaging Organization estimates that the global

packaging industry today is valued at approximately 500 billion dollars annually.[18]

The packaging industry uses large quantities of natural and energy resources. These resources are global in the sense that they are extracted, produced, used, and traded around the world. The primary materials currently used to manufacture packaging include paper and paperboard, plastic, metals, glass, and wood. Emerging alternative materials for green packaging include corn, potatoes, sugar, tapioca, palm oil by-products, and wood pulp.

Global demand for the use of bioplastics in packaging is growing for several reasons. First, the dramatic increase in the price of petroleum has led to increased prices for plastics. Second, consumer demand for natural products in natural packages is growing. Third, production capacity of bioplastics suppliers is increasing. As a result, the profit incentives of many suppliers are currently consistent with the social incentives of environmental sustainability. Wal-Mart's recent initiative to increase their use of sustainable packaging is an example of this consistency. The initiative seeks to increase the use of sustainable packaging along the supply chain and to increase profits through decreasing costs.

The Global Purposes of Packaging

Decisions about what materials to use in packaging depend in part on the purpose of the packaging. There are several standard purposes of packaging. First, packaging serves to protect the product for storage and distribution. That is, packaging ensures that the product reaches the consumer in the desired condition. Second, packaging serves to market the product. That is, packaging affects consumer choices. Third, packaging facilitates consumer use. For example, packaging can enhance the safety or convenience of the consumer in using the product. Finally, packaging serves an environmental performance purpose, which is related to the ability to dispose of packaging after it has served its other purposes. The choice of packaging materials influences the success of packaging in serving these purposes.

In a global market, there is an additional complexity to the purposes of packaging and decisions about materials. For example, packaging materials suitable for international transport may be different than those suitable for domestic transport. The materials suitable for marketing to consumers may differ across national cultures. The infrastructure for reusing, recycling, or disposing of packaging may differ across nations. Finally, the laws regarding information and

markings on packaging may differ nationally. These are just a few examples of the areas where packaging must meet additional requirements for serving its purposes in a global market.

Global Laws Affecting Packaging

The laws that affect packaging for a global market differ from those for a domestic market. Packaging in a global market must conform to the laws of both the exporting and importing countries. These laws include general laws that apply to all products, as well as product-specific laws (such as those that apply uniquely to food and drugs). The purposes of these laws are diverse. They include national security, control of products in short supply, compiling trade statistics, administration of trade laws, protection of endangered species, ensuring product quality, assessment of taxes, protection from hazardous pests and diseases, packaging and labeling requirements, and recycling and waste recovery. Each of these areas of law affects the character of the global packaging market.

In summary, the globalization of the packaging market expands the complexity of the supply chain, material use, purposes, and legal requirements of packaging. To move toward sustainable packaging in such a complex global environment, a clear vision of the current state of global packaging trade is required. For example, who are the dominant countries trading packaging? Are developing countries impacted? Which countries trade the materials used in packaging? Which countries trade the waste materials from packaging? The next subsection unwraps these questions.

> **To move toward sustainable packaging in such a complex global environment, a clear vision of global trade is required.**
>
> **Who are the dominant countries, and are developing countries affected? Which countries trade in packaging materials; which trade in packaging waste?**

The Scope of Global Trade in Packaging

One reason to examine packaging trade is to determine the economic impact of the industry in different countries. This knowledge is a prerequisite to determining which countries would be most affected by policy changes. However, determining economic impact is difficult because of the multiple steps in the supply chain.

For example, Germany may export plastics to China, where plastic containers are manufactured. China may then export plastic containers to Mexico, where the containers are used to package a product. Mexico may then export the packaged product to the United States, where the product is consumed. The United States may then export the waste plastic to China for disposal, reuse, or recycling. If China then uses the waste plastic to manufacture plastic containers, then the trade cycle can repeat. Furthermore, the trade at all steps may be transported in wood packing containers and pallets that are exported from Poland, Germany, or Canada. Alternatively, metal or glass containers from Germany may be used at various steps along the supply chain.

This example illustrates the complexity of determining the impact of the packaging industry. Even so, let's consider the value of annual trade in a subset of the markets along the supply chain. First, we consider trade in manufactured packaging (step 2 in the supply chain). Second, we consider trade in the material inputs used to manufacture packaging (step 1). Third, we examine trade in the waste materials from packaging (step 5). For this purpose, we will use trade data from the United Nations.[19]

Trade in Manufactured Packaging

This subsection considers trade in manufactured packaging. Specifically, we identify countries that are dominant exporters and importers of packaging. We also consider the impact of the trade of these countries on developing countries.

The value of world trade in packaging was 60.2 billion dollars in 2005. This packaging includes containers made of either plastic, paper and paperboard, metal, glass, and/or wood.[20] The associated values of trade in each type of packaging are:

29.1 billion dollars — Plastic
12.9 billion dollars — Paper and paperboard
11.1 billion dollars — Metal
4.9 billion dollars — Glass
2.1 billion dollars — Wood

So, which countries are the sources and recipients of this packaging? Tables 1 and 2 on the following pages provide the answer. Table 1 reports the value of exports of packaging and Table 2 reports the value of imports. These tables both focus on the five countries that dominate each market. The tables also report each country's share of the world export and import markets. These shares describe the relative dominance of countries in packaging trade.

Consider the market for plastic packaging the largest packaging market. The five largest exporters are the United States, Germany, China, France, and Canada. Alternatively, the five largest importers are the United States, Mexico, Germany, France, and the United Kingdom. Jointly, these countries comprise 44 percent of the export and import markets for plastic packaging. Separately, the United States is the leading exporter and importer of plastic packaging. The United States

Table 1. Exports and shares of packaging by select country and material type in 2005

COUNTRY	EXPORTS	SHARE	COUNTRY	EXPORTS	SHARE
PLASTIC PACKAGING			**GLASS PACKAGING**		
USA	3,437,095,214	11.80	Germany	807,791,000	16.39
Germany	3,290,927,000	11.30	France	727,290,787	14.76
China	2,835,545,780	9.73	Italy	484,820,272	9.84
France	1,782,722,961	6.12	Mexico	265,485,994	5.39
Canada	1,587,107,875	5.45	China	259,183,153	5.26
PAPER AND PAPERBOARD PACKAGING			**WOOD PACKAGING**		
Germany	2,207,581,000	17.09	Poland	256,348,158	12.50
USA	1,517,162,759	11.74	Germany	200,885,000	9.80
Italy	864,597,313	6.69	Canada	156,635,369	7.64
China	770,382,515	5.96	Belgium	120,935,011	5.90
Canada	716,356,514	5.55	Czech Republic	110,624,533	5.40
METAL PACKAGING			**ALL PACKAGING**		
Germany	1,361,507,000	12.23	Germany	7,868,691,000	13.08
USA	948,466,314	8.52	USA	6,193,129,283	10.29
Italy	766,895,079	6.89	China	4,434,932,088	7.37
France	720,148,919	6.47	France	3,837,856,101	6.38
Spain	577,052,346	5.18	Italy	3,504,046,884	5.82

Exports are measured as the dollar value in 2005.

Shares are measured as a country's exports as
a percent of total world exports by material type.

The select countries reported are the five largest exporters.

Source: The original data are from the UN Comtrade
dataset.

Table 2. Imports and shares of packaging by select country and material type in 2005

COUNTRY	IMPORTS	SHARE	COUNTRY	IMPORTS	SHARE
PLASTIC PACKAGING			**GLASS PACKAGING**		
USA	4,701,759,428	15.83	USA	754,717,614	15.82
Mexico	2,323,431,978	7.82	France	558,540,909	11.71
Germany	2,102,367,000	7.08	Spain	363,897,834	7.63
France	2,020,827,658	6.80	Belgium	258,671,220	5.42
United Kingdom	1,972,743,937	6.64	Italy	252,448,960	5.29
PAPER AND PAPERBOARD PACKAGING			**WOOD PACKAGING**		
USA	1,594,273,461	12.57	Germany	320,588,000	17.29
France	1,241,807,748	9.79	USA	196,959,406	10.62
Mexico	1,031,661,000	8.13	France	190,459,394	10.27
Germany	894,932,000	7.05	Belgium	148,927,918	8.03
United Kingdom	648,373,383	5.11	Italy	95,005,811	5.12
METAL PACKAGING			**ALL PACKAGING**		
USA	875,529,775	8.95	USA	8,123,239,684	13.82
Germany	730,271,000	7.47	France	4,679,568,515	7.96
France	667,932,806	6.83	Germany	4,217,957,000	7.17
Belgium	604,012,648	6.18	Mexico	3,658,634,199	6.22
United Kingdom	517,119,763	5.29	United Kingdom	3,371,660,487	5.74

Imports are measured as the dollar value in 2005.

Shares are measured as a country's imports as a percent of total world imports by material type.

The select countries reported are the five largest importers.

Source: The original data are from the UN Comtrade dataset.

exports 3.4 billion dollars of plastic packaging and imports 4.7 billion dollars of plastic packaging.

Indeed, many of the largest exporters are also large importers. This pattern of two-way trade is often referred to by economists as "intraindustry" trade, which is typically characterized by imports and exports of different varieties of the same product. For example, the United States may export different varieties of plastic packaging than it imports. Examples of varieties may include water bottles versus yogurt containers. The prominent economic explanation for such intraindustry trade is that countries specialize in and trade different varieties in order to extract the benefits of economies of scale. Economies of scale are efficiencies that result from the large size of a firm or industry within a country.

Tables 1 and 2 show a similar pattern of trade in packaging markets other than plastics. Consider, for example, trade in paper and paperboard packaging. The largest exporters are Germany, the United States, Italy, China, and Canada. The largest importers are the United States, France, Mexico, Germany, and the United Kingdom. These countries comprise 47 percent of the world export market and 43 percent of the world import market for paper and paperboard packaging. As shown, countries such as Germany and the United States are both large exporters and importers. Again, the intuition is that these countries export and import different varieties of packaging in order to extract the benefits of economies of scale.

The tables also show that trade in packaging is highly concentrated in a relatively small number of countries. Consider, for example, trade in packaging of all material types. Dominant participants include European countries (Germany, France, Italy, United Kingdom), North American countries (the United States, Mexico),

and China. These countries are either dominant exporters, importers, or both. The country shares of the global market demonstrate that packaging trade is highly concentrated among these few countries.

The countries that dominate the packaging market are developed countries. The outstanding exceptions are China, Mexico, and Poland. But are other developing countries impacted? To consider this question, we can look at the value of trade relative to the overall economic activities of a country. One way to do this is to measure each country's net trade as a percentage of their gross domestic product (GDP).[21] This measure provides a sense of how economically sensitive a country is to changes in global packaging trade.[22] That is, if trade in packaging is a large share of a country's overall economic activities, then the country would be impacted by changes in the packaging market.

The findings show that trade in packaging is indeed a larger share of the economic activities of developing countries. For example, Togo is a developing country that has a comparative advantage in packaging. Togo's net exports of packaging are 1.01 percent of the value of its GDP. This means that Togo's net exports of packaging are $1 out of every $100 of economic activity. Another example is Guyana, which has a comparative disadvantage in packaging. Guyana's net imports of packaging are 2.07 percent of its GDP. That is, Guyana's net packaging imports are more than $2 out of every $100 of economic activity. Indeed, quite a few developing countries (like Guyana) have sensitive import markets for packaging. Examples include Seychelles, Dominica, Suriname, Kiribati, Belize, St. Lucia, Jamaica, Republic of Moldova, and Namibia.

The implication is that many developing countries are strongly impacted by the packaging market and changes to the market. These countries do not dominate the market in absolute terms (as do countries like Germany, the United States, and China). However, these countries are economically sensitive since their packaging trade is a large share of their economic activities.

Trade in Packaging Materials

When assessing global impact, it is useful to assess the markets in the supply chain that are linked to packaging. For example, what is the relationship between packaging trade (step 2) and trade in material inputs (step 1)? Which countries are the sources and recipients of the materials used to produce packaging? How sensitive are countries to trade in the materials market?

Consider the case of materials used to manufacture plastic packaging. These materials include "plastics," such as polymers of ethylene, styrene, and vinyl chloride. An examination of the data shows that the direction of trade in these plastics is opposite of trade in packaging. Specifically, plastics are exported out of the United States and Germany, and imported into China. At the same time, plastic packaging is exported out of China, and imported into the United States and Mexico. Thus, the United States exports the material inputs and imports the manufactured outputs. Conversely, China imports the material inputs and exports the manufactured outputs. This pattern reflects the strong link between trade in plastic materials and trade in plastic packaging.

The dominant countries that trade plastics have large economies and are relatively insulted from changes in this market. In contrast, countries for which plastics trade is a large share of their overall economic activity are sensitive to changes in the market. Plastics exporters that are economically sensitive include Singapore, Belgium, Netherlands, Saudi Arabia, Thailand, and the Republic of Korea. Plastics importers that are economically sensitive include Ghana, Syria, Costa Rica, Malawi, Malta, Jordan, Turkey, Honduras, Republic of Moldova, and United Republic of Tanzania. For these countries, plastic materials constitute a large share of their overall economic activities.

The implication of these findings is that developing countries are trade sensitive as both importers and exporters of the material inputs into packaging. Another implication is that policies that impact the market for packaging will impact developing countries directly through the packaging market and indirectly through the materials market.

Trade in Waste Materials

Let's next consider the link between packaging and waste materials. One can consider these materials in two ways. If the materials are not reused but are disposed of, then the market for waste materials represents the last step in the supply chain. Alternatively, if the materials are reused as inputs into new packaging, then the materials market represents both last and first steps in the supply chain. This is the case of the "closed loop." In both cases, the used packaging may be traded to another country for disposal, reuse, or recycling.

Analysis of the global waste market is challenging. The international trade data includes measures of trade in waste plastic, and waste paper and paperboard. However, the data do not describe whether the trade in waste materials is for the purpose of disposal, reuse, or recycling. What the data does tell us is which countries are leading this market. These countries have the most interest in shaping policy toward the use of waste materials. The data also give us a sense of the magnitude of the waste market in absolute terms and relative to the market for new materials.

In the aggregate, global trade in waste paper and paperboard is approximately 5.6 billion dollars in 2005. Global trade in waste plastic is approximately 4.4 billion dollars. Together these waste markets are valued at 10 billion dollars. This is the value of waste that is traded across national borders. The figures do not include waste that remains within a country's borders. To provide context, trade in waste paper and paperboard is 19 percent of trade in the broader category of pulp materials. Trade in waste plastic is 2 percent of trade in the broader category of

---

Table 3. Exports and Imports of waste materials by select country and material type in 2005

COUNTRY	IMPORTS	SHARE	COUNTRY	IMPORTS	SHARE
WASTE PAPER AND PAPERBOARD			**WASTE PAPER AND PAPERBOARD**		
USA	1,720,765,624	35.09	China	2,457,178,461	43.49
United Kingdom	505,097,934	10.30	Germany	351,870,000	6.23
Japan	436,627,974	8.90	India	303,426,563	5.37
Germany	337,998,000	6.89	Indonesia	288,419,506	5.10
Netherlands	330,365,369	6.74	Mexico	273,851,874	4.85
WASTE PLASTIC			**WASTE PLASTIC**		
Hong Kong	859,447,099	24.87	China	1,928,435,289	44.10
USA	451,864,139	13.07	Hong Kong	1,385,527,016	31.69
Japan	396,598,216	11.48	USA	253,659,227	5.80
Germany	245,927,000	7.12	Canada	110,260,749	2.52
Mexico	200,968,872	5.81	Italy	90,640,024	2.07

Exports and imports are measured as the dollar value in 2005.

Shares are measured as a country's exports or imports as a percent of total world exports or imports by material type.

The select countries reported are the five largest exporters and importers.

Source: The original data are from the UN Comtrade dataset.

primary-form plastics. Thus, waste paper is a larger share of the traded materials market than waste plastic.

Which countries dominate the waste market? On page 124, Table 3 provides the answer. Table 3 reports the value of exports and imports of waste paper and paperboard, and waste plastic. The table focuses on the five countries that dominate each waste market, and also reports each country's share of the world export and import markets. As shown, the United States and China dominate the market for paper and paperboard waste. In 2005, the United States exported 35.09 percent of world exports of waste paper and paperboard (or 1.7 billion dollars). These exports go primarily to China. China imported 43.49 percent of the world's imports of waste paper and paperboard (or 2.5 billion dollars).

Further, Table 3 shows that the market for waste plastic is dominated by China and Hong Kong. Hong Kong is both a major exporter and importer of waste plastic. Hong Kong has 24.87 percent of the export market and 31.69 percent of the import market. This finding is consistent with Hong Kong's serving as a hub for trade in waste plastic into and out of Asia. Separately, China is the largest importer of waste plastic with 44.10% of the world import market. Thus, China and Hong Kong jointly import 75.79 percent of world imports of waste plastic.

The implication of these patterns is that the United States has a strong interest in policy that affects exports of waste paper while China has a strong interest in policy that affect imports of waste paper and plastic. Interestingly, developing countries appear to be insulated from trade in these waste materials at this time. That is, the value of their net trade in these waste materials is a small share of their gross domestic product.[23]

Summary of Facts on Packaging Trade

The facts on global trade in packaging today are:

— The global packaging market is concentrated in a relatively small number of countries. These include North America countries, European countries, and China.

— Developed countries dominate the global packaging market, but there are select active participants from the developing world. Dominant developed countries are the United States and Germany. The dominant developing country is China.

— Countries that dominate the global packaging market both import and export packaging. This pattern is consistent with intra industry trade, where countries export different varieties of packaging than they import.

— Developing countries are affected by trade in packaging and by trade in the materials used to manufacture packaging. That is, trade in packaging and material inputs are a relatively large share of the overall economic activity of developing countries. Examples are Togo and Guyana.

— China imports packaging materials and waste, and exports manufactured packaging. In contrast, the United States exports packaging materials and waste, and imports manufactured packaging.

— The markets for packaging materials, manufactured packaging, and packaging waste are linked through trade.

The Scope of Environmental Impact of Packaging

The facts on packaging trade highlight which countries dominate and are impacted by the global packaging market. The facts also highlight the interconnectedness of the markets along the packaging-supply chain. Understanding these trade patterns and linkages is a prerequisite to designing policy. Understanding the scope of the environmental impact of the packaging market is also a prerequisite to policy design.

Thus, this subsection now unwraps the issue of environmental impact. The discussion does not provide answers or recommendation, but rather provides a way to think in economic terms. To this end, we consider three questions. First, how can we think "economically" about the environmental impact of packaging? Second, what is the role of governments? Third, what are the optimal policies?

The Economics of Environmental Externalities

How can we think "economically" about the environmental affects of packaging? In economic terms, packaging creates an externality. An externality is a side effect of production or consumption. This side effect impacts someone other than the producer or consumer. That is, the side effect impacts society as a whole or a subset of society. The scope of the societal impact may be local, national, regional, or global. For example, packaging that enters the waste stream has a negative side effect on society by damaging the environment. Local landfills are an example of a side affect that impacts a subset of society in the local community. Another example is global warming, where the side effect impacts global society as a

whole. In these cases, neither the producer nor the consumer has an economic incentive to change their behavior because they indirectly experience the side effect borne by society.

Externalities such as environmental damage are a classic case of market failure. Market failure describes the case where markets do not generate the socially optimal levels of production and consumption. In the case of packaging, firms tend to overproduce packaging because they do not take into account the social cost of their production on the environment. Similarly, consumers tend to overconsume packaging because they do not take into account the social cost of their consumption on the environment. This excess production and consumption is relative to the socially optimal levels of production and consumption. Socially optimal levels take into account the environmental impacts (i.e., the externality).

Externalities such as environmental damage are a classic case of market failure.

The Role of Government Policy

What is the role of government in addressing the environmental impact of packaging? The role of government in the case of a market failure is to adopt policies that provide incentives for producers and consumers to produce and consume the socially optimal levels of a good such as packaging. Typically that means adopting policies that legally require the producer and/or consumer to bear the cost of the externality (environmental damage). Examples in the case of packaging include government policies that require producers to pay fees up front to cover the cost of disposing of packaging after it has served its purpose. Examples also include government policies that require consumers to pay fees for disposing of packaging. The former policies create incentives for producers to decrease the quantity of their supply of environmentally damaging packaging. The latter policies create incentives for consumers to decrease the quantity of their demand for environmentally damaging packaging.

So, who is responsible for packaging waste, the consumer or the producer? In economic terms, consumers are responsible if their behavior generates packaging that damages the environment. Consumer behavior includes decisions about which packaged products to purchase and decisions about the disposal of packaging. In the global environment, consumer behavior related to packaging and its disposal varies widely. Alternatively, producers are responsible if their behavior generates packaging that damages the environment. Producer behavior includes decisions about the amount of packaging and materials used in packaging. Again, in a global environment, producer behavior related to packaging and its disposal varies widely.

Further, the interaction between consumers and producers over time can affect the environmental impact. For example, as consumer demand for natural products in natural packaging increases, consumers are willing to pay higher prices for such goods and packaging. In a competitive market, the higher prices allow producers to use more costly material inputs that may generate smaller negative

environmental externalities. These preferences also vary widely in the global market.

In each of the cases above, governments can adopt policies to decrease the consumption and production activities that generate environmental externalities. The next logical question is, Which policies are most effective toward this end?

Optimal Policies

Governments have a wide range of policy instruments to choose from in addressing externalities such as environment damage. In economic terms, a first-best policy is one that corrects the domestic market failure (such as environment damage) without introducing a new distortion in the market. A second-best policy is one that corrects the market failure, but simultaneously introduces a new distortion. An example of a distortion is when a policy targeting manufactured packaging creates an inefficiency in a linked market such as the materials or waste markets. Thus, designing a policy solution to create incentives that reduce the overproduction and/or overconsumption of environmentally damaging packaging is challenging.

One particular challenge in the case of packaging is the issue of policy scope. In economic terms, a first-best policy is one with a scope that matches the scope of the externality. That is, if the environmental damage of packaging is domestic, then the first-best policy is a domestic policy. An example would be national directives on packaging waste reduction. However, if the environmental damage is global, then the first-best policy is a global policy. An example would be a global treaty that addresses packaging waste reduction. In both cases, the national and global policies aim to affect the consumption and/or production behavior of those who generate the externality (environmental damage). If the scope of the policy does not match the scope of the externality, then new inefficiencies are introduced as a result of the policy.

In the case of packaging, the scope of the environmental impact varies widely. The packaging waste that adds to a local landfill represents an externality at the local level. At the other extreme, the contribution of packaging to global warming represents an externality at the global level. Thus, a portfolio of policies coordinated among local communities, national governments, and international organizations is required. The goal of policy coordination would be to address the externalities in an economically efficient way that minimizes new distortions.

Current sustainable packaging systems focus on minimizing waste by reducing, reusing, recycling, or recovering packaging materials. Developed countries have taken the lead in adopting policies that focus on the environmental aspects of packaging. An example is the European Union Directive on Packaging and Packaging Waste. The directive requires packaging producers to recover packaging waste from their production or make the waste available to a waste recovery organization. This requirement reflects the principles of "polluter pays" and "extended producer responsibility." These policy principles are consistent with the notion that producers be responsible for the externalities they generate.

Developing countries face many challenges in initiating sustainable packaging systems. The challenges include the absence of coordinating bodies, information sources, and adequate legislation for packaging. There is also an absence of infrastructures for collecting, disposing, and/or recycling packaging in developing economies. To address these challenges, development programs are emerging to assist firms in developing and transition countries to learn and adopt sustainable packaging practices. An example is the initiative of the International Trade Center (ITC), a joint technical cooperation agency of the United Nations Conference on Trade and Development and the World Trade Organization.[24] The ITC has initiated programs for sustainable packaging practices in Colombia, India, Jamaica, Malawi, and Zimbabwe.

These national and regional initiatives are the first "building blocks" toward constructing broader global initiatives. The optimal future policies (from an economic perspective) are those that match the scope of the policy to the scope of the externalities. That is, global policy is optimal for addressing global environmental externalities associated with the packaging market.

In the case of packaging, the scope of the environmental impact varies widely. The packaging waste that adds to a local landfill represents an externality at the local level. At the other extreme, the contribution of packaging to global warming represents an externality at the global level.

Looking Forward

The goal of this article was to unwrap the global packaging market today. In looking forward, several global vantage points are useful for designing policy.

The first is the scope of the supply chain and submarkets. Policies that impact one step in the supply chain can positively or negatively impact other steps in the supply chain. For example, a policy to reduce waste in the packaging market can impact the materials market. Linkages also exist across the submarkets for packaging made from different materials. For example, a policy to reduce waste in the market for plastic packaging can impact the market for paper and paperboard packaging. Thus, policy design requires an understanding of the interconnectedness of the markets along the supply chain and the interconnectedness of markets for different varieties of packaging. Optimal policies would match the scope of the policy to the scope of the impact across the supply chain and submarkets.

The second vantage point is geographic scope. The data show us that the geographic distribution of the packaging industry varies depending on the step in the supply chain. For example, the market for waste materials is more highly concentrated than the market for manufactured packaging. And the market for plastic packaging is distributed geographically differently than the market for paper and paperboard packaging. Furthermore, even though developed countries (plus China) tend to dominate the packaging market, developing countries are impacted. Their packaging trade represents a larger share of their overall economic activity. Thus, policy design requires an understanding of the impacts of the packaging market across economies at different development levels. Optimal policies would match the scope of the policy to the geographic scope of countries involved.

Finally, the third vantage point is the scope of the environmental impact. Economics tells us to match the scope of the policy to the scope of the externality. That is, global (rather than domestic) policy is most effective to address a global market failure such as global warming. Economics also tells us to target policy at those who generate the externality. The intuition is to create "socially optimal" incentives for consumers or producers when the market has failed to do so. Thus, policy design requires understanding the scope of the environmental impact. Optimal policies would match the scope of the policies to the scope of the environmental impact across countries, and across consumers and producers within countries.

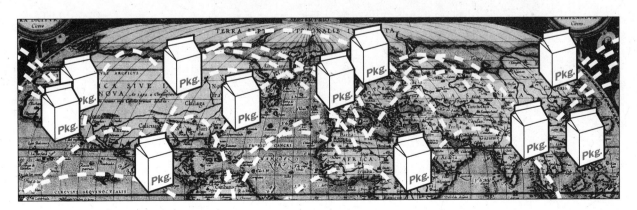

Case Study: UsedCardboardBoxes

A great example of applying a creative business approach to what was otherwise considered a resource drain can be found in the variety of reusable materials exchanges popping up around the world. One such operation is UsedCardboardBoxes.com (UCB). In the 3Rs, Reduce, Reuse Recycle, *recycle* is last as it's the most energy intensive. Though second-hand stores have been a part of our economy nearly from the start, reuse of goods to create new products or service channels is difficult to implement well, and is still not as ubiquitous as recycling. The big question UCB asked was: How do you get stuff from the people who have boxes, to the people who need boxes with the least hassle and best quality, and be profitable?

UCB's idea was to capitalize on paperboard's over 100-year recycling history, and "green it" by getting more energy saving miles out each box by inserting a viable reuse cycle into the mix. Today, UCB sells quality used boxes that cost less than new and are more eco than boxes that go right from forest to landfill.

UCB's Marty Metro originally tested the concept of buying and selling used boxes within a four-store retail chain. Though it was a big hit with customers, retail overhead made it unsustainable. After years of struggling to turn a highly successful concept into a profitable one, Metro shut down the retail stores and completely changed gears. In just eighteen months, his new Internet-based company, UCB expanded across the United States and into Canada.

Why did they do it? Every year, over $40 billion worth of paperboard boxes are produced in the United States, with nearly $120 billion produced worldwide.

Virtually everything in our global economy today came in a box at some point. Most boxes are used once, then go to landfills or incinerators. Recyclable boxes in the United States are mostly sold to China as scrap. Before a box makes a trip to a faraway land to be groundup though, UCB "rescues" usable boxes by the truckload. This not only keeps usable resources in its domestic market, but revenues and jobs as well. One of the really elegant aspects of UCB's business model is the simple idea of supply and demand. For businesses looking to reduce their environmental footprint, UCB helps shippers take a proactive and cost-effective role in a more responsible domestic resource management system. Over the years, UCB has found that people who buy from them are not just customers, but supporters. After all, UCB points out, "You don't have to cut down a tree to make a used cardboard box!" Using EPA guidelines, UCB estimates that by selling used boxes vs. virgin it has already saved:

Wood	= 6,709 trees
Energy	= 2,625,920 kWh of electricity (or 1,600 barrels of oil)
Greenhouse Gases	= 1,775,680 lbs CO2
Wastewater	= 3,485,760 gallons
Solid Waste	= 618,560 lbs

Metro and UCB have shown that their "Rescue, Resell, Recycle" model could not only be successful, but very profitable as a nationwide e-commerce company. His company embodies the eco motto: *Green is the new black.*

⑤ Systems Thinking

Curt McNamara, PE
Minneapolis College of Art and Design
Sustainable Design Certificate Program

With additional contributions from:
Tim McGee and Dr. Dayna Baumeister, Dan Halsey, Terry Gips,
Sustainable Packaging Coalition,[SM] MBDC's Cradle to Cradle[SM]

The systems approach begins when first you see the world through the eyes of another.

C. West Churchman

Humankind has excelled at taking the world apart and reassembling the pieces to do our bidding. This process is called reductionism. It has allowed humans to harness the atom, ship fuel around the world, and cure disease. For all its power to force Nature to our will, reductionism has failed to help us address our biggest problems. Today, reductionism is giving way to a larger picture of the world where designers are beginning to find ways to restore Earth's systems by putting things back together.

Nature's systems in action
Photo: Curt McNamara (c.mcnamara@ieee.org)

The Systems View

The damages from reductionism now exceed the benefits. Assembling pieces without considering the whole has yielded highly concentrated, inefficient, and damaging materials. Earth systems can't break down and safely absorb the concentrated materials or process wastes. For example, materials from nuclear power plants are unsafe for the environment. They are too concentrated to be safely broken down and must be stored for many thousands of years.

The by-products of reductionism are the massive environmental changes occurring today. Chemicals designed for a specific purpose without regard to their breakdown almost wiped out the bald eagle. There are areas of the world unsafe for habitation due to pervasive pollution. The atmosphere is changing to a new state brought about by our emissions, and the result will be less friendly to the people, animals, and habitation we are accustomed to.

In contrast, living systems continuously recycle materials and regenerate life. Designs modeled after natural systems can repair the damage while adding value to end users, designers, and corporations.

How does a designer do this? One response is to proceed as usual, but gain and use more knowledge of material effects. This "do less bad" approach is good as it broadens awareness and expands focus, yet there is much more that can be done.

An alternative point of view as old as civilization called holistic is represented in Daniel Pink's *A Whole New Mind*, where the age of systems is brought about by design, story, symphony, empathy, play, and meaning. Design by using a big picture view that includes other perspectives.

The holistic view is also called the systems view. Rather than seeing design problems as something to be divided down into the smallest bits, the systems view sees them as opportunities for interconnecting the world.

While this view can be traced back to early cultures in all parts of the world, R. Buckminster (Bucky) Fuller, a modern designer, epitomized this idea. Fuller came of age in the early part of the twentieth century and had experience in the Navy, leading him to consider navigation, efficiency of materials, and energy usage as the key components in a design situation. He was inspired by the elegance of nature's design, and his focus on nature's operating system gave him a dislike for the typical results of our processes.

We are on a spaceship; a beautiful one. It took billions of years to develop. We're not going to get another. Now, how do we make this spaceship work?

R. Buckminster Fuller

He is most well known for the geodesic dome, a high-efficiency lightweight structure that could span any distance. Domes consist of regular polyhedra coupled together to form a partial sphere. Set upon a simple foundation, a dome weighs as little as a pound per square foot.[1] Fuller's designs were intended to be mass produced for low cost.

Fuller saw housing as benefiting from the practices of automobile and aircraft manufacture with optimized components and efficient structure.

Yet Fuller was also a philosopher who believed that we all had the capacity to do great things, and that the world could work for all if we changed our priorities from weaponry to livingry (using technology to help humanity).

In World War II he catalogued the essential materials of civilization and concluded that there was enough if we simply recycled material and made the best use of what we had.

Fuller's designs included a high-efficiency car, low-flow shower (in the 1930s!), and a map that doesn't distort the shapes of the continents.[2] Since this is a spherical world, he taught that we have six degrees of freedom at every instant (radiate/converge, spin, orbit, invert, torque, precess), not the illusory three (xyz) of "flat earth" thinking.

Bucky inspired thousands of designers across several generations, and left us with a marvelous catalog of universal principles that can be used to design ever more elegant and sustainable solutions.

As a result, Fuller inspired generations of students and designers:

> Jay Baldwin
> (portable domes, teaching Bucky)
>
> Paul MacReady
> (human-powered flight)
>
> John Todd
> (water purification systems)
>
> Hunter Lovins, and Amory Lovins
> (energy systems)

> Stewart Brand
> (design information for all)
>
> Medard Gabel and Howard Brown
> (success for all humanity)
>
> William McDonough
> (green architecture, Cradle to Cradle[SM] design)

This brief list shows many of the leaders and ideas in sustainable design. Throughout the last half of the twentieth century many were aware of the trends and doing good work that is still relevant today.

Universal Principles

"The world is not flat, it is spherical. There is no up and down, just in and out." Humans have a flat world mentality from time immemorial. However, the world is a rotating sphere whirling around the sun while the solar system moves 52 million kilometers along with the Milky Way. Movement is not up in this world, it is out.

TECHNIQUE: Consider designs from the center — expand out, contract in.

"Nature doesn't calculate pi to 20 decimal places when she designs a flower." Fuller often observed that the basic mathematical "objects" were in fact illusions. There are no straight lines, planes, or circles in the real world. Pi proves that our coordinate system is wrong and that the circle is a mathematical illusion. Sustainable design is aligned with the coordinate system and energy cycles of the universe, enhancing effectiveness by acting in accordance with universal principles.

In the real world there are no idealized objects, but structures whose fine detail comes from individual nodes. As an example, consider the coastline of the United Kingdom. At one level of scale it appears to be a given length. Zooming in closer reveals more detail, and the length increases. This process occurs to the finest level of detail (the coast is a fractal, an object with similar structure regardless of scale). The coastline is not a "line," but rather an object composed of many nodes. All of nature is constructed this way.

TECHNIQUE: Rather than boxes, designs can be structures of fine detail mimicking natural systems. Grow designs to fit the world by using fine details. There is no flat in nature. Boxes are not a design solution.

Precession: Bees do not intend to pollinate, yet by collecting pollen they ensure that new flowers bloom. In a similar way Fuller pollinated heads with ideas and expected the universe to provide. If the universe did not provide, he adjusted his pollination strategy.

TECHNIQUE: If the package is nectar which attracts the buyer bee, what is the pollen? The brand? Sustainability? If the package fits customer values, it can carry the product along. What else does the shopper pick up? How does this information inform her next actions? Can package protection and information yield respect and learning about the earth? How can a package change a life?

Synergy: Alloys and composites show material properties not predicted by the behavior of individual components, or even the addition of individual component properties. "The whole is greater than the sum of the parts." Perhaps the most fundamental property of systems is that they can't be understood by taking the pieces apart, but only by looking at everything together. Similarly, design done by taking things apart to the smallest level will not result in sustainable designs.

TECHNIQUE: Use and create interconnections when designing. Test combinations of design elements to find unexpected gains.

Ephemeralization: Humanity increasingly does more with less. Consider the cell phone network, which allows developing countries to gain communications infrastructure without building miles of telephone wires and poles.

TECHNIQUE: How thin can that package be?

Trimtab: An ocean liner is a huge object requiring a large rudder. In turn, the rudder requires much force to move. Naval designers use a smaller rudder called a trimtab to move the larger rudder.

TECHNIQUE: Look for trimtabs to move a company or society. The sustainable story on the package might be able to move the company.

Tensegrity: Most efficient structures use tension and compression in balance. Bridges could only be built so far when they relied on compression columns to support them. Using cables (suspension = tension) allowed structures to span much larger distances using less material.

TECHNIQUE: Packages can use tension and compression, creating a web of support.

Triangulation: Along with the illusion of a flat world, humans have a "box" mentality that pervades design. Constructing a cube of toothpicks with clay corners shows there is no structural stability in such a design. If a structure is made of triangles, then it has stability and strength regardless of what the corners or nodes are made of. Boxes come from a flat earth worldview.

TECHNIQUE: Design by expanding out from the product and add more elements (higher frequencies) as required.

Tools not politics. People's behaviors only change when they have the right tools. This book is not about changing minds through legislation, but rather changing the world through design.

Universal principles are laws that work everywhere and anytime. For example, gravitation pulls inwards (contracts) toward the center. It is not a property of either object, but exists only as a relation between the two objects.

TECHNIQUE: What are the forces of relationship that exist between and not in the parts? How can the design use these forces?

Other principles: Life regenerates itself continually. Nature runs on loops. Systems are not static. Interconnection is the law.

Universal principles of life (adapted from Hoagland):

— Builds from the bottom up. Cells form organelles, individuals form society. Flocks of birds and schools of fish emerge from simple rules.

— Assembles itself into chains. How do packages link together?

— Needs an inside and an outside. One side of a boundary faces in, the other faces out.

— Uses a few themes to create many variations. Invertebrate, vertebrate, clamshell, web.

Nothing exists outside of a relationship. The grass holds the dunes that harbor the shoreline's ecosystem.

Photo: Curt McNamara (c.mcnamara@ieee.org)

— Organizes with information, not energy. The abalone self assembles in seawater without heat or waste, yet is stronger than any ceramic.

— Encourages variety by reshuffling information and creates with mistakes. Make deliberate and accidental design combinations.

— Occurs in water and runs on sugar. Design the process first, the package second.

— Works in cycles. Packages are alive, whether Frankenstein or butterfly.

— Recycles everything it uses. There is no waste in nature, but food for you or another. Return wastes to earth safely, or find a partner who can use it.

— Renews itself by turnover. Can a package be refreshed or expire? Don't design for perpetuity, take advantage of decay. The package should not last longer than the product.

— Optimizes rather than maximizes. Optimal is neither worst case nor forever. Rather it is a balance of forces and requirements.

— Is opportunistic. Look for openings and test with small changes. Experiment.

— Competes within a cooperative framework. Work with peers and team with competitors to increase markets and knowledge. Both parties will gain. "Whatever you want, give it away" (Ford teamwork principle). No design or designer is an island.

— Is interconnected and interdependent.[3]

Perhaps Fuller is most well known today for buckyballs, carbon crystals consisting of sixty atoms arranged in a sphere composed of pentagons and hexagons (similar to his geodesic dome designs).

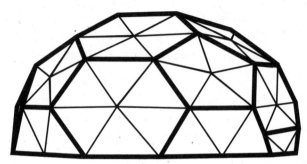

Fuller's geodesic dome design

Buckyballs are assembled into carbon nanotubes and the structures are advancing materials science.

Fuller's combination of positive philosophy, elegant design, and the capability of the individual made him an inspiring speaker. His design approach was a bridge between science and the needs of humanity, convincing listeners there were solutions to the big problems. At the time knowledge of environmental problems was increasing while industry seemed decoupled from the issues and needs of society.

The preceding paragraphs summarized a set of principles that allow a designer to align with the universal coordinate system of the universe.

TECHNIQUE: Knowing location and orientation allows a designer to move along universal dimensions. The world is an ocean and all are sailors.

Design decisions set the direction for packages, people, and the company. To take advantage of the systems view, align designs with universal principles.

It is a human tendency to view systems as external and static. In reality all are enmeshed in creating, utilizing, and designing dynamic systems every moment. The movement from reductionism to seeing systems is a change in perspective. Once that change is made, there are several ways to utilize the systems view:

- The properties of systems and how they can improve designs

- Considering work and design itself as a system process

- Using the cycles and properties of natural systems as inspiration for design

Bridging the Gap with Systems

How can design leave the world in better condition? One lesson of reductionism is that if designs are improved along just one dimension, other aspects may degrade in ways that were not foreseen. Examples would be a highly efficient package that requires toxic materials, or a material from plant fiber that uses large amounts of water or chemicals for processing.

The implication is that sustainable design can't be done by optimizing just one design attribute. As an example, several sustainable accounting methods use a three-part approach which includes social, environmental, and economic factors (aka Triple Top Line — People, Planet, Profits).[4] Sustainability may be shown as the intersection of these three domains with the economic system embedded in the environment.

In the systems view, designs are connected to their environment at all times — from production to processing to sale to end of life. These connections are package attributes — materials they were created with, energy used for processing, connections to the designer and customer, and decay at end of life.

Packages exist inside the economic system, yet the economic system is embedded in society and the environment. The connections of material, produc-

tion, and end of life extend out into the environment as they pass through society. A material might appear to have a nice loop within the economic system, yet affect workers in the societal system and have negative impacts on the environment.

Contrast this with appropriate materials that benefit the workers and the environment while still fulfilling an economic function. This kind of design builds value at all levels.

The three-part accounting method is a reminder to designers of primary constituencies. However, the parts can't be considered individually! Rather, all must be dealt with at the same time. Connections are the key principle behind the nested circles of sustainability.

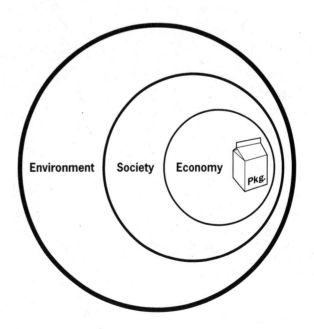

Packages exist inside economic, societal, and environmental systems.

Systems Properties

There are multiple perspectives where the systems view can be used: package designs, the design process, or even the structure and relations of a department or company.

The systems view at the design level focuses on linkages, boundary, and function.

In the real world, nothing can contract nor expand without limit. A stable system has forces to increase and forces to decrease. The force to increase is termed positive feedback, while the force to decrease is negative feedback. Their balance creates stability.

System edges and exchange points are at boundaries, the places where they connect to each other and to the world. A package has many boundaries or edges: physical, informational, and visual.

Functions are the ways a system responds to or modifies the environment. Packages protect, inform, and sell, and these functions can be assigned to components of the system. For example, protection against light can come from package reflectance. The type of function often gives insight into the structure required to perform that function. A boundary function could be to protect, respond, or permit entry.

Loops and interconnections are visible when perspective changes from images (a leaf bud or a rusting automobile) to cycles, changing from snapshots in time, to steps in a cycle looping from creation to life and return. This is a life cycle, and all products have it. They are created from the earth, live on materials and energy from natural systems, and return to nature via landfill or incineration. It is not possible to know the true costs or values or benefits of a design without considering the life cycle.

TECHNIQUE: Seeing the life cycle can inspire a package service system where customers pay for the service of packaging rather than packages.[5]

The systems perspective looks beyond the current way of doing business and permits designers and managers to imagine future systems that benefit both company and planet. If all current designs are made from primary materials and landfilled, the alternative choices look meager. Instead, a systems perspective allows the company to imagine the packages becoming an asset to attract customers, improve the working life of employees, and increase margins and market share.

The next few sections show how to move to the systems design perspective.

Systems and Design

Designers need three types of information to capture a system: visual, descriptive, and relational. Designers are visual thinkers so the first way is natural. Description benefits by using one of the following perspectives: dimension, function or boundary. Relations are graphical elements that illustrate linkages, forces, or movement.

TECHNIQUE: To use the systems perspective, draw an image of the package. Now divide it into its components, and connect each package component to the earth as a source material. Show the materials being processed and delivered as a finished package. The next step is transport, then sale and arrival in the customer's hands. Create an image of the customer and the package. The package is opened. Now what happens?

The diagram may show a cycle returning materials to the source to create a loop, or it may show a package ending up in the landfill. At each stage, diagram the relations of the package materials to the earth and to the people associated with that step in its life. Now write a description of each stage. This is a systems description of the package.

Make a large copy, post it, and invite comments. Document another design — how does it compare? Do the images show places to add connections? Do they show the potential to use alternative materials?

The image shows system properties — dimension, function, boundary, linkages, and interconnection exist in every system and its elements:

The Package

— Material

— Processing

— Life cycle (creation to use to end of life and rebirth)

— Stakeholder connections (customer to production staff)

The design process is also a system with interconnections, loops, feedback, energy, and information flows. Consider documenting the design process and how it connects to the stakeholders.

— Package design process

— Design environment (information sources, peers, competitors)

— Package requirements

— Design tools

— Design representation (CAD, point design vs. systems view)

— Product design process

— Package <-> product interconnection (consider the larger system)

— Team learning (teaching and learning from each other)

— Company function

— Commercial ecology (customers and suppliers)

— Industrial ecology (interconnections with other firms)

— Departmental ecology (human systems)

There are several systems viewpoints and perspectives:

— Technical approaches

— Philosophical approaches

— Design guidelines

The following sections cover a range of systems perspectives on packaging, the design process, and the relation of the package to the environment.

Package as a System

Where does the system perspective start, and how can it be utilized effectively?

As a first step, what is a package? If the first thought is enclosure, advertisement, or product information, then the design has been viewed from a single perspective. The design solution will not be a system but a "point solution." While it may do an excellent job in one area, it might have unintended consequences in others. This type of design solves a situation that is limited in scope, leading to problems in other areas.

Lead paint on children's toys is one example. While it was a good choice for the initial cost, the consequences of this material specification went far beyond a product recall. Companies took more steps to ensure safety, suppliers went under, and there were responses from the government. The total impact is huge and ongoing. In addition to risk reduction, there are economic and competitive advantages to sustainable design as well.

A related example is a company with high failure rates on shipped product. Adding more packaging did not help, and the failures continued until they looked deep enough into the product design and found that a rubber stop, costing only a few pennies, positioned inside the product kept the components from vibrating destructively. This allowed them to decrease packaging to the bare minimum, saving material dollars and transportation costs.

These situations are part of a continuum, illustrating how designers and managers have the chance to make decisions from a narrow or wide perspective. In many cases, using the larger perspective only takes a little more time and money, yet the payoff is huge. It has been said that up to 80 percent of the material and energy impacts of a package are determined by the design decisions.

How can design practice be enlarged to make the larger perspective automatic? Consider each design (and its elements) as a system.

Adapt to the Environment

How do we get from here... — point solutions, doing designs that oppose natural systems.

...to there? — comprehensive solutions that benefit companies, society, and the environment.

The systems perspective is an excellent entry point. This may sound surprising if the word *system* brings to mind complex equipment or regimented organizations. This type of system design comes from a view of the world as a static entity with many layers. Such designs can be brittle and unable to adapt as the environment changes.

Buckminster Fuller said, "Extinction happens when the environment changes and the organism doesn't adapt." We are now in times of extreme environmental change, and many products, organisms, and organizations will become extinct.

What are the environments a package lives in?

Regulatory (ISO 14000, RoHS, WEEE)

Workplace (company culture and changes)[6]

Competitive (the company and the competition)

Marketplace (packages are flowers designed to attract buyer bees)

Consumer (their mind space)

Cultural (media, books, and music)

Physical (protection against water, heat, theft, and pathogens)

Economic (costs and advantages)

Biosphere or natural environment

These are all changing and evolving. A package is the boundary between product and all these environments, so it needs to evolve as well or become extinct. Design of the package as a system occurs when the perspectives of others are included and life cycle is considered.

The creation, distribution, and disposal of every package impacts the physical environment here on earth. There are many ethical reasons to "do the right thing": regulations, leaving the planet better for the children, preserving the health of neighbors. Adapt to the biosphere.

Typical package design requirements

Protect

Against environments, pathogens, and shock

Against theft or tampering

Inform

About the product

About the company

Sell

The contents

The company

Examples of design for the wrong environment

Protection: needed for storage time of weeks, yet persists for decades in nature

Sell: designed to please stakeholders, yet doesn't connect to customers

Inform: makes sense internally but end user doesn't understand

The design for protect/sell/inform needs to work for all the environmental interfaces. So the first benefit of the systems perspective is to enlarge design thinking to include other environmental interfaces. This larger picture makes designing and designs more adaptive, giving competitive advantage.

The design has to fulfill the technical objectives! An earth-friendly package that falls apart in the store helps no one.

Consider how often designs are updated. At the time of design adaptation to the environment happens, and improvements occur. Just as organisms have new offspring, designers have new packages. The environment acts on those packages, rewarding the best.

— Increasing market share for package

— Better health of planet and people

— Enhancing the designer's career

To make this work, try several design options and let the market select.

Designs, companies, and designers can also become extinct. How does a designer track and adapt as the environment changes? By updating skill sets and being open to new information. Being open to new information means searching outside the current way (personal or company) of doing things. The new information will be from different perspectives than the present one. Beware of the view that it is safe to go back automatically to the tried and true ("nobody ever got fired for choosing IBM").

Properties of Systems

Along with the environment, other systems properties that can transform package designs are:

— Boundary

— Function

— Linkages: feedback and interchange

Boundary

What is a package? It is a boundary or skin between the product and the environment.

What is a system? Something with a boundary that persists as the environment changes, yet is connected to the world.

The boundary of a package serves all the diverse environments noted above. Yet it is often designed for one. Is the package boundary alive or dead? Is it seen as an adaptive system, changing as required?

To take a biological example, the cell is a system, and the cell boundary is a system as well. Like every other boundary, the cell membrane divides the world into two: the system inside the boundary and the world outside.

The package also divides the world in two: the product inside and the world outside. Seen this way, it is similar to a cell boundary.

Does this sound familiar? A little more detail: The cell boundary is composed of molecules called phospholipids, which have one end that prefers water and the other that rejects water. The molecules snap together with the water-loving ends outside and the water-hating ends inside. A second layer forms inside, and a boundary is created.

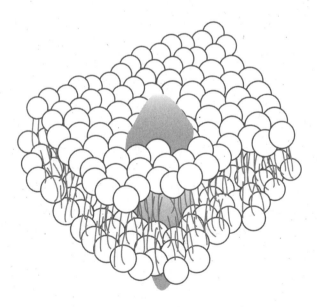

A boundary showing the interlinked molecules that form the inner and outer layers

The cell boundary protects the contents inside, and permits some substances and energies to enter while rejecting others. This seems more complex than a package, yet there are similarities. A package boundary allows radio frequency identification (RFID) signals (and perhaps also light) to pass through, while keeping fingers and moisture out. With the appropriate signal, the boundary lets other signals pass through.

A cell boundary responds to molecular triggers that fit the shape of its openings. The trigger initiates an action inside the cell boundary. Cell boundaries pump water to create one set of environmental conditions inside regardless of external conditions.

At a larger scale, the cell boundary looks like the eggshell or the banana peel. Both are elegant packaging solutions that return to nature and restore the earth in the process.

If there are similarities between the cell wall and the package, what can be learned from this?

Like the cell, can the package

— be grown;

— pump pressure;

— respond to stimulus;

— indicate internal conditions?

The package is a boundary, with one controlled environment inside and another environment outside.

What doesn't the typical package do that the cell boundary does?

— Renew itself

— Valve or regulate substances and energies

— Decay

— Self-assemble

How can insights from cell boundaries be used to improve designs? The cell boundary has an inside surface (cell to membrane) and an outside surface (membrane to environment). Can package designs be improved by considering the two interfaces separately? Start by defining the ideal boundary from the inside looking out and from the outside looking in.

Cell boundaries self-assemble when their fundamental components are close enough to allow interconnection. What materials and processes would mimic this?

One approach is to start thinking at minimum complexity with a two-piece package (clamshell) snapping together. How can that be changed to four parts? To eight? This is similar to the innovative process at 3M, where they learned many small lenses are better than just one, then invented technology to create the products and the processes. This was then spun off into adhesives and a variety of other product lines.

> This cross-fertilization is perhaps best exemplified by 3M's micro-replication process, a technology developed for the manufacture of lenses for overhead projectors. The process enables the creation of tiny, precisely shaped structures that can be used to tailor the physical, chemical, and optical properties of a surface.

> These perfectly replicated structures, which range in size from nanometers to millimeters, have since been used to create reflective prisms on safety clothing and light enhancement films for display screens, as well as in structural adhesives and a number of abrasive products.[7]

As packages come into alignment with the dimensions of the universe they will be less like flat earth boxes and more like webs and skins. This process could be started by replication, with similar shapes fitting together to cover any surface. Packages need not be flat or square. If the package is unique, then the buyer and the product are unique by association.

Cell boundaries are composed of organic molecules that need to be renewed or they will decay and be carried away by scavengers. In the urban environment valuable packages (aluminum cans) are carried away by scavengers once the contents are emptied. What other material choices could decay after use or be valuable enough for collection? Perhaps the package is high value, guaranteeing collection and return.

Consider designing the system for collection first. What would make a package valuable enough for scavengers to arise? In Brazil one city rewards with food residents who bring in recyclable garbage. Janine Benyus in Biomimicry tells how she brought secondhand store employees into a manufacturer so they could look at wastes and decide which had potential for reuse. The industrial design program at The University of the Arts in Philadelphia sends students out to companies to collect a barrel of whatever they consider waste. The students return and figure out ways to use the material.

Contrast this approach to one that makes the boundary ephemeral and easily decomposed. In the one case make it valuable and recapture it, in the other make it easy to return to nature. This is similar to biological and technical nutrients in Cradle to Cradle.

Function

The functions of a system are the ways that it reacts to inputs or responds to the environment. In some cases this is simple: Persist in the face of environmental changes.

Other functions are to support, guard, preserve, seal, prevent oxidization, show, hide, reveal, draw attention, open, hang, stack, nest. There are more — make a list for the company.

For each function, describe whether it is accomplished through materials, forming, or graphics. Many functions will be a combination or sequence of these elements.

TECHNIQUE: Describe all package functions graphically. Break each function down into materials and processing. Show how several functions are contained in one structure. What functions stand alone, or are the result of a single processing step or material selection?

Lightening: Now take the step of lightening the package. Can the function be accomplished with less material? With lower-impact processing? Moved from structure to information?

Elimination: Are there functions that are not mandatory? Perhaps something designed for worst case can be lightened, yet still fit 85 percent of the market. Make a trade-off comparison to see if the savings outweigh the market fit. If necessary, create one package for the majority and a more expensive one for the minority.

Splitting: If one material choice or processing step is used to achieve more than one function, split the functions apart. Does this allow less material or lower-impact processing to be used for part? How could the secondary function be achieved?

Combining: As before, now look at combining functions in a single material or process step. Perhaps two previously combined functions should be split and one recombined with a new partner.

Level up: What are the functions of the package/product combination? Brainstorm with the product team to see if there are functions that could be assigned to the package. If the package does more, can the product do less? What is the interface between package and product? If the package is a subsystem, how does it relate to the product?

Level down: Can package functions be accomplished by the product? Would this make a better product? If the package does less, can the product do more?

This process of fine-tuning function relates to life cycle assessment (LCA). The first step in LCA is to define the function, followed closely by the system that bounds that function.

TECHNIQUE: For each function ask, How does nature do it? Can the function or its expression be minimized? Is it possible to eliminate that function? Can the function be transformed into information?

A typical design process might view the package's function to be a skin added at the last minute for protection. Yet skin is a complex structure tightly coupled to the tissue underneath: protecting, breathing, growing, and dying. The metaphor of skin (or seed or shell) can give many ideas, and there may be an advantage in coupling the package more tightly with the product.

Design function can be reimagined

— Package function
      expands out
      contracts in

— Package does
      more functions
      less functions

— How minimal can the package be?

— What is the maximum package?

— How valuable can the package be?

Packages can be "overdesigned." Product damage during shipment can in some cases be traced back to the product design. In these cases, improvements in product design yield a more robust product while lowering packaging costs and weight. Instead of design for worst case, design for nominal and accommodate special needs.

What is required of the product if the package is minimized?

In other words, can the package be rethought in terms of total product design? Perhaps overdesigning the package can be good if it reduces product materials or costs. Maybe the product can be designed in a way that minimizes the package. The package could be grown around the product, or be essential to the end user. Packages lead users to sustainability since they are first to be returned to the earth. Doing the right thing with the package carries over to other areas of life and design.

If the package persists in a useful way, it serves as another constant reminder of the company. Many companies are thinking of their products as composed of "technical nutrients"[8] and want them returned.

They reward customers for this and gain repeat buyers, increasing sustainability. The package can lead this as well.

Package functions can be expanded, contracted, or transformed in ways that increase sustainability.

Design strategies

— Look at the package/product pair as a system.

— Grow the package, decreasing requirements on the product.

— Shrink the package, increasing product requirements yet decreasing total costs.

— Transform the package function.

— Can it survive after shipment in a useful way?

— Can it be returned to the manufacturer in an exchange that benefits both?

A package that persists after use can be a detriment not only to the environment, but also to the company when it becomes trash in the woods or ocean with your logo on it. Create packages that inspire closing the loop.

When designing, consider the actual package environments: manufacturing or production, shipment or transport, point-of-sale, consumer transport, home, and end of life. Each is a different environment with different requirements. Tune in and design for the best case.

Packages can be transformed to increase sustainability....Tune in and design for the best case.

Feedback and Interchange

Feedback brings thermostats to mind: If the temperature is too low, turn the furnace on. If the temperature is too high, turn the furnace off.

Feedback in package design is deeper and richer. For one example, certain colors provoke certain associations. These might be confirming the identity of the buyer, or they might be a "hook" to catch new users. Just like product design, the package design communicates core values that resonate with end users.

The package also has interchange with the product: It may simply provide a controlled environment or it may allow certain interactions while prohibiting others.

One direction of feedback and interchange is package to product: What is that interface? Skin, shell, husk, house, or box? Is it coupled like the banana skin? Or decoupled via inert atmosphere like the space station?

The other direction is package to customer. In some cases the package lets the product shine through and make its own connection to the user. In other cases the package aids or obscures this. The idea here is not to think of the package as a filter but rather another piece to create better solutions.

Valving or regulating energy has potential to expand beyond light (advertisements) and RFID (product tracking). What if the package responded to customers and opened? Then perhaps oxygen could start the package decomposing.

The connection to sustainability is obvious: Certain package designs attract those customers. Other designs can educate customers who have been attracted by some other feature.

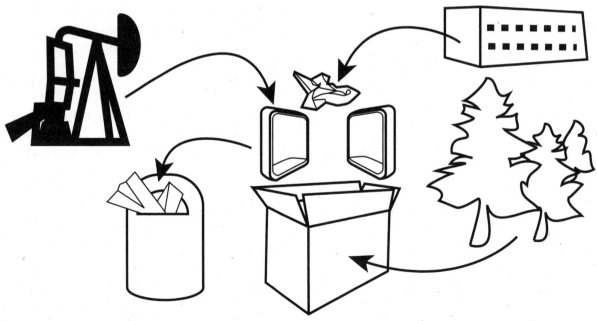

What's in a box?

In many ways the package is the unit of interchange: The price is marked, indicating the transaction fee to the buyer and the seller. The package can affirm core values to the buyer, and the inclusion of sustainability can attract new customers.

Levels

Point of view determines the structure, order, and relation of a system. For example, the view of a corporation is different among the worker, manager, owner, and customer. A designer often views the package from outside the product, and perhaps even outside the product design team. Consider the package-level view — what does the product need and want from the package? Looking in, what does the package want from the product?

This view automatically reminds one of levels, from the product through package to end user.

The package often consists of several levels:

Protection
  Shock
  Moisture
  Theft
  Consumer safety

Information
  Consumer
  Company
  Regulatory

Housing
  Box
  Support
  Moisture barrier
  Sensing (RFID)

Levels include external enclosure, product supports, informational inserts, labeling, and inner protection. Graphics may be combined on another level (printing in external enclosure), which can help or hinder sustainability. For example, a toxic ink may appear lower cost, yet contaminate the packaging material.

TECHNIQUE: Make a contents chart of a complex package. What physical levels are there? What informational levels? Which levels are combined into one physical level? Explore combining or separating the levels.

Can two levels be combined into one? Perhaps the functions of one level can be subsumed in the next, requiring less energy and materials to produce. Conversely it may be possible that one layer should be split into two. The idea of "platform design," where a standard set of materials is customized for different products, can allow lower impact designs in a variety of ways: Economy of scale can allow use of more appropriate materials; less time and energy is needed for new designs; standardization allows refinement instead of inventing the same wheel over and over again.

The package can affirm core values to the buyer, and the inclusion of sustainability can attract new customers.

149

Taking Advantage of the Systems View

Besides the systems perspective, how can a package designer take advantage of systems approaches?

There is competitive advantage to considering package design as a system. There are several ways to do this: marketing vs. the competition, increasing best practice inside the company, and evolving in the product niche.

Consider the Niche

What is a niche? In ecology, it is the area an organism occupies, and has dimensions for position in the food chain, habitat, life history, and geographic range. The parallels to packages are the consumers who buy it, the places it is sold, where it goes when it dies, and how it competes against other packages. Two packages can't occupy the same niche.

TECHNIQUE: Map the forces that describe the niche the package lives in. How do these link to the consumer? To the earth? What are the commonalities and differences between the package and the competition?

Products are organisms inside niches where they compete for food (energy or dollars) against other products. Organisms can't live just anywhere, as they adapt or evolve to the niche they are found in. This could be a kind of soil, a type of insect, a sequence of temperatures, and moisture. Some birds can live in wider ranges than others because they can eat insects or seeds, similar to a car that can run on more than one kind of fuel.

Consider the niche in the marketplace: Where is the product placed (high or low on the shelves); how does it attract customers; what is the value for price? Some products only appeal to a small set of customers but have high rates of return. Others are like the house sparrow, which can live almost anywhere.

TECHNIQUE: Describe the niche for the package and for the competition. How do they compare and differ? How can your package move away from the competition and toward the customer?

Questions to Consider

How can product/package adapt to niche changes?

Niches
Consumer mind-set
Regulatory environment
Competitive

Nutrients
Money
Information
Materials

Cycles
Consumer
Regulatory
Company
Earth (sport products change with seasons)

Design Strategies

— Minimize structure (more efficient in the niche)

— Maximize function (better return vs. competition)

— Use cycles (pay attention)

— Identify with the customer as opposed to compete with others

— Adaptive design (changes after release)

— Evolve design practice

— Select design strategy from several options

— Use variation (design alternatives) and let the market select

— Increase iterations of the design system

In other words, is the focus on the consumer (the source of energy/dollars) or on the competitors? Two organisms that compete for the same resources have to share a niche.[9] This is not a long-term strategy — most companies move products to new niches where there is little or no competition.[10] This forced evolution takes into consideration both customer and product characteristics.

Design Practice

How does the process start? A package can be the last thing in the production process, or it can be integrated into the design cycle. Early work improves the results. For example, the design of the package can optimize the package/product system.

Design improvements are proportional to effort.

Techniques that encourage excellence and multiple viewpoints are:

— Team learning

— Design dimensions

— Use constraints to improve package designs

— Checklists

— Best practice

— Design language

— Systems design approaches

— Biology as inspiration

The Package/Product Team

It has been said that there are no single-brain problems anymore. Rather, excellent designs come from environments with multiple diverse viewpoints. Thinking back to the original examples of lead paint

and product support, a different viewpoint in the decision process would have saved much time and money.

How can this be accomplished? In many companies there are reviews and checkpoints where other departments are involved. Unfortunately, these happen once the design is fairly structured (don't want to show unfinished work) and their format can be adversarial so that design decisions are defended instead of taking in the new view. The best antidote is to walk around with the design ahead of time. Find a good person in each department to share ideas with. These informal reviews can be much more productive than the formal ones.

This approach comes from biology — acting as a tree, extending roots out into the organization to get nutrients and to give back value. Interestingly, the interconnection will benefit both departments.

Team Learning and Decision Making

All effective teams have members with different problem-solving styles. While other styles may not "mesh" with each other, there is gain from seeing each distinct perspective in action. Knowledge obtained through working together helps with decisions.

Decision-making styles are a mixture of energy source (extrovert vs. introvert), information management style, information language, deliberation style, and decision closure style. The bottom line is that if the leader can recognize and acknowledge these differences, then the team decision will be much stronger than any individual effort. It will be impossible to obtain consensus on all design decisions. If team members can state the problem clearly along with the decision criteria and why the decision was made, then the team effort has been effective.[11]

Involve the Stakeholders

Each design has several stakeholders: the production team, the product team, company finance, product sellers, and customers. Each design has to work for all these parties, and their needs may be in conflict. As one example, regulatory may want more product margin while finance doesn't want to spend the money. The good news is that this wider team will give more perspective, enabling better and more sustainable solutions.

Stakeholders

> Package designers
> Management
> Customers
> Product designers
> Marketing
> Sales
> Regulatory
> Finance
> Production
> Service
> Maintenance
> Manufacturing

It can feel overwhelming to guide a design to the finish line with all these people involved. To help the process, consider defining package requirements for each stakeholder, and rank or prioritize these requirements to evaluate the design against.

A good tool in this situation is to catalog product "dimensions" or characteristics, for example, package weight, material cost, security, and advertising. The design alternatives can then be ranked by stakeholders (on a scale of 1 to 5) and a score assigned. It may be necessary to prioritize the dimensions to weight one characteristic against

another. A great practice is to make a brief description of the desired solution or design situation and have stakeholders comment on and revise it.

Design Dimensions

As noted above, it can be critical to identify key product characteristics.[12] If the design doesn't fit the essential goals, it doesn't matter if the materials are sustainable.

Physical lifetime

> Use time
> Reliability
> Safety
> Economy

As one example, packages may need to last a long time (physical lifetime), yet customer use time is very brief (from purchase to opening). This leads to a conflict as the designer works toward a long physical lifetime, resulting in material choices that don't decompose and return to nature once the use phase is over. In contrast, a seed can travel a long distance (long physical lifetime) yet have a short use phase (water causes the seed husk to open and it then decays). Sometimes the seed casing (package) provides materials for the seed (product) to grow.

Annie Chun's: Noodle Bowl

Annie Chun's noodle bowls are made from a corn-based bioplastic, with a recyclable paperboard outer sleeve. The company won a 2004 Environmental Achievement Award from the Environmental Protection Agency (EPA). Going a step further, its 1Bowl Campaign (1bowl.org) is working to help raise funds for the UN World Food Program.

A structured creativity technique called Triz[13] looks at design dimensions from a variety of perspectives: weight, strength, loss, amount of material and energy, complexity, manufacturability, response to variation; and ease of use.[14]

Human-centered design uses a triad of use, usability, and meaning as design dimensions. Use corresponds to function, usability to the ways a consumer interacts with a product, and meaning is the complex of associations with the product.[15] For example, a tiny MP3 player signifies independence and love of music.

Design Checklists

Having a standard checklist ensures that all critical characteristics (material toxicity, ease of opening, requirements for new processing) are considered. These should be continuously updated along with examples of how previous teams have used this approach to improve designs. Besides the common questions about materials and processing, it should list the design dimensions mentioned above, and state how each was satisfied. Designs that meet the most stringent environmental goals but fail to meet the fundamental design dimensions are not sustainable.

Best Practice

To work with best practice, interview designer peers or determine your best design. What is the best package for this type of product? What characteristics does it have, and what should be carried on to other designs? Keep a chart of package essentials: cost, weight, environmental impact, market attributes. Use this to document design practice and compare new designs to old.

What is the state of the competition? What lessons can be learned from them? How can a better design be marketed against them?

There is good industry buy-in for this approach: The Energy Star[16] rating and ISO 14000 require examinations of company designs against other products. If clear energy savings are shown against the typical product, the Energy Star can be used in marketing materials.

Finally, compare company packaging approaches. Is one design strategy clearly better than another? Why? Can continuous improvement be done in this area? What are the intangibles? Can an improved product be marketed to give advantage over the competition?

A good way to share best practice is to have design meetings (perhaps over lunch) where each individual shares information about design approaches, new techniques, or their current project.

Design Language

Patterns are set ways of seeing and relating to the world, giving great power along with risk. Patterns are a characteristic of the design process, making it possible to scaffold previous learning to the next generation of products and designers.

A design language is a set of patterns that describe the standard way of solving problems. Every company has one, whether it is explicit or implicit. For example, consumer products designed to hang on a peg may use a two-part, heat-sealed, plastic shell. This approach may be "the way things are done around here" or it may be the best solution based on years of experience.

At a basic level, a design language consists of three part descriptions:

— Text description of the situation

— Relational diagram of forces in and outside the design situation

— Design solution with a visual representation[17]

The above example can be mapped as follows:

Sealable, transparent packaging is required for a high-volume low-cost consumer product.

Forces

Customer requirement: See the product

Retailer requirement: Sealed package to reduce theft and presale damage, low cost, hangs

Product requirement: Keeps moisture out

Solution

Two-part plastic shell of heat-sealed transparent material

Readers will note several things about this. First, an enormous amount of information is still left out. What types of plastic are appropriate? How is the shell designed for the lowest cost manufacture? What design details are required for effective heat sealing? Why does it have to be heat sealing at all?

These are documented in further design patterns, forming a multilevel structure that can easily be grasped by new employees. This reveals assumptions about the design which may not have been visible, and draws attention to parts of the design process that can be improved.

As just one example, adding a requirement on material type to the pattern on transparent materials will create a new set of patterns. In a similar way patterns for the separation of package components for recycling or reuse can be added.

The company language may be unwritten and may depend on the current mix of employees. Aspects of it may be due to the implicit understanding of company constraints and expectations. Readers in management will recognize the difficulties with this — as company direction and priorities change, it can be hard to mold the "hidden forces" existing within product groups.

The patterns developed this way consist of design solutions to conflicting forces within the situation. Showing how conflicting forces were resolved gives both context to standard design solutions, and inspires new work in documenting new design situations.

Writing down a design language is a very freeing process. Designers and others can see what forces are at work in a particular design and get feedback. As the language propagates through the company, new patterns and details are added. This becomes a rich repository of design information — it is intellectual property. New employees can more quickly come up to speed, and they have a neutral environment to express their ideas.

Writing down a design language is a very freeing process. Designers and others can see what forces are at work in a particular design and get feedback.

Using Systems Thinking in the Design Process

The systems approach enables many possible viewpoints of package design.

Package/product co-design. Complement the product design by working with that design team. This will give an advantage to both product and package, reducing costs on both sides.

Package boundary. What passes the boundary? What is rejected at the boundary? How is the boundary created? Can it self-assemble?

Package life cycle. When does the package decompose? What starts the process? Can the results be used as food for another cycle?

System feedback. What is the loop from the consumer to the product? Is there one loop at purchase time and another at use time? How about the loop to the seller? What aspects of package design are most important to each design customer, and can they be integrated to benefit both?

Package as a level of design. Does the package live above or below the product? Is the package itself a product? Do people want the package more than the product (e.g., commemorative cereal boxes)?

Package as structure. Does the package have a use apart from the product? Does it complement the product? Does it have an entirely different use? Will people buy the product for the package?

Package as attachment. Are people attracted more to the package or to the product? Is this a two-step process?

A bee is a customer, attracted to the flower's "packaging."

Photo: Curt McNamara (c.mcnamara@ieee.org)

Shield. Communities often provide a buffer zone between themselves and their surroundings. For example, a forest has an edge area where species that can't survive in the forest itself flourish. These areas serve as a transition between one kind of environment and another. As one example, there may be high winds outside the forest while it is relatively calm inside. Bird life will differ considerably between these two environments, and species will migrate along the boundary, allowing them access to either environment. How is the package the bridge between product and consumer? Can the package link to other products, creating a community?

Advertisement. Plants advertise themselves to pollinators by a variety of colors and shapes. The arrangement serves both well, as the flowers get pollinated while the bees get nectar.

The customer is a bee, attracted by the package to the product. A good package experience inclines them to try another product (flower) from the garden.

Security. The hard exteriors on some organisms protect them from many predators, yet there is always something that evolves to overcome this defense. The same is true in our networks ("spam" and computer viruses). A package design may have embedded RFID, be bulky, or hard to open in an effort keep away predators. Each approach is effective in a given environment, yet may add high ecological costs to the design. How can we use natural inspiration to accomplish this?

Support. Organisms may have internal structures (like vertebrates) or external structure (invertebrates). A package design may be that external structure (the jelly jar). What can the crab shell teach us?

Product/package as seed. If the product is a seed, how does the package "catch on" (as burdock inspired hook and loop closure tape) and connect to the customer, carrying the product along? If the package is a seed, what causes it to open? (In nature it may be water or fire.) After it opens, what happens to the seed covering? What are the correct environments for the seed to return to nature? Could the package nourish the product after it opens?

Shell. There are plastic packages called clamshells, but how effective is the metaphor? The clamshell is grown in seawater at normal temperatures with readily available materials and no waste. It consists of two parts that open readily when the organism wants, yet is very resistant to being opened by others. When open the organism pumps water through as it filters food.

How is the package the bridge between product and consumer? Can the package link to other products, creating a community?

Biomimicry

by Tim McGee and Dr. Dayna Baumeister

From baskets and bins to blister packs and bubble wrap, our society is awash in a sea of packaging. But we're not the only ones on this planet who shield our goods from a tempestuous world. Consider seed pods, cheek pouches, snakeskin, and eggshells — all perform the same functions as our modern packaging: They contain loose objects, protect contents from harm, and communicate to the outside world what the package may contain. Uniquely, they meet these critical functional roles without causing harm to themselves, the contents, or the environment. Given the similarities, might we learn about sustainable packaging from the natural world? This process of looking to life for sustainable design advice is called biomimicry.

A rapidly emerging discipline, Biomimicry has found innovative solutions for many human design challenges, including fiber optics, advanced materials, automotive and robotics, green building, the food industry, software, and, of course, packaging. We explore here the possibilities of what we, as co-inhabitants on this planet, might learn from the other 30 million species about sustainably containing, protecting and communicating about our goods.

Contain

One of the first and most critical roles of packaging is to contain the contents. Holding sloshy liquids or multiple items together represents several subtle

---

Clamshell packaging comes in many forms and materials.

challenges. Faced with changing volumes, numbers, sizes, or shapes of items over time, nature has evolved some innovative and adaptive packaging solutions.

Expand and Collapse

Flexible containers are popular in nature since the size or number of the contents isn't always predictable. If you've ever seen a pregnant woman you are aware of the need for flexible containers. Likewise, the kangaroo's pouch, which carries a pea-size joey until it's two very squirmy years old, and the gular pouch of the pelican, which can rapidly expand to catch gallons of water and fish, represent some flexible membranes we might learn from. But these animals can't compare to the expansion capabilities of the tick. Some species are known to ingest up to 624 times their body weight, blowing up to over four times their original size. Unique coils in their abdomen allow for this incredible expansion. Imagine a water bottle that could easily fit in your pocket when dry, but hold several liters of water when you find a source. What about a container for cleaning products that could ship small as a concentrate but grow in size upon reconstitution?

A Matrix Solution

Fruits and vegetables are one of nature's most common containers, particularly of liquids and seeds. For example, strawberry, watermelon, and eggplant are 92 percent water by weight (lettuce is almost 98 percent water), but when you cut one, fluid doesn't leak out all over the counter. This amazing trick is accomplished with a fibrous matrix that retains water against the force of gravity. What if we could store flammable or dangerous fluids in just such a container? Many packaging materials are thick in order to avoid a leak; could we save on mate-

rial weight by building matrices? Researchers have discovered that by infusing hydrogen gas through just such a matrix it lowers the pressure needed to contain the gas, greatly increasing the safety and decreasing the cost of a hydrogen fuel car.

Optimal Shape

Whether you are packing a truck or a pillbox, figuring out how to ensure the greatest number in the smallest space is as much a part of the packaging as the product. Nature optimizes packing on many scales. When it comes to optimizing space, sunflower seed heads arrange their seeds in a spiral to allow for the most seeds per unit area as the seed head grows. Likewise, plants have tremendous space issues. One of the best examples is looking to see how a leaf can unfold from a bud. Leaves have devised numerous strategies, from rolling up like an umbrella, to folding like perfectly pleated skirt. These folding strategies from leaves have been mimicked into deployable structures by aerospace corporations for folding structures into the smallest space possible, ideal for a shuttle launch into space. These high-tech solutions could filter down to consumer applications, just as origami has influenced Japanese consumer packaging.

Nature optimizes packing on many scales. The sunflower seed heads arrange their seeds in a spiral to allow for the most seeds per unit area as the seed head grows.

Dispersal

Even the best containers need to release their contents at some point, hopefully with ease and at exactly the time needed. For nature, this is often accomplished with specific materials for the packaging itself. Take a virus, which depends on a strong and resilient structure that can contain genetic information. Viruses are tough, yet when they find the right conditions they need to quickly open to take advantage of the opportunity at hand. To accomplish this packaging task some viruses adopt an icosahedral symmetry (a fancy way of triangulating a dome into twenty pieces). This architecture is one of the best ways of creating a dome — like shell with equally stressed bonds — break one and they all break, for an easy accessible payload. Seeds that break open at maturity (dehiscent) optimize the structure of their seed coat so that as it dries while maturing, the coat easily breaks open to reveal the matured seed inside. In contrast, most species in the plant Aizoaceae family possess what is known as a hygrochastic capsule. When the capsule gets wet, it opens and explodes the seeds by jet action away from the plant. Ideally, packaging would contain and protect while needed but open with a simple trigger, like water, when desired.

For some organisms, the packaging itself serves a dual purpose, both containing and protecting the contents in one form and then serving another purpose once opened. For example, many insects will eat their egg sac after hatching for an immediate source of nutrition. Many water-dispersed seeds (think coconut!) find their seed coat acting as a boat to carry them to drier ground. Imagine a package that is designed to be opened to facilitate the use of the product itself, a cereal container that opens into a recyclable bowl, or concentrated laundry detergent balls that dissolve when wet and enhance the cleaning abilities of the detergent.

Protect

Ideally, once contents are contained, they need to be protected from the forces of impact, abrasion, and tearing, as well as water and oxygen penetration. Additional issues of theft, dirt, and microbial invasion add to the list of functions that packaging must perform. Despite this long list of demands, the same needs face nature's packaging and like containment, innovative solutions abound.

Impact

One place a bioinspired designer could look for sturdy packaging design resistant to impacts is in the rough and tumble environment of the intertidal zones. Here we find soft-bodied invertebrates, mussels, and snails resisting the pull of ocean waves, intense direct sunlight, and blasting sand. Their secret? A hard outer shell, resistant to the forces required of most packaging. The abalone is particularly adept at avoiding shell breakage. Their shells self-assemble from the same minerals as chalk in the seawater through a process called biomineralization. The organic/inorganic composite that is mother-of-pearl is over 3,000 times tougher than the materials it is made from. The secret is in the ability of the shell to distribute force between the composite layers so it doesn't fail from one crack. Instead the shell is resilient to all but the most brutal damage. The material of many other shells isn't as strong, but they make up for it through the shape of the shell. Spiral-based shells like those found in the cone snail or nautilus build on previous material, resulting in a shell that resists many impact forces.

Out of the water, the toucan's beak has been shown to be a lightweight material that absorbs high impact. The outside of the beak is constructed of overlapping tiles of keratin, while the inside is made of rigid foam. Using these simple strategies, we could create lightweight tough packaging materials that easily absorb shipping and handling bumps and bruises, or crack-resistant materials for durable and strong packaging needs.

Just-in-Time Protection

Packaging that can change from soft to hard in the blink of an eye would be something to behold. The sea cucumber long ago evolved this valuable trick to avoid predation. Upon first sensing a potential bite, the sea cucumber's skin instantly hardens from a consistency of soft gelatin to an apple. A protein in the skin can reversibly group collagen fibers. This matrix-forming capability is what gives the cucumber skin its unique properties. Even the common potato has a few tricks up its sleeve. When stressed, the potato actually creates a harder cell structure to protect its valuable starches. Imagine packaging that becomes more ridged when vibrated in a truck, or a box that is soft when you pack it to fit whatever space is available but then becomes rigid to protect its contents during transport.

Abrasion

For abrasion-resistant packaging, we might venture to the desert to ask the sandfish lizard. The lizard moves by swimming through rough sand. Its skin has evolved to decrease friction between the lizard and the sand. Remarkably, it outperforms steel as an abrasion-resistant material. This feat is achieved through a special glycosolated (sugar) surface on the keratinized scales of the skin. Mimicking this unique chemistry could pointing the way to abrasion resistant coatings tougher than steel, yet made out of keratin (the same stuff as your fingernails or hair) and sugar.

Naturally, abrasion resistance, common in most reptiles — particularly those that drag their bellies over the ground — also means the skin is less likely to tear.

Self-Repair

Inevitably, even durable skins and packaging will tear. Nature's solution is to use self-healing materials, which have inspired humans for millennia and which are a holy grail of materials science. Tree bark and human skin demonstrate the possibilities. But you don't need blood or sap to create a self-healing material. The mussels that live in the intertidal zone (the very same ones you eat in the restaurant) use a self-manufactured thread to hold tight through the rough waves. The nonliving threads are self-healing. The thread uses reversible sacrificial bonds to dissipate the energy of ocean waves. This enables several small extensions that stretch the thread without breaking it or causing permanent damage. After having broken the bonds, when the stress is gone it simply re-forms those energy bonds to bring the material back to its original elasticity. Likewise, rhino horns are also nonliving and exhibit similar self-healing strategies. Imagine flexible packaging that is tough, yet heals itself, and after use you simply throw it on your compost pile.

The ultimate solution for durable goods is to use no packaging at all.

Failing with Grace

One clever way to avoid abrasion or tearing is to use a tough material. Another way is to have sacrificial layers that dissipate the stress without compromising the integrity of the material. A horse's hoof is designed so that the outer layers of the material slough off under pressure. The ponderosa pine uses plate like tree bark that crisps up during a quick forest fire, but protects the rest of the tree from burning. It is possible that the amount of packaging on products designed to protect them in transit could be reduced by a coating that may wear off during the process of getting from manufacturer to consumer. Waxes on many fruits currently serve this purpose. Of course, the ultimate solution for durable goods is simply not to use packaging at all, but design the product to age gracefully with time. You don't buy jeans in packaging, right?

Protection from Air and Water

Packaging that needs to inhibit the flow of moisture or air across the barrier is quite common in the natural world. Most organisms need to stay moist, and by thinking of their moisture barriers in reverse, a suite of packaging solutions becomes visible. Think about snails, which are mostly water. Dehydration would kill the snail, and as such they depend on their ability to seal in the moisture they have, while keeping the hot dry air on the outside by the use of a quick forming barrier. Once it rains again, they dissolve their barrier and resume normal lives. Snails have a built-in system for an organic, tough, biodegradable, nontoxic sealant that easily fits unusual shapes or openings.

Frogs and other amphibians that lay eggs out of water must also find ways to keep them moist. Several tropical frogs known as foam nesters build nurseries out of bubbles. The outer bubbles harden to form a protective case that encloses the foamy core of eggs. The foam provides shelter from predators, bacteria, and sunlight, as well as preventing dehydration. The nest then disintegrates when the time approaches for the young to emerge. By understanding the chemistry behind the foam and mimicking it, we could create a similar moisture-retaining packaging.

The egg is a miracle of packaging. The developing chick needs to inhale oxygen and exhale carbon dioxide, all within the shell of the egg. The egg provides this service through a membranous sac that develops in the embryo. Fish with swim bladders face the opposite problem. Fish need to prevent the gas in the bladder from entering their bloodstream and leaving the animal. They use a layer in their swim bladder that provides an effective barrier to the passage of oxygen. What if we could protect our perishable items in the same way, by adding an organic membrane that can keep oxygen out, or allow for the controlled exchange of gas like the egg? We could extend shelf life, and improve the medical packaging and health of our products — all with just basic organic building blocks.

Protection from Microbes

What if your package needs to protect the contents from microbial invasion? Often the solution is to add preservatives to the contents, or an antibacterial coating to the packaging. Both have their share of problems including the taste and health effects of preservatives and antibiotic resistance in bacteria in response to the overuse of antibiotics. But not all of nature plays this game. An Australian seaweed, Delicia pulchra, is rarely covered in biofilms. Professors Staffan Kjelleberg and Peter Steinberg noticed this remarkably clean surface, and discovered that instead of killing the bacteria, the algae secretes a compound called a furanone that inhibits the ability of the bacteria to congregate by interfering with their communication system. This way, the algae remains free of bacteria, and the bacteria never become resistant. The two professors began Biosignal[18] to help commercialize this technology. Their molecule can be coated or embedded on or in most materials.

Protection from Dirt

A good deal of packaging serves as a means to keep a product clean while in transit from manufacturer to consumer. We've even gone as far as shrink-wrapping new cars to send to dealerships. We aren't the only ones with the need to stay clean, and often Nature does it not with packaging, but with self-cleaning surfaces. Leaves, for example, need to absorb light, and to do this they must remain clean. To solve this problem, many leaves have evolved the ability to self-clean. Examine a self-cleaning leaf very closely with a microscope and you will often see mountains and valleys. The phenomena on this nanoscale create a surface that cleans dirt and grime with just a little rain. Known as Lotus-Effect™ it's showing up in many products worldwide including exterior paint, glass, stainless steel, and roofing tiles.[19] The latest? Plastic! This means the last bit of ketchup, jam, or sauce in food packaging will flow out for another meal, and no more rinsing before dropping that item into recycling. This ease should lead to less food waste and higher recycling rates.

The egg is a miracle of packaging. Could we do things the same way?

Communicate

An occasionally overlooked role of packaging is how it communicates. Bar codes, bright colors, and catchy logos are on every candy bar wrapper in the checkout line. Nature also advertises, yet it is very careful with how it communicates. It uses efficient methods that don't waste time or energy whenever possible, as well as only sending out the right signals at the right time. Life will often take its communication cues based on its local environment, actively interfacing with the flow of life around it. How are we able to learn from nature here?

Color Without Paint

Paint or ink that advertises the contents can be the Achilles heel of an otherwise earth-friendly package. Life avoids this sticky situation, often by creating color without dye. Beetles, one of the most diverse groups of insects on earth with over a million species, have mastered generating color without dye. By micro-structuring the outer surface of their exoskeleton, beetles are able to create an impressive array of color displays via reflection. A wide variety of animals use this technique, from the multiple colors of the peacock, to the blackest black on the Papilio butterfly and the brilliant blue of the Morpho butterfly. Taking inspiration from the Morpho, Qualcomm's new Micro Electronic Memory Systems (MEMS) display are a technology based on the reflec-tion of light from butterfly wings, using the micropatterning to allowing a low power screen that can be viewed in bright sunlight. Recently, UV-activated cholesteric crystals that create color like many iridescent beetles have been used in advertising billboards in Japan, which can be used over and over again by simply resetting the crystal structure. Imagine if the materials in the packaging were embedded with crystals, allowing for communicating the right message to the right person.

Active Interface

Responsive packaging surrounds us in nature, yet is rare to find in our markets. Interfacing with the world is a challenge for modern packaging, but not for nature's packaging. Plants open and close their stomata to optimize gas and water vapor exchange. Human skin sweats to keep cool on a hot day. The hagfish exudes one of the wettest slimes known to protect itself from predators. Designing packaging that responds to its environment is an entirely new market. What if packaging could stay cool on a summer day by opening pores, or change color to let the storekeeper know the product is too warm? How about a milk carton that lets you know how full it is? Ultimately, these designs for packaging would help change our relationship to the packaging and the packaging to the contents allowing for a more systemic approach and hopefully less waste.

Mother Nature: Banana Packaging

Mass produced, this self-packing food product comes from the factory (the tree) in large transport bundles (a 200-unit bunch).

Transport units are easily broken down into retail clusters (a 4 to 5 unit bunch), and can be sold by weight or consumption unit.

To consume, the end user breaks off a single serving unit, with the remaining units held together until needed. These single units make up the primary packaging for the fruit.

The primary packaging protects the delicate food product contained inside and is easily opened with a tamper-evident tear closure.

The primary packaging offers plenty of facing area for branding or promotion. The primary packaging also provides distributors, retailers, and end users an indication of the food product's freshness state without opening the primary package, disrupting the sanitary seal.

Additionally, the primary package is water and light tight, gas permeable, biodegradable, and compostable.

Past Due

Nature didn't create the Twinkie, with an unlimited shelf life. Natural products tend to have life spans that connect them with seasons or events. Fruit ripening on the tree, falling to the ground, and decomposing are readily observable simply by looking at the color and quality of the packaging itself. Imagine if packaging were tied into events and seasons. What if the package changed color depending on how "hot" an item was, or how fast it needed to move off shelves? What about a change in packaging to denote rough handling? Bruised or old fruit turns brown due to the oxidation of limited-life pigments such as anthocyanin. Imagine a similar mechanism used to indicate if a box was damaged in shipping — you would know before you open it if it has been damaged.

Burrs ready to hitch a ride
Photo: Rick Gutierrez (n8studio.com)

Going My Way?

Life uses the free energy of wind, sun, waves, and even other animals for transport. Winged seeds sail to distant lands. Burrs hitch a ride on passing animals, spreading themselves far and wide. Further, the burrs are often designed to match the coats of their would-be transporters. Could we design packaging that would enable a dispersal process? What if a box could catch a ride on a car, truck, or subway — taking advantage of the free energy provided by the commuter flow of a city?

Mimicking Deep Principles

Innovative solutions abound by observing individual species, but not everyone knows a biologist or watches critters and learns. Could we learn from life in general about sustainable packaging? Not surprisingly, the list of sustainable packaging principles from the Sustainable Packaging Coalition^SM (SPC) listed here in this book as well as lists produced by others include operating principles that all of life embraces. These principles have allowed life to prosper on this planet. Biomimicry provides us the opportunity to compare how life works with how our designs should work. The Sustainable Packaging Coalition postulates that sustainable packaging embodies the characteristics as outlined in the table in this section, coupled with each characteristic is one of life's principles, as developed by the Biomimicry Guild. (Note: Life has many more principles not found in the SPC list.)

Let's look at these principles in more detail. Life has many working principles that allow it to adapt to a dynamic world while creating conditions conducive to life. For example, life is locally attuned and responsive. Imagine if our packaging was made from local materials to fit with local conditions, rather than a one-size-fits-all approach. Life also embeds cyclic processes in manufacture and use of its products. Life's packaging is designed from the start to return through natural cycles to the environment. Built from the bottom up by basic building blocks common to all life, the materials are easily reincorporated into almost any living organism. How many of our packaging manufacturers have systems in place to reuse preconsumer waste? Other than corrugated cardboard, which can be recycled almost anywhere, how much of the materials in our packaging makes it back into packaging once again? Not only are these building blocks common, but Nature has shown us how these simple materials can be used as a quantum energy conduit in photosynthetic plants, or as fireproof material in a redwood tree.

Using life-friendly materials doesn't mean we have to compromise our technological prowess; in fact we may be able to achieve greater innovation through fitting in with the rest of the natural world.

Not only can Nature help us innovate to deliver sustainable packaging, but it can also reconnect our world with the natural world. Using local materials and the energy at hand, living organisms evolve solutions to an incredibly diverse range of habitats and functions. Bacteria digesting methane at the bottom of the ocean, or withstanding the high heat in Yellowstone National Park's thermal pools and geysers, shows us how life thrives in diverse environments. Learning how life adapts and evolves to the diversity of habitats can enable our ability to recognize a local resource, and how we can use our local

Life's principles coupled with characteristics embodied by sustainable packaging

Biomimicry Guild Life's Principles	Sustainable Packaging Coalition Definition of a Sustainable Package
Creates conditions conducive to life	Is beneficial, safe, and healthy for individuals and communities throughout its life cycle
Locally attuned and responsive Resourceful and opportunistic	Meets market criteria for performance and cost
Uses free energy Uses self-assembly	Is sourced, manufactured, transported, and recycled using renewable energy
Recycles all materials Uses simple, common building blocks	Maximizes the use of renewable or recycled source materials
Uses benign manufacturing	Is manufactured using clean production technologies and best practices
Uses water-based chemistry Uses life-friendly materials	Is made from materials healthy in all probable end-of-life scenarios
Optimizing rather than maximizing	Is physically designed to optimize materials and energy
Recycles all materials	Is effectively recovered and utilized in biological and/or industrial Cradle to Cradle cycles

free energy. By rethinking our packaging and manufacturing processes as locally dependent on the environment, we once again establish ourselves as citizens of our world.

Ultimately, by looking to the other 30 million species and asking, "How do you package?" we might discern some innovative solutions. Yet, by matching these solutions with our best practices and mimicking life's principles, then we can confidently say that our packaging fits in, adapting and evolving to a dynamic world, all the while creating conditions conducive to life.

Go Outside!

Life has been creating packaging on earth for 3.85 billion years, leaving behind no landfills, no wasted materials, and no toxic sludge. For almost any problem that vexes you there is a solution. Imagine what you can discover, if you just slow down and take a walk outside. Imagine the packaging just outside your window.

Nature's systems, just waiting to be learned from
Photo: W. Jedlička

Permaculture Principles in Package Design

by Dan Halsey

Nothing exists outside a relationship. Everything is related in the working systems of nature, economics, or package design. Designers that do not take into account the effect their plan will have on users, resources, or society deplete the design's potential and future viability. Systems thinking requires a developed awareness and skills to define and design the Functional Relationships,[20] which reduces waste and enhances yield from existing relationships. Permaculture is a practice that uses a set of principles to assure the long-term viability of self-sustaining systems in agriculture. Permanent + agriculture = permaculture.

In the 1970s, Australian ecological activist, Bill Mollison,[21] retreated from popular culture to study and develop a set of principles that would assure success in ecological-minded farming. Over twenty-five years of practice, his resulting thirty-four principles for Permaculture were refined by his close associate David Holmgren.

In his book *Permaculture: Principles and Pathways beyond Sustainability* (2002) Holmgren lays out his refined list of twelve principles for sustainable living systems. These powerful concepts, here applied to package design, can open a new worldview of responsibility as designers and possibilities as people. The principles can be viewed as *passive*, *proactive*, or *progressive* in nature and difficulty.

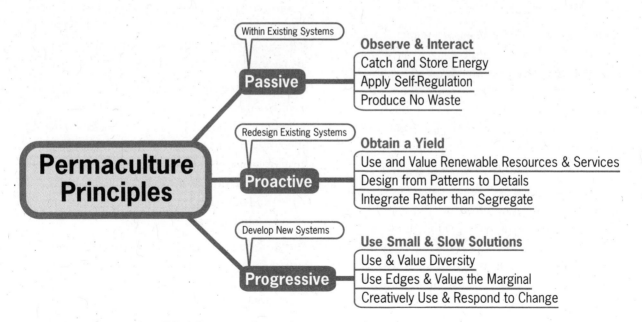

An Overview of Permaculture Principles

Adapted by Daniel Halsey from David Holmgren's original list.

Passive Permaculture Principles

Observe and Interact:
The Omnipresence of Relationships

In the natural world millions of relationships are occurring. From the lowest levels of living soil to the tops to trees and beyond are the answers to how people can flourish and not just survive. People already interact with everything around and although it is not limited to things within close proximity, trying to observe firsthand everything affected is impossible. In permaculture observing the things around us, like the cycles of seasons and weather, gives valuable information when designing a garden or ecosystem. For example, where water collects after a rain, how long it stays on top of the soil, and what direction it flows can provide information about the best place for some plants and where to avoid placing others. It also tells where the water is to use, catch, or store it.

To successfully observe means to interact. Stand in the rain, dig a hole, touch the soil, and dig deeper. Stand in the wind on a winter day. Feel the breeze in summer. Where does it come from? Where is it warmest in the winter and coolest in the summer? Where do mushrooms grow? Where do gophers burrow? All these things give important information, but only if we gently interact.

Careful observation of the environment in which a work is used gives power to respond with new ideas for design, materials and integration. Knowing the environment that materials, come from, and the ultimate end of the product is an important step in defining the parameters of a packaging strategy. The life cycle of a package cannot be ignored in the process. Interaction with consumer or warehouse is not the end of the relationship. The package lives on in an environment as inert or toxic waste, fuel, or a second extended life in another purpose, as an extension of the designer interacting through it.

Catch and Store Energy:
The Real Life Cycle, Assets, and Waste

For most of us; water, fuel, and electricity flow freely from spigots, pumps, and outlets. The energy is produced somewhere, stored somewhere, and transported (at a huge loss) to places of work or home. Other free energies that exist right outside the door dissipate unnoticed. For economic reasons that are also dissipating, local sources can appear more expensive than mass-generated ones. However, when the observant consumer sees the energies and resources that wash over their property only to be consumed by the ground or wind, the potential for that energy is realized.

Rain from a season can supply a whole family with bathing and laundry water and then piped to the garden as part of the morning routine. The water is soft and clean, and only needs limited treatment: the cleanest water that needs no well.

Catching this energy and delaying its passing makes it work and build value. Roof water can also be collected in a fish pond, flushing the accumulating effluents out to an orchard or garden. The fish get fresh oxygenated water and the garden gets nutrient-rich moisture. Add swales (a level ditch to collect water) and the water stays even longer, buffering drought and temperature changes.

The Sun's energy can also be caught and stored. Evacuated tube solar panels catch enough sunlight to raise their temperatures above 350 degrees, (at which point they shut down for safety). An array of these panels then transfers the heat to a large storage tank. One device: free fuel.

As one example, a machining company in Minnesota developed a process to purify lubricating oil used in their milling machines. The oil had been previously filtered but was soon contaminated in the closed system, unusable, and expensive to dispose. Engineers at the company developed an in-house distilling process that removed the impurities and moisture, making the final oil as pure as new stock. The water from the process was so clean, they ran it to their drinking fountains and the lunchroom. Solving one problem to catch lost resources (energy) brought new opportunities and savings in other areas as well. They bought less new oil, paid less fees for waste removal, and built their company reputation using the talent and resources already at hand.

The "paid" time spent in developing designs and the funds invested in the ultimate container create an asset. If the ensuing container is seen as "stored energy," a potential marketing resource beyond the trash bin, and having a second purpose beyond its initial use, it has additional stored potential for the end user. Harnessing this stored potential for marketing and extended customer interaction increases the return on the packaging investment. Being short-sighted leaves lost opportunity if the life of the package is ignored. What can be done with the unused potential? Where is the stored energy potential in a package?

Imagine people saying, "I have enough!" It's almost un-American.

Apply Self-Regulation and Accept Feedback

Imagine limiting consumption. People actually saying, "I have enough!" It's almost un-American. From all sides and even in the depths of tragedy citizens are instructed to shop, buy, and consume. It is what America lives on, ironically consuming itself. Buying everything offered would leave nothing to live on in a very short time. The body self-regulates temperature with perspiration and available energy with heartbeat. If not given the means to regulate with water and healthy food, it cannot. Self-regulation does not mean deprivation. It means knowing the difference between enough and too much, healthy food and empty calories, long-term effects and short-term benefits.

Information needed for self-regulation comes from feedback. Everything can be viewed as positive feedback. Feelings, words, sensations, pain, and happiness are feedback. If it influences change, it is positive. Negative feedback is silence: no message, no response, apathy. If actions or energies are returned with apathy or no response, that is negative. But if a person screams horrid insults, a pipe bursts, or yields increase, that is a pretty good dose of positive feedback and encouragement for change.

In an office setting, years of experience or schooling build in self-regulation. The most creative designer uses internal guides in composition and aesthetics. Innumerable options are assessed and personal creativity blends with good design. Effort is used to find suitable materials. Personal ethics specify which materials are acceptable. Then clients, supervisors, and associates need to give feedback. Pushing the envelope, a proposal is made to use ecologically minded vendors and resources. Questions are asked of consultants and suppliers. Excessive waste is minimized. Attempts are made to have the process self-regulate. All will elicit feedback.

Produce No Waste

Nothing goes to waste in nature. It is not allowed. Everything gets chewed up, spit out, decomposed, and reabsorbed into the relentless cycle of nutrients and biomass. Waste comes from underusing or over-using energy and materials. Most things never have to leave a system if used efficiently. Everything from the kitchen can be composted and made into soil, along with grass clippings, leaves, and weeds. Give something a second use or life and it isn't waste. Like magic, waste disappears in the shadow of reuse after the recycling bin is full and the thrift shop or garage sale gets the rest. What could there be? Perhaps the things were unneeded in the first place. Perhaps the consuming of a natural resource and the energy it takes in transport is the real waste. Perhaps the best thing to do when producing no waste is to limit consumption from the start. Do more with what you have.

In the electronic age, paper is run through printers as if it came from the sky — which it does, by sunlight, water, nitrogen, and carbon dioxide. From that point, however, waste starts, in processing, trimming, ship-ping, and disposal. Keeping proofs to a minimum and using electronic documents surely diminishes wasted paper. Then putting the computer to sleep or off when out of the office reduces more. In the quest to produce no waste one must ultimately limit con-sumption. Don't buy it, wrap it, bag it, transport it, unwrap it, or toss it. There is no waste. If an item can be sold without a dead end package (absolute heresy), where is the waste? Again, the second life of all things can extend its useful period and catch and save energy otherwise used in its disposal.

Proactive Measures

Obtain a Yield

When a permaculture designer works on a project, aesthetics is not the main design driver. Each element yields a beneficial if not tangible product. Many produce multiple yields. A few examples are:

— A perennial plant (overwintering) that shields annual plants (vegetables) while itself producing fiber or food.

— A ground cover plant that keeps soil moist and attracts pollinating insects, also eaten as salad greens and used as compost.

— Alpine strawberries that share nutrients, build soil, and attract bees to flowering fruit trees without competing.

Each element yields benefits to the system beyond its initial purpose. Rain falls on a hill; on its way down its energy runs a small hydroelectric generator, its temperature cools a house, its velocity aerates a pond of fish, and its mass carries away nutrients to plants. The more functions it has, the longer it stays on the property working. Each characteristic has a function.

All efforts in producing packaging must ultimately produce results. The engineering, marketing, corpo-rate, and government requirements for "allowable" designs must be met. Yet the ultimate function of the package is not a result of any of these singular dic-tates. Because of these, the package has multiple functions and thus multiple yields. Some of these are structure to protect and hold the contents until used, shelf or appetite appeal to increase or keep sales, brand recognition for other products, and regulated or standardized information for public safety. Once these are secured, the designer determines the final yield(s) in the life cycle few others may be aware of.

Use and Value Renewable Resources and Services

Like trees, renewable resources are in themselves limitless. They grow and grow, yet it takes four to eight years for pulpwood and at least one if not three human generations for building lumber. Corn ethanol is renewable, but with a 10-percent return of net energy after processing, is it practical?

In his book *The Essence of Permaculture*, David Holmgren says, "Renewable resources are like sources of income while nonrenewable resources are like capital needed to generate that income." Assets are to be maintained, increased, and held. A nonrenewable asset like soil is limited and needs maintenance if crops are grown on it. Not maintaining the soil asset will leave no place to grow the renewable crops. To value the renewable resource means taking care of its underlying and supportive asset.

Using renewable resources for transient purposes such as short-lived packaging may seem practical. However, valuing the materials as limitless is naïve. The cheapest paper has value and uses nonrenewable energy to be produced, processed, and shipped. A large portion of renewable material's inherent cost is in production and transportation. Understanding the source of material and its processing methods is central in understanding the ecological cost or sustainable value of the material.

For example, making the package shape to nest with others reduces partitions and carton materials, which makes more material, money, and time available for other packaging. It also reduces carton size and space used in trucks and warehouses.

In *Beyond Backpacking* Ray Jardine[22] talks of cascading benefits from using ultralight backpacking systems. If the backpack weighs less from prudent equipment decisions, the hiker can walk further in less time, and needs less food. Thus the pack itself gets smaller, and the hiker is more comfortable, and enjoys the trip more. An eighty-pound pack will cause more injury to the ankles, knees, and back than a twenty-five-pound pack that provides the same features. Pretrip and prepackage decisions cannot be based on a tendency to fear the unknown and overbuild rather than understand and adapt.

Design from Patterns to Details

Permaculture is "the conscious design and maintenance of productive ecosystems that have the diversity, stability and resilience of natural ecosystems. It is the harmonious integration of landscape and people providing their food, energy, shelter, and other material and non-material needs in a sustainable way."[23] Base maps are used in permaculture design to understand a landscapes' characteristics. Dimensions are drawn with topography, plants, and soil. As the map develops, structures and information are added with increasing detail. Decisions are made from the patterns of the land and refined as the details are discovered. Placement of ponds, gardens, orchards, and livestock is based on the pattern of the land. Plant and animal species in those groups are chosen from the details in the area placed. Gradually over time the land is repatterned, enhancing its properties. But it will be the details that change the pattern. A pattern is but the details at a distance.

Changing the pattern in a department or corporation is difficult. Yet one person can make small adjustments each time as opportunity arises and affect change. Broad patterns of corporate culture can be shifted with small details. A pattern is made of small details that repeat over and over. Gradual shifts in materials, modest requirements of suppliers, and eco-options for revisions will set the corporate culture on a course for change. An award for a green design goes a long way. Observation of trade trends to eco-minded design can be highlighted in trade journals.

The workflow of design is a pattern. It varies in each company, department, and office. Choices of materials are at times mind-numbingly predictable. Mapping out the patterns in all these can help discover the details and thus opportunity to make change. Making assumptions about a supplier's materials or techniques without asking for their creative solutions wastes a good resource. Let the pattern be innovation in the details. Innovation begets innovation.

Integrate Rather Than Segregate

Diversity builds sustainability. Situating landscape plants in close relationships opens opportunities for new efficiencies and added benefits. Although centuries-old European styles of landscape design still influence American landscape design, placing elements in close relationships (rather than isolated areas) helps them integrate and mutually benefit. Large expanses of grass only serve to deplete resources and suppress the natural benefits available from distant companion plants. Experiments with side-by-side planting have shown increased yields. Like people, some plants are proven competitors while others thrive in groups.

Compartmentalized resources in a company also delay potential solutions. Designers working with engineers at the inception of a product can add to the functionality and aesthetics while engineers contribute material options and mechanical parameters. The status quo rationale for engineering design can be opened to other possibilities by simple questions. Designers can understand basic concerns of engineers. Integrated teams with diverse disciplines add

value and understanding, solving problems before they have a chance to exist. Competition from a distance is replaced with appreciation for the talent each area brings to the group.

Progressive Measures

Use Small and Slow Solutions

Wet basements are a problem when surrounded by clay soils with temperate climates. Homeowners are required to put drain tile around foundations to catch the water before it enters the house. Most of this water comes off the roof from rain. Since the house is in the way and built in a hole, the water has an obvious route. Yet moving the water away from the foundation before it has a chance to seep in seems to be problematic.

If a house is built on clay soil and the rainwater overflows the sump pump, options are to add further drain tile, pumps, and buried drainpipe at large expense. It's a quick, expensive solution that will need maintenance and electricity. Or do two other things: Extend the downspout of the gutters ten feet from the house and plant a willow tree or two in the wettest areas. The extensions solve most of the immediate problem, but the long-term solution is the fast growing willow trees that pull moisture form the soil. Planting more trees as time goes by will reduce further soil saturation. A good-sized tree will transpire 2,000 gallons of water a day. The small solution is downspout extension, using a system that already exists and enhancing it. The slow solution was the tree that absorbed the water and created a new route for rainwater.

Using the smallest, cleanest, simplest solution to a problem makes for less waste and faster turnaround. Answering the basic question, "What does this really need to do?" through observation may help define the solution, and then gradually make opportunities to advance new design improvements. Build momentum with gradual changes and small efficiencies when revisited. Map future possibilities.

Use and Value Diversity

Solving a problem using a single solution, with no diversity, may make it vulnerable to outside influences. In the 1970s a drought after intense farming caused rapid desertification of Niger. The sands began to consume the landscape, swallowing up the fertile land and grazing areas. The government acted swiftly with millions of tree plantings. The army was mobilized to achieve a defensive line of sand-catching forests. The solution was heralded as brilliant and ecologically sound. Years later the monoculture of trees, all a single species, was decimated by disease and insects. Since the forest was so limited in diversity, there was no deterrent to either threat. The rapid loss of trees threatened the project's sustainability.

Mono means *one*. Poly means *multiple*. A monocrop in agriculture exposes the plants to disease and insects, making access to needed food sources by insects without natural deterrents, like diversity, causing the crops to be under stress. When dominoes are set side by side they fall fast. If spread apart, things are less likely to be affected by other failures. Diverse sources of revenue, supplies, and talent make a strong and interconnected unit.

Using only one supplier, one method, and one material makes design vulnerable to outside forces and internal disturbances. For logisics it may be easier and comfortable to have all materials come from one warehouse, but any disturbance in infrastructure leading to the warehouse renders it useless, and holds all inventory there hostage.

Marketing communicators do not rely on a single sales tool, market sector, or industry for revenue. A diverse source of intelligence and design resources ensures a broad scope of reference. One plastic may have worked for a series of packages, but not the next, and a favorite medium may not be the best as new materials evolve. Appreciate diversity in sources and materials, and blend the benefits of each. Keep up with improved and eco-friendly materials.

Use Edges and Value the Marginal

Clean lines is a term used to describe style and design. The lines are edges that define space. Most edges are points of transition, from sea to shore, field to woodland, lake to wetland. The edge is a place where energies, nutrients, and biomass collect. Leaves blow across a smooth field, are stopped at the edge of a forest, then the leaves decompose, turn to soil, and feed the forest edge. The forest expands its species into the new soil and increases. Small, quick-growing trees take root shielding the inner forest from dry winds; while slowing the wind's rush silt, dust, and leaves drop to the forest floor. Floodwaters enter a river island where edge trees slow the current, building soil with each new surge of silty water. The edge collects, protects, and filters.

To be definable one needs to be extreme. To ride the edge of technology, design, and engineering means to be noticed: the leading edge, with all its resistance and polishing; the bleeding edge, where new ideas are tested and challenged. Resources collect at the edges waiting for a purpose or the excitement. Win or lose, there is knowledge to be gained. Nothing is wasted on the edge, the highest point of concentration.

The marginal areas are to be explored. Opportunity missed and resources ignored are in the margins. Both edge and margin are places on transition. The edge is where the action is. The margin where things are waiting for change, can be wide or narrow.

Creatively Use and Respond to Change

With all the above principles, tactics must be able to change. Change means new life, energy, and purpose. Change can be seen as a roadblock to some and a catapult to others. Most times it's quite obvious, like the weather, seasons, and parenthood. Signs show something is about to need a bit of attention. Signs of change may show the end of one phase of life and the beginning of another. Change can cause stress to those unprepared or unaware of the signals. Seeing the signs of change is almost as important as the change itself. The reflection on the roadway surface signals a need to change speed, steering, and the expected time of arrival. The price of a material drives designers to adapt budgets or technique. Change is opportunity for the forward thinking, creatively seeking the benefits the change may bring, while mitigating the negative aspects.

If recycled plastics move to corn-based PLA and major fast-food chains want compostable materials, designers see the perceived value and make opportunity, leveraging this change. They take the popular notion from adversity to opportunity. They ride the paradigm shift others avoid.

Vertically integrated resource management: A bean vine uses a nearby corn stalk to get off the ground and into more sunlight.

Photo: Dan Halsey (halsey1.com)

Some change is about defensive measures. Trying to survive change with the least amount of damage gives the affected parties time to adjust and regroup. Some short-term expenses may need to be taken on in order to protect an asset in the long-term: burning forest A to save forest B; flooding a town to keep a dam from failing, destroying more towns; pulling infested vines to stop disease from spreading to the whole vineyard. The Tylenol Murder case in the early 1980s is a classic example. Johnson & Johnson, the makers of Tylenol brand pain reliever, pulled millions of bottles off the store shelves, and suffered a huge market share loss, but ultimately saved their brand. The wake-up call helped expose a distribution weakness, and the standard for packaging for all brands in this sector changed within a year.

Nothing sits still for very long. Everything is moving and adjusting position, the ups and downs are time to be creative. Nature fills all voids. Untapped skills suddenly find use. Solutions shelved long ago, find a need. It is an opportunity to be creative while the paradigm shifts and scripts are being written. A disturbance in the "natural order" is an opening for both weed and flower. The seeds have always been there or will soon blow in, catching on the bare soil. Even if the weeds take hold, they are but placeholders while the deeper plants make roots and prepare to emerge. Nothing is wasted, unless there is nothing to respond. In time, something always will.

Change means new life, energy, and purpose. Change can be seen as a roadblock to some and a catapult to others.

Change Management

Given the wide variety of information and approaches on sustainability, many readers will wonder how to implement this in their companies. Change management techniques can help turn what seem like insurmountable obstacles into a logical path for strategic growth.

In many environments, one designer or manager is ready before their peers. How can they serve their organization as a change agent and provide an environment for the new information to grow in? Several strategies can be successfully used:

— Teaching each other

— Leading by example

— Bringing others to the team

— Generating alternative designs on a consistent basis

— Being aware of the process and possible reactions[24]

Change agents often find that the challenge with change is that people are "locked in" to one way of thinking. The change agent then needs to help them "unfreeze" their old ways of thinking (paradigms) and "refreeze" to operating the new way.

What this all comes down to is patterns. Humans are "wired" for pattern matching. In fact, brain elements (neurons) learn from real world situations to recognize familiar shapes and objects like faces. From an early age, patterns quickly become essential for survival: moving object, door, food, loud animal, stairs. Each of these images provokes strong associations that persist into adulthood, and in many cases help survival.

The downside of patterns is that humans keep them in areas where flexibility would give greater opportunities. For example, a sales department may have always done things a certain way that was well known and comfortable to the employees. Some can see that a new way will bring new opportunities and greater sales, but the change is seen as threatening to those comfortable with the old ways.

This ties especially well into sustainability, where many things are changing and old patterns no longer fit. How can the change agent present information about change that guides people through the transition to the new way?

Managing change need not be like managing cats.
Photo: W. Jedlička

There are several approaches depending on what position the change agent finds themselves in.

Role 1: Change Agent as Peer

Change agents may find themselves in the position of persuading their organizational peers to change their thinking regarding sustainability. In this instance, the change agent may be "self-identified" as an early adopter. What does that mean? Years ago the United States Department of Agriculture (USDA) spent a lot of time and energy trying to convince farmers to try new techniques and seeds. They were puzzled by the range of responses, and researched it.

They found that in any community, there are several kinds of folks:

— Innovators find the next new thing.

— Early adopters will try most any of those new things.

— Early majority or pragmatists pay attention to the early adopters and try what they were successful at.

— Late majority and laggard farmers would wait until most everyone was doing something before they tried it.[25]

The result for the USDA was to focus on finding and supporting the early adopters, so they got similar results with far less expenditure.

Assuming the reader is an early adopter and wants to reach the early majority of product designers or managers, what can be done?

First, avoid triggering the "corporate immune response." Most readers have seen this: A new idea appears and it is so foreign that employees gang up to defeat it. How to avoid this? Communication to the masses is key. Selling your new ideas cannot be overdone at this stage, especially to your peer group. Tie the idea into corporate goals, and reinforce the benefits of doing things more sustainably. Demonstrate to your peers how this new way will also benefit them individually. For example, the new package design lowers costs and risks. It has inspired designers to create new approaches. Marketing has indicated the package can gain new customers if appropriately marked.

To communicate the change and propagate ideas, try some of the following:

— Talk to (and thereby influence) an opinion leader.

— Hold lunch talks to pass on information.

— Use some of the techniques in a project and publicize the benefits.

— Understand that new ways of doing things challenge old patterns:

> Support those whose ways of working are changing.

> Talk to them about the old patterns. dissolving and new ones forming.

— Get management buy-in and use it to advance a key project.

— Share information freely and praise those who take advantage of it.

— Be flexible about how sustainability can be implemented.

— Ask about best practices. Publicize these, tying them in to sustainability.

— Diagram the forces for and against change. Use the insights to strategize.[26]

— Determine the feedback loops keeping the old system stable. There will be one positive loop tending to grow the system, and another negative loop tending to contract the system. It is the interaction of those two loops which creates stability. Use the insights to create or change loops to move the system to a new way of designing.

Role 2: Change Agent in a Position of Authority

Recall that all companies are systems, and that departments within the company are systems as well. Systems of people are often referred to as open systems since they are adaptive. So there are two tasks here: help the individuals change their patterns; help the groups change their systems.

Utilize some of these techniques influence people regarding the change in your organization:

— Convincing people (rational approach)

— Changing the social environment (alter norms and values)

— Changing the reward system (use power and implement consequences when necessary)

— Changing the environment (create a new structure for them to move to)[27]

Utilize these twelve ways to change the operation of systems in your organization:

1. Subsidies, taxes, and standards. Payback for the good thing, increased cost for the bad thing, rate designs.

2. The size of buffers, relative to their flows. Buffers are stored materials, energy, and information. Larger buffers slow down the system but can help in times of change. Faster flows allow the system to respond faster. Consider stockpiles of

packages vs. the frequency of design updates. Cost vs. adaptability?

3. The structure of material stocks and flows. Stocks are physical entities like packages or products. What flows increase or decrease a stock?

4. The length of delays. Systems have delays that "even out" response, yet slow it down, and can affect stability. For example, only asking for feedback on designs at release gives stability to the design process while potentially causing problems in other areas.

5. The strength of negative feedback loops. Negative feedback brings the system to a set point like a thermostat controls the temperature. Design reviews and customer comments are feedback.

6. The gain around positive feedback loops. Positive feedback can move a system to a new state or grow the system until the limits are reached. Positive and negative loops must be balanced for a stable system.

7. The structure of information flow. Who sees the information about inventory, sales, and growth of product lines? What information is seen? How does the designer know if the work was good?

8. Incentives, punishment, constraints. Constraints actually force more creativity since without constraints things are done the same way they always were, or the way things are done in other places. With constraints designers have to search for new solutions, inspiring innovation.

9. Adding, changing, or evolving system structure. Adding new feedback loops or buffers, giving more information to employees.

10. Goal of the system. Create a new mission statement for the department. Encourage employees to create their own mission statement.

11. Mind-set or paradigm that the system arises out of. The design department exists to customers.

12. The power to transcend paradigms. Set up forces to renew vision and direction.[28]

Role 3: Individual in a Changing Organization

Finally, some readers may be in the position of navigating the changes brought about by others or by the marketplace. In this case, you can still be a change agent but your first task may be to change your own mind-set.

Some possible approaches:

— Consider one new idea each day.

— Find someone in the innovator group and ask them for help in adjusting to the change.

— List points of connection to the new system.

— Discover your own reaction to the change: Are you in support of it or are you resisting it?

— Identify how your actions are supporting or manipulating the change.

— Compose a plan of action for how you will succeed in this change.

— Create an image of the existing system and another of the new system. What would it take to move there?

This last point applies to all the approaches. Change agents need to know the current state of things as well as the desired future state. Knowing these two states gives the end points for a path that is created much as a wide and shallow stream is crossed.

Each day the current state and the desired state change so the path must be frequently updated.

To make this effective, the change agent needs to know:

> What are the new system functions, and how can they be implemented?

> What communication systems keep the old system in place?

> What new communication systems are required?

> How can new channels be created?

It can be important to view the new situation as an opportunity and the present situation as a problem. This can make it easier to identify communication channels, and as others get involved in "mapping" the new and old situations the change agent gets buy-in or commitment to the process.

Nature optimizes packing on many scales. The sunflower arranges their seed heads in a spiral to permit the most seeds per unit area as the seed head grows.

Technical Approaches

Industrial Ecology

While there were many approaches to design for the environment before the 1990s, the birth of industrial ecology symbolizes the approaches in place today.

The fields of study in industrial ecology are:

— Systems analysis

— Industrial metabolism: flow of materials and energy, and their transformation

— Using perspectives from other fields

— Study of natural systems

— Closed-loop systems

Today we might term these fields as:

— Systems thinking

— Life cycle assessment

— Stakeholder involvement

— Biomimicry

— Cradle to Cradle designs (C2C)

Both perspectives are useful, and each will attract a different type of designer. For some areas the industrial ecology descriptions give a larger viewpoint.

Systems analysis is the view of designs as systems, with life cycles, interconnections, boundaries, and relations to the stakeholders. There are a great many tools for systems analysis, and they allow the design team to capture a large amount of information in a structured way, and to ensure that this information is part of the process.

As one example, requirements engineering is an excellent tool to capture the needs of the various stakeholders on a complex team. Once the requirements are captured, they can be mapped to parts of the design, and it can be proven that each requirement has been addressed.

Industrial metabolism and the study of natural systems go farther than life cycle assessment by looking at industrial ecosystems to see how complex production processes are structured and interlinked. The study of transformation brings in viewpoints from other industrial processes.

Perspective from other fields includes legal, health, biology, management, engineering, and resource management. Making these groups explicit, results in their becoming stakeholders whether or not they exist within the company.

Closed loop systems are the goal of industrial ecology — moving from I to II to III.

> *Type I* systems take energy from the environment and dump wastes back
>
> *Type II* has internal process loops so energy and wastes are minimized
>
> *Type III* has closed loops, utilizing wastes as food and running on solar income.

The field is alive and well with journals[29] and dedicated teaching staff at a variety of institutions.[30] It is out of the scope of this chapter to cover all the facets, so the reader is encouraged to seek out additional sources of information.

Typical design processes from industrial ecology follow the phases of needs analysis, design requirements, design strategies, and design analysis. Here are some design strategies:

Strategies for Meeting Environmental Requirements[31]

Product Life Extension

extend useful life

make appropriately durable

ensure adaptability

facilitate serviceability by simplifying maintenance and allowing repair

enable remanufacture

accommodate reuse

Material Life Extension

specify recycled materials

use recyclable materials

create closed loop material strategies (C2C)

Material Selection

substitute materials

reformulate products

change material type

alter material processing

Reduced Material Intensity

conserve resources

Process Management

use substitute processes

map process inputs, outputs, and storage losses

increase energy efficiency

process materials efficiently

control processes

improve process layout

improve inventory control and material-handling processes

plan efficient facilities

consider treatment and disposal

perform life cycle assessment

Efficient Distribution

- choose best method for transportation
- reduce packaging
- use low-impact or reusable packaging

Improved Management Practices

- use office materials and equipment efficiently
- phase out high-impact products
- choose environmentally responsible suppliers or contractors
- label properly
- advertise demonstrable environmental improvements
- measure and manage for sustainability

Product Service Systems[32]

- transform from a product to a service
- instead of making physical packages, sell packaging as a service

Design Practice

Good design practice involves multiple viewpoints and is adaptive to new information. Along with this, there are a variety of design aids.

It is essential to eliminate toxic materials, and the sooner material impacts are known, the better the response will be. When looking at materials, it may be difficult to decide on one type of plastic vs. another, or on how to compare glass (with higher transport costs but higher recycling) with plastic (lower transport costs, possible recycling, and higher potential impact on earth systems).

As a first step, put some math behind this. What is the equation for packages? Isn't the package price just a cost per unit sold with some tooling?

This is a typical approach, and gives "cost" at some instant in time without regard to where things come from, what it takes to get them here, and what it takes to retire them. These costs are part of the bigger picture, and the universe takes them into account. Is there an advantage in using the universe's viewpoint?

First, look at what this would entail. What materials are in the package and where did they come from? How much waste and energy was lost in creating the raw materials? Now, what happens to the materials? Were they injection molded? What did that take? A mold had to be created and designed, and energy was used for each instance. Next, the package has to be transported. It may seem tiny on an individual basis, but consider the refrigerator or the millions of MP3 players. A tiny improvement in each one gives a huge overall reduction. Now, consider the consumer. Is that the final chapter in the package? If thrown away, the landfill is an additional cost. Recycling reduces end of life cost, and reuse gives, yet another improvement. Litter has a negative impact overall on the company.

This process is called life cycle thinking. In order to quantify environmental impacts a life cycle assessment (LCA) is conducted. There are both public domain and commercial tools for it (see reference section and sidebar example). It is most useful to think of LCA as a comparative tool: Does one approach have less impact than another? There is no perfect package, just a constantly evolving landscape of packages moving toward our design goals.

The advantage of an LCA is that it gives independent confirmation of material impacts, and designers are forced to consider each step in the process. It is also a key tool in trade-off analysis, allowing designers and management to contrast design approaches (for example, compare durability and recyclability). LCA is well suited to identify trade-offs and helps to avoid shifting environmental impacts from one environmental compartment to another. It can also be used in combination with multicriteria decision tools (for example, the Analytic Hierarchy Process)[33] not only to improve the design strategy but also to communicate with different stakeholders.

Users of LCA find that their design thinking may not have extended to end of life, or may not have considered transport costs. Each of these pieces of the puzzle has impacts beyond what the accounting department might consider:

— Marketability: Excessive packaging is considered a negative by consumers.

— Economics: Transport cost is not in control, rising, and can be a competitive advantage.

— End of life: Reduced risks from landfill issues, and increased consumer satisfaction from recycling the packaging (vs. a larger trash bag).

— Growth potential: Just like organic food, sustainable designs are increasing in share much faster than the average product.[34]

— New customers: Good packaging attracts new customers and makes a statement that inclines buyers toward the company's product. Bad packaging may keep old customers through familiarity but is not a sustainable strategy.

An LCA analysis goes beyond regulation. Looking closer gives improvements against internal designs as well as the competition. Beating those means beating the market. Think the boss is interested?

If presented the right way — cost reductions, process improvements, competitive advantage — then most anyone will sign up.

ISO 14000

Just as many companies joined the quality revolution by embracing ISO 9000 as a quality system, many have now embraced sustainability by becoming ISO 14000 certified.

ISO 14000 encompasses a range of quality activities, but at its heart is the requirement to do life cycle assessment on company products. While the detailed impacts of each material are beyond the standard, the requirements are clear: Define the product system, identify the product functions, and perform life cycle assessment continuously as an improvement practice. Record the results of the LCA and make them available to auditors.

A requirement of ISO 14000 is that a company has an environmental management system with the following characteristics:

An Environmental Management System (EMS) for ISO 14001:2004 is required to:

— Document and manage the environmental impact of activities, products, or services

— Continually improve environmental performance

— Establish a system to set environmental goals, to accomplish them, and to document the performance.[35]

Levels of environmental performance are specific for each business and type of activity so they are not specified in the standard. The intent of the standard is to enable a consistent framework for reporting and managing environmental issues.

There are many other ISO standards for environmental issues, but ISO 14001:2004 is intended to provide a comprehensive and consistent approach on environmental issues, as generic EMS's can be effective regardless of business type or activity.

Given a consistent approach to environmental management systems, there is now a consistent approach to the communication of environmental issues.

Since the levels of environmental performance are not specified, organizations in a variety of fields and stages of development can use the standard. As with other quality standards, organizations must commit to comply with all applicable environmental legislation and regulations. In addition, the standard requires continuous improvement as a practice.

As the reader can see, the standards require that each company adopt continuous monitoring and improvement policies with regard to the environment.

Life Is Cycles

As many have noted, life works in cycles. The Earth rotates, seasons change, and everyone grows up. Material is recycled the same way that water evaporates from the oceans and lakes, condensing in clouds and raining back on the earth where it flows to watersheds and starts the cycle over again. Some have said that each of us shares atoms with the Egyptians!

What does this mean for products? If they are designed without thinking through their whole life, the company is at risk in several ways:

Unforeseen Costs	*Risks*
Material sources	Product liabilities
Processing issues	Regulatory actions
End of life issues	

In addition, the designer misses out on one of the most powerful tools for increasing value.

Life cycle management (LCM) is part of the start of the process, and simply put, it follows a product from inception in raw materials through end of life. It does not attempt to assess impacts, but rather it is a big picture view of the product costs over the total lifetime of that product. For example, an LCM approach to a printer would consider the acquisition cost, the cost of supplies (paper and ink), the cost of maintenance, the impact of product downtime, and the costs to dispose of the product at end of life. This approach is popular with managers of large systems, as their true cost is only known when the total life cycle is quantified.

Life cycle assessment (LCA) is an integrated procedure to quantify the impact of a product life cycle. After the area of analysis is defined, material and energy flows are identified. Each material and energy flow then has an impact number assigned to it, and the total impact can be calculated. Life cycle assessment is divided into four major steps:

1. Goal and scope definition
   (define functional unit and system boundary)

2. LC inventory (allocation procedures and inventory analysis)

3. LC impact assessment

4. Interpretation

In accordance with ISO a peer review is required if the results of the LCA are communicated to the public. The LCA report should include assumptions and limitations.

LCA Steps

Identify the function of the product system, and the functional unit. What is the main use or utility of this product? Many products have several functions, and this step can help identify product aspects that could complicate design decisions. Some companies use this information to "pare down" functionality, feeling that the most efficient product is the one that fits a single function.

Define the product system and boundaries. What are the product boundaries? Does this analysis include the consumables? Are all life cycle stages considered? Generally the answer is *yes,* but it is crucial to document. Only after the boundaries are defined can the material and energy transfers be established. Does the system include transport? Once again, the answer is generally *yes* and the results can be surprising. For example, a European study showed the costs of transporting reusables back to the factory dramatically changed the results.[36]

Perform a life cycle inventory. To assess impacts, the designer needs to know what transfers of material and energy take place over the life of a product. Using the example of the printer, the inventory would identify the material components used in the creation of the printer parts and the energy required to process those materials. Similar steps would be taken for the paper, ink, energy, and maintenance supplies. At end of life, the components that make up the printer would either be classified as recyclable, needing disposal in a landfill, or capable of being incinerated. The components would be shown entering each of these end of life destinations. This step creates a flow diagram showing connections between product steps, energy, and materials entering the product system, and wastes exiting the product system.

Document material impacts. Use either a public domain or commercial database to quantify the material and energy impacts. The place of manufacture can change the results, as energy in one part of the world may have less impact than in other parts. Processes to be considered are acquiring raw material, material conversion into finished parts, transport, use characteristics (consumables and energy), recycle/reuse or waste management.

Analyze the results. The main value of the LCA is thinking through the process. The number does not indicate either a perfect or a horrible product, rather it allows the designer to compare one design approach to another, and to make trade-offs that benefit both the company and the environment. It is also an excellent tool to document design improvements.

Compare alternatives and optimize. As noted above, comparing two ways of doing something is one of the more powerful advantages of LCA. Look at lightweight packaging (recyclable plastic) vs. glass. The glass may look better on the materials side, yet worse once transport is included. Consider different materials, or change the type of processing to reduce the impact.

Publish and critique. Put the results on a public server, schedule a lunch meeting, or present the findings at a department meeting. Getting others to look at it gives several key advantages:

— Shared understanding of the product system

— Ideas about changes that could benefit both the company and environment

— Increased knowledge for authors and reviewers.

— Provides transparency of decision processes

Note on sustainability matrixes. These are decision support tools used to compare the impact of one project to another approach. For each project a variety of dimensions are listed: use of energy, amount of pollution, impact on groundwater, and the like. The alternate designs are rated on each dimension and the totals used to get a better picture of overall project impact. While these are more commonly used in building design or development projects, they can be used for product and package design as well. The limitation is that each dimension is ranked using a small range of numbers, sometimes 0:5 or -2:+2. While this does give information about how projects compare at a high level (and it is quick), it doesn't give enough information about the details of a design and it is not tied to the impacts of specific materials. It can be a reasonable way to summarize data for a high-level presentation.[37]

SimaPro[38] was used to model a simplified life cycle for glass bottles. This illustration shows a network that includes bottle manufacturing, transport to the refiller, bottle washing, and disposal in US municipal waste. The thick lines show where the major impacts are coming from. In this model, we see that almost 25 percent of the impacts are coming from natural gas production and distribution used to manufacture the bottle. Graphical presentations like this network allow the user to pinpoint "hot spots" — areas where improvements have the most potential to make a difference.

The graph on page 188 shows a different way of looking at the glass bottles modeled in the network illustration. We see that fossil fuel use is the largest impact for the bottle's life cycle, with both manufacturing and bottle washing playing a role. Because so much glass is recycled in the United States, the end of life gives a small credit for displacing the need for virgin material.

The Eco-costs Approach

An LCA is a somewhat complex tool that requires the material characteristics of a product to be known before analysis can proceed. This creates difficulties for designers in several ways:

— Package components may not be known when the design process is started.

— Composition and chemistry of package components may not be known.

— There may not be support (staff and software) for the LCA process.

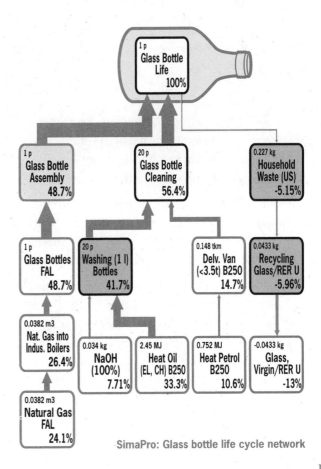

SimaPro: Glass bottle life cycle network

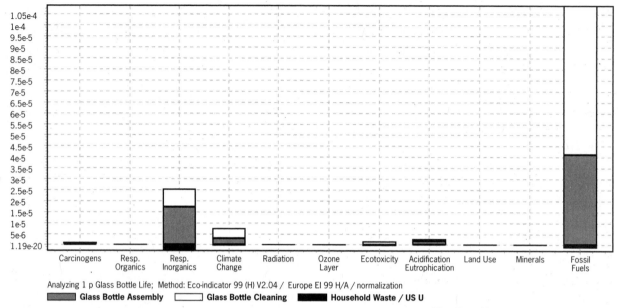

Analyzing 1 p Glass Bottle Life; Method: Eco-indicator 99 (H) V2.04 / Europe EI 99 H/A / normalization

▨ **Glass Bottle Assembly** ▢ **Glass Bottle Cleaning** ▮ **Household Waste / US U**

SimaPro: Glass bottle life cycle graph

The result is that designers often look for nontechnical approaches to package impacts, either with a philosophic approach or with higher-level tools. One higher-level tool is eco-costs.

An eco-cost summarizes all the effects on the environment from a given material. The eco-cost for a material is the "extent to which a product or production process is not yet environmentally sustainable."[39]

Why does a business use an eco-cost? To fulfill this mission: "The delivery of competitively priced goods and services that satisfy human needs and bring "quality of life," while progressively reducing ecological impacts and resource intensity, throughout the life cycle, to a level at least in line with the earth's estimated carrying capacity" (WBCSD, 1995).[40]

Eco-costs may be in the same range as material costs and include the impact of emissions, energy, and materials. Similar in a way to an LCA, however, they give one totalized number for each component of the design over the whole range of product life (simplifying calculations).

In design decisions it is useful to relate the eco-costs to the (customer) value. The ratio of eco-costs to value is termed the EVR. Products with low EVR numbers have large impact or low value compared to the environmental impact. Conversely, products with high EVR numbers give good value for their impact. Product decisions can be made based on EVR: dropped if it is low; material substitution or increase value if it is medium; keep as core product if it is high.

Product value (to the customer) can often be increased faster than eco-costs. Labor has lower eco-costs than materials or energy, so reducing high impact materials while increasing labor content will improve EVR.

Teaching materials on the Delft University of Technology Web site (ecocostsvalue.com) note that in product decisions, environmental sustainability is a second-level filter after quality and price. This reinforces the earlier point that sustainable products have to meet quality goals along with reduced impact.

At this time eco-costs are an optional exercise allowing a company to evaluate design decisions in terms of environmental impact. However, these voluntary calculations will become a matter of regulation at some future time.

Products with high eco-costs may appear profitable today but are not good investments in the long term. Rather, look for products with lower eco-costs and a good value-to-cost ratio. For existing products, decrease eco-costs where they are high and increase product value where it is high. A product with increased value may have a lower eco-cost–to-value ratio and be a better design even if its eco-costs are higher than the original design.

Note that life cycle costs (LCC) or whole life costs (WLC) are the totalized amounts from an LCA analysis, and compare to an eco-cost calculation. Also, the eco-costs are the marginal prevention costs of making materials sustainable, and are not the same as the external costs, which represent damage to the environment.

In summary, an eco-cost is an LCA-based indicator for environmental burden. Each material has an associated eco-cost, which is the cost required to make use of that material sustainable. The eco-costs–to-value ratio (EVR) is an easy way to visualize which designs have the best strategic fit.

The eco-costs are "virtual:" These are measures to make (and recycle) a product "in line with the earth's estimated carrying capacity."[41]

Systems Approaches

LCA analysis is a powerful tool to measure and compare the impacts of a particular design. What way of thinking will guide designs to the opportunities beyond the current situation? The Sustainable Packaging Coalition[SM] draws on a number of philosophies that address sustainability, including industrial ecology, natural capitalism, The Natural Step, and Cradle to Cradle, to name just a few. Their definition of what a sustainable package could be is a great starting place for any man-made effort.

The Sustainable Packaging Coalition[SM]

A project of the nonprofit institute GreenBlue[SM], The Sustainable Packaging Coalition (SPC)[42] is an industry group committed to creating and implementing sustainable packaging solutions.

The Sustainable Packaging Coalition envisions a world where all packaging is:

— Sourced responsibly

— Designed to be effective and safe throughout its life cycle

— Meets market criteria for performance and cost

— Made entirely using renewable energy

— Once used, is recycled efficiently to provide a valuable resource for subsequent generations

In summary, we envision a true Cradle to Cradle system for all packaging.

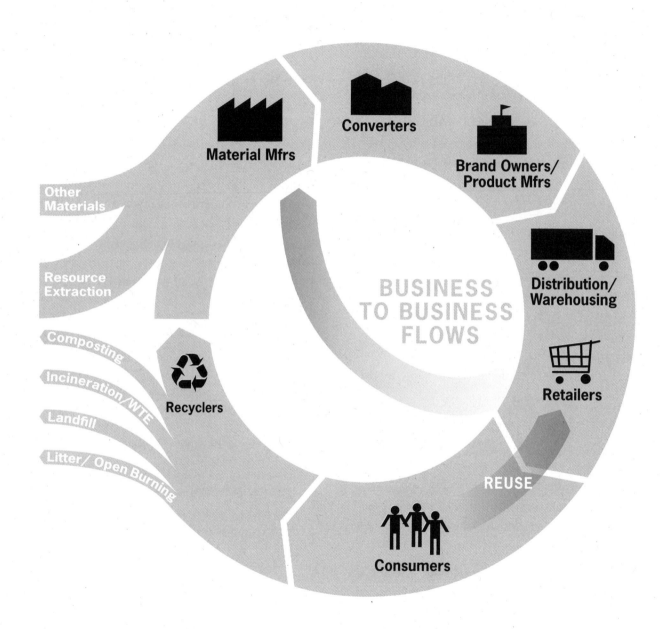

The Cycle from Material Creation to End of Life
Used with permission of Sustainable Packaging Coalition^{SM} / © Green Blue^{SM}

The SPC Approach

— Provide a forum for supply chain collaboration

— Share best practices and design guidelines

— Support innovation and effective, new technologies

— Provide education, resources, and tools

The SPC is made up of leading companies seeking consensus on approach and best practice in packaging design. The SPC seeks to engage the entire packaging supply chain; members include raw materials suppliers, converters, consumer product goods companies, design firms, retailers, and recyclers.

In addition to the packaging guidelines, the SPC creates:

— Case studies that document the strategies, business justification, and environmental impacts of sustainable packaging.

— Environmental briefs that summarize the environmental impacts related to the production, use, and end of life of packaging materials.

— A package design tool that allows designers to assess the environmental impact of their packaging designs. This tool is a simplified life cycle assessment tool that uses life cycle inventory data for basic packaging materials. It provides comparative environmental profiles for packaging designs based on metrics such as fossil fuel consumption, water consumption, and greenhouse gas emissions.[43]

Definition of Sustainable Packaging

The Definition of Sustainable Packaging[44] is reprinted here with the permission of the Sustainable Packaging Coalition. To get up-to-the-minute information on sustainable packaging, and to get a copy of their *Design Guidelines for Sustainable Packaging*,[45] or visit their Web site at sustainablepackaging.org.

Sustainable packaging

1. Is beneficial, safe & healthy for individuals and communities throughout its life cycle;

2. Meets market criteria for performance and cost;

3. Is sourced, manufactured, transported, and recycled using renewable energy;

4. Maximizes the use of renewable or recycled source materials;

5. Is manufactured using clean production technologies and best practices;

6. Is made from materials healthy in all probable end of life scenarios;

7. Is physically designed to optimize materials and energy;

8. Is effectively recovered and utilized in biological and/or industrial Cradle to Cradle cycles.

Packaging accounts for a third of the waste stream in developed countries. How can that be reduced while increasing market share and brand loyalty?

In many ways "doing the right thing" lets the customer feel good about their product choices — reinforcing brand loyalty. Keep the buyer, eliminate the remorse.

What does that take?

— Use the right materials by considering the health of workers, customers, and the planet.

— Restore the Earth: Put back resources.

— Create systems and solutions that are long term and forward thinking.

— Use renewable resources (energy and materials).

— Favor reuse rather than virgin sources.

— Increase efficiency: all costs — logistics, materials use, transport, end of life.

— Confirm that all components are doing what they're supposed to do.

— Protect/Inform/Sell. *Protect* includes the planet.

The criteria are a goal, not gospel. As new products are designed or systems are improved, the criteria provide a benchmark. Sometimes all the marks are hit, sometimes just a few. But in all cases movement is in a forward direction.

Design Guidelines from the SPC

The following concise reminders of key design guidelines are presented as an overview with permission from the Sustainable Packaging Coalition Design *Guidelines for Sustainable Packaging*.[46] It is recommended that readers download the actual guidelines from the SPC Web site to get the full utility of the work.

Design with a larger view of the product: Expand the definition of quality (traditionally package design quality is based on a small set of dimensions):

— Technical performance (How the package does its job: protect, inform, and sell.)

— Cost

— Appearance

— Regulatory compliance

Looking closely at these parameters and continually doing a better job can be one way to make a better package. However, the parameters are limited in the same ways mentioned before. For example:

Optimizing for costs alone may be shortsighted and impact environmental performance and therefore increase risk at the corporate, manufacturing, and consumer levels of the system.

Expand the definition of quality to do the following:

— Optimize resources — use less materials and energy, use better materials and energy.

　Practice source reduction.

　Use recycled content.

　Design for transport.

— Conduct responsible sourcing — talk to your vendors and make judgments as to who is best.

　Use environmental best practice as a yardstick.

　Confirm they adhere to fair labor and trade practices.

　Design with virgin renewable materials from sustainably managed sources.

— Material health

　Know the chemistry of the materials in your package.

— Ask questions, research, compare approaches. Use an LCA.

　Know the potential health and environmental impacts over the life cycle of your package.

— Resource recovery

　Design for reuse, recycling, composting, or energy recovery.

The definition of a "design well done" is bigger but also better. Employees, stakeholders, and the customer base will appreciate the focus.

Do the right job: Avoid overengineering. The industrial revolution mind-set didn't care about material and energy usage if the job was done. As a result, packages often are more than needed — stronger (Grandma can't get in), longer lasting (decades or centuries in the landfill or ocean gyre), and larger (excess packing material in a huge box).

Consider carefully and design appropriately:

— What physical product protections are required?

— Consider the package life cycle.

— Can the product protect itself?

— What are the actual constraints and requirements in manufacture, transport, and storage?

— Can transport packaging reduce package requirements?

— Chart all the environments the package lives in between birth and death.

— Optimal designs use less resources and energy, saving money for the producer.

— Consider the channel (distribution, point-of-sale) the product lives in.

— Consider add-ons (RFID, foil, electronics) as added burdens at end of life.

Expand the definition of quality... The definition of a "design well done" is bigger but also better.

Design Simply: Graphics

Move marketing and other information from packaging to signage.

Add recovery/recycling signage on all packaging.

Design appropriately for the product target markets.

— Check regulations.

— Consider costs for packaging and disposal.

— Verify design requirements for content.

— Confirm prohibitions on materials.

— Use appropriate labeling.

Consider using the strictest set of requirements to reduce design variety and increase volume.

Checklist of Design Strategies for Sustainability

Practice continuous source reduction:

— Use materials with lower production energy levels.

— Use the minimum number of materials.

— Choose the best suppliers and converters.

— Work with the product designer to reduce one and/or the other.

— Reduce size, weight, and thickness.

— Minimize void space.

— Optimize primary vs. transport packaging.

— Consider the transport energy.

Expand the use of recycled content:

— What are the package requirements, and can they be met with recycled content?

— Change the package design so requirements meet capabilities.

— Consider the markets for recyclables in your markets.

— Work with marketing to help advertise and avoid conflicts.

— Set internal goals for content.

Design for transport at the front end:

— Optimize primary vs. transport packaging.

— Change one design to minimize the other, calculate savings.

— Eliminate primary or transport packaging through design.

— Use source reduction.

— Use all the transport package space.

— Consider truck and container dimensions for most efficient packing.

— Make transport packaging reusable or recyclable.

— Choose transport suppliers with good environmental performance.

— Work with logistics experts.

Adapt and expect environmental best practice:

— Demand compliance with all reporting requirements.

— Set goals to minimize hazardous and increase reuseable and recyclable materials.

— Use of closed-loop systems in production processes.

— Set goals for continuous improvement beyond compliance.

Practice design for equity:

— Ask suppliers to provide their labor and trade practices.

— Check how often compliance is verified.

— Confirm their policies match the one at your company.

Use renewable virgin material from sustainable sources:

— Require certification for sustainable management.

— Where possible, use local or regional sources.

Support green chemistry:

— Choose a supplier that practices it.

— Know your material impacts, and choose the lowest-impact materials.

Know your materials:

— Use an LCA tool.

— Ask for contents of each material you use.

— Use confidentiality agreements if necessary to get details.

— Choose vendors that are easy to work with.

— Check material impacts both in use and end-of-life phases

— Scan for updated materials of concern.

McCormick Distilling: Earth Friendly Distilling Co.

Earth Friendly Distilling's 360 Vodka bottle is made from 85% recycled glass. Looking further at the total package though: the label is from New Leaf Paper's 100% Post Consumer Waste paper, and printed with water-based inks. In addition, each bottle carries a postage paid envelope that lets customers mail back the flip-top closure for reuse, increasing use cycles for every metal closure mechanism, rather than going to landfills.

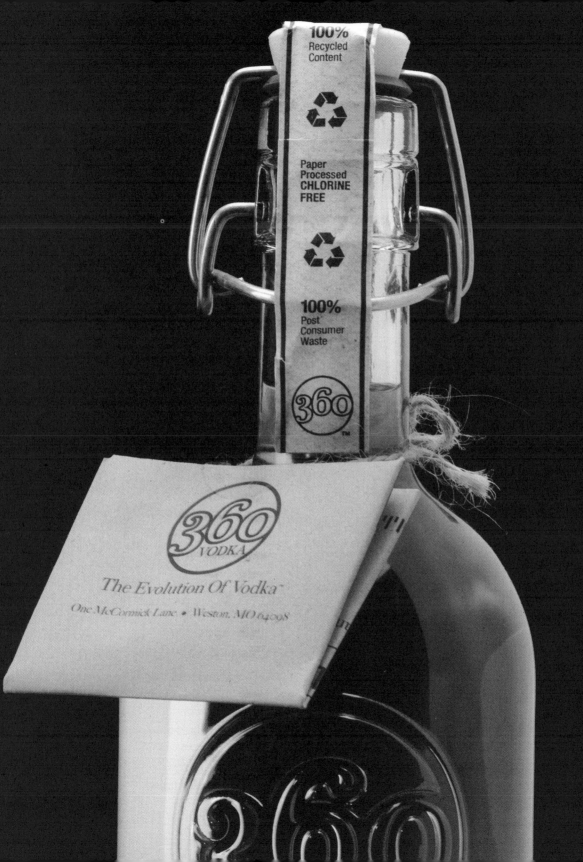

— Check plasticizers, heat stabilizers, compatibilizers, dyes, pigments, fillers, UV stabilizers, antioxidants, and flame retardants.

— Consider all package components including add-ons such as RFID, inks, coatings, and adhesives.

Design for reuse.

— Confirm if it will work for your package requirements (food in particular).

— It can result in overdesign if the customer or transporter won't close the loop.

— Create incentives to help close the loop.

— Consider the transport costs for reuse vs. one way.

— Consider end of life for reusable packages.

— Work with suppliers and process personnel from the start on a reuse design.

Design for recycling.

— Select the best materials.

— Consider add-ons as they can affect recycling.

— Use appropriate labeling.

— Check with suppliers in the design process.

— Use single materials, or design for disassembly.

— Design graphics to increase recycling rates.

— Design a take-back program so customers return and recycling rates increase.

— Paper/cardboard: Watch for plastic films, foil stamping, adhesives, inks, wax.

— Plastic: Watch for single or compatible materials, attachments, inks, foils.

— Biopolymers: Watch for additives such as coupling agents, plasticizers, fillers, dyes, and pigments.

— Steel: Watch for inks, added features, plastic components, paints and coatings.

— Aluminum: Watch for coatings, and laminations.

— Glass: Watch for pigments like cobalt blue, metal rings, and inks for on-glass printing.

Design for composting.

— Degradable may only mean "separates into small pieces."

— Biodegradable means "it will be consumed by microorganisms."

— Compostable means "biodegradable within constraints." Check standards.

— Can compostable packaging meet technical needs?

— Confirm that all components (add-ons, printing) are compatible.

— Test the package to confirm biodegradability.

— Check for infrastructure.

— Possible materials suitable for composting where facilities exist include natural fibers and fiber-products such as hemp, kenaf, wheat straw, palm fiber, agripulp, kraft paper, molded fiber, paperboard, and plant-based plastics such as PHA, PLA, and starch-based products.

The approaches used by the Sustainable Packaging Coalition are made up of ideas, philosophies, and frameworks that have a long history of providing real and actionable solutions. The world is a very complex place, so there can be no one-size-fits-all solution for putting sustainability into practice. Rather than blindly following the SPC definitions as gospel, the SPC asks everyone to dig deeper, to discover for themselves how they arrived at their definitions and formed the ideas put into their design guidelines — then joins with them in taking these ideas to the next level. "The criteria presented here blend broad sustainability objectives with business considerations and strategies that address the environmental concerns related to the life cycle of packaging."[47] They are a goal, a guide, and are themselves organic — growing and developing over time as our understanding grows.

The Natural Step Framework

A Sketch for Designers

The Natural Step Framework (NSF) is a compass or guide to sustainability. It can be viewed at many levels: as a tool for creating a shared understanding, vision, and sustainability action plan among everyone in an organization; as a checklist for assessing the current status; as a yardstick to measure designs against; and as a way of seeing into the future and responding proactively.

One of the most elegant ways to enhance each design is to examine it against basic sustainability principles, breaking difficult and intertwined systems down into actionable choices. This simple step takes much of the uncertainty out of the process and free designers up to do the thing they do best — create.

To allow this to happen the designer has to be forward looking, making sure each design decision holds up in the light of future society. Typically a designer is tied tightly to the present moment and the demands of the design situation as it exists today.

The beauty of the Natural Step Framework is that the key principles are easily recalled, allowing the designer to quickly assess options and create breakthrough designs.

The NSF uses four lenses to focus attention on the effects of design decisions: TAKE, MAKE, BREAK, and NEEDS. This high-level approach can easily be used to examine actions, improve strategies, and make choices that can save money while being environmentally and socially responsible.

The Natural Step Framework
Four Sustainability Principles

By Terry Gips

The Natural Step Framework (NSF) is based on scientific consensus principles developed by physicist Dr. John Holmberg and Dr. Karl Henrik Robert (medical doctor and TNS founder), and consists of four basic "system conditions" for sustainability.

The principles state that in a sustainable society, nature won't be subject to systematically increasing:

1. concentrations of substances extracted from the earth's crust;

2. concentrations of substances produced by society;

3. degradation by physical means;

And, in that society,

4. ...human needs are met worldwide.[48]

In other words, not systematically increasing:

What we TAKE from the Earth: mining of metals and burning of fossil fuels

What we MAKE: pesticides, plastics, and chemicals

What we BREAK: ecosystems and biodiversity

While meeting human NEEDS worldwide.[49]

Design strategies include:

— Dematerialization or ephemeralization (using less resources to accomplish the same task)

— Substitution of alternatives

— More efficient use of materials

— Better materials and material processing

— 3 Rs and 1 C: Reduce, Reuse, Recycle, and Compost

The simplicity of the four system conditions allows the designer to quickly evaluate options and make a decision on the best approach.

1. What is taken from the Earth (Take)

Mining and fossil fuels: Avoid systematically increasing concentrations of substances extracted from the earth's crust.

Use renewable energy and nontoxic, reusable materials to avoid the spread of hazardous mined metals and pollutants. Why? Mining and burning fossil fuels release a wide range of substances that may continue to build up and spread in our ecosphere. Nature has adapted over millions of years to specific amounts of these materials. Cells don't know how to handle significant amounts of lead, mercury, radioactive materials, and other hazardous compounds from mining. Unwanted chemicals can lead to learning disabilities, weakening of immune systems, and improper development of the body. The burning of fossil fuels creates smog, acid rain, and global climate change, and living things cannot evolve fast enough to adjust to such changes: millions of years vs. hundreds of years for such dramatic human-created changes.

Packaging Design Actions

Use lower-impact materials, reduce package energy use, and create designs that conserve energy and/or use renewable energy.

— Material selection

Use renewables instead of fossil fuels.

Use reused materials instead of primary sources extracted from the earth.

Replace metals with materials that require less energy and pollution.

— Reducing energy use

Choose materials that require less energy to produce.

Use local materials as transport costs are lower.

Increase processing efficiency.

Increase efficient use of materials — webs instead of boxes.

— Reducing transport costs

Lighten packages — saving a gram on a million packages is a ton!

Improve transport packaging.

Use reusable transport packaging.

— Recycling

Design for disassembly.

Choose materials with the largest markets.

Select recycling processes that don't downcycle materials to a lower quality.

Overall the aim is to reuse and reduce consumption. Use the general principles to guide actions: Choose the renewable energy source over the coal plant, the renewable biomaterial over the metal from across the world.

2. What is made (Make)

Chemicals, plastics, and pesticides: Nature must not be subject to systematically increasing concentrations of substances produced by society.

Use safe, biodegradable substances that don't cause the spread of toxins in the environment. Why? Since World War II, our society has produced more than 85,000 chemicals, such as DDT and PCBs. Many of these substances don't go away, but spread and bioaccumulate in nature and the fat cells of animals and humans. Cells don't know how to handle significant amounts of these chemicals, often leading to cancer, hormone disruption, improper development, birth defects, and long-term genetic change. This system condition tells a designer they cannot use these chemicals in anything they create at any level. Perform design differently to keep these things out of the system.

Packaging Design Actions

— Consider the lifetime of the package material.

> If it ends up in the ocean or woodland how long does it last?

> If it is landfilled or incinerated, will toxic components escape?

— Support green procurement policies. Work with better vendors.

— Replace high impact materials with biobased, reusable, or compostable ones.

— Develop product return policies.

— Design for disassembly and recyclability.

— Utilize recycled materials.

— Design production processes that minimize air and water pollution.

— Use nontoxic inks.

— Materials processing.

> Low-impact forming (check LCA databases for details).

> Minimize production steps.

> Minimize material waste.

3. What is done to the Earth (Break)

Biodiversity and ecosystems — Nature must not be subject to degradation by physical means.

Protect soils, water, and air, so all are able to eat, drink, or breathe. Why? Forests, soils, wetlands, lakes, oceans, and other naturally productive ecosystems provide food, fiber, habitat and oxygen, waste handling, temperature moderation, and a host of other essential goods and services. For millions of years they have been purifying the planet and creating a habitat suitable for human and other life. Destruction or depletion of these systems endangers current livelihoods and the likelihood of human existence. Make design decisions that enhance diversity. Choose materials that enhance the earth instead of depleting it. Consider material sources: Did it come from virgin timber or sustainable forestry? Perhaps it doesn't come from a slow-growing tree, but from an annual plant source.

Packaging Design Actions

— Reduce paper use during the design process.

— Use earth-friendly processes for printing the package.

— Purchase certified, sustainably harvested forest products.

— Use 100% post-consumer recycled content paper.

— Decrease water use and runoff by carefully examining the impacts of production processes.

— Encourage smart growth in the company and community.

— Examine material choices carefully to minimize impact on natural systems.

4. Meeting basic human needs (Needs)
"Human needs are met worldwide."

Use less stuff and save money while meeting the needs of every human on this planet. Why? Developed countries make up only a small percentage of the world's population but consume a disproportionately high percentage of its resources. Just to survive, people in underdeveloped countries see no choice but to cut down their rainforests, sell endangered species, and use polluting energy sources. As a designer, act to reduce the impact of designs by choosing materials and energy sources that benefit human systems.

Packaging Design Actions

— Designs can be examples of meeting goals while minimizing impact on the earth.

— Being public about design approach spreads design knowledge and promotes the company.

— Encourage the company and peers to make socially responsible investments and purchase fair trade products.

— Create designs with an understanding of the market they will be sold in.

— Design the package to add value to the user and their community.

— Create designs that aid the local economy.

Tools to Implement the Natural Step

The sustainability "tunnel" shows society moving from a region where resources are used without regard into a region where these materials appear scarce, expensive, or regulated. The other side of the tunnel has light coming from increased product efficiencies, worker-friendly processes, design innovations, and a more sustainable work environment.

The sustainability "tunnel" moving into the future.

Designers are often focused on the present design situation and the forces at work today, along with knowledge of past designs. It is an inspiration to have awareness of the upcoming situation, but it is more powerful to imagine being on the other side of the tunnel where the solutions have been implemented. These ideal designs can then be projected back to today (back-casting from a desired future).

This powerful technique "pulls" the design team through the current situation. Companies that use this approach report impressive gains — with decisions made today benefiting both current and future efforts.[48]

The Next Level in the Picture

The Natural Step provides four ways of seeing the impact of design decisions. These ways are qualitative allowing nearly anyone in the company to add value to the process. From a systems viewpoint, the Natural Step is a philosophical framework focused on the interaction between design and environment. To focus on putting these ideas into action, we begin to examine frameworks that take a more prescriptive approach to design impacts and strategic thinking.

o2's 5Rs of Great Design

The o2 International Network for Sustainable Design (o2.org) undertook the task many years ago of updating the classic Three Rs of Reduce-Reuse-Recycle. Initiated by the United States Upper Midwest chapter (o2umw.org), their goal was to tap into ideas already in common use, create a resource ordered list (least to most energy/resource consuming), and to have the Rs include ideas that would help shift from a world where designers are only asked to do less "bad" to one where they can create more "good," moving toward a *Restorative Economy*.

What is a Restorative Economy?

— A way to add diversity back into natural systems.

— Industrial plants where the water coming out is better than the water going in.

— Products whose life cycle aids natural cycles, allowing the designer to calculate restoration instead of quantifying impact.

— Industrial operations that clean the air.

— Organizations that rebuild themselves to a higher level of functioning as employees increase their own capabilities.

The 5Rs are simple guidelines that guide actions of an organization, from one end to the other: energy sourcing to design and marketing to package. Here the organization is viewed as an organism that takes in food, produces a useful product, emits waste, and has an internal structure to respond to the environment. While not as metrics oriented as the SPC's eight criteria for a sustainable package, the 5Rs represent the next level in thinking about product impacts, and are used as a tool for quickly moving through design ideas in the brainstorming phase.

Restore

Ecological systems create new information and continually expand diversity. Use biological inspiration for design to create package diversity. For example, use variation and selection, allowing package environments and energy sources to determine the parents for the next generation. Choose suppliers and sources that add diversity back to natural systems, particularly where it has been depleted. Other sources of biological diversity are:

— Variation (sexual recombination): Genetic mixing produces new organisms that have differing abilities.

— Selection: The environment acts on those organisms to favor the ones who best match the niche.

— Food sources: Waste materials and unused energy can become food sources, allowing some designs to propagate more widely and fill the niche.

— Migration: As the niche changes, organisms migrate to follow the changes.

— Boundary regions: Allow intermixing of species, leading to competitive exclusion where two organisms try to occupy the same niche, leading to evolutionary changes.

— Using all the biomes: In the tropics there are species at each level, from tree canopy to undergrowth.

— Succession: Other species can colonize new territory, while a mature ecosystem has few spaces for new designs. The new territory changes as some species win out over others, creating an environment with gradations from full sun to shade.

The world as it exists is the result of millions of years of evolution and interconnection. Over many thousands of years, the processes above will bring products of the industrial economy into natural systems. To make this happen in human lifetimes, restoring the state of the world will require positive actions to bring industrial and natural cycles back together. Designers are in a unique spot to take these actions since their decisions affect as much as 90 percent of energy and material impacts over the design lifetime.

Pick raw materials from sustainably managed sources, and design to return the package at end of life into either the production process or the biosphere.

In other words, use materials (and support firms) that help reverse damage or add to natural capital. Natural capital represents the embodied information and energy in natural systems. What did it take to grow that tree, and how much value does that tree add to the local environment? Along with cleaning the air and recycling water, the tree gives habitat to animals, reduces the impact of the sun on hot days, and provides useful materials (leaves and twigs) to develop new soil. Natural capital is the bank account humanity has inherited from the earth, to be used wisely for all humans and their descendants. The value of genetic information in the rainforest is one way to visualize natural capital.

Other actions that help restore:

— Retiring carbon credits.

— Purchasing renewable energy or using vendors who do.

— Supporting organizations that do ecological restoration.

Respect

Design like you give a darn.[49] This means thinking of all the people in the supply chain from material extraction to manufacturing to assembly to sales to end user to end of life. Is mining required to obtain the raw material, potentially damaging streams that others make their livelihood from? What chemicals are required in the production process that could impact health today or generations from now (bioaccumulation)? Does the production process involve chemicals that are harmful to workers? Is it possible for Grandma to open that package (Universal Design)?[50] Is rushing to an "easy" solution creating an economic shift with broader socioeconomic impacts (like the move to a corn economy)? In other words, examine impacts the item will have on all stakeholders, as well as ecosystems. Examine the triple top line for economic health, environmental restoration, and social equity.

Bring images of nature and world citizens into the design environment. Update monthly. Get outside every day.

Reduce

Fuller: Do more with less! Make the structure minimal by using triangulation instead of a massive box. Consider the package a web not a box. Use compression and tension to create minimal structures. Combine layers of a complex package and reduce some of the layers to information (from material). Examine all package functions and reduce the material and energy needed, including less raw feedstocks, less weight to transport, and less energy to manufacture, less energy to store (aseptic pack vs. refrigerated milk), less energy to use (LED bulbs vs.

incandescent). Examine all materials and choose ones with reduced toxicity (moving toward zero).

In the natural world, "extra" requires more energy to create and support. How would Nature package?

Reuse

The best use of energy in a manufactured item is reuse. Each pass through the material recapture system takes energy and can result in materials being downcycled (most plastics do not become the same thing again). Design for reuse by making the package robust and creating a system to take advantage of that durable good: Even though it may cost more the first time, the overall life costs are lower and the customer becomes a participant in satisfying need, rather than just consuming goods. Savings in customer retention can easily outweigh any increase in packaging cost. Identify the reusable item and reward those who return it. Create packaging thatn is the product. Yet consider the system carefully: If the item is not reused, then energy and materials were wasted. Returnables work well only when systems are in place for them to be effective.

Recover

Recover replaces *Recycle* in this last slot, as recyclable without recovering those resources is just waste. Recovery can happen in one of two ways: The materials are fed back into the production process or the materials can be returned to Nature directly. Design the pathways intentionally and label the package to aid the end user. To enable this, the item needs to be created with the production process or Nature in mind. Recovered materials can retain customers as reuse does. Recovered materials that return to Nature are noteworthy and will increase product visibility.

The minimum level of recovery is to use recycled substrates, decreasing loads on earth systems, increasing the market for materials, and increasing marketability. However, just because materials can be recycled doesn't mean they will be.

Strategies to increase recovery/recycling:

— Team with other companies to increase market demand for the recycled material.

— Design with materials that have the maximum recovery/recycling potential. These have the most value to manufacturers and the largest markets.

— Give customers an incentive to return the package: Rebates, recognition, and rewards.

   Design for recyclability using noncomposite materials and easily separable components.

   Label correctly as to material type. Clearly communicate disassembly instructions.

The last resort for a recovered product is incineration (waste to energy). If this is the end case, design carefully to avoid any trace toxic materials. A few milligrams of a toxin multiplied by many millions of containers can be serious contamination.

Recycle has no meaning unless the material is selected to fit a real recycling market and the material is actually collected. Recover/recycle is last on the 5R list, as remanufacture (without any interim reuse) is the most energy intensive of the Rs.

When manufactured free of toxins, paper, paperboard, and pulp (wood, kenaf, bamboo, agripulp) are great examples of renewable, biodegradable resources that make many useful reuse and/or remanufacture trips (*C2C technical nutrient*) before it's time to retire as compost fodder for the next growing cycle (*C2C biological nutrient*).[51]

The Wal-Mart 7Rs

Over the past several years Wal-Mart has learned that working toward sustainability makes good business sense from a variety of perspectives: less risk, increased profits, and increased customer goodwill and market share. As just one example, they have made a commitment to sell 100 million compact fluorescents in a year, benefiting themselves, customers, and the environment — the classic *Win-Win-Win* of eco-business.

This business direction has extended into packaging as an area where costs can be decreased while also reducing toxics and impact on the environment. In a first of many initiatives, the "Wal-Mart Scorecard" system for packaging, asks suppliers to enter product information to determine their impacts.

To help Wal-Mart achieve its sustainability goals, suppliers are to consider these seven Rs for packaging:

Remove Packaging: Eliminate unnecessary packaging, extra boxes, or layers.

Reduce Packaging: "Right size" packages and optimize material strength.

Reuse Packaging: Pallets (use CHEP, IFCO, etc.) and reusable plastic containers (RPC).

Renewable Packaging: Use materials made of renewable resources; select biodegradable or compostable materials.

Recyclable Packaging: Use materials made of highest recycled content without compromising quality.

Revenue: Achieve all above principles at cost parity or cost savings.

Read: Get educated on sustainability and how we can all support it.

Like many sustainability ideas in use today, Wal-Mart's seven Rs are goals, subject to continual improvement and change.

The official scorecard is software creating a score weighting these factors:

— Greenhouse gas emissions (15%)

— Amount of materials used (15%)

— The ratio of the product to the packaging (15%)

— Efficient packing into shipping containers (cube utilization) (15%)

— Amounts of recycled content (10%)

— Innovation (5%)

— Quantity of renewable energy used in manufacture (5%)

— Value of the raw materials that could be recovered (10%)

— Calculations of emissions used for transport of the package (10%)

Note: Categories and percentages are subject to change as the scorecard evolves.

There is and will continue to be a vigorous debate about the scorecard. On one side, some will say that it doesn't go far enough and should not become a standard, while others argue that it goes too far and is not realistic.

The truth will be somewhere in the middle, and the main benefit will be that these factors are now visible to suppliers, purchasers, and the end user. It is likely that over time the debate will cool down, and as suppliers comply with the scorecard system they will benefit from decreased costs, increased market share, and a motivated workforce.

Readers will also observe that the 7Rs can be matched to the fundamental principles outlined here as well: Removing packaging levels, reducing packaging weight and size, and creating minimal package structures are examples of ephemeralization (doing more with less) as well as triangulation (designing with minimal struc-tures) and tensegrity (using tension and compression in tandem).

In 2008 Wal-Mart announced a major partnership with the Environmental Defense Fund with the goal of raising environmental performance standards throughout their supply chain. The *Green Supply Chain Initiative* will include targets for the reduction of energy and water use, reductions in packaging (already in place with the scorecard) as well as commitments to develop more sustainable products and supply chain practices.

Cradle to Cradle[SM]

Cradle to Cradle (C2C[SM]) is the idea of nature's systems made tangible by William McDonough and Michael Braungart, in their book, *Cradle To Cradle: Remaking the Way We Make Things.*[52] The basic precept is that items of human use can be manufactured so that the biological and synthetic components are retained and reused safely and independently in endless recycling loops. The Cradle to Cradle approach is being used on designs ranging from packaging to buildings. A building using Cradle to Cradle ideas, for example, focuses on the effective use of energy and resources along with the creation of safe and uplifting environments for human occupation.

McDonough and Braungart define the "eco-effective" design methodology of Cradle to Cradle as one that strives for products and places that are "more good,"

in distinction from "eco-efficient" design, which strives for products that are "less bad." A truly Cradle to Cradle product is considered to be "100% good" in every category of evaluation.

Life works in cycles, yet it is all too common for a product's life to end in the landfill or be incinerated. This approach to design is called *cradle to grave.* Recall that many materials either:

— Do not break down in the environment

— Are captured in a landfill where decomposition is not possible

— Only break down over decades or centuries

— Emit harmful wastes or toxins if incinerated

This end of life does not close a loop but rather locks up materials and energy in forms that are not usable in the cycles of nature or technology and often pollute.

The alternative strategy is for package end of life as a new beginning, looping back either into the production process or into the biological system.

This is the idea of Cradle to Cradle: Model industrial cycles on natural processes, and ensure that these cycles are tied safely back to the earth

A life cycle assessment (LCA) shows a negative cost at product end of life if it ends up in the landfill and a positive cost if it is recycled. Costs can also be higher for materials that come from nonrenewable sources.

In contrast, a C2C modeled process intentionally reuses or recycles materials for another round of production, avoiding the life cycle costs of package landfill or incineration, along with reducing the manufacturer's costs for source materials. To take this design approach further, it is possible to have positive impacts if end of life results in materials that are returned directly to the earth and enrich soils.

Using this systems approach means that market growth is good, as designs could actually improve ecosystems instead of doing less damage to them.

A systems approach example is Rohner, a Swiss manufacturer of industrial textiles. Their processes required many dyes produced by chemical manufacturers not always forthcoming about the chemicals used, putting the company into a difficult position as the Swiss authorities then designated their process scraps as toxic waste. In addition to disposal and handling requirements, a toxic waste designation also meant the company could not use their scrap to fuel their internal heating system.

Luckily for Rohner, their customer Susan Lyons of Designtex was looking for a low-impact line of materials, and employed William McDonough and Michael Baungart Design Chemistry (MDBC).[53] They contacted all the dye manufacturers and were finally able to find one willing to share their data on dye composition. After analyzing many thousands of dyes, they found enough that met the Cradle to Cradle requirements for human and ecological health to start the new product line. The results:

— New market opportunity

— Elimination of a regulatory burden

— Production scraps now sold as compost

— Reduced health risk for factory workers (since the new dyes are safe)

— Effluent water cleaner than the water coming in to the factory

It is possible to create products with lower negative or even positive impacts by careful design and appropriate information about materials, without new inventions or custom processes.

A key perspective from Cradle to Cradle is that the original industrial revolution was not designed to create waste and pollution. Rather, these were side effects as easy access to energy and improved machinery allowed processing of materials in new ways. The results were effective economically, but since there was no design intent other than efficiency, there were many unforeseen results.

Today the impacts of material production, processing, and disposal are known. Using ideas such as Cradle to Cradle it now becomes possible to design products with positive impact on earth systems.

This is a huge benefit psychologically, enabling designers to see sustainable design as a creative tool, a way to expand design freedom, and that growth can be good.

Cradle to Cradle looks at two cycles — the *technical cycle* and the *biological cycle*. A key viewpoint in Cradle to Cradle is that product life cycles should not end by materials simply dumped into natural systems, and provides two alternative approaches:

The technical cycle uses the end products (products of service) as input to a new production cycle. This creates a technical metabolism similar to the biological metabolism of the earth.

Alternatively, design products so the materials can be returned safely to the ecosystem in a way that improves natural systems. This is the biological cycle, and these are products of consumption since they get "used up" in the product life cycle. An example is the banana peel returned to the compost pile.

Key Design Goals of Cradle to Cradle

Waste = food. Traditional industrial production saw waste as extra, not useful, to be thrown away. Today industry knows there is no "away." Everyone lives in the same biosphere, and what goes out one pipe comes in another. The result is that waste is now risk and cost. Cradle to Cradle takes note that nature continuously evolves to take advantage of material and energy flows. Instead of waste being cost and risk, could it be transformed into something useful that reduces risk and cost? What can waste be used for? Can it be transformed into something safe? Perhaps it can be looped back into the production cycle to make new products. Waste then becomes an asset. Consider having the customer return the product. Even if this is not as profitable in the short term as other approaches, it brings customers back, increases their satisfaction, and can help with operations in other parts of the company. Consider the scavenger, living on the scraps that other species do not want.

Use current solar income. Virtually all variety on earth was created with energy from the sun. The industrial revolution discovered stored solar energy as fossil fuel. For the past century society has been on a wild ride spending the bank account. The by-products of this are climate change, increased energy costs, and vulnerability to supply disruptions. Cradle to Cradle suggests that designers instead examine all processes to increase efficiency or lower energy usage. Move operations progressively toward a balance with current solar income. Luckily, enough sunlight hits the earth every day to fuel society for a year.[54]

Celebrate diversity. In the rainforest there are species at every level from the ground to the treetops. This diversity allows the ecosystem to maximize capture of solar energy, and the interconnections make the system stronger and less vulnerable to changes. In contrast, a company with a single product is a monoculture and is very sensitive to environmental changes, in some cases becoming extinct when that environment changes.

Encouraging diversity benefits both the human and the natural community. There are a multitude of approaches to encourage diversity. Start by considering the kinds and sources of materials used in designs. Are they all from the same basic sources? Does the extraction of creation of that material affect ecosystem diversity? Specify material sources that are more diverse and that enhance diversity in natural systems. A more diverse system is more robust and resilient to changes.

Cradle to Cradle Design Strategies

To move a design toward Cradle to Cradle it is essential to examine these process steps:

— Material sources

— Material processing

— Package creation (putting it all together)

— Package transport:
  To manufacturer
  From manufacturer to retail outlet to end user

— Package use

— Package end of life

The "dimensions" of each process step are waste=food; solar income; diversity. As one example, material sourcing may require the use of natural resources. Are these sources managed in a way that is sustainable and that will encourage diversity? What about the energy used to extract the materials?

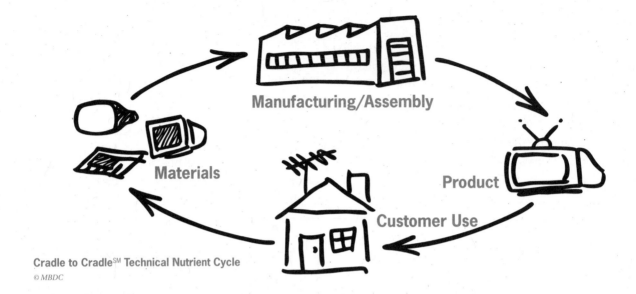

Manufacturing/Assembly

Materials

Product

Customer Use

Cradle to Cradle^{SM} Technical Nutrient Cycle
© MBDC

Can this be done on a solar equivalent basis (for example, the energy comes from wind power)?

Similar examinations are done with material processing, considering the other chemicals entering the process. Where do they come from, what are their impacts?

It is useful to draw a process diagram showing where materials and energy come into the process at each step. Then move outside the product cycle and create a process diagram for each of these external inputs.[55]

Along with the process diagram for the overall product, consider assembly of components, how items are attached to each other, and what types of inks and extra materials are in the package. These items can affect the end phase of the package by impeding recycling or reuse.

Another perspective on Cradle to Cradle is to view the product life cycle and look for areas where particular tools can be employed. For example:

— Material impacts (toxicity, source reduction) in material acquisition, processing, manufacturing, and end of life

— Design for reuse, recycling, and composting in material selection, acquisition, processing, and end of life

— Energy use in material processing, material acquisition, and transport

— Use of recycled materials in materials acquisition, processing, and end of life

— Biological diversity in material acquisition

— Weight reduction and design for transport in manufacturing and end of life

— Choose best practice when selecting materials and suppliers

Know the chemistry of your package. Ask about green chemistry and engineering when checking supplier performance.

Cradle to Cradle Strategies to Close the Loop

— *Return to nature.* To make this possible, the materials, processing, and any extra components in the packaging have to be benign and able to break down readily in normal environments. Returning the product safely to the Earth enhances biological productivity, as in the Rohner fabric example.

— *Reuse of packaging.* This gives the highest return value as no extra energy is needed and there are no landfill or incinerator costs. Packaging must be designed to withstand being cycled through the distribution system.

— *Recapture of packaging.* This uses the package as a technical nutrient and requires coordination with manufacturing personnel. For example, virgin packaging materials have one set of process conditions while recaptured packaging materials have another. It is important to design this cycle effectively so the recaptured material is not down-cycled (changed into material of lower value).

As one example of this recapture of technical nutrients, Shaw Contract Group leases their carpets to maintain a closed loop system. Besides the positive environmental impacts, they get return customers, who gain benefits from using a better product.[56]

When presenting the Cradle to Cradle concept to others, recall that present day design processes are based on a world where constraints, impacts, and the end of the cycle weren't considered. This is not so much wrong as a simple view based on a past version of the world. Now more is known. This knowledge doesn't restrict design freedom; rather it gives new paradigms and approaches to benefit both the company and the Earth.

Cradle to Cradle suggests that designers move away from "doing less bad" to inventing new systems where the product life cycle is tied to natural cycles and the results improve Earth systems. This is a deeper and more powerful approach than sustaining. Imagine an industrial system where the waste products actually improved the Earth's ability to grow the crops required to build the product. This is an example of the carbohydrate economy, getting raw materials from plant-based systems.[57] The Carbohydrate Economy Web site notes:

> Carbohydrates, the building blocks of plant matter, can be converted into chemicals, energy, textiles, building materials, paper, and many other industrial products. We call this new materials base a "carbohydrate economy." A carbohydrate economy reduces pollution, builds stronger rural communities, and supports a rooted farmer-owned manufacturing sector.

The Cradle to Cradle approach sees intelligence and learning in natural systems ranging from sensitive use of materials, to efficiency, to solar energy. Industrial designs can benefit from that knowledge and create new loops that benefit the Earth.

As with Shaw, a variety of other manufacturers have learned that getting materials back from customers minimizes production costs and risks, while also giving another point of contact that encourages repeat business and brand loyalty.

Cradle to Cradle asks that we don't just do "less bad," but try to create "more good."

Checkpoints for Cradle to Cradle Designs

When considering the original source of materials and the impacts of processing, the following are critical points in the packaging system:

— What systems are needed to procure and process package materials?

   Do the material systems use C2C guidelines?

— What are the material characteristics, and what is the impact on ecological and human health?

   Use C2C design protocol[58] or LCA data.

— Design the package to aid recycling and recovery.

— Think of the package as resource instead of a waste product.

— Reuse the package instead of recycling it. Reuse retains more value.

— What systems are required for reuse?

— Return the package to a biological cycle by composting.

— Eliminate anything impacting reuse or recycling.

— Design the package to be an asset with user value.

— Worst case: Design the package so it can be safely burned to recover energy.

— Make the customer your partner when they return or compost the package.

— Work with other companies to:

   Educate big box retailers and distributors

   Increase market share of recycled and/or recyclable materials.

   Create larger recycling opportunities

   Teach each other about inks, additives, labels, and decoration that hurts recycling

   Take a proactive stance, avoiding regulation

Summary of Cradle to Cradle

Sustainability requires that the three domains of economy, society, and environment are satisfied. To aid in remembering this requirement, Cradle to Cradle uses a "fractal triangle" that illustrates the interconnection of ecology, economy, and equity. The larger triangle is divided into smaller triangles, each of which is a combination of the aspects along that edge of the triangle. By using several triangles along each edge, the designer considers multiple interactions with the paired principles in each triangle alternating in strength — for example: Economy/Equity, or Economy/Ecology. In this way two kinds of interaction are gained from each pairing. The essential question of each pair: How can these two forces be resolved to add value? In practice the areas with the most conflict offer the most opportunities for improvement.

Cradle to Cradle design principles are:

— Waste = food (evolve a system to use it).

— Use solar income (don't spend down the bank account).

— Celebrate diversity (the world is full of niches).

The US Postal Service made it a priority to earn Cradle to Cradle Certification at the Silver level for human and environmental health, from McDonough Braungart Design Chemistry (MBDC).

By air mail | Priority
Par avion | Prioritaire

INTERNATIONAL
EXPRESS
PRIORITY

™

PRIORITY MAIL
POSTAGE REQUIRED

Flat Rate Box
For Domestic and International Use

Cradle to Cradle Certification is awarded to products that pursue
an innovative vision of ecologically-intelligent design
that eliminates the concept of waste.
This USPS® packaging has been certified for its material content,
recyclability, and manufacturing characteristics.

Please recycle.

cradletocradle
SILVER

Cradle to Cradle Certification is awarded to
products that pursue an innovative vision of
ecologically-intelligent design that eliminates the
concept of waste. This USPS® packaging has
been certified for its material content, recyclability,
and manufacturing characteristics.

Please recycle.

nation: Pays de destination:

Flat Rate Box
For Domestic and International Use

PLEASE PRESS FIRMLY

0-FRB2

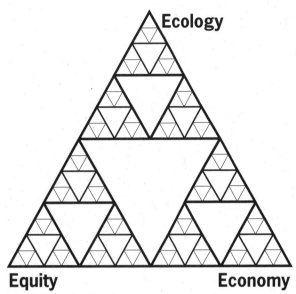

Ecology

Equity **Economy**

The fractal triangle of economy, environment, and society.

Text adaptation of Sierpinski Triangle to reflect Triple Top Line ideas ©MBDC.

There are two key material types in Cradle to Cradle:

— Biological nutrients can return to earth systems safely.

— Technical nutrients can be recaptured and used again safely without degrading in value.

Key aspects in the Cradle to Cradle design process:

— What effects does a material have on human and earth systems?

— Can a material be recaptured, recycled, or composted?

— How much energy is embedded in the material?

— Design to intentionally improve innovation, value, and impact.

The net effect is that Cradle to Cradle designs intentionally for best impact instead of minimizing negative outcomes. It is known as design for the triple top line (profitable designs that benefit humanity and nature)[59] as opposed to the triple bottom line (people, planet, and profits). In his 2002 article, *Design for Triple Top Line*, William McDonough notes:

> Typically, meeting the triple bottom line is seen as a balancing act, a series of compromises between competing interests played out in product and process design. The key insights offered by the fractal triangle turn this notion on its head: Intelligent design, rather than balancing economy, ecology and equity can employ their dynamic interplay to generate value.

Cradle to Cradle[SM] and C2C[SM] are Service Marks of MBDC, LLC. For more information on the book "Cradle to Cradle" or to get details on Cradle to Cradle Design Protocol, Cradle to Cradle Business benefits, Product Co-Marketing, or Cradle to Cradle Certification, visit their Web site at: mbdc.com or c2ccertified.com.

Product Design Perspectives

Is sustainable design a new set of requirements and processes? Or can it be related directly to things a company is already doing? Design is the first stage in a set of operations to create and deliver a product. Designers pass their art to manufacturing for replication, and they deliver the package to the next stage. On the production side there have been many techniques that advanced sustainability in practice.

As just one example, production has always considered the material sources and characteristics. The "dimensions" they consider can be enlarged just as the definition of quality was enlarged in previous discussions. Bottom line: Any of these practices can be the way to implement sustainability. With a few exceptions (materials bans, changes in pollution laws, and so on) there is no requirement saying companies must start from scratch or add new processes, simply start by reexamining current systems.

Design for Environment

There is a large body of material available under this name. How can it inform design process?

The Minnesota Pollution Control Agency did just that by researching best practice and creating a design guide that covers biomimicry, the basics of LCA, checklists, and information on how to design for recyclability.[60]

Design for disassembly. To be effectively recycled, products must be able to be taken apart with minimal effort. How are materials joined in the design? Can the RFID tag be taken off and discarded (safely!)? Can adhesives be eliminated?

Design for recyclability. Similar to the above, are the components recyclable in the local system? Can they be disassembled easily to allow this to happen?

Design inspiration. Note the biomimicry chapter — can the design use these principles to reduce material or energy costs?

Reduce process steps. Each step adds energy.

Confirm that the product is designed to:

— avoid the need for using hazardous or restricted materials

— optimize assembly (relates directly to disassembly)

— avoid energy-intensive processes (for example, multiple heat/cool cycles)

— minimize waste (avoiding surplus coating, cut-aways, trimming, by-products)

Consider changing the product to a service. Some copier makers changed their business model from selling copiers, to leasing machines that make copies.

The core idea is that nature, imaginative by necessity, has already solved many of the problems we are grappling with. Animals, plants, and microbes are the consummate engineers. They have found what works, what is appropriate, and most important, what lasts here on Earth. This is the real news of biomimicry: After 3.8 billion years of research and development, failures are fossils, and what surrounds us is the secret to survival.

Janine M. Benyus,
Biomimicry: Innovation Inspired by Nature

Design for the environment surprisingly coincides very well with design for manufacturability. (With) design for the environment, we have a lot of components and pieces of the hardware that snap together or can come apart easily, and that also benefits our manufacturing assembly time as well as the throughput rate of all of our products on the production floor. So not only do we get the environmental benefits, but we get the manufacturing benefits at the same time.

*Greg Vande Corput, Hardware Development Engineer, IBM (*Better by Design video, *2004)*

After 3.8 billion years of research and development, failures are fossils, and what surrounds us is the secret to survival.

Okala Design Guide

Also sprouting out of an Industrial Designers Society of America (IDSA) and EPA partnership is the 2007 edition of the *Okala Design Guide*.

Two other stakeholder groups in packaging's creative process, graphic designers and industrial designers, are making timely steps forward in the development of tools to help them navigate a project's options and impacts, and to broaden their creative possibilities in a quickly changing landscape.

Helping product designers do things right is the newly revised *Okala Design Guide*, written by design professionals and educators Philip White, Louise St. Pierre, and Steve Belletire. Though the guide addresses the design process from the product designer's perspective, the background and methodologies that make up the bulk of the guide are immediately useful for any design application.

Okala (from the Hopi Indian word *oqala*, meaning "life-sustaining energy") is an easy-to-understand primer for the teaching and practice of eco-conscious design. It introduces broad concepts behind eco-design, with detailed methods for estimating design impacts, and features thoughtful explorations of such subjects as environmental ethics, eco-design business planning, and green marketing.

Making an ecologically responsible decision can often be a daunting challenge, as designers must juggle a mind-boggling array of variables to create even the simplest products. Especially useful are tools and tips on practical topics such as how to use biomimicry in design, and plan for end of life disassembly and recycling. The guide also calculates the contribution of products and processes to global warming, the most eminent environmental challenge of our time.

Because packages and products are often manufactured in quantities numbering in the millions, even seemingly benign products can have enormous downsides for the air we breathe, the water we drink, and the soil we cultivate. The Okala guide, notes coauthor Philip White, helps "designers understand the implications of their decisions for the natural environment and, in doing so, the future of human society."

Key attributes of this edition include:

— Updated life cycle impact assessment methods that include use the newest environmental impact characterization methods and normalization data from the US EPA, as well as the newest weighting values from the National Institute of Standards and Technology (NIST)

— Okala impact factors (incorporating the aforementioned methods) for 240 materials and processes, which enable estimation of the ecological performance of any product or system

— Global climate change values (in CO_2 equivalents) for the same 240 materials and processes

— Design guidelines for disassembly and recycling

— Expanded explorations in environmental ethics, biomimicry, and design to stop climate change

— Additional references to socioeconomic relationships

— Green marketing data and product life cycle costing analysis

The guide can be ordered through the IDSA Ecodesign Section (idsa.org).

Since hindsight is 20/20, why not take advantage of it?

Your Nearest Advantage May Be Behind You

Bad blueprints make bad houses, regardless of vision. Yet a good blueprint only becomes a great house when there are good workmen to build it. An excellent architect learns from the workers what is practical and how to design for success. Since hindsight is 20/20, why not take advantage of it? If the following ideas sound familiar, the company is already on the path to make sustainable design part of the business model.

Note: Each production or quality approach has a parallel from Nature associated with it. The hope is that this will encourage readers to integrate the core principles with their design insights and strategies.

TQM

In Total Quality Management, or the house of quality, practitioners focus on continuous improvement of processes (visible, repeatable, and measurable in both production and design). Yet they also check to make sure the right product is being built and that all parts of the company are in agreement on that product. There is focus on making products work as they are supposed to, improving products by looking at how customers use them, and making an excellent product aesthetically. In effect, sustainability means listening closer to the customer and bringing those concerns into material and processing choices. This is in agreement with TQM practice.

Parallel from Nature: Symbiosis as one organism adapts to the other, the production of millions of seeds and leaves from simple patterns, changes in organisms as the niche changes.

5S

This is an improvement process involving five steps (Sort, Set in order, Shine, Standardize, and Sustain) to create and maintain a clean, neat, and orderly workplace. Some organizations add a sixth "S" for Safety.

Parallel from Nature: Scavengers reduce the waste materials in the bloodstream, creating an environment where the desired recombination can take place. Most biological processes take place by diffusion, requiring the presence of the correct materials in all locations without direct control of their motion.

Standard Work and Visual Controls

Standard work represents the best ("least-waste") way to perform a given operation. Visual controls are used to reinforce standardized procedures and to display the status of an activity so every employee can see it and take appropriate action. This is similar to the design language example where best practice is written down for all to see and learn from.

Parallel from Nature: Organisms using the least materials and energy can survive in more environments. Visual cues (leaves sprouting, flowers blooming, and reflections of fish in water) trigger actions.

Cellular Manufacturing

Manufacturing work centers (cells) have the capability to produce an item or group of similar items. Changes in production requirements can easily be handled by adding parallel cells to produce more product.

Parallel from Nature: All life is divided into cells and work is distributed in parallel between them. Nutrients arrive "just in time" for absorption.

Just in Time (JIT) / Kanban

This scheduling concept requires that any item needed for an operation — whether raw material, finished product, or anything in between — is available precisely when needed. Kanban (signals) are used to control levels of inventory and work in process. In effect, this reduces the buffers in the system, allowing the production system to respond more precisely to changes.

Parallel from Nature: Living systems only use what is present in front of them. Growth and change occur when triggered.

Antiparallel: Humans excel at storing materials and energy "for a rainy day."

Total Productive Maintenance (TPM)

Enlist operators in the design, selection, correction, and maintenance of equipment to ensure that every machine or process can perform its required tasks without interruption. This process puts the production stakeholders in charge of the most critical parameters of production. Knowledge of production capabilities enables optimal designs.

Parallel from Nature: Cells persist by continually renewing each element, avoiding decay. Most human cells are replaced within seven years. This requires both a cell regeneration process as well as a scavenger process. The scavenger process can find unused materials and resources in your organization, improving efficiencies and increasing profitability.

Six Sigma

Six sigma reduces product variation and thereby scrap, yet it is also a design practice that looks carefully at choice of materials, fit between design and customer need, material processing, and how to minimize variation. Six sigma has experts (black belts) that move from project to project, doing optimization and spreading knowledge.

Parallel from Nature: RNA/DNA copying is amazingly precise in general, and has a comparable error rate. Bees pollinate as they move from flower to flower.

Advanced Lean Enterprise Methods

Pre-Production Planning (3P) is the lean method for product and/or process design. It designs and implements production processes, tools, and equipment that support one-piece flow, are designed for ease of manufacturing, and achieve appropriate cost, quality, and lead time. Minimize energy and material use in the manufacturing process by looking at every step of the process from design to material acquisition to material processing to product quality. For every step, determine where efficiencies can be improved, material reused, or energy use decreased. This step reduces costs along with environmental impact.

Parallel from Nature: Evolution produces organisms ideally suited to their niche like the hummingbird.

Lean Enterprise Supplier Networks

This is a set of buyer-supplier relationships where organizations apply lean production concepts across the supply chain to reduce costs, delays, and other wastes.

Parallel from Nature: There is little less lean than the mollusk, growing its shell in seawater using available chemicals with no toxic waste.

Backstory on Production Processes

Life evolves by recombination of functional units. For example, there are only twenty amino acids but hundreds of proteins. Compare it to the English language of twenty-six letters and a few rules of grammar. Yet out of it comes Shakespeare and rap!

Designers create using the existing functional units, combining them to come up with new solutions. When the design is approved it heads to production where the rules are different. Now the design needs to be replicated reliably over and over again. This takes more than a good print. If the design calls for capabilities that aren't present in the production process it will not succeed. Design must be done in an environment of full production knowledge.

If design is sexual recombination, production is the DNA/RNA transcription happening in our cells constantly.

Innovation Heuristics

The systems approach can be used to transform packages from static "things" into flows within natural cycles. This is the basis of innovation in packaging. The flow is the system — from material creation through processing, assembly, sale, and recycling.

Flow is dynamization, making a process more dynamic or flexible. Design the system first, and the package to live within it. This dynamic process starts by dividing the package into pieces (segmentation) and moves through ever finer gradations until packages are replaced by service.

Lightness is closely related to flow. How light can the package be? Can the materials be chosen for the lowest impact?

The material in this section covers a variety of approaches to transform packaging.

Design Rules

Stopping the use of inappropriate materials: Packages shall not last longer than their contents.

Expand the space of design knowledge: Use the power of teams and diversity.

Use evolution as a guide: Experiment continuously.

All packages live in ecological niches: Listen and be guided by the user.

Move beyond local limits: Harness the power of open source to improve knowledge and networks.

TECHNIQUE: Create your own set of 5 to 7 innovation heuristics and share them.

The Basics of Innovation

Innovation is applied creativity. Some fundamental areas for innovation:

— Location: Where (design, designer, user)
— Direction: Why (what your principles are)
— Materials: What they are (good and bad)
— Cycles: How to use them
— Users: Who they are, their needs, desires, and interactions

Innovation occurs in:

— People: Changing design practice, changing package use
— Process: New ways to produce products and designs
— Products: Providing a function with greater advantage

Innovation can be:

— Incremental: Increasing the good qualities

— Decreasing the bad qualities

— Transformational: Providing a service instead of a product

— Disruptive: Changing the nature of the industry

Movement toward a goal or ideal design can occur at the level of people, process, or products.

At the level of people, a designer needs to know where they are. This can only happen when their methods and means of interaction with the world — the design principles — have been documented.[61]

TECHNIQUE: Create your own set of design principles.

Ecological Design Principles

Sim van der Ryn[62]

— Solutions grow from place: Keep it local.

— Ecological accounting informs design: Know your material and energy flows.

— Design with nature, not against it

— Everyone is a designer: Take advantage of different viewpoints and knowledge.

— Make nature visible: Let it shine in the design.

John Todd[63]

— The living world is the matrix for all design.

— Design should follow, not oppose, the laws of life.

— Biological equity must determine design.

— Design to reflect bioregionality.

— Base projects on renewable energy.

— Use the integration of living systems to design.

— Design as evolution along with the natural world.

— Design to heal.

Process Innovation

At the level of process, designers need to know material qualities and transformations.

Materials are the world of form. What can be made? What effect does it have? Can it be cycled back into production or left in the environment? Is it possible to let it "evaporate," leaving a web?

Transformations occur via energy, organization, or information. For example, plastics may be transformed with heat and pressure (energy). Companies can be transformed by organization as levels of hierarchy are reduced and interconnections formed. Societies can be transformed as information about the results of processes (industrial or political) are made available.

Package Innovation

At the level of package, designers work with function, system, and end users. To innovate with function, consider providing the package as a service rather than a tangible good.

Systems can be designed to transform the world as it exists, or to create new structures via interconnection. For example, sharing products (like power tools) creates new systems as well as new opportunities for product design.

The practice of user-influenced design requires that a designer forget their unique knowledge and typical techniques and solutions. Instead, explore and define the functions the user is most interested in. Ask the user how they are using the existing product and what features are missing.

Translating themselves into the users' world, designers can project those needs and desires back to innovate. The users can be interviewed (lead user process)[64] to find out preferences and how they use the package.

Innovations can be classified as quality improvement, new market creation, product range extension, reduction of labor or material or impact or energy, improvements in process, replacing products with services, or adapting to constraints (including regulation).[65]

Design Mindfulness (Thackara)[66]

— Think about the consequences of design. Most impacts come from design decisions.
— Consider the material and energy flows of package creation and use.
— Give priority to humans.
— Deliver value to people.
— Know that place, time, and cultural differences are positive values.
— Create services, not things.

Other Design Strategies from Thackara:

Learning from users

Innovation is becoming user led, as exemplified by Wikipedia and open-source solutions. Use that same power of multiple intelligences by being open to design solutions from users. Enlarge design thinking by including the Earth and the end user. Quiet down the "maker" mind-set that knows all about solutions and jumps to design decisions.

Following user needs

Users have needs: How does the package satisfy the need? What is excess? What is an irritant about the package? The creativity tool Triz[67] notes that there are two ways to improve a product: Increase the good factors or decrease the bad factors.

Studying how the package lives

Use context. How is the package used? Get it home, tear it open, toss it? Consider the egg carton with seeds that the kids want to plant. Think they will remember that brand?

Solution space

Enlarge the thinking space in the company. Bring in ideas from Nature (biomimicry). Encourage others to see the package as a spaceship or alien.

Mobility

The Internet has sped up the material economy and its flows. Now the book arrives overnight and goods come from the other coast. On an individual basis, lower environmental impact by thinking more and driving less. From a company perspective the same holds true — this is the lesson from operations research, where the activities at a company are studied to make optimal decisions about resource allocation. Consider where materials come from, the processing location, and how packages get from the company to the next step in the chain. Perhaps transport packaging isn't a layer on top of individual packaging. Make all packaging local.

Locality

Instead of moving things faster, make them closer. Local products are a growing market, and the package is a big part of that. Make the package itself local and it will sell the product (package made right here in Lake Wobegon!). Consciously design for going deeper instead of searching farther. Everything is particular: Design for each situation.

Experiment

Design implies intent, knowing the outcome. Evolution shows that variation and selection lead to variety and solutions that optimize fit into the local environment. Practice experimentation, not design. Start with small experiments. Try several, don't invest everything in one.

Appropriate use case models

Don't design for the worst case — 80 percent of all traffic is local, 15 percent is continental, and 5 percent is international. This holds for everything from cars to the Internet.

Consider the time cycle of packaging: Design to represent ideal package life.

Connect packages, products, and people

Life is structured via connections — use webs, chains, and networks. Most people want big city amenities and a small city pace.

Design Approaches

Design tends to converge on single (point) solutions. Rather, diverge outward from the center (Fuller's dimensions).

Innovation thrives in adversity, creating the most novel adaptations. Design without constraints can look like last year's, or worse, a competitor's box.

Requirement changes are part of life. Learn how to adapt to, and anticipate, changing requirements.

Pay attention to the flow: Packages, information, mindset of peers, changes in the economy. Emulate the flexibility of agile software development strategy. Teams meet every morning for a few minutes to determine top priorities for the day and to track requirements changes.

Design friendly packages — pieces that bring people together and create community.

Move from package as product to package as service.

Consider local exchanges and trades, sharing resources, time, and skills: Extend family to community. Use social and business networks to enlarge your design community.

Design using the universals of culture. If the package seems to fit in one market, consider what other context it is used in. For example, household articles might be used in play and recreation, or creating a beautiful sustainable package could define a new market.

Consider how package designs fit one or more of these areas: Alice Ann Cleaveland, Jean Craven, and Maryanne Danfelser, have extended the work of George Murdock on cultural universals:[68]

1. Material culture: Food, clothing, tools, housing, transportation, possessions

2. Arts, play, and recreation: Music, arts, design

3. Language and nonverbal communication: Books, language, video

4. Social organization: Societies, families, networks

The information space of the designer and user are different: Consider how to make messages "sticky" and how to represent the message of sustainability.

Design Using Universal Principles

Gravitation: What pulls the package into the Earth? What grounds the design and designer?

Dimension: Spin, radiate/converge, orbit, invert, torque, precess.

Trimtab: Use a small rudder to change the big rudder.

Boundary, flows and loops: Chart package flows.

Use viral or meme design techniques: What would cause a message or package to attach to a user? Consider hook and loop tape or sticky seeds. Similar to these examples, a meme is a behavior or piece of information that passes from one person to another. For memes to propagate, one user exhibits a behavior that others copy. The rapid popularity of white MP3 player earbuds is a good example. The idea jumps from one mind to the next, and behavior is copied and reinforced.

Other Design Strategies

Consider how the user interacts with the package and product. Design as a teacher: How can the package promote learning or literacy in general terms or in sustainability?

Biomimicry asks us to follow Nature by exchanging complication for biological inspiration. Consider the state of the industry: How does it mirror the ecosystem maturity level? Is it a stable mature forest? Or are there open areas where new species are growing rapidly? Should the products (and business) move toward or away from areas like these?

Consider life cycle as a means to innovate.

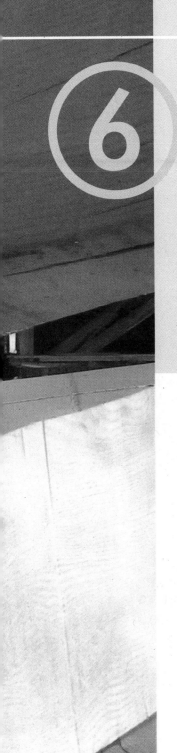

⑥ Materials and Processes

Wendy Jedlička, CPP

o2 International Network for Sustainable Design

With additional contributions by:
Jeremy Faludi, Eureka Recycling, National Recycling Coalition, Environmental Paper Network, Organic Design Operatives, Sustainable Packaging Coalition,[SM] *Packaging Strategies*

In theory, picking an eco-material is a better move than picking an un-eco one.

But if one doesn't know why a material is eco, how to apply its use correctly, or even if it actually *is* eco, taking a typically shallow replacement approach can end up with impacts far worse than the thing being replaced.

Using the simple replacement approach, too many companies seem to think they'll have done their part if they can just locate a list of magic green materials, pick something off the menu for their project, and cross "get eco" off their to-do list.

"Back in the day" there was no such thing as waste.
C.A. Thayer Restoration, 2007. Photo: W. Jedlička

Paper or Plastic? Neither!

Like so many things man has made over time, what was once a handy nicety has become an environmental nightmare. Eco-minded businesses, communities, and even whole countries around the world are banning one-use totes with increasing frequency, particularly plastic bags. Unlike paper bags, which do break down on their own and have the same impact on wildlife as eating paper, plastic bags stay in the environment for 400 to 1,000 years, clogging up drainage (making flooding worse), and killing wildlife (killing and rekilling after the animal's body decomposes and the bag is reingested by another hapless victim). Due to their longevity in the environment, plastic bags accumulate, and have gone "from being rare in the late 1980s and early 1990s to being almost everywhere from Spitsbergen 78° North [latitude] to Falklands 51° South [latitude]," notes David Barnes, a marine scientist with the British Antarctic Survey.[1] *Trashing the Oceans*, by Thomas Hayden, in the November 4, 2002, *U.S. News & World Report*, gives a particularly sobering account of plastic's impact on marine life.

Another really strong reason for not using one-use bags is a simple one. Why spend the money? Why use resources for a thing we have really handy, durable goods solutions for? Australia alone spends $175 million or so just for one-use totes each year. But this is only a small fraction of what is spent in the United States. According to *The Wall Street Journal*, American retailers spend $4 billion a year on one-use plastic bags. Imagine if that money were spent instead on renewable energy, or sustainability education?[2]

As the debate rages on, when the question of paper vs. plastic comes up, careful examination of the "facts" are in order.

Comparing the Numbers

Two life cycle studies — from production to disposal — of paper vs. plastic bags showed opposite results.[3]

Study 1

— Plastic uses 23% less energy than paper.
— Plastic produces 76% less solid waste.
— Plastic contributes 57% less air emissions.
— Plastic has 96% fewer water emissions.

Study 2

— Paper uses 80% less energy than plastic.
— Paper contributes 96% less to global warming.
— Paper contributes 52% less air emissions.
— Paper contributes 29% less water emissions.

An analysis of the two studies showed that location and scope of the assessments can result in drastically different conclusions.

Deeper review would require addressing who funded each study and so on. There is also the issue of recyclability not illustrated in the comparison above. Paper bags are recycled wherever paper recycling facilities exist (very common): Plastic bags, as well as plastics in general, don't enjoy the same recycling rates that paper manages. One-use paper bags sequester carbon from today's carbon cycle for the whole time they remain as paper, no matter how many times they are reused and recycled. One-use

---

Whole Foods Market®: Reusable Bags

This reusable tote, made of 80 percent post-consumer recycled plastic bottles, makes appropriate use of plastic's longevity, while also helping the consumer "close the loop."

plastic bags from nonrenewables are resurrected carbon from millions of years ago, and simply add to today's carbon and toxin load when burned, as is their fate in many markets.

When the question is paper or plastic for a one-use bag the answer is, should be, and should have always been — neither.

What Are We Trashing?

What we throw away says a lot about a society. Archeologists base whole careers on finding and analyzing ancient peoples' castoffs. What will future generations think of us when they crack open a landfill? Today discards range from packaging, food scraps and grass clippings, to old sofas, computers, tires, and refrigerators. In 2006, the US EPA released their most recent review of municipal solid waste. Of the things we throw away, containers and packaging made up the largest portion of waste generated, with 31.7 percent or 80 million tons. The second largest portion came from nondurable goods, which amounted to 25.5 percent or 64 million tons. Durable goods make up the third largest segment, accounting for 16 percent or 40 million tons. In all, though, Americans recovered 61 million tons of resources through recycling, which is 2.4 million tons more than in 2005. These figures exclude composting, still way underused in the United States but very popular in other countries.

In 2004, according to data collected by Packaging Strategies, packaging materials used in general were distributed as follows: paperboard 40 percent, plastics 26 percent, metal 16 percent, paper 10 percent, wood 4 percent, glass 4 percent.

Paper and paperboard recovery in the United States according to an EPA report, rose to over 50 percent (44 million tons), while metals were recycled at a rate of just over 36 percent, and 62 percent of yard trimmings were recovered. By recycling nearly 7 million tons of metals (which includes aluminum, steel, and mixed metals), the EPA calculates Americans eliminated what would otherwise have been about 6.5 million metric tons of carbon equivalent (MMTCE) greenhouse gas (GHG) emissions. This is equivalent to removing more than 5 million cars from the road for one year. Imagine the impacts if the recycling rates for mixed metals were at 100 percent, rather than only around 36 percent.

Materials: 2006 Percentage Recycling Rates

Auto Batteries	99.0
Steel Cans	62.9
Yard Trimmings	62.0
Paper and Paperboard	51.6
Aluminum Beer and Soda Cans	45.1
Tires	34.9
Plastic HDPE Milk and Water Bottles	31.0
Plastic PETE Soft Drink Bottles	30.9
Glass Containers	25.3

Before we get too enthusiastic about the numbers, though, these are national averages. In states taking a much more aggressing stance on resource management the numbers are much higher.

The California Department of Conservation's *Six-Month Report of Beverage Container Recycling & Significant Carbon Reductions* shows California's beverage container recycling rate rose to 71 percent over the study period of January to June 2007, up from 65 percent for the same period in 2006. Glass container recycling was up six percentage points from the previous year as well, reaching 71 percent.

The figures for glass container recycling in California are almost three times higher than the national average. In the United Kingdom recycling rates for glass containers (like bottles and jars) is around 50 percent. That's doubled over the last five years but still lags behind other countries — for example, Switzerland and Finland recycle more than 90 percent of their glass containers.

According to the Six-Month Report from the California Department of Conservation, each year California consumes 657 million barrels of oil and emits 492 million metric tons of greenhouse gases. California's beverage container recycling effort from January through June 2007 saved the equivalent of 2.5 million barrels of oil and reduced the equivalent of 293,000 metric tons of carbon in greenhouse gas emissions. The impact of the increase of nearly 800 million beverage containers alone saved the equivalent of 183,000 barrels of oil and reduced the equivalent of 21,000 metric tons of carbon in greenhouse gas emissions, which equates to removing 16,000 passenger cars from California roads each year.[4] Imagine what it would be like if the successes in California could be duplicated all over the United States! America, with California's example showing it can be done within a United States market system, might begin to approach the impact reductions other countries have already achieved.

RockTenn: Recycling and Conversion

Since 1908, RockTenn has been turning waste paper and paperboard board into cereal boxes and other packaging — helping to supply local food and consumer goods producers with local resources.

Paper

Recycling 1 ton of paper saves

— 17 trees (35' tall)

— 7,000 gallons of water

— 2 barrels of oil
(enough fuel to run the average car for 1,260 miles or from Dallas to Los Angeles)

— 4100 kilowatts of energy
(enough power for the average home for 6 months)

— 3.2 cubic yards of landfill space
(one family sized pick-up truck)

— 60 pounds of air pollution

— 4.2 MWh of energy
(enough energy to power a computer for almost a year)

Statistics from recyclebank.com

Benefits at a glance

— Renewable resource (current solar income)

— Can be made from a variety of pulp fiber plants, including annuals

— More and more mills are switching to renewable energy

— Sequesters carbon through to end of life

— Readily recycled in most markets

— lightweight and durable

— Virgin annual fiber crops typically require little bleaching

Primary uses for packaging: Extremely versatile, serving a vast array of functions from food to consumer goods, to transport packaging — with paper versions of common metal and plastic forms as well.

Drawbacks at a glance

— Supply chain not universally certified as sustainable

— Industry still very dependent on one pulp source (wood)

Typical toxins: Dioxins (bleach for virgin wood pulp or recycled pulp) and biocides (prevent bacterial growth).

Energy use impacts: Papermaking is the fourth highest user of electricity in the United States. Mining/drilling impacts, and combustion pollution, from fossil fuel generated electricity is at issue.

Wood-Based Paper

Paper, the American Council for an Energy Efficient Economy notes, is one of the few basic materials for which per capita demand has not saturated in the United States. The increase in per capita consumption averaged 1.8% per year from 1960 to 1980, 1.6% per year from 1980 to 1993, and has been projected at 0.6% per year for 1990 to 2040.[5] In spite of the drive to "go paperless" paper use remains one of the key resources needed for development in underdeveloped countries. Paperboard packaging and associated paper products from primary packaging (what you see on the store shelf), to labels and manuals, to shipper boxes, form the bulk of consumer goods packaging in use around the world today. Paper/paperboard products are what make our market economy possible. Most of the paper/paperboard products in use today are made from wood pulp.

Why What's In Your Paper Matters

Making responsible paper choices is one of the most significant environmental choices we make on a daily basis. The world's still growing appetite for paper, and the climate, forest, and social impacts of its production, are one of the planet's greatest environmental challenges. Global paper consumption is currently running at more than 350 million tons per year and fast approaching an unsustainable one million tons per day. Right now, paper production is expanding deeper into the world's last endangered forests and more frequently coming in conflict with local and indigenous communities over land, water and public health. However, when we examine our paper choices we can find opportunities to be more efficient, and to choose high-quality paper with environmentally advantageous qualities that add value to our design work. Making these responsible paper choices is something we all must do if we desire a sustainable future.

Paper is a wonderful asset to all of us, from designers to just about any other person in the world. Its natural texture, versatility, and availability are among its many positive attributes that make it so abundant in our lives, and will continue to for the foreseeable future, despite the "digital revolution." Paper will at times be the appropriate material for your project, and that's why knowing what's in your paper matters.

Much like the urban cliché of the child who responds, "The grocery store," to the question "Where does food come from?" most of us don't really know where paper comes from. Unfortunately, if we don't ask ourselves what is in the paper we are using, there is a very good chance it is coming from unsustainable sources, resulting in major negative impacts such as the loss of endangered forests, pollution to air and water, and accelerating climate change.

Paper still comes primarily from trees. The industry accounts for over 40 percent of the world's industrial wood harvest, threatening the world's last endangered forests and the habitat they provide for endangered species. Paper companies are currently cutting deeper into ancient and endangered forests such as the Canadian Boreal Forest, the Russian Taiga, and the tropical rainforests of Indonesia. They are replacing native forests with sterile, monoculture tree plantations across biologically significant areas in the southern United States, Tasmania, and South America. With less than 20 percent of the world's original forest still intact and undisturbed (less than 5 percent in the United States), the situation is critical for the world's endangered forests. These forests provide unique habitat for endangered species, store carbon and regulate the global climate, and ensure fresh water for millions, among many other benefits.

The paper industry is the fourth largest greenhouse gas contributor among manufacturers and a huge consumer of energy, making it a major culprit in climate change. In addition, paper that ends up in landfills releases methane, a greenhouse gas with twenty-three times the heat-trapping power of carbon dioxide. Landfills are the largest human source of methane and paper is the single largest component of our landfills, despite the fact that about half of paper waste is recovered for recycling.

Paper choices don't just affect the fate of our climate and our forests, they also impact the immediate livelihoods and health of people around the world. As paper companies seek cheap land, cheap labor, and limited regulation in new regions of the world, they are increasingly directly impacting the land, air, and water of local and indigenous communities. The land rights of indigenous peoples and rural communities must be respected, but in some regions they are violated in the course of activities by pulp and paper corporations. When paper companies are granted concessions to log forests and/or establish fiber plantations without gaining the full and informed prior consent of local communities or indigenous peoples with customary rights on that land, this is an abuse of the land rights of those people and communities. Unfortunately these abuses are far too widespread. Indigenous people are struggling for their rights in many paper-producing regions, from the Sami in Finland to the Maori in New Zealand, from the Haida in Western Canada to the Udege in the Russian Far East.

In Brazil, for example, there is bitter conflict in the state of Espírito Santo, Brazil, surrounding the acquisition by Aracruz Cellulose, the world's biggest producer of eucalyptus pulp, on land claimed by indigenous peoples. In Brazil, there is now more than 5 million hectares (11 million acres) of eucalyptus plantation growing in vast monocultures, termed "green deserts" by their opponents, who complain that the plantations consume vast quantities of water, causing rivers to dry up and leading to erosion, deterioration of water quality, and loss of fishing and water resources to local communities.

The pressure on our planet from paper production is clear, but what can we realistically do about it? First, be efficient. Designing paper-use efficiency into products has the most significant impact. It can also result in significant cost savings for manufacturers and clients and set products apart from others in a competitive marketplace. Just as a unit of conservation/efficiency is the most economically valuable unit of "alternative/clean energy," the same applies to paper use.

Second, make a responsible choice. Today, like never before, opportunity abounds to find high-quality paper produced with responsibility in mind. Today, there are more products containing recycled paper content than ever, with new innovations demolishing old perceptions and bringing quality and performance on par with virgin-fiber paper. Today, there is the Forest Stewardship Council, third-party certifiers who can provide a credible assurance that forest fiber was harvested in a sustainable manner and local communities were not negatively impacted. (Note: Beware of other certification schemes that have not yet established credibility.) Today, there is paper produced without chlorine bleaching. Today, there are paper products produced using clean energy, reducing the impact on our climate. Today, it is not just a nice idea, it is truly possible to choose socially and environmentally responsible paper.

The Environmental Paper Network is a community of conservation organizations that can connect you with tools and resources to make socially and responsible paper choices. Their Web site, WhatsInYourPaper.com, provides a wealth of information and people ready to help. When you're thinking about your next project, remember to think about and ask, "What's in your paper?"

Article by Joshua Martin, Network Coordinator, Environmental Paper Network. For more information visit their Web site at environmentalpaper.org.

Alternative Papers

A 1998 100% Recycled Paperboard Alliance (RPA-100%) national survey of US primary shoppers indicated that preference for 100 percent recycled paperboard products had reached an extremely high level: 92 percent believe they are doing something for the environment when they buy it, 84 percent feel better about companies that use it as packaging material, and 73 percent are more inclined to buy products from companies that use it.

With such high, and long established, consumer support for forest-free (100% recycled) or even virgin pulp reduced (partially recycled) packaging documented over ten years ago, the opportunities are ripe for companies looking to integrate the positive consumer perception advantages found in tree-free products. The fact that no trees were used at all, and that most alternative pulp products come from annually harvested crops and residue (agripulp), is a simple idea the consumer can easily get. In this time of transition, with companies issuing varied and confusing eco-marketing claims, companies that find simple ways of connecting with the consumer are best positioned to profit the most in an ever greening market.

In their 2000 report, *Toward a Sustainable Paper Cycle*, the International Institute for Environment and Development talk about nonwood fibers, in developing countries, where nonwood fibers account for over half the virgin pulp production, and are important to their paper industry. In addition to importance as a materials resource, their report notes there may be social and economic benefits to be gained by expanding paper production from nonwood fibers.[6] Tree-free/nonwood fibers for paper products in production today include bagasse, cotton, flax, old jeans, mulberry, kenaf, hemp, agripulp (wheat, rice, corn, straw), banana, and bamboo.

Like any material though, simple substitution should not be the primary go-to mode in the decision-making process. Materials selected should be ones that will provide advantages on a variety of levels. Is the material considered special for the purpose? What are the greater impacts of selecting this material (agricultural, social, waste management)? What does the material's process and supply chain look like?

Selecting any material needs to be undertaken with considerable thought. One high spot in otherwise bleak discussions of rampant consumption is that to meet increasing demand, both in the developed and developing world, all pulp sources will require serious attention.

In his 1999 book, *The Guide to Tree-free Recycled and Certified Papers,*[7] author Dan Imhoff explains:

> ...a tree-free paper industry promotes the goal of keeping old-growth forests and trees growing on United States federal forest lands out of the paper stream. A tree-free paper industry could greatly benefit rural economies as well.

Imhoff goes on to describe several regions in the Unites States (the world's biggest consumer of paper) that could support pulp demand, as well as talks about the development of mini-mills to keep transport fuel use down. Local crops serving local needs is one of the cornerstones of sustainability systems thinking.

Distant Village Packaging makes use of a huge variety of recycled and tree-free pulp sources, paper types, and paperboard options.

Plastics

Nonrenewable Plastics

Recycling 1 ton of plastic saves

— 5,774 Kwh of energy

— 685 gallons of oil

— 98 million BTUs of energy

— 30 pounds of air pollutants from being released

Statistics from recyclebank.com.

Benefits at a glance

— Very lightweight and durable

— Some types retain recycling value vs. downcycling

— Moisture and gas barrier properties

Primary uses for packaging: Extremely versatile, serving a vast array of functions from food to consumer goods, and medical applications.

Drawbacks at a glance

— Not renewable; not from current solar income, increasing today's environmental burden by adding ancient toxins to current load.

— Not all types readily recycled in all markets. Currently only PETE (1) and HDPE (2) enjoy strong recycling levels.

— Common materials flow is for downcycling rather than true recycling.

— Some additives can make plastic toxic.

Typical toxins: Depends on the type of plastic. Some are currently subject to phase out due to high toxin loads, and offgassing throughout their life. Careful review is required before making any commitment.

Energy use impacts: Plastics are the fifth highest user of electricity in the United States. Mining/drilling impacts, and combustion pollution, from fossil fuel generated electricity is at issue.

Plastics Overview

Since the late 1980s, plastic products used for packaging have been labeled with one of seven codes indicating the type of material they're made from. Familiar to most people now, these labels appear as numbers and letters inside *chasing arrows* on the bottom of each container. The types most commonly recycled by a wide margin are PETE/PET (1) and HDPE (2), with the remaining plastics with very low recycling, if they are accepted at all.

Note: The current numbering system does not include bioplastic types yet.

On their *Greener Choices* Web page, *Consumer Reports* provides an overview of nonrenewable plastics based on 2004 data:[8]

#1 Polyethylene terephthalate (PETE or PET)

Common packaging uses: beverage and food bottles and containers

Amount recycled in 2004: 22 percent

Common recycled use: textiles, clothing, and carpet; luggage; film, food, and beverage containers (rPET)

#2 High density polyethylene (HDPE)

Common packaging uses : beverage and food bottles and containers; dish and laundry detergent bottles; grocery, trash, and retail bags

Amount recycled in 2004: 26 percent

Common recycled use: plastic lumber, pipe, buckets, crates, flowerpots, film, recycling bins, floor tiles; nonfood containers including laundry detergent, shampoo, conditioner, and motor oil bottles

#3 Polyvinyl chloride (PVC or vinyl)

Common packaging uses : food and nonfood packaging; medical tubing; siding, window frames, floor tiles, and carpet backing

Amount recycled in 2004: less than 1 percent

Common recycled use: packaging, loose-leaf binders, decking, paneling, gutters, mud flaps, film, floor tiles and mats, electrical equipment, traffic cones, garden hoses, mobile home skirting

#4 Low-density polyethylene (LDPE)

Common packaging uses: dry cleaning, bread and frozen food bags, squeezable bottles

Amount recycled in 2004: less than 1 percent

Common recycled use: shipping envelopes, garbage can liners, floor tile, plastic lumber, film, compost bins, trash cans

#5 Polypropylene (PP)

Common packaging uses: food and medicine containers and bottles

Amount recycled in 2004: 3.2 percent

Common recycled use: automobile battery cases, signal lights, brooms, brushes, ice scrapers, oil funnels, bicycle racks, rakes

#6 Polystyrene (PS)

Common packaging uses: cups, plates, cutlery, compact disc jackets, egg cartons

Amount recycled in 2004: (data not available)

Common recycled use: thermometers, light switch plates, thermal insulation, egg cartons, vents, rulers, license plate frames, foam packing, and dishware

#7 Other

Often polycarbonate, but also the current designation for any plastic not 1 to 6, like bioplastics

Common packaging uses: reusable water bottles, beverage and food bottles

Amount recycled in 2004: (data not available)

Common recycled use: bottles, plastic lumber

Pictured here, glass vs. plastic. Plastics offer similar properties such as clarity and moldability, while being lighter weight. All types though, may not be accepted for recycling.

Biobased/Renewable Plastics

Benefits at a glance

— Primarily made from renewable resources (current solar income)

— Very lightweight and durable

— Various types closely resemble traditional nonrenewable plastics

— Moisture and gas barrier properties, some have gas permeable advantages.

Primary uses for packaging: Extremely versatile, serving a vast array of functions from food to consumer goods. Forms in common use today include trays and containers for fruit, vegetables, eggs, and meat; bottles for soft drinks and dairy products; window films for paperboard bakery cartons and bags; and blister foils for fruit and vegetables.

Drawbacks at a glance

— Various types closely resemble nonrenewable plastics causing disruption to established recycling materials flows, if proper collection facilities are not in place to receive the new material.

— Not readily recycled or composed in all markets.

— Some additives can make plastic toxic.

Typical toxins: Depends on the type of plastic. As they are made primarily from plants, as with food, toxin loads then would come from farming, transport, and processing. Careful review is required before making any commitment.

Energy use impacts: Plastics in general are the 5th highest user of electricity in the United States. Mining/drilling impacts, and combustion pollution, from fossil fuel generated electricity is at issue.

At this point in their development making production ever more efficient, plus increases in crude oil prices, biobased plastics compare favorably to nonrenewable plastics. Biobased plastics can also show a comparative advantage when studies include costs for collection and processing of raw materials in the calculation as well (*assessing true costs*).

Common Bioplastics

For more information see biopolymer.net.

Bioplastics/biopolymers, an alternative to petroleum-based polymers (nonrenewable plastics), are polymers generated from renewable sources. As they are made from many of the same sources as food, they are usually biodegradable and generally considered nontoxic.

They can be produced by biological systems like microorganisms, plants, and animals, or synthesized from biological starting materials like sugars, starch, natural fats, or oils.

In general, biopolyesters, the group commonly used for packaging, have properties similar to traditional polyesters.

CA — Cellulose acetate

Currently made from wood or cotton, this is one of the oldest bioplastics still in production today. Cellulose acetate (CA) is used for transparent and translucent films for packaging. It is especially suitable for coatings requiring a high melting point, toughness, clarity, and good resistance to ultraviolet light, chemicals, oils, and greases.

PHB — Poly — beta hydroxy butyrate

PHB is derived from bacterial fermentation of sugar or lipids. A very basic polymer, it has physical properties comparable with polypropylene (PP). A PHB copolymer called PHBV is tougher and more flexible, making it useful for packaging.

PHA — Polyhydroxyalkanoatesas

PHA is produced in nature by bacterial fermentation of sugar and lipids. Through photosynthesis in a controlled environment these tiny biofactories combine carbon dioxide, water, and sunlight to create a biodegradable, renewable alternative to petroleum based plastic. Metabolix, PHA's developer, is building the world's first plastic biorefinery in Clinton, Iowa, scheduled for completion by the end of 2008.

Potential adaptations for PHA are numerous, and range from food serviceware to orthopedic sutures and fasteners.

PLA — Polylactide acid

PLA resembles clear polystyrene and is currently made from corn, but can be made from a variety of plants, including residuals, making it possible with further development to make this bioplastic from agricultural waste rather than competing with food crops for land and other resources. According to NatureWorks, PLA's developer and producer, PLA can deliver a fossil fuel savings of between 25 and 68 percent compared with polyethylene, using renewable energy certificates for its manufacturing energy needs. PLA can be processed like most thermoplastics into fibers or films, and can be thermoformed or injection molded.

Starch-based polyesters

Starch-based polymers can be used as is, or a blend of starch (from corn, wheat, rice, and potatoes) and other plastics or minerals (like clay) for enhanced environmental or use properties. Current products made from starch include food serviceware and loose fill for transport packaging.

Foamed starch (StarchTech, National Starch & Chemical) is naturally antistatic, insulating, and shock absorbing, and can be either composted or dissolved in water, making it a preferable replacement to polystyrene foam in most applications.

Cereplast Compostables™ consist of certifiable, biodegradable plastic alternatives derived from starch-based feedstock such as potatoes, corn, and wheat. Cereplast Hybrid Resins™ is identical, except it uses a 50-50 mixture of starches and petroleum.

Bioplastics Overview

To really get a handle on renewable plastics, one needs to look at plastics in general. Though a relatively new invention, plastics have become a key part of our existence in the West — touching on nearly every aspect of modern life.[9]

The ages of man are broken down into key technological developments for each era: the Stone Age, the Bronze Age, the Iron Age, and Steel Age. Today, the total volume of plastics produced worldwide has surpassed that of steel and continues to increase. By the definition of "key technological development" we refer to our current era as the Information Age, but one could just as easily call it the Plastics Age.

The plastics driving our current successes are made from nonrenewable resources such as oil, coal, or natural gas. As they aren't renewable, all of these will eventually become exhausted. Rather than treat these nonrenewable resources like the precious things they are, products made from them have been reduced to a quick use and one-way trip to landfill or incinerator at an ever increasing rate. As the use of plastics grows, the important question must be asked: How can we balance the convenience we've found through the use of plastics and minimize or eliminate their long term environmental impact? To get a better feeling for what the answer might be, let's look at what makes plastic so useful.

In his book, *Green Plastics: An Introduction to the New Science of Biodegradable Plastics*, author E. S. Stevens helps explain.

A material can be called a plastic if it satisfies three conditions: Its main ingredient must be a polymer material, it must be fluid at some point during processing (usually processed using heat), and it must be solid in its final form. Plastics can be made up of many different kinds of polymer, and can be processed in many different ways, but as long as they satisfy these three conditions, they are bona fide plastics.

The main ingredient of any plastic is a polymer, a type of molecule that takes the form of a long chain. Polymers can come in different shapes, and some polymers are synthetically produced, such as nylon and polyester, while others can be found in nature: Silk, hair, natural rubber, and even starch are examples of polymers. In principle, any of these polymers could be used to produce plastics; in practice, however, over 90 percent of all plastics are made from just five polymers, all of which are synthetic.

Over 90 percent of all plastics produced today are made from only five polymers: polyethylene, poly(vinyl chloride), polypropylene, polystyrene, and poly(ethylene aveterephthalate). All of these are synthetic polymers, and may contain additives such as plasticizers and coloring that are added to a polymer to change its flexibility, strength, color, and texture, giving it the qualities desired in the final product.[10]

The use of natural polymers (bioplastics) is not entirely a new idea. Natural resins like amber and shellac have been mentioned throughout history, and are in common use still today. Commercial use of bioplastics began in the middle of the nineteenth century when American inventor John Wesley Hyatt, Jr., was looking for a substitute for ivory, then used in the manufacture of billiard balls. However, this first application of the materials, had flammability issues. Balls would occasionally burst into flames when near a lit cigar — a common indulgence in pool halls. Hyatt continued development, eventually creating celluloid, the first widely used plastic, now best known for its use in photographic and movie film.

In the 1920s, Henry Ford experimented with soy-based bioplastics for car parts. Looking for nonfood applications for agricultural surpluses and to better assure homegrown solutions to resource demands, he applied soy plastics for automobile parts like steering wheels, interior trim, and dashboard panels. Eventually Ford was able to produce a "plastic car," exhibiting the prototype in 1941, though never putting it into production. As petroleum emerged as a cheap source of carbon, development of bioplastics was replaced by synthetic polymers, with World War II wartime technology demands driving development even faster.

One notable exception is cellophane, a sheet material made from cellulose (commonly wood derived). It survived the growth of the synthetic, nonrenewable plastics industry and is still used in packaging today for candy, cigarettes, and other articles.

Today's US plastics industry includes over 20,000 facilities, employs over 1.5 million workers, and ships over $300 billion in products each year. The magnitude of the plastics industry, however, is itself a cause for concern Stevens points out in his book:

> The pressures of increasing waste and diminishing resources have lead many to try to rediscover natural polymers and put them to use as materials for manufacture and industry. As a result, there is increasing interest in the promise of a new generation of green plastics.

> For bioplastics to become practical, they must have properties that allow them to compete with the current plastics on the market: Bioplastics must be able to be strong, resilient, flexible, elastic, and above all, durable. It is the very durability of nonrenewable plastics that has helped them in the marketplace, and has been a major goal of plastics research throughout the years. However, it is exactly this durability that now has people increasingly worried. Now that we wrap our sandwiches in bags that will still be around when the sandwich, and even the person who ate it, are long gone, many people are wondering: Have we gone too far?

> Current research on bioplastics is focusing on how to use Nature's polymers to make plastics that are programmed-degradable: in other words, how to make products that allow you to control when and how it degrades, while insuring that the product remains strong while it is still in use.

Stevens's book calls out three factors that affect how environmentally friendly a material is:

Renewability: How quickly are the ingredients that go into making the plastic created in the environment?

A material that is made from soybeans, for example, could be more environmentally friendly than one made from wood, because nature can produce soybeans faster than it can produce trees.

Degradability: How quickly can the plastic be reintegrated into the environment after it is no longer in use?

Production: How much pollution or waste is created during the process of actually making the plastic? Traditional, nonrenewable, plastics, Stevens points out, fail on all three of these points.

Bioplastics offer so many advantages to help build a more sustainable society. However, like any material, just because they are renewable, they must not be considered "free," meaning they too can have enormous environmental impacts.

Bioplastics share many of the same issues as farming — where impacts of pesticide use, synthetic fertilizers, and other impacts of intensive agriculture are a major environmental issue, with eutrophication being a major ecosystem threat (example: Hypoxic Zone of Gulf of Mexico, epa.gov/msbasin).

On the social impact side, conversion to a "corn" economy it has been argued, sparks competition for resources (land, water, labor) between crops grown for food and those for industry. Some argue further, that commodity price spikes result in unbearable prices for staple items in the countries that can least afford cost increases.

In addition, increases in industrial demand for agricultural products may be putting even greater space demand pressure on old growth forests and other areas of natural, irreplaceable biodiversity.

Cellophane, one of the first bioplastics, is still used today to package a variety of food products.

Metals

Aluminum

Recycling 1 ton of aluminum saves

— 1,663 gallons of gasoline
(amount of fuel needed to provide a typical home with electricity for a period of 10 years)

— 14,000 Kwh of energy

— 238 million BTUs of energy

— 10 cubic yards of landfill space

Statistics from recyclebank.com.

Benefits at a glance

— Lightweight and durable

— High recycling value, with wide acceptance

— Can be recycled into same forms nearly indefinitely

— Moisture, gas, and light impermeable

Primary uses for packaging: beverage cans, canned foods, foils, nonfood structures, closures.

Drawbacks at a glance

— Not renewable; not from current solar income.

Typical toxins: Environmental and health issues associated with the manufacture of metals; mining and processing of raw materials; furnace emissions; coatings; and process chemicals. Most of the human health and ecological concerns of aluminum are associated with alumina refining, anode manufacture, and the emissions and wastes associated with the electrolysis process.

Energy use impacts: Pollution and collection impacts from fossil fuels are used for manufacture.

It takes 95 percent less energy to make an aluminum can from recycled than from virgin sources.[11] A high "recycled to virgin" ratio is a good indicator of just how high the energy need was for creating the original virgin product.

Steel

Recycling 1 ton of steel saves:

— 642 Kwh of energy

— 76 gallons of oil

— 10.9 million BTUs of energy

— 4 cubic yards of landfill space

Statistics from recyclebank.com.

Benefits at a glance

— Durable; has weight advantages over similar items packaged in glass

— High recycling value, with near universal acceptance

— Can be recycled into same forms nearly indefinitely

— Moisture, gas, and light impermeable

Primary uses for packaging: beverage cans, canned foods, nonfood structures, closures.

Drawbacks at a glance

— Not renewable; not from current solar income.

— Not the lightest weight option for some uses.

Typical toxins: Environmental and health issues associated with the manufacture of metals; mining and processing of raw materials; furnace emissions, coatings; and process chemicals.

Energy use impacts: Pollution and collection impacts from fossil fuels are used for raw materials collection and manufacture.

Overview

Many of the leading causes of death in quickly industrialized developing countries are being attributed to the use of fossil fuels (coal) and metals production. Ore and mineral extraction, as well as coal mined to fuel refining furnaces, all carry a high environmental impact burden.

The rate of impact increases for nonrenewable resources is unnecessarily boosted by low recycling collection rates worldwide. It is important to remember, though, there is no *one* superior material for all cases. Metals packaging has enjoyed a long history of service to the food industry, and continues to be an important part of the distribution system we use to feed ourselves. In areas with no refrigeration, shelf-stable foods provide access to nutrition, with metal packaging often a welcome addition to their metals resource stream.

Surface mining operation
Photo: Jeremy Faludi

If It Can't Be Grown, It Must Be Mined

Where does your cell phone, your furniture, your shoes, all your stuff come from? Before the store, before the factory, where is the real beginning? If it isn't made of wood, cloth, or other living matter, it was dug out of the ground. Number one of The Natural Step's four system conditions is: "In the sustainable society, nature is not subject to systematically increasing concentrations of substances extracted from the Earth's crust." So ultimately, one day our industrial economy will be made up entirely of recycled and biologically grown material. That day, however, is a long way off. How do we get there, and what is the world of mining like today? How rapidly are we depleting the minerals we have, and how do we get to sustainable mining?

Current Usage

The Robinson Mine in eastern Nevada (also called the Liberty Pit mine) was one of the biggest copper mines in the world. A shadow of its former self, the mine is now mostly piles of tailings (leftover rock and dirt that doesn't contain ore). Climbing up a pile of tailings, one can seen they are gigantic, stretching over a mile wide and over four miles long. A future civilization stumbling on them might think them earthen-mound architecture like Cahokia. Literature available at the site at the time (2005) says: "Every year 40,000 pounds of minerals must be provided for every person in the United States to maintain [their] standard of living." Providing additional insight into the magnatude of the issue, according to 2007 statistics from the Mineral Information Institute (mii.org), the US requires about 46,000 pounds of minerals for each person, each year, to maintain their standard of living.

911 lbs. of lead	1,398 lbs. of copper
1.546 Troy oz. of gold	32,654 lbs. of iron ore
5,417 lbs. of bauxite (alum.)	773 lbs. of zinc
18,447 lbs. of phosphate rock	31,909 lbs. of salt
20,452 lbs. of clays	75,047 lbs. of cement
82,169 gallons of petroleum	578,956 lbs. of coal

5.71 million cu. ft. of natural gas

1.72 million lbs. of stone, sand, and gravel

Plus 68,0341 lbs. of other minerals and metals

The numbers above do not include tailings; the ratio of tailings to ore can be huge. The concept of an "ecological rucksack" measures how many kilos of material must be mined (or grown) to produce one kilo of end product.

According to a report by NOAH, the Danish Friends of the Earth, every 1 kg of gold in your hand carries an invisible history of 540,000 kg of material in its ecological rucksack.[12] A few other notable metals in the report: Polyethylene's rucksack is a mere 2.4 kg of "abiotic" material per kg of end material, copper's is 356 kg/kg, stainless steel's is 23 kg/kg, and virgin aluminum's is 66 kg/kg, while recycled aluminum is just 1.2 kg/kg. Ecological rucksack calculations in NOAH's report also include water and air, comprising a more comprehensive measurement of ecological footprint than is usually found in impact reports that focus on narrow impacts. In addition to the ecological rucksack, there is sometimes a social cost as well.

Everyone is familiar with "blood diamonds," but gold is often mined under inequitable circumstances. In the 1990s tantalum, used in high-temperature applications, such as aircraft engines; electrical devices, such as capacitors; surgical implants; and handling corrosive chemicals, was often responsible for much

bloodshed and endangered species habitat loss in the Congo.

The phrase "maintain standard of living" is often called out as a reason for continuing certain practices. Most people would probably assume that using fewer minerals means lowering our standard of living, but the phrase is carefully neutral. If we find organic alternatives to these materials, our standard of living might even improve. For instance, as *ScienceDaily* has pointed out, carbon nanotubes can exhibit "electrical conductivity as high as copper, thermal conductivity as high as diamond, strength 100 times greater than steel at one sixth the weight, and high strain to failure."[13] Although nanotubes are currently very resource intensive to make, the field is still in its infancy, and carbon to make them is the most common element on earth.

A more immediate example is renewable energy. Over 22,000 lbs of the mining listed above is for energy: oil, gas, and coal. Growing biodiesel from algae to replace petroleum mined from the Earth shows how our standard of living could actually improve with less mining, by having safer vehicle emissions and less CO^2 buildup in the atmosphere. Wind power replacing coal shows how our lives could improve while radically reducing mining impacts. The Mineral Information Institute offers some interesting facts on mineral use in daily life. Did you know your computer screen uses feldspar and your hair tie uses clay and phosphorus?

The USGS has an excellent report, *Materials in the Economy — Material Flows, Scarcity, and the Environment,* with legions of data.[14] While much of it seems grim, it offers hope as well. For instance, today only about 5 percent of material used in the United States was from renewable sources, but in

1900, 40 percent was renewable, showing that it is possible and doesn't even require high technology. Much of the nonrenewable material in use is invisible to us: "Crushed stone and construction sand and gravel make up as much as three quarters (by weight) of new resources used annually." The average person probably doesn't go out and buy gravel; it's mostly used to build and repair the roads you drive on. So one of the simplest way to reduce mining impact is to simply drive less, reducing the need for more or expanded roads, as well as reducing the demand for fossil fuels.

The report also has some good news about metal recycling:

> Recycling contributed 80.7 million tons of metal, valued at about $17.7 billion, or more than half of metal apparent supply by weight in 2000...recycled sources supplied 63 percent of lead; 55 percent of iron and steel; 50 percent of titanium; more than 30 percent of aluminum, copper, and magnesium; and more than 20 percent of chromium, tin, and zinc.

Peak Minerals

How much mining can the Earth sustain? The answer is not quite zero, as you might think from the Natural Step principle (page 198). Mineral compounds can slowly return to the Earth's crust on their own. Steel can rust away in a few decades, and aluminum takes between 200 and 500 years to degrade. Estimates vary widely, but a page by the state of Nevada has a well-illustrated list of how quickly various materials degrade — compare an aluminum can's degradation rate (500 years) to a Styrofoam cup ("May be around forever").[15] But minerals and ores are clearly a nonrenewable resource on the time scale of our lives —

they are not current solar income by any stretch of the imagination. Some researchers have begun to argue that just as we are hitting peak oil, we will soon be hitting peaks for other mined resources, and have already passed peaks for some. Italian chemist Ugo Bardi published a research paper, "The Oil Drum: Europe," whose abstract follows:[16]

> We examined the world production of 57 minerals reported in the database of the United States Geological Survey (USGS). Of these, we found 11 cases where production has clearly peaked and is now declining. Several more may be peaking or be close to peaking. Fitting the production curve with a logistic function, we see that, in most cases, the ultimate amount extrapolated from the fitting corresponds well to the amount obtained, summing the cumulative production so far and the reserves estimated by the USGS. These results are a clear indication that the Hubbert model is valid for the worldwide production of minerals and not just for regional cases. It strongly supports the concept that "peak oil" is just one of several cases of worldwide peaking and decline of a depletable resource. Many more mineral resources may peak worldwide and start their decline in the near future.

The resources Bardi and co-author Marco Pagani found to be peaking were mercury, tellurium, lead, cadmium, potash, phosphate rock, thallium selenium, zirconium, rhenium, and gallium — most of which are key components in computers and other electronics. How serious is "peak minerals"? *New Scientist* released a report with excellent charts plotting expected years to depletion for twenty of the most-used minerals, as well as the percent recycled, the amount an average US consumer will use in their life, and a map of the world showing where the various metals are mined.[17] According to the report, copper has between thirty-eight and sixty-one years left before depletion, indium (used in LCD monitors) has between four and thirteen years, silver (used in catalytic converters and jewelry) has between nine and twenty-nine years, and antimony (used in flame retardants and some drugs) has between thirteen and thirty years. The market already knows this in a dim way: Copper prices have tripled in the past decade, and as the report points out, indium is even worse: "In January 2003 the metal sold for around $60 per kilogram; by August 2006 the price had shot up to over $1000 per kilogram."

As with peak oil, the economics of this situation both help and hurt. They hurt because higher ore prices make it more economically viable to do larger-scale mining at lower rates of return, causing more destruction per unit of product. The economics of scarcity help because mining for virgin materials becomes more expensive, so alternative materials and recycling become more economical by comparison. British geologist Hazel Prichard discovered in 1998 that platinum dust from cars' catalytic converters covers roadsides in the United Kingdom in high enough concentrations that sweeping up road dust and extracting the platinum will soon be cheaper than mining and refining the ore. The *New Scientist* article says she and fellow researcher Lynne Macaskie are "developing a bacterial process that will efficiently extract the platinum from the dust." The report also suggests pulling copper pipes out of buildings and replacing them with plastic, effectively mining buildings.

Greening the Mining Industry

How sustainably run are mines? It varies wildly, both by country and by industry. A 2006 *Geotimes* article described the current situation in the United States as being a mess, but with several other countries doing well:[18]

> The current impasse between environmentalists and industry, however, is unique among advanced nations. The US conflict contrasts especially sharply with policy in Sweden, where a dynamic mining and mineral industry coexists with a strong national environmental commitment in a high-wage, strong economy. The Swedish policy model, as well as Canadian and Finnish models, may not be applicable to current US sociopolitical conditions, but they offer important perspectives on potential ways to break out of the current standoff.

Pressure is being put on mining companies, thanks to organizations like the Environmental Working Group, which makes information more available to activists. They have a Google Maps mashup of the western United States that maps literally hundreds of thousands of mines and mining claims; existing mines can even be viewed in Google Earth on its 3D terrain. They point out that there are "815 mining claims within 5 miles of Grand Canyon National Park." And the Grand Canyon is hardly unique: Arches, Dinosaur, Capitol Reef, Death Valley, and many other parks are in areas where mining is the backbone of the local economy.

Mining is already getting cleaner, though it has a long way to go. In 2000, the US EPA's Toxics Release Inventory[19] listed metal mining as being responsible for a whopping 47 percent of all toxic waste released by industry in the country; their 2005 report listed metal mining at just 27 percent. And it's not due to other industries dumping more; 2000 releases were a nationwide total of 7.1 billion pounds, while 2005's total was 4.34 billion pounds, over 30 percent less. A significant amount of this savings is no doubt due to offshoring environmental burdens to mines and manufacturing facilities in poorer countries, but a significant amount is due to better practices as well, and recycling is growing. The *Encyclopedia of Earth* talks about one of the world's largest mining companies, Noranda, Inc., of Canada, which investigated ways to make their smelters more profitable. Through their study, they found recyclable materials to be as important to the operation's profitability as essential ore concentrates.[20]

Several organizations are dedicated to more sustainable mining. Good Practice (goodpracticemining.org) is an informational Web site. The Initiative for Responsible Mining Assurance is a multisector effort to develop a voluntary system to independently verify compliance with environmental, human rights, and social standards for mining operations. Participants in IRMA include Wal-Mart, World Wildlife Fund, DeBeers Group, Oxfam America, and Tiffany & Co. (responsiblemining.net).

The strategies for sustainable material use are the classics: reduce, reuse, recycle on a massive industrial scale. The USGS report recommends the classic three Rs, as well as remanufacturing (a mixture of reuse and recycling) and landfill mining. Landfills will soon have higher concentrations of useful ores than virgin ground; for some elements, as mentioned above, they already do. We must also look to grow alternatives to many of the materials we now mine. This is where McDonough and Braungart's concepts of "technical nutrients" and "biological nutrients" come into sharp focus.

Technical nutrients are things that at some point needed to be mined, but in the long run must be used in a closed loop, not confounding themselves with biological nutrients (because separate they are useful, but conjoined they are garbage). Biological nutrients are those that can be farmed or otherwise grown, but these also need to not exceed the available land's carrying capacity, so even if we could replace all minerals in industry with functional equivalents grown from organic matter, it still might not be the wisest course of action. The wisest course is to close the resource loops and keep them easily separable, so all ingredients can retain their value. Both sustainable harvests and closed-loop recycling are needed to create a viable system. There is no single answer to meet all needs.

In 1900, 40 percent of US materials used were renewable; now the standard of living is much higher, but renewable materials have fallen to 5 percent. In many poor rural parts of India and Africa today, the vast majority of materials used are renewable and local, but the standards of living are low, and much of the younger generation leaves for cities when given the opportunity. We must find ways to make the best of the resources we have, to create a universal quality of life even higher than today's and shared by all.

Article by Jeremy Faludi. Original article concept appeared on worldchanging.org, December 25, 2007.

SPC Member: Crown Holdings, Inc. (Crown)

Their SuperEnd® can is an innovative lightweight aluminum beverage can. This redesign of the classic pop-top can not only reduced source materials required by 10% compared with competitive ends, the new product offers improvements to pourability, drinkability, ease of opening, and appearance — all of which makes this alternative more attractive to customers, the company and, the environment.

Glass

Recycling 1 ton of glass saves

— 42 Kwh of energy

— 5 gallons of oil

— 714,000 BTUs of energy

— 7.5 pounds of air pollutants from being released

— 2 cubic yards of landfill space

Statistics from recyclebank.com.

Benefits at a glance

— Readily recycled in nearly all markets

— Can be recycled into same forms nearly indefinitely

— Moisture and gas impervious; chemically inert

Primary uses for packaging: preserved food, beverage containers.

Drawbacks at a glance

— Nonrenewable, though fairly abundant

— The heaviest option compared to alternatives for typical uses, resulting in additional environmental impacts associated with transportation energy

— In the United States, low recovery rate of a highly recyclable material

— Glass contamination of other recyclable materials, particularly single-stream recovery

Typical toxins: The majority of human and environmental health issues are associated with the manufacture of glass, furnace emissions, coatings, and process chemicals.

Energy use impacts: Pollution and collection create impacts from natural gas use for manufacture, and additional environmental impacts are associated with higher transportation energy demands due to weight issues.

Overview

New glass is made from four main ingredients: sand, soda ash, limestone, alumina (bauxite), and other additives for coloring or special treatments. This mix of soda-lime-silica is the classic composition of container glass. There is no shortage of these raw materials at this time. But they have to be dug from the ground, which is harmful to the environment if traditional mining methods are used.

Glass is an easy material to recycle. It can be recycled again and again without losing its clarity or purity, and making new glass from recycled cullet uses less energy than making new glass from scratch. Currently, though, there are issues around the supply of glass collected for recycling not being able to keep up with the demand for new recycled glass products. Having to import cullet from thousands of miles away would negate any energy savings gained by not making new glass from raw materials more locally available.

A major barrier to recycling glass in many markets is the shortage of appropriate glass colors to match the materials flows demand for a given economy. For example, the United Kingdom has particular issues that would be different than one would find in the United States.

Glass materials flows and issues for the United Kingdom

Clear glass: A major barrier to recycling glass in the United Kingdom is the shortage of clear cullet available to be recycled. The United Kingdom produces plenty of clear glass, but exports a lot of it as spirit bottles. Clear glass in the United Kingdom is constantly leaving its market and never accumulating long enough to meet local demand.

Green glass: By comparison, the United Kingdom imports a large amount of green glass but do manage to recycle it — so the green bottles made in the United Kingdom contain at least 85 percent recycled green glass. The surplus is either exported to make new green bottles or is used in alternative markets within the United Kingdom, such as in fiberglass insulation or brick manufacture or as filtration media in effluent treatment works.

In contrast to the difficulties and impacts associated with manufacturing and recycling glass, refill programs using glass containers coupled with regular pickup of empties and drop off of refilled product (extended producer responsibility systems) have a long history of success. Once transportation and remanufacture energy are taken out of the equation, glass really is an ideal material choice.

The Beer Store in Ontario, Canada, is happy to talk about their global leadership in the practice of extended producer responsibility. Their program is designed to take back all the packaging material they sell — from paperboard to glass bottles to bottle caps, and then either recycle or reuse it. Through their impressive packaging and recovery system, The Beer Store aims to recover 100 percent of beer packaging sold in Ontario. Cartons, bags, plastic bottles, and other associated materials are welcomed back at The Beer Store. With environmental leadership as part of their core values, in eighty years, they have diverted approximately 70 billion beer bottles from

Ontario landfill sites — enough to stretch to the moon and back about twenty-five times.

The Beer Store was the first company to be presented with Canada's Eco Logo award, given for its efficient environmental package management systems.

How they earned their recognition:

— The Beer Store pioneered the first returnable bottle system in 1927 — a user-pay system paid for by beer customers, for beer consumers.

— The Beer Store's system wide recovery and reuse rate of 99 percent for the industry standard bottle, which is then reused twelve to fifteen times.

— The Beer Store takes back everything it sells: bottle caps, photodegradable high-cone plastic rings, PET bottles, plastic bags, and all of the different types of paper and paperboard used.

— The Beer Store picks up over 100,000 metric tons (220,462,262 lbs) of beer packaging each year from over 17,500 licensed establishments.

To read more, go to their Web site at thebeerstore.ca.

Energy Changes Everything

There are nearly endless variables to consider when choosing a packaging material. But perhaps the one attention area designers can immediately sell and bank on is energy. Energy in the equation (and so greenhouse gas impacts and bottom line energy costs) changes everything.

Milk comes in a variety of packages with differing energy needs: Shelf-stable aseptic packaging requires no refrigeration before opening, while round-trip milk jugs provide local consumers energy-efficient material use. No one package is perfect, all have advantages and disadvantages.

Understanding Energy

Embodied energy refers to the quantity of energy required to manufacture and supply to the point of use a product, material, or service. When reviewing options, these are a few ideas to help weigh not only materials choices, but structure options:

Weight: Heavier weight means more transport energy costs. If the transport fuel is a fossil fuel, every gram of extra weight means that much more energy is needed to move the thing at every point of its life from manufacture through end of life. Concentrates are a great example of products that deliver all of the use at a fraction of the weight. Why spend the fuel, time, and money, to add and move water around when the consumer can do that at the point of use?

Size: How many units will fit on a pallet? Pallet optimization has impacts for both transport energy demands (how many per truckload), as well as warehouse space/energy demands. How many will fit on a shelf? Must the product also inflate retailer, and end user's space/energy demands? Concentrates are a great example of products that deliver all of the use at a fraction of the size. Again we ask: Why spend the fuel, time, and money, to add and move water around, when the consumer can do that at the moment of use?

Distance: The farther a good has to travel from materials sources, to manufacturer, to buyer, the more energy it uses. A Leopold Center study of energy use in the food system[21] found that, for a Des Moines, Iowa, processing plant to make a tub of strawberry yogurt, using current food distribution systems brings in strawberries from California (1,811 miles), milk from out of state (205 miles), and sugar from Minnesota and North Dakota (524 miles).

A total of 2,540 miles was burned to make a product that could have been produced from local sources.

Quality: Create goods that will do the job well. How many "cheap" products have we all purchased to meet a need — with all the associated manufacturing, transport, and disposal impacts attached to each purchase — when one really good, but more expensive version would have served in place of the string of broken wannabes?

Efficiency: Over 90 percent of the energy that goes into an incandescent bulb is converted to heat energy. That's why a child's toy oven functions with only a 100-watt bulb as its heat source. Compact fluorescent lamps (CFLs) deliver the same light output as incandescent lightbulbs but use 75 percent less energy. A typical household can save $200 to $500 in a year by switching to more energy-efficient lighting and appliances.

Energy use: For packaging this would mean the total amount of energy to deliver a good. An example of a product that eliminates a whole level of energy use is aseptic packaging and canned goods. Milk packaged in aseptic bricks is shelf stable and doesn't require refrigeration for months until opened. Traditionally packaged milk, on the other hand, needs to be refrigerated from the moment it's packaged, and through all of its short shelf life — requiring larger refrigerated storage areas for the store, and more frequent trips to the store for the consumer.

Source: Papermaking is the fourth highest user of electricity in the United States. Mining/drilling impacts, and combustion pollution, from fossil fuel generated electricity is at issue. Because of their high energy demand and to make their processes more sustainable, eco-minded paper mills as well as eco-printers that use their products are switching to windpower, eliminating one of their bigger manufacturing impacts. For areas that use the mining technique known as "mountain topping" — a particularly impactful method that is environmentally destructive with lingering long-term regionally destructive economic impacts, common in the southeast region of the Unites States — power using coal extracted this way carries additional negative perception baggage. Companies in these coal burning regions that go out of their way to generate their energy using renewable sources, would be easily looked on as comparative super champions.[22]

Carbon Accounting

Though the debate about climate change has been going on for decades, 2006 was considered a pivotal year with the publication of the *Stern Review on the Economics of Climate Change*, and the release of Al Gore's film *An Inconvenient Truth*. Now the question of climate change is no longer just a theoretical exercise for the select few — public and business attention finally has become focused on the realities of what that debate means today on a personal level.

Though impacts are felt in countries all around the world, in Australia and the western United States, prolonged drought periods are contributing to public concerns that the climate appears to be getting hotter and drier. In the US Gulf States, Hurricane Katrina and her ever more violent siblings, coupled with the collapse of government support systems to deal with the magnitude of these disasters, has the public demanding a deeper look at the causes of hurricane intensity and frequency.

According to the Stern Review

The damages from climate change will accelerate as the world gets warmer. Higher temperatures will increase the chance of triggering abrupt and large-scale changes.

— Warming may induce sudden shifts in regional weather patterns such as the monsoon rains in South Asia or the El Niño phenomenon — changes that would have severe consequences for water availability and flooding in tropical regions and threaten the livelihoods of millions of people.

— A number of studies suggest that the Amazon rainforest could be vulnerable to climate change, with models projecting significant drying in this region. One model, for example, finds that the Amazon rainforest could be significantly and possibly irrevocably damaged by a warming of 2 to 3°C.

— The melting or collapse of ice sheets would eventually threaten land that today is home to one in every twenty people.

While there is much to learn about these risks, the temperatures that may result from unabated climate change will take the world outside the range of human experience. This points to the possibility of very damaging consequences. The impacts of climate change are not evenly distributed — the poorest countries and people will suffer earliest and most. If and when the damages appear it will be too late to reverse the process. Thus we are forced to look a long way ahead.[23]

Concerns over how to deal with these issues quickly have given raise to an ever-growing selection of schemes promoting carbon offsets. These plans use a variety of methods including using monies collected to help support renewable energy develop-ment and implementation; carbon sequestering, helping to make old growth forests economically attractive left intact; and carbon trading, allowing eco-forward companies a chance to recoup more quickly the costs of their improvement investments.

Many companies around the world have announced plans to become carbon neutral. In January 2007, United Kingdom retail giant Tesco, announced its intention to put carbon labels on all of their products to provide information on their carbon footprint from production to consumption. In the Unite States, Frito-Lay has added the Green-e logo, a designation from the Center for Resource Solutions used to indi-cate that a product offsets its carbon emissions, across the full line of its SunChips snacks.

One of the problems facing companies trying to meet various guidelines and scorecards, and then adding carbon issues into the mix, are the complexi-ties involved in minimizing the environmental impacts of a product. There is no straight line to "goodness" and there may be significant trade-offs to weigh between recycling or energy consumption that look good on a particular scorecard, but overall may have impacts that are outside of that metric. Recycling for example, a common feature for favor-able scores, is only part of the story, and must not be considered in isolation. Recycling, like any decision variable must be weighed as part of a comprehensive environmental objective to achieve goals for reduc-tions in pollution, greenhouse gas emissions, and better resource management throughout the whole product and packaging life cycle.

Carbon labels have received a lot of attention in recent years. A 2007 study from L.E.K. Consulting in the United Kingdom found that more than half of UK consumers want information about the carbon foot-print of the products they purchase — with nearly half indicating a willingness to switch to brands with smaller carbon footprints.[24] In July 2007, Carbonfund.org launched a CarbonFree Certified Product label that companies can use to promote their products as being climate neutral.

Paying attention to carbon impacts needs to be added to the overall impact strategy with the same care as any impact variable. As Timberland found out, impacts are complicated to calculate, as well as to articulate to give a complete picture. Today, Timberland footwear carries a "nutrition facts" label detailing the product's impacts:

— Manufactured Section: gives the name and factory location where the product was made as a tool for maintaining production transparency

— Environmental Impact: reports how much energy was needed to produce Timberland footwear and the amount of Timberland's energy generated from renewable resources such as the sun, wind, or water

— Community Impact: details the percentage of factories assessed by the company's code of con-duct standards, the percentage of children in the workforce, and total number of hours Timberland employees volunteer in the community

To measure the true environmental costs of Timberlands's products, though, one would have to go all the way back to the cow that supplied the leather. In fact, Timberland found the vast majority of their product's carbon footprint is accrued before its shoes are even produced.

At this point there are a variety of carbon offset schemes, but no comprehensive regulation.

In a July 13, 2007 article, "How to Green Your Carbon Offsets," Team TreeHugger asks:

> What will your offsets go to? Are their projects certified? Does any independent authority audit them to ensure your money is going to the projects mentioned in the marketing? Do they have a solid client list? Contact some of those clients and see what they thought of the service? What is the price per ton? How does this compare? Do they use any recognized guidelines to prepare their calculations? Are your funds supporting new projects, not "business as usual"? As *The Guardian* newspaper put it, "There is nothing but the customer's canniness to stop a company claiming to be running a scheme which does not exist; claiming wildly exaggerated carbon cuts; selling offsets that have already been sold; charging hugely inflated prices.[25]

For more information on carbon offsets, review *Clean Air-Cool Planet Guide: A Consumer's Guide to Retail Carbon Offset Providers.*

Printing

This section on printing is offered by the Organic Design Operatives (themightyodo.com).[26] Though not all packaging is paper based, most have printing of some sort, and even glass and metal packaging commonly uses paper labels. This overview of printing in a sustainability context could apply to any project, and is a solid look at the considerations to be made at every step of the process.

1. Define the Problem

Begin by answering a few questions about the project. Purpose (inform, sell, and so on)? Audience (social, economic, and so on)? Restrictions (budget, format, regulations, and so on)? Special requirements? Useful lifespan (a week, a year, and so on)? Quality of life (durable vs. consumable, fixed vs. changeable, and so on)?

2. Plan the Life cycle

Everything you create has a past, present, and future. Now that you have defined the problem, begin planning for a closed-loop, sustainable life cycle.

Resources. Source reclaimed (used, recycled) and renewable (for any virgin content) resources that are

It was a restaurant, now it's just a roof. Biloxi, MS.
Photo: Jeremy Faludi

sustainably managed. Resources should also be recoverable after end use. Don't just use recyclable materials; use materials that actually will *be* recycled in the target market.

Production. Seek out socially responsible manufacturers that utilize clean production technologies, resources, and practices. Choose manufactures that are nearest the end user when practical to reduce transportation impacts.

End Use. Seek out the cleanest, most efficient, and most effective solution.

Recovery. Begin to plan for your project's end of life. Think about how you can enable end users to complete the cycle by designing for resource recovery (i.e., label recyclable materials and include any needed instructions).

3. Design the Solution

As a designer, you can have far more positive impact at the creative stage, long before anything is recycled.

Start with a powerful idea. Creative, deliberate solutions can be far more effective than those that rely solely on the excessive use of resources.

Carefully select a medium/format. Take what you have learned from defining the problem and brainstorm the most effective and least resource-intensive medium/format in which to solve it. For instance, a problem may resolved just as well with an e-mail as with a postcard. For packaging do you really need a polybag with header card to sell a T-shirt, or would a reusable hanger work just as well?

Estimate scale based on content. Using volume of content as a guide, determine the approximate scale of a chosen format. For example, it would be wasteful to design a twenty-four-page brochure for twelve pages of content. For packaging, avoid overpackaging. The consumer doesn't appreciate it, and it just adds cost.

Determine actual size. Working backward from stock press sheet sizes, determine the most efficient final dimensions for your design. Minimize trim waste through imposition or by avoiding bleeds. Ask your printer for help with special requirements like gripper margins, grain direction, and the like. For packaging, consider transport needs from the start of the product design process. Can we make the product just a bit stronger to avoid exponentially larger packaging to move too fragile an item?

Use resources wisely. Utilize both sides of paper, limit number of inks and ink coverage, gang projects together on press when possible, and so on. Choose materials appropriate to function, life span, and quality of life.

Maximize functionality. Combine otherwise separate functions into a single piece (i.e., postcards with a built-in, pop-out Rolodex card and brochures that incorporate a mailing panel — eliminating the need for an envelope). Expand function by building in a second use (i.e., paper swatch books that also function as sketchbooks). Extend the useful life of a piece by designing it for reuse. Remember that reusable materials must also be recovered at the end of their useful life. For packaging, refillable milk bottles are the classic reuse success story. But be careful not to simply make overbuilt one-way packaging. To be reusable, it needs to make sense to reuse.

Avoid frills. Don't add extras (i.e., foil stamping, thermography, UV coatings, lamination, varnishes, embossing, and diecuts) unless they will greatly extend the functionality or effectiveness of a design. Extras can be overkill from a design standpoint, consume additional energy and resources, and, in some cases, can be problematic in the resource recovery process.

Work smart. Proof onscreen. Use e-mail, PDFs, and the Internet where appropriate. Reuse office paper: Print on both sides and/or use for scratch paper. Set up an office recycling program. Create an office purchasing policy to buy recycled, recyclable and/or nontoxic products, and energy-efficient computers (Energy Star) and lighting. Turn off idle computers and utilize/support renewable energy sources such as wind and solar. Support vendors that do the same.

4. Specify Resources

Paper. Specify papers high in post consumer recycled content (non-deinked when possible) and processed chlorine free (PCF). Any virgin content should be derived from tree-free fibers (kenaf, hemp, and the like) and whitened totally chlorine free (TCF). Look for papers that are produced cleanly (i.e., renewable wind energy).

Ink. Specify vegetable oil-based, low-VOC (volatile organic compound) inks. Avoid colors that contain heavy metal compounds. Use recycled inks where possible.

Adhesives and bindings. Specify pasted binding (similar to saddle stitch binding but without metal staples, which must be removed during recycling) over saddle stitching when possible. Ask your printer to source paste that is water based, vegetable based, nontoxic, and that disperses in water. When saddle stitching is a must, consider specifying one instead of two staples. Keep in mind, anything made from metal must be mined and processed, so should be used sparingly. When perfect binding is appropriate, specify water-soluble over solvent-based glues, hot-melts, and toxic vinyl acetates (found in many padding compounds).

Labels. Gum arabic is an alternative to crack-and-peel pressure-sensitive adhesives that may hinder recycling and employ a throwaway, silicone-coated liner sheet. Gum arabic, the same type of compound used on the back of lick-and-stick stamps, is water soluble, starch based, and easily removed during recycling.

5. Get It Produced

Preparation. Work closely with your vendors throughout the process. A well-conceived production plan minimizes surprises, waste, added costs, and mistakes.

Before sending your final design out to be produced, create a list of instructions and specifications. This gives you a chance to double check dimensions, ink, paper, and so on, while also providing the vendor with clear written instructions.

Carefully determine quantities to be printed in order to avoid overruns or reprints. Miscalculation here can be a large source of waste.

Printing. Work with certified printers (PIMN.org or ISO 14000). These printers go beyond compliance with environmental, health, and safety requirements to reduce waste and pollution in day-to-day printing plant operations.

Reduce the negative impacts of lithographic printing: dryography (waterless), computer-to-plate (CTP), direct imaging (DI), vegetable-based, low-VOC press washes.

Specify only when it greatly increases functionality or effectiveness: embossing. die-cutting engraving.

Avoid whenever possible, may make paper difficult to recycle: spot varnish (specify vegetable-based) aqueous coating.

Avoid altogether, generally renders paper unrecyclable: foil stamping, lamination, UV coating, thermography

6. Send It Out

Use targeted, updated mailing lists and request address corrections.

Avoid air and rush delivery when possible.

Specify addresses to be applied directly onto pieces via ink-jet. Demand water-based, high-resolution ink jet technology over solvent-based ones.

7. Follow Up

Seek feedback. Talk to your client, vendors, and so on, about what was successful and what could be done better next time.

Stay up to speed. To make wise choices, you must know your facts and options.

Keep learning. Get active, and exchange information with others; support and participate in relevant organizations — like ODO!

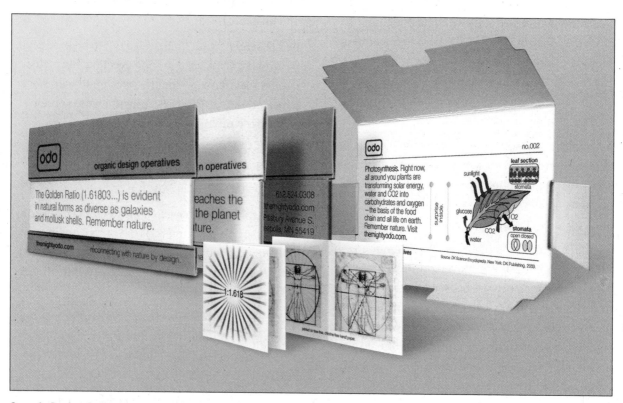

**Organic Design Operatives: Pea Pod business cards — recycled, recyclable, but way too cool to throw out.
Awards: *Print Magazine* 2006 Regional Design Annual, AIGA/MN Green Leaf 2006.**

The Wonderful World of Waste

The Economic and Environmental Benefits of Recycling

Recycling creates economic and environmental benefits at the local, state, and national levels. National Recycling Coalition's Recycling Economic Information Project demonstrated the importance of the recycling and reuse industries to our national economy.

Consider these facts:

Well-run recycling programs cost less to operate than waste collection, landfilling, and incineration.

The more people recycle, the cheaper it gets.

Two years after calling recycling a $40 million drain on the city, New York City leaders realized that a redesigned, efficient recycling system could actually save the city $20 million and they have now signed a twenty-year recycling contract.

Recycling helps families save money, especially in communities with pay-as-you-throw programs.

Well-designed programs save money. Communities have many options available to make their programs more cost-effective, including maximizing their recycling rates, implementing pay-as-you-throw programs, and including incentives in waste management contracts that encourage disposal companies to recycle more and dispose of less.

Recycling creates 1.1 million US jobs, $236 billion in gross annual sales, and $37 billion in annual payrolls.

Public sector investment in local recycling programs pays great dividends by creating private sector jobs. For every job collecting recyclables, there are twenty-six jobs in processing the materials and manufacturing them into new products.

Recycling creates four jobs for every one job created in the waste management and disposal industries.

Thousands of US companies have saved millions of dollars through their voluntary recycling programs. They wouldn't recycle if it didn't make economic sense.

Recycling is one of America's best environmental success stories. Consider these facts:

Recycling results in a net reduction in ten major categories of air pollutants and eight major categories of water pollutants.

Recycling saves energy, which can help the United States reduce its dependence on foreign oil.

The amount of lost energy from throwing away aluminum and steel cans, plastic PET and glass containers, newsprint, and corrugated packaging each year is equivalent to the annual output of fifteen medium-sized coal power plants.

Increasing the recycling rate of these commodities by 10 percent would save enough energy annually to heat 74,350 million American homes, provide the required electricity for 2.5 million Americans, and save about $771 million in avoided costs for barrels of crude oil.

Manufacturing with recycled materials, with very few exceptions, saves energy and water and produces less air and water pollution than manufacturing with virgin materials.

It takes 95 percent less energy to recycle aluminum than it does to make it from raw materials. Making recycled steel saves 60 percent, recycled newspaper 40 percent, recycled plastics 70 percent, and recycled glass 40 percent. These savings far outweigh the energy created as by-products of incineration and landfilling.

A national recycling rate of 30 percent reduces greenhouse gas emissions as much as removing nearly 25 million cars from the road.

Recycling conserves valuable natural resources, which are often dangerous to obtain, while protecting natural habitats and ecosystems.

Mining is the world's deadliest occupation. On average, forty mine workers are killed on the job each day, and many more are injured. Recycling reduces the need for mining.

In the United States, processing minerals contributes almost half of all reported toxic emissions from industry, sending 1.5 million tons of pollution into the air and water each year. Recycling can significantly reduce these emissions.

Recycled paper supplies more than 37 percent of the raw materials used to make new paper products in the United States. Without recycling, this material would come from trees.

Every ton of recycled newsprint or mixed paper is the equivalent of twelve trees. Every ton of recycled office paper is the equivalent of twenty-four trees.

When one ton of steel is recycled, 2,500 pounds of iron ore, 1,400 pounds of coal, and 120 pounds of limestone are conserved.

"The Economic and Environmental Benefits of Recycling" was provided with permission by the National Recycling Coalition.

The National Recycling Coalition (NRC) is a 501(c)(3) membership organization of recycling professionals and advocates from every region of the country, in every sector of the waste reduction field. Local

recycling coordinators, state and federal regulators, corporate environmental managers, environmental educators and advocates, and waste management professionals are all members of NRC. Founded in 1978, NRC's objective is to eliminate waste and promote sustainable economies through advancing sound management practices for raw materials in North America. NRC hosts the Annual Congress & Exposition each year in a different city to bring its members and others together for several days of outstanding educational and networking opportunities. NRC also works closely with nineteen affiliated state and regional recycling organizations around the nation.

Greenhouse Gas Emissions and Waste

Currently the US Environmental Protection Agency (EPA) defines four main stages of product life cycles, all of which provide opportunities for GHG emissions and/or offsets: raw material acquisition, manufacturing, recycling, and waste management.[27]

Raw material acquisition. All products use inputs of raw materials, such as metal ore, petroleum, trees, and so on. Extracting and transporting these materials entails the combustion of fossil fuels for energy, which results in carbon dioxide emissions. These fossil fuels must be extracted themselves, which requires additional energy use.

Manufacturing. The processes that transform raw materials into products require the combustion of fossil fuels for energy. Again, energy use produces GHG emissions both directly from the combustion of fossil fuels (mainly in the form of carbon dioxide) and from the upstream energy used to obtain and transport those fossil fuels. In addition, some manufacturing processes release other GHGs, although the type and amount of these emissions are specific to the manufacturing processes for each material.

Recycling. Once a product has been used, it can be recycled into new products. While manufacturing products from recycled inputs still requires energy, fewer raw materials are necessary. GHG emissions are therefore offset by the avoided fossil fuel use for raw material acquisition. In addition, for products that require wood or paper inputs, recycling reduces the need to cut down trees, increasing carbon sequestration in forests.

Waste management. If a product is not recycled at the end of its useful life, it goes through one of three waste management options: composting, combustion, and landfilling. All three use energy for transporting and managing the waste, but they produce additional GHGs to varying degrees.

Composting — an option for organic materials such as food scraps and yard waste — releases some non-biogenic carbon dioxide associated with transporting and turning the compost. However, some of the carbon contained in organic materials is returned and stored in the soil and therefore not released into the atmosphere.

Combustion releases both carbon dioxide and nitrous oxide (a GHG that is 310 times more potent than carbon dioxide). However, some of the energy released during combustion can be harnessed and used to power other processes, which results in offset GHG emissions from avoided fossil fuel use.

Landfilling, the most common waste management practice, results in the release of methane from the anaerobic decomposition of organic materials. Methane is a GHG twenty-one times more potent than carbon dioxide. However, landfill methane is also a source of energy, and some landfills capture and use it for energy. In addition, many materials in landfills do not decompose fully, and the carbon that remains is sequestered in the landfill and not released into the atmosphere.

In an effort to reduce methane emissions from landfills, the US EPA's Landfill Methane Outreach Program (LMOP) is a voluntary assistance program that encourages the recovery and use of landfill gas as an energy resource. LMOP forms partnerships with communities, landfill owners, utilities, power marketers, states, project developers, tribes, and nonprofit organizations to overcome barriers to project development by helping them assess project feasibility, find financing, and market the benefits of project development to the community. The EPA launched LMOP to encourage productive use of this resource as part of the United States's commitment to reduce greenhouse gas emissions under the UN Framework Convention on Climate Change.[28]

Landfill tapping (extracting methane from landfills as fuel) and landfill mining (extracting resources literally "just sitting there") are some of the ways people are starting to look at garbage as a new revenue stream rather than a burden.

In 2002, then New York City Mayor Michael Bloomberg ended New York's costly plastic and glass recycling program in an effort to balance the city's budget. Part of the problem was not the program per se, but the fact that people were participating at a fraction of the level needed for the program to work. Trucks going out to collect were coming back only a quarter full, leaving the city obligated to pay the difference for the cost of operations. Patrick Fitzgerald, then a law student at Fordham University, started wondering how to get people committed to and actually following through on recycling. Fitzgerald concluded: Pay them.

"There are a lot of companies out there, like Starbucks and Home Depot, that are spending a lot of money on environmental programs, but [most] people don't know about them," Fitzgerald said in a December 19, 2006, *Forbes* article. "If I could get those companies to reward households that are recycling, I could increase recycling rates."[29]

After being awarded a $100,000 grant in 2003, Fitzgerald, and high school friend Ron Gonen, launched RecycleBank in Philadelphia. Their goal was very straightforward: to increase municipalities' recycling rates, and lower their landfill costs. To do this they created a scheme where participants could earn coupons good for products from big companies such as Starbucks, Bed Bath & Beyond, Staples and Whole Foods Market, as well as a whole host of smaller participating businesses in the area. To keep the business end sustainable, RecycleBank collects a modest facilitation fee, less than the amount saved by the municipality. The advantages for the community are a healthy and profitable addition to their waste management scheme, as participating customers are highly motivated to recycle consistently seeing their actions converted into goods they would buy anyway. Participating companies get to connect directly with their customers, showing them their positive environmental efforts — reinforcing brand satisfaction and fostering loyalty.

To keep things running smoothly, and on the up and up, RecycleBank's system uses customer tracking collection containers embedded with radio frequency identification tags. At the curbside come pickup time, scanners and scales on the trucks record the weights into RecycleBank's database and credit the contribution into the customer's account. With solid success in their home market, and connection to an impressive array of national retail partners, RecycleBank has begun to look at increasing their service area throughout the northeastern United Sates.

Starch Foam Packing Peanuts

Foamed starch is naturally antistatic, insulating, and shock absorbing, and can be either composted or dissolved in water, making it a preferable replacement to polystyrene foam in most applications.

⑦ Innovation Toolbox

This chapter is a quick and handy, all-in-one-spot, *Field Guide* to ideas and resources referred to throughout this book.

Eco-Packaging in Three Easy Steps

1. Know what the market expects your package to do then exceed those expectations.

   What is your package (and product) saying about how you feel about the consumer, and the environment?

   Is it well researched? Do you really understand your end user as well as competitive market?

2. Know what the package actually needs to do, the Package/Product Team.

   Is it well researched. Do you really understand your supply chain as well as end-of-life and rebirth possibilities?

3. Connect with the consumer and foster brand loyalty with the true quality and deep integrity of your product and message. Empower the consumer to make good decisions that ultimately benefit us all.

Taking the first steps into the future

Definition of Sustainable Packaging

The definition from the Sustainable Packaging Coalition[SM] is just a starting point. To get a copy of their *Design Guidelines for Sustainable Packaging*, visit their Web site at sustainablepackaging.org.

Sustainable packaging

1. Is beneficial, safe & healthy for individuals and communities throughout its life cycle;

2. Meets market criteria for performance and cost;

3. Is sourced, manufactured, transported, and recycled using renewable energy;

4. Maximizes the use of renewable or recycled source materials;

5. Is manufactured using clean production technologies and best practices;

6. Is made from materials healthy in all probable end of life scenarios;

7. Is physically designed to optimize materials and energy;

8. Is effectively recovered and utilized in biological and/or industrial cradle to cradle cycles.

The criteria blend broad sustainability objectives with business considerations and strategies that address the environmental concerns related to the life cycle of packaging. Many working in packaging believe that by successfully addressing these criteria, packaging can be transformed into a Cradle to Cradle flow of packaging materials in a system that is economically robust and provides benefit throughout the life cycle — a sustainable packaging system.

Consumer's Shopping List for Positive Change

Consumer advocates use these ideas to help buyers better align their purchases with their ethics.

— **Choose products/packaging that use sustainably renewable or recycled materials first.**

Encourage manufacturers to do the right thing. Help make those eco-choices part of their competitive advantage.

— **Buy locally.**

Help cut down on fuel for transportation, and keep jobs in local communities.

— **Choose products currently recycled in your area, plus look for those that close the loop.**

Stay familiar with the recycling rules, not all areas take all materials. Give preference to products that allow you to close the loop.

— **Use common sense.**

Concentrates are more cost-effective than ready to use. Do you really need cheese in individually wrapped slices? If the package is plastic, is it adding a positive user feature, like shampoo in a shatter-proof bottle for safety? If it looks wasteful, it is.

— **Be an advocate for change.**

If you regularly buy a product that's overall really good, but has un-eco packaging, drop the company a letter. Be an eco-purchasing activist. Tell them you'd like to keep buying their product but their un-eco packaging is making it hard for you. If there's a competing product packaged in a more responsible way, point that out too. Support manufacturers who are proud of their eco efforts (usually printed right on their packaging with more details on their Web site).

At Home

— Encourage family and friends to use eco-alternatives.

— Teach your kids why good buying choices and recycling are important.

At the Office

— Give your company's purchasing department alternatives for more eco-friendly products. Most people will pick a more eco product if given the option, make it easy for them.

Consider life cycle as a means to innovate.

Innovation Heuristics

The systems approach can be used to transform packages from static "things" into flows within natural cycles. This is the basis of innovation in packaging. The flow is the system — from material creation through processing, assembly, sale, and recycling.

Flow is dynamization, making a process more dynamic or flexible. Design the system first, then the package to live within it. This dynamic process starts by dividing the package into pieces (segmentation) and moves through ever finer gradations until packages are replaced by service.

Lightness is closely related to flow. How light can the package be? Can the materials be chosen for the lowest impact?

The Basics of Innovation

Innovation is applied creativity. Some fundamental areas for innovation:

— Location: Where (design, designer, user)

— Direction: Why (what your principles are)

— Materials: What they are (good and bad)

— Cycles: How to use them

— Users: Who they are, their needs, desires, and interactions

Innovation occurs in:

— People: Changing design practice, changing package use

— Process: New ways to produce products and designs

— Products: Providing a function with greater advantage

Innovation can be:

— Incremental: Increasing the good qualities

— Decreasing the bad qualities

— Transformational: Providing a service instead of a product

— Disruptive: Changing the nature of the industry

Movement toward a goal or ideal design can occur at the level of people, process, or products.

At the level of people, a designer needs to know where they are. This can only happen when their methods and means of interaction with the world — the design principles — have been documented.

TECHNIQUE: Create your own set of design principles.

Design Rules

Stopping the use of inappropriate materials: Packages shall not last longer than their contents.

Expand the space of design knowledge: Use the power of teams and diversity.

Use evolution as a guide: Experiment continuously.

All packages live in ecological niches: Listen and be guided by the user.

Move beyond local limits: Harness the power of open source to improve knowledge and networks.

TECHNIQUE: Create your own set of 5 to 7 innovation heuristics and share them.

Jedlička Design Ltd.: Mybackyard Seed Flower

Design Criteria: Create a unique giveaway for trade shows and other promotional opportunities. The solution must reflect the natural purity and respect for the earth that is the core of the mybackyard philosophy. In addition, the item must have uncommon value and a touch of fun.

Solution: The package "flower" opens to reveal five small seed packets inside. Sell-copy on the packets and flower back label outline the mybackyard product line the flower color represents. The back label layout is designed to allow the user to pull the plant marker off the "flower" and use as a ready-labeled garden marker.

Eco-aspects: Plant markers used for the "stem" are sourced from Certified Sustainable Forestry suppliers. "Flowers" and seed packets are made from high post-consumer waste or tree-free papers. The "leaves" are made from natural raffia. All label stocks are recycled paper with no or low-solvent glues as available.

Fabrication of the marker was designed to allow the seed flower to be a low-cost, as-needed promotional item, without huge sunk costs in materials or vendor services.

Use/Reuse: In addition to the intended second life as a garden marker, the "flower" portion can be reused as a mailable "bow" for holiday packages or a wide variety of craft/gift applications.

Ecological Design Principles

Sim van der Ryn

— Solutions grow from place: Keep it local.

— Ecological accounting informs design: Know your material and energy flows.

— Design with nature, not against it

— Everyone is a designer: Take advantage of different viewpoints and knowledge.

— Make nature visible: Let it shine in the design.

John Todd

— The living world is the matrix for all design.

— Design should follow, not oppose, the laws of life.

— Biological equity must determine design.

— Design to reflect bioregionality.

— Base projects on renewable energy.

— Use the integration of living systems to design.

— Design as evolution along with the natural world.

— Design to heal.

Process Innovation

At the level of process, designers need to know material qualities and transformations.

Materials are the world of form. What can be made? What effect does it have? Can it be cycled back into production or left in the environment? Is it possible to let it "evaporate," leaving a web?

Transformations occur via energy, organization, or information. For example, plastics may be transformed with heat and pressure (energy). Companies can be transformed by organization as levels of hierarchy are reduced and interconnections formed. Societies can be transformed as information about the results of processes (industrial or political) are made available.

Package Innovation

At the level of package, designers work with function, system, and end users. To innovate with function, consider providing the package as a service rather than a tangible good.

Systems can be designed to transform the world as it exists, or to create new structures via interconnection. For example, sharing products (like power tools) creates new systems as well as new opportunities for product design.

The practice of user-influenced design requires that a designer forget their unique knowledge and typical techniques and solutions. Instead, explore and define the functions the user is most interested in. Ask the user how they are using the existing product and what features are missing.

Translating themselves into the users' world, a designer can project those needs and desires back to innovate. The users can be interviewed (lead user process) to find out preferences and how they use the package.

Innovations can be classified as quality improvement, new market creation, product range extension, reduction of labor or material or impact or energy, improvements in process, replacing products with services, or adapting to constraints (including regulation).

Consider the time cycle of packaging: Design to represent ideal package life.

Design Mindfulness (Thackara)

— Think about the consequences of design. Most impacts come from design decisions.

— Consider the material and energy flows of package creation and use.

— Give priority to humans.

— Deliver value to people.

— Know that place, time, and cultural differences are positive values.

— Create services, not things.

Other design strategies from Thackara:

Learning from users

Innovation is becoming user led, as exemplified by Wikipedia and open-source solutions. Use that same power of multiple intelligences by being open to design solutions from users. Enlarge design thinking by including the Earth and the end user. Quiet down the "maker" mind-set that knows all about solutions and jumps to design decisions.

Following user needs

Users have needs: How does the package satisfy the need? What is excess? What is an irritant about the package? The creativity tool Triz notes that there are two ways to improve a product: Increase the good factors or decrease the bad factors.

Studying how the package lives

Use context. How is the package used? Get it home, tear it open, toss it? Consider the egg carton with seeds that the kids want to plant. Think they will remember that brand?

Solution space

Enlarge the thinking space in the company. Bring in ideas from Nature (biomimicry). Encourage others to see the package as a spaceship or alien.

Mobility

The Internet has sped up the material economy and its flows. Now the book arrives overnight and goods come from the other coast. On an individual basis, lower environmental impact by thinking more and driving less. From a company perspective the same holds true — this is the lesson from operations research, where the activities at a company are studied to make optimal decisions about resource allocation. Consider where materials come from, the processing location, and how packages get from the company to the next step in the chain. Perhaps transport packaging isn't a layer on top of individual packaging. Make all packaging local.

Locality

Instead of moving things faster, make them closer. Local products are a growing market, and the package is a big part of that. Make the package itself local and it will sell the product (package made right here in Lake Wobegon!). Consciously design for going deeper instead of searching farther. Everything is particular: Design for each situation.

Experiment

Design implies intent, knowing the outcome. Evolution shows that variation and selection lead to variety and solutions that optimize fit into the local environment. Practice experimentation, not design. Start with small experiments. Try several, don't invest everything in one.

Appropriate use case models

Don't design for the worst case — 80 percent of all traffic is local, 15 percent is continental, and 5 percent is international. This holds for everything from cars to the Internet.

Consider the time cycle of packaging: Design to represent ideal package life.

Connect packages, products, and people

Life is structured via connections — use webs, chains, and networks. Most people want big city amenities and a small city pace.

Move from package as product to package as service.

Design Approaches

Design tends to converge on single (point) solutions. Rather, diverge outward from the center (Fuller's dimensions).

Innovation thrives in adversity, creating the most novel adaptations. Design without constraints can look like last year's, or worse, a competitor's box.

Requirement changes are part of life. Learn how to adapt to, and anticipate, changing requirements.

Pay attention to the flow: Packages, information, mindset of peers, changes in the economy. Emulate the flexibility of agile software development strategy. Teams meet every morning for a few minutes to determine top priorities for the day and to track requirements changes.

Design friendly packages — pieces that bring people together and create community.

Move from package as product to package as service.

Consider local exchanges and trades, sharing resources, time, and skills: Extend family to community. Use social and business networks to enlarge your design community.

Design using the universals of culture. If the package seems to fit in one market, consider what other context it is used in. For example, household articles might be used in play and recreation, or creating a beautiful sustainable package could define a new market.

Consider how package designs fit one or more of these areas: Alice Ann Cleaveland, Jean Craven, and Maryanne Danfelser, have extended the work of George Murdock on cultural universals:

1. Material culture: Food, clothing, tools, housing, transportation, possessions

2. Arts, play, and recreation: Music, arts, design

3. Language and nonverbal communication: Books, language, video

4. Social organization: Societies, families, networks.

The information space of the designer and user are different: Consider how to make messages "sticky" and how to represent the message of sustainability.

Design using universal principles

Gravitation: What pulls the package into the Earth? What grounds the design and designer?

Dimension: Spin, radiate/converge, orbit, invert, torque, precess.

Trimtab: Use a small rudder to change the big rudder.

Boundary, flows and loops: Chart package flows.

Use viral or meme design techniques: What would cause a message or package to attach to a user? Consider hook and loop tape or sticky seeds. Similar to these examples, a meme is a behavior or piece of information that passes from one person to another. For memes to propagate, one user exhibits a behavior that others copy. The rapid popularity of white MP3 player earbuds is a good example. The idea jumps from one mind to the next, and behavior is copied and reinforced.

Other Design Strategies

Consider how the user interacts with the package and product. Design as a teacher: How can the package promote learning or literacy in general terms or in sustainability?

Biomimicry asks us to follow Nature by exchanging complication for biological inspiration. Consider the state of the industry: How does it mirror the ecosystem maturity level? Is it a stable mature forest? Or are there open areas where new species are growing rapidly? Should the products (and business) move toward or away from areas like these?

Fair Trade Essentials

Packaging and product are not just about materials alone. Fair Trade is one of the key elements employed by today's sustainability leaders. Ethics-based companies need to be sure their talk is walked. Part of a company's vertical supply chain management system would use fair trade practices to help assure the integrity of a company's message is carried through — from the growers in the field and sewers at the factory to the product on the store shelf. Aligning a company's supply chain on more than a simple materials level can seem like a daunting task at first, but finding ethical suppliers (or helping established suppliers realign their priorities) is getting easier every day, and there are a variety of groups serving various industries to help make the job easier still. Co-op America is one of the oldest and most respected groups working with both businesses and consumers.

Founded in 1982, Co-op America is a nonprofit membership organization working to harness economic power — the strength of consumers, investors, businesses, and the marketplace — to create a socially just and environmentally sustainable society. For a free download of the full version of Co-op America's Guide to Fair Trade go to fairtradeaction.org.

To get started understanding what fair trade is, below is a basic overview of fair trade principles and practices from *Co-op America's Guide to Fair Trade.*

A Fair Price

Fair Trade Certified™ product prices are set by the Fair Trade Labeling Organization. Prices set not only cover the cost of goods, but strive to provide a fair living wage for the people involved in the production process.

Investment in People and Communities

Often Fair Trade producer cooperatives and artisan collectives reinvest their revenues back into their communities — strengthening local businesses, building health clinics and schools, supporting scholarship funds, building housing and providing leadership training and women's programs. All working to build stronger, healthier communities.

Environmental Sustainability

Fair Trade producers respect their natural habitat and are encouraged to use sustainable production methods. Example: Nearly 85 percent of Fair Trade Certified™ coffee is also organic.

Empowering Stakeholders

Fair Trade promotes producer empowerment in their communities and in the global marketplace. For Fair Trade coffee producers, their cooperatives or associations are transparent and democratically controlled by their members. For estate grown products like tea and bananas, Fair Trade provides revenue that is invested in a fund, managed and controlled by the farmers, and used for the interests of the community — providing education, access to health care, and so on.

Empowering Women

Recognizing the untapped potential of all stakeholders in a community, Fair Trade encourages participation by women in local cooperatives and in leadership roles. Fair Trade revenue is also often used to support or promote women's programs.

Direct, Long-Term Relationships

Those who import Fair Trade Certified™ products and other fairly traded goods contribute to the endeavor to establish long-term stable relationships with producer groups. Not only helping to create healthier communities, but providing a more stable, and sustainable economic base allowing entire regions to benefit.

Use the opportunity for creating trust (and foster brand loyalty) by actually being trustworthy.

Overview of Environmental Marketing Claims

Making the FTC *Guides for the Use of Environmental Marketing Claims* easier to understand, TerraChoice Environmental Marketing's Six Sins of Greenwashing is a handy heuristic to keep in mind.

Green-wash (green'wash, -wôsh') — verb: The act of misleading consumers regarding the environmental practices of a company or the environmental benefits of a product or service.

Sin of the Hidden Trade-off

E.g., paper (including household tissue, paper towel and copy paper): "Okay, this product comes from a sustainably harvested forest, but what are the impacts of its milling and transportation? Is the manufacturer also trying to reduce those impacts?"

Emphasizing one environmental issue isn't a problem (indeed, it often makes for better communications). The problem arises when hiding a trade-off between environmental issues.

Sin of No Proof

E.g., personal care products (such as shampoos and conditioners) that claim not to have been tested on animals, but offer no evidence or certification of this claim.

Company Web sites, third-party certifiers, and toll-free phone numbers are easy and effective means of delivering proof.

Sin of Vagueness

E.g., garden insecticides promoted as "chemical-free." In fact, nothing is free of chemicals.

Water is a chemical. All plants, animals, and humans are made of chemicals as are all of our products. If the marketing claim doesn't explain itself ("here's what we mean by 'eco' ..."), the claim is vague and meaningless. Similarly, watch for other popular vague green terms: "nontoxic," "all-natural," "environmentally friendly," and "earth friendly."

Sin of Irrelevance

E.g., CFC-free oven cleaners, CFC free shaving gels, CFC-free window cleaners, CFC-free disinfectants.

Could all of the other products in this category make the same claim? The most common example is easy to detect: Don't be impressed by CFC-free! Ask if the claim is important and relevant to the product. (If a lightbulb claimed water efficiency benefits you should be suspicious.) Comparison shop (and ask the competitive vendors).

Sin of Fibbing

E.g., shampoos that claim to be "certified organic" but for which our research could find no such certification.

When we check up on it, is the claim true? The most frequent examples in this study were false uses of third-party certifications. Thankfully, these are easy to confirm. Legitimate third-party certifiers — EcoLogo,™ Chlorine Free Products Association (CFPA), Forest Stewardship Council (FSC), Green Guard, Green Seal, for example — all maintain publicly available lists of certified products. Some even maintain fraud advisories for products falsely claiming certification.

Sin of the Lesser of Two Evils

E.g. organic tobacco, "green" insecticides and herbicides.

Is the claim trying to make consumers feel "green" about a product category of questionable environmental benefit? Consumers concerned about the pollution associated with cigarettes would be better served by quitting smoking than by buying organic cigarettes. Similarly, consumers concerned about the human health and environmental risks of excessive use of lawn chemicals might create a bigger environmental benefit by reducing their use than by looking for greener alternatives.

Consumers are looking for "good" products; the right labels can help them find them.

Eco Seals, Certifications, and Claims

Compounding the confusion of what is eco is a long list of terms and "seals" both real or created as a marketing tactic with no official meaning. To help better communicate valuable information to the consumer, presented here is a list of commonly accepted terms and certifications in current use for packaging. This is not a complete list by any means, and, like a nutrition facts panel for food, packaging must accurately reflect the contents of any product it contains. This means all product attributes called out on the package must be carefully researched and correctly applied for product disclosure to be in compliance.

This list was compiled from resources found at coopamerica.org/programs/woodwise, ecoLingo.com, and greenerchoices.org. Please visit these Web sites for additional information.

Alternative or Tree-free Papers

Paper made from tree-free fibers include: bagasse, cotton, flax, old jeans, mulberry, kenaf, hemp, agripulp (wheat, rice, corn, straw), banana, and bamboo.

Currently there are no official certifications for tree-free fibers, but certified organic growers for these fibers are becoming more common.

Ancient Forest Friendly (AFF)

Ancient Forest Friendly paper is Totally Chlorine Free (TCF) or Processed Chlorine Free (PCF) and contains only the following fibers: post-consumer recycled fiber (PCR), deinked recycled fiber, agricultural residue or tree-free virgin fiber, or Forest Stewardship Council (FSC) certified virgin fiber.

Biodegradable / Compostable

The Federal Trade Commission (FTC) has issued general guidelines on how the term should be used. Claims that a product is "degradable," "biodegradable," or "photodegradable" mean that the materials will break down and return to Nature within a reasonably short time after customary disposal. What a "reasonably short time" is depends on where the product is disposed. In addition it is important to understand the difference between the terms "biodegradable" and "compostable."

A material labeled as "biodegradable" can be broken down completely under the action of microorganisms into carbon dioxide, water, and biomass. It may take a very long time for a material to biodegrade on its own depending on its environment (e.g., hardwood in an arid area), but it ultimately breaks down completely without human assistance.

Compostable materials biodegrade substantially with the help of specifically designed systems into carbon dioxide, methane, water, and compost biomass, and are a subset of "biodegradable." Compostable materials for packaging usually require the controlled environment of an industrial composting facility. Unlike a backyard/home composter, the industrial composting facility generates much higher temperatures and maintains other specifically monitored conditions that include attention to microbe types, plus carefully controlled moisture and air levels not possible in a home compost setup.

Blue Angel

The Blue Angel is the first and oldest environment-related label in the world for products and services. About 3,850 products and services from approximately 550 label users in Germany and abroad are entitled to bear the Blue Angel seal.

Carbon Labeling

Currently several products have begun carrying a label disclosing their carbon footprint. This disclosure is still in its early stages with several labels in use. Carefully research any label before committing to its use. Carbonfund.org offers a CarbonFree Certified Product label that companies can use to promote their products as being climate neutral.

Contains no CFCs or Other Ozone-Depleting Substances

Regulations in countries around the world, prohibit CFC propellants in aerosols. Companies who wish to use the claim are required to submit a notification to the US EPA for review. There are additional qualifications for adding the claim "or other ozone-depleting substances."

Chasing Arrows

Variations of this world-recognized recycling symbol can provide important information at a glance — or be extremely misleading. Unfortunately the common impression for any item carrying a chasing arrow logo means it is recyclable and has recycled content, when this impression couldn't be further from the truth on both counts.

The chasing arrow logo with the white outlined arrows means that the package may be recycled where appropriate recycling programs exist. The solid version is a variation on the theme and is often shown in green or other colors.

Solid or white arrows in a black circle indicate that the product contains recycled content. Often it will be accompanied by the symbol and a qualifying statement, for example, Contains 50 percent Post Consumer Fiber. When the solid black symbol with white arrows is used alone, it means that the product is 100 percent recycled.

Note: This recycling logo should not be used on printed material unless the paper contains a minimum of 30 percent post-consumer waste.

Additional Chasing Arrow Variations

Since the first recycling symbol was designed and plastic resin codes were introduced, certain groups have developed unique symbols specific to their industry. For example, industry associations for glass, paperboard, and corrugated materials have all developed, and in some cases trademarked, their own recycling symbols. On plastics, the chasing arrow logo is used along with a numbering system (1 to 7) to help designate plastic resins used in the product, but this does not mean the item has been recycled or is even accepted for recycling in the market the product is sold in.

For aluminum, steel, and glass it is common to find a note (X) Recycles. This generic statement can only be used for items that are commonly accepted for recycling, but doesn't provide the buyer with information about recycled content. This can be confusing to the consumer who is being asked to "buy recycled," but is then not provided with an indication of an item having been recycled. Information available to put on packaging is becoming availble now from more forward looking aluminum, steel, and glass suppliers. Buyers whose corporate ethics require transparency and disclosure, should give preference to vendor partners willing to provide recycled content detail.

Chlorine Free (TCF / PCF / ECF)

Totally Chlorine-Free (TCF) is paper made with a bleaching process that uses no chlorine-based compounds; currently TCF refers only to 100% virgin paper.

Processed Chlorine-Free (PCF) is recycled paper made with a bleaching process that uses no chlorine-based compounds.

Certified TCF products require: No chlorine or chlorine compounds were used in the papermaking process, all virgin components need to be certified as total chlorine free and require a chain of custody for all fiber, the mill has no current or pending violations, and the mill does not use old growth forest for any of the virgin pulp. In addition to the TCF criteria, certified PCF products require: the product contains at least 30% post-consumer content, and the mill details post-consumer content sources.

For more information about TCF, PCF, and Chlorine Free Products Association Certification visit their Web site at chlorinefreeproducts.org.

Elemental Chlorine-Free (ECF) is a bleaching process that substitutes chlorine dioxide for elemental chlorine in the bleaching process. Compared to elemental chlorine bleaching processes, ECF bleaching reduces the formation of many chlorinated organic compounds. However, as chlorine is still used, effluent quality remains an issue mills using these processes must address.

Earth Smart or Eco Safe

There are no official definitions for these terms and no organization behind these claims other than the company marketing the product.

EcoLogo

www.ecologo.org

Launched by the Canadian federal government in 1988, EcoLogo has grown to serve buyers and sellers of green products throughout North America and around the world. EcoLogo is North America's oldest environmental standard and certification organization (and the second oldest in the world). It is the only North American standard accredited by the Global Ecolabeling Network as meeting the international ISO 14024 standard for environmental labels.

The Global Ecolabeling Network (GEN) is a nonprofit association of third-party, environmental performance labeling organizations founded in 1994 to improve, promote, and develop the *ecolabeling* of products and services.

Eco Mark

www.ecomark.jp

The Eco Mark program by the Japan Environment Association is managed in accordance with the standards and principles of ISO 14020 and ISO 14024. Certification criteria for every product category has taken the environment and product life cycle (resource extraction, manufacture, distribution, use, disposal, recycling) into consideration.

Environmentally Friendly, Environmentally Preferable, Environmentally Safe

There are no official definitions for these terms and no organization behind these claims other than the company marketing the product.

Fair Trade Certified

www.transfairusa.org

TransFair USA is currently the only certifier of Fair Trade goods in the United States, a nonprofit organization, and one of twenty members of Fairtrade Labeling Organizations International (FLO), the umbrella organization based in Bonn, Germany, that sets certification standards.

Forest Stewardship Council (FSC)

www.fscus.org

The Forest Stewardship Council (FSC) is an independent, nonprofit organization devoted to encouraging the responsible management of the world's forests. The FSC sets high standards that ensure forestry is practiced in an environmentally responsible, socially beneficial, and economically viable way.

The FSC Logo identifies products that contain wood from well managed forests certified in accordance with the rules of the Forest Stewardship Council.

Products carrying the FSC label are *independently certified* to assure consumers those products come from forests that are managed to meet the social, economic and ecological needs of present and future generations.

FSC has offices in more than 46 countries, and provides standard setting, trademark assurance and accreditation services for companies and organizations interested in responsible forestry.

Of interest to those who spec paper and paperboard, FSC certified products are now readily available in North America from both small, independent paper companies and large paper mills.

To view links to certified paper merchants and certified printers with FSC chain-of-custody certification visit the FSC Web site.

Green

There is no official definition for this term and no organization behind this claim other than the company marketing the product.

Green-e
www.green-e.org

Green-e is the United States's leading independent consumer protection program for the sale of renewable energy and greenhouse gas reductions in the retail market. A program of the Center for Resource Solutions, Green-e offers certification and verification of renewable energy and greenhouse gas mitigation products.

Green Seal
www.greenseal.org

Green Seal is an independent organization that certifies a wide variety of environmentally focused products.

The certification criteria are publicly available. The Green Seal logo found on paper products must also contain a description of the basis for certification.

Grüne Punkt / Green Dot
www.gruener-punkt.de

In Germany, producer responsibility has been served through the Green Dot license program in response to the 1991 German Packaging Ordinance. Once packages have served their purpose, manufacturers, vendors, and importers are required to take them back, arrange for eco-friendly recovery, and finally document the procedures involved. The Green Dot logo now used throughout Europe has a different meaning than recycling symbols commonly used in North America. Packages bearing the Green Dot indicates the manufacturer of that package has purchased a license for the right to use the Green Dot trademark and is obliged to abide by the regulations that license imposes, with fees funding the recovery and recycling system. In addition, manufacturers must design to minimize material use, while making recovery easy.

Natural

The USDA has defined this term holding manufacturers accountable for proper use, but does not yet have a verification system. The Natural Products Association (NPA) though, is helping address this issue for personal care products through their certification program.

Nontoxic

The claim "nontoxic" implies that the product will not cause adverse health effects. There are no specific standards for the "nontoxic" claim.

Post-Consumer Recycled (PCR) or Post-Consumer Waste (PCW)

These terms refer to materials that were used for their intended purpose, put into a recycling bin, and then recycled into new products.

Pre-Consumer Waste

This refers to scraps leftover from manufacturing, converting or trimming at point of manufacture, cycled back into the materials stream. It may also include unsold magazines and newspapers. Although the paper and scraps are being reused, this paper has never made the journey to the consumer and back again.

Recyclable

This claim means that products can be collected, separated, and recovered from the solid waste stream and used again, or reused in the manufacture or assembly of another package or product through an established recycling program. Unless otherwise third-party certified, there is no organization behind this claim other than the company marketing the product.

PLEASE RECYCLE is likely to convey to consumers that the package is recyclable, where in fact it may not be. Some labeling laws allow for this statement's use when recycling is available to a majority of areas.

Recycled

Recycled claims may be used for products or packaging that contain either pre-consumer or post-consumer recycled materials. Unless the entire product is recycled, the percent of recycled material should be indicated. However, listing the type of recycled material or the portion of post-consumer content is not required. True recycled content papers though, are defined as papers containing a minimum of 30 percent post consumer fiber by weight.

Currently there is no global consensus on what the term "recycled" means beyond the fact that it may contain either post- or pre-consumer materials. Just saying that a thing is recycled is not enough, as this could vary from 1 percent to 100 percent, but not necessarily from post consumer waste that has actually been recycled. Look for data-sheets that provide the breakdown of post consumer waste and pre-consumer waste content. For paper, those that contain 50 to 100 percent PCW (post-consumer waste) are more significant environmentally.

Sustainable Forestry Initiative (SFI)
www.aboutsfi.org

Sustainable Forestry Initiative (SFI) is composed of members of the American Forest and Paper Association (AF&PA) who are required to comply with SFI defined standards, though currently third-party certification is voluntary, indicators must be certified in order to use the SFI label.

Vegetable-Based Ink / Soy-Based Ink

Vegetable-based ink contains varying amounts of oil from annual crops like soy to replace petroleum in the mix, making it lower in volatile organic compounds (VOCs), which react with other atmospheric pollutants, as well as pose potential health risks from their use. The American Soybean Association has developed standards for soybean content in soy inks and the appropriate use of the Soy Seal or "Printed with Soy Ink" logo.

Materials Choices at a Glance

When it's time to pick materials, just ask yourself these simple questions:

— Are you picking your material because it's the best one for your application or the same as it's always been done?

— Are you choosing materials that have long-term benefits and a solid systems approach, or just grabbing from a list of happy-sounding buzzwords?

— What are the end-of-life materials handling systems currently in place for your product in your target market?

— If you're displacing an actively recycled material, are you ready to help create a new materials stream for your product?

— If you're not able to accept responsibility for the full cycle and true cost of your product, can you provide an alternative that makes better use of the existing infrastructures?

McCormick Distilling: Earth Friendly Distilling Co.

Earth Friendly Distilling's 360 Vodka bottle carries a postage paid envelope that lets customers mail back the flip-top closure used to seal the bottle. The *Close the Loop Program* is part of the company's "green friendly" initiative, and donates one dollar to recognized environmental causes for every closure returned.

Eco-Resources at a Glance

This list is provided by EcoPackaging.net to help you get started finding groups and resources that will go deeper into topic areas that impact packaging. Each is a gateway to even more resources, materials options, and service vendors.

E-News, Online Publications, and Resources

Biomimicry Institute
www.biomimicryinstitute.org

BrandChannel.com
www.brandchannel.com

Carbonfund.org
www.carbonfund.org

Consumer Reports: Greener Choices
www.greenerchoices.org

Cradle to Cradle^{SM}
www.mbdc.com/c2c

EcoPackaging.net
Sustainable packaging, marketing, and print.
www.ecopackaging.net

Environmental Defense
Alliance for Environmental Innovation
www.environmentaldefense.org

GreenBiz
www.greenbiz.com

GreenBlue^{SM}
www.greenblue.org

Green Marketing
www.greenmarketing.com

The LOHAS Journal
www.lohas.com

Natural Step Canada
www.naturalstep.ca

Package Design Magazine
www.packagedesignmag.com

Packaging Digest
www.packagingdigest.com

Packaging Strategies
www.packstrat.com

Packaging World
www.packagingworld.com

Rocky Mountain Institute
www.rmi.org

Roper Report
National Report Cards on Environment Attitudes, Knowledge and Behavior
www.neefusa.org

Sustainable is Good
www.sustainableisgood.com

Sustainable Packaging Coalition^{SM}
www.sustainablepackaging.org

Treehugger
www.treehugger.com

Watershed Media
www.watershedmedia.org

LCA/LCI Tools and Databases

UNEP International Life Cycle Partnership for a Sustainable World
www.lcinitiative.unep.fr

MERGE database
www.sustainablepackaging.org

NREL U.S. Life-Cycle Inventory Database
www.nrel.gov/lci

SimaPro
www.simapro.com

Sustainable Minds
www.sustainableminds.com

Wal-Mart Stores, Inc.
Package Modeling
www.packagemodeling.com

Materials

Glass

Glass Packaging Institute
www.gpi.org

Metals

Aluminum Association
www.aluminum.org

American Iron and Steel Institute
Steel Packaging Council
www.steel.org

Steel Recycling Institute (SRI)
www.recycle-steel.org

Paper and Paperboard

Tools

Calculate the environmental impacts
of your paper choice.
www.environmentaldefense.org/papercalculator

Co-op America Wood Wise Project
www.coopamerica.org/programs/woodwise

Ecological Guide to Paper
www.celerydesign.com

Rainforest Alliance
A SmartGuide to Paper & Print Sources
www.rainforest-alliance.org/programs/forestry

Groups

100% Recycled Paperboard Alliance
www.rpa100.com

Chlorine Free Products Association
www.chlorinefreeproducts.org

Corrugated Packaging Council (CPC)
www.corrugated.org

Environmental Paper Network
www.environmentalpaper.org

Forest Certification Resource Center
www.certifiedwood.org

Forest Stewardship Council (FSC)
www.fscus.org

International Molded Pulp
Environmental Packaging Association
www.impepa.org

Sustainable Forestry Initiative (SFI)
www.sfiprogram.org

Technical Association of the Pulp
and Paper Industry (TAPPI)
www.tappi.org

Plastics: Biodegradable, Biobased, Recycled

Association of Postconsumer Plastic Recyclers
www.plasticsrecycling.org

Biodegradable Plastics Society
www.bpsweb.net

Biodegradable Products Institute (BPI)
www.bpiworld.org

BioEnvironmental Polymer Society (BEPS)
www.beps.org

Biopolymer.net
www.biopolymer.net

Center for Biodegradable Polymer Research
www.bprc.caeds.eng.uml.edu

National Association for PET Container
Resources (NAPCOR)
www.napcor.com

Packaging and Packaging Design

IoPP Sustainable Packaging Technical Committee
www.iopp.org

Packaging Association of Canada
www.pac.ca

Sustainable Packaging Alliance (SPA)
www.sustainablepack.org

Sustainable Packaging Coalition^{SM}
www.sustainablepackaging.org

Printing and Print Design

American Institute of Graphic Arts
www.sustainability.aiga.org

PIM Great Printer Environmental Initiative
www.pimn.org/environment/greatprinter.htm

Printer's National Environmental Assistance Center
www.pneac.org

Institute for Sustainable Communication
www.sustaincom.org

Organizations

Governmental

Environnement Canada
www.ec.gc.ca

European Commission Environmental
   Marketing Claims Guidelines (EU)
www.europa.eu.int

US Environmental Protection Agency
www.epa.gov

Nongovernmental (NGO)

Carbonfund
www.Carbonfund.org

Caux Round Table / Principles for Business
www.cauxroundtable.org

Center for a New American Dream
www.ibuydifferent.org

Earth 911
www.earth911.org

Environmental Defense
Alliance for Environmental Innovation
www.environmentaldefense.org

Environmental Paper Network
www.environmentalpaper.org

GrassRoots Recycling Network
www.grrn.org

GreenBlue^{SM}
www.greenblue.org

International Standards Organization
www.iso.org

o2 International Network for Sustainable Design
www.o2.org

Rainforest Action Network
www.ran.org

Rocky Mountain Institute
www.rmi.org

Union of Concerned Scientists (UCS)
www.ucsusa.org

World Resources Institute
www.wri.org

Sustainable Business

Businesses for Social Responsibility
www.bsr.org

Center for Environmental Leadership in Business
www.celb.org

Ceres
www.ceres.org

Ethical Consumer
www.ethicalconsumer.org

GreenBiz
www.greenbiz.com

Natural Capital Institute
www.naturalcapital.org

Sustainability Consultants

Jedlicka Design Ltd.
www.jedlicka.com

Organic Design Operatives
www.themightyodo.com

J. Ottman Consulting
www.greenmarketing.com

Techlogic, Inc.
ISO 14000 Consulting
www.techlogicinc.com

Sustainability Associates
www.SustainabilityAssociates.us

Sustainability Education

Design:Green
www.designgreen.org

IDSA Ecodesign
www.idsa.org/whatsnew/sections/ecosection

Minneapolis College of Art and Design
MCAD Online: Sustainable Design Certificate
www.mcad.edu/sustainable

Packaging Strategies
www.packstrat.com

Sustainability Associates
www.SustainabilityAssociates.us

Sustainable Packaging Coalition℠
www.sustainablepackaging.org

Sustainable Purchasing

Certified Forest Products Council
www.certifiedwood.org

Environmentally Preferable Purchasing (EPP)
www.moea.state.mn.us/lc/purchasing

Solid Waste Management Coordinating Board
www.greenguardian.com/business

Waste Issues

The Annenberg/CPB Project
www.learner.org/exhibits/garbage

Bureau of International Recycling
www.bir.org

Container Recycling Institute
www.container-recycling.org

Eco-Cycle
www.ecocycle.org

EPA/WasteWise
www.epa.gov/wastewise

Eureka Recycling
www.eurekarecycling.org

"If not you, then who?" / MPCA
www.moea.state.mn.us/campaign

Natural Resources Defense Council
www.nrdc.org/cities/recycling

New York WasteMatch
www.wastematch.org

Recycling Laws International
www.raymond.com

RecycleBank
www.recyclebank.com

Recycler's World
www.recycle.net

SEEK / Sharing Environmental Knowledge
www.nextstep.state.mn.us

Solid Waste Association of North America
www.swana.org

Strategies for Waste Minimization
www.cfd.rmit.edu.au/waste

Waste News
www.wastenews.com

Waste Wise / EPA Program
www.epa.gov/wastewise

Glossary of Basic Packaging Terminology

Wherever possible, definitions from other sources or associations have been maintained in order to achieve as much alignment as possible with the large diversity in the packaging industry.

Absolute Humidity

The actual weight of water vapor contained in a unit volume or weight of air. Referred to also as relative humidity.

Absorbent

A substance that has the ability to soak up or retain other substances, such as sugar or salt, absorbing water when exposed to high relative humidity atmospheres.

Acid

A substance, usually a liquid, that increases the concentration of hydrogen ions (H+) in water and reacts with a base to form a salt. On a pH scale, an acid has a pH value of <5; a pH value of 7 indicates a neutral substance. As the pH value declines from pH <5, the substance becomes more acidic and generally more corrosive.

Accumulation

An accumulation apparatus is a device that deliberately amasses inputs or products into one place for the next required operation or process. Taking a single line of product and collating the products into multiple rows to go into an oven, cooler, or similar operation is an example of accumulation. Accumulation should not be confused with buffers. The definition of buffer is to shield or cushion (via conveyor length or off-loading areas such as tables or conveyors to let the inputs gather) an upstream machine from a downstream machine that stops.

Generally, a buffer is a technique used as a positive modulating effect on utilization. The two definitions should not be used interchangeably.

Achievable Run Speed

That speed or rate as tested during commissioning (which also verifies the packaging line design criteria of needs) to be the needed sustainable steady-state speed or rate on a per-minute or per-hour basis with a wastage factor of <0.01. It is generally 20 percent less than the packaging line capacity and 50 to 70 percent less than the packaging line capacity for a true just-in-time (JIT) packaging line. The proposed run speed, the achievable run speed, and the design run speed can be used interchangeably.

Activity

An individual step or piece of work that is part of the job being scheduled.

Activity-Based Costing (ABC)

The use of cost accounting tools that attempt to allocate indirect or overhead costs on the basis of related activities, rather than using surrogate allocation bases such as direct labor or machine hours, floor space, or material costs.

Actual Set Run Speed

That target speed or rate as set or fixed for a given package run cycle on a per-minute or per-hour basis that is subjectively set by the operator or management. It is generally equal to (ideal) or less than the achievable run speed (usually). It is the dialed run speed set by the operator or management. On dynamically controlled automated packaging lines, it is the instantaneous steady-state target output rate. The effects of wastage rework and stoppages have not been considered.

Additive

Any substance, the intended use of which results or may reasonably be expected to result, directly or indirectly, in its becoming a part of or otherwise affecting the characteristics of any input.

Adsobent

The material on whose surface adsorption takes place.

Adsorption

The adhesion of a substance to the surface of a solid or liquid.

Adulterant (Adulteration)

Foreign material in the product, especially substances that are aesthetically objectionable or hazardous to health, or indicate that unsanitary handling or manufacturing practices have been employed.

Aeration

The bringing about of intimate contact between air and a liquid by bubbling air through the liquid or by agitation of the liquid.

Aerator

A device used to cause or that unwittingly causes the promotion of aeration.

Aerosol

The colloidal suspension in which gas is the dispersant. Dispersion or suspension of extremely fine particles of liquid or solid in a gaseous medium.

Affordable Capital Limits (ACLs)

The specified cost or "cap" for a project to achieve maximum value. The ACL is based on the economic facts associated with a specific business need, not a "wish" or arbitrary "grab number."

Agglomerate

To gather, form, or grow into a rounded mass, or to cluster densely.

Allocated Inventory

Materials in inventory or on order but that have been assigned to specific production orders in the future. These materials are therefore not available for use in other orders.

Aluminum, 2P

Aluminium cans are generally two piece cans (2P), made of a top and a body. The body is made from a sheet of aluminium stamped to the specified height. Bodies can decorated in the round (up to six colors) and coated internally, or labeled after filling. The customer will add the top (second piece) after filling.

Anaerobes

Microorganisms that grow in the absence of oxygen. Obligate anaerobes cannot survive in the presence of oxygen. Facultative anaerobes normally grow in oxygen but can also grow in its absence.

Anaerobic

Living or active in the absence of free oxygen.

ANSI

American National Standards Institute.

Antimicrobial

A compound that inhibits the growth of a microbe.

Aseptic Processing and Packaging

The filling of a commercially sterilized cooled product into presterilized containers, followed by aseptic hermetical sealing, with a presterilized closure, in an atmosphere free of microorganisms.

Asset Utilization

Fraction of time of a 24-hour day, 7 days a week potential time, that is actually used in producing quality packages until the package run cycle is completed (package run cycle start point to the next package run cycle start point). If the package run cycle (start to next start) takes exactly 3 days, then the total asset utilization time is $24 \times 3 = 72$ h, even though only one shift per day may be used.

Autoclave

A vessel in which high temperatures can be reached by using high steam pressure. Bacteria are destroyed more readily at elevated temperature and autoclaves are used to sterilize food, for example, in cans.

Automation

A technique of making industrial machinery, a process, or a system operating in an independent or self-controlling manner. This is the generic definition of automation. With regard to packaging, this definition should be adjusted to reflect the objectives of packaging, as follows: Automation is controlling the packaging line by using the optimum technique to cause the process to operate at a steady-state pace in a self-controlling manner. These definitions say nothing about eliminating labor or guaranteeing profitability, but they both imply that automation will optimize labor and give the potential of profitability.

Availability

The total available time for which a machine or system is in an operable state or between failures divided by the sum of the mean time between failures plus the mean time to repair plus the mean preventive maintenance time. Simply put, it is the fraction of time the machine is in an operable state to the total time period defined. An operable state is the condition that allows the machine or system to function at its achievable run speed in a manner that produces an outcome or an assemblage of inputs within the stated specifications and conformance to customer's needs.

Available Inventory

Materials in inventory or on order that are not safety stock or allocated to other uses. This available inventory is on immediate call to sustain the needs of production on a timely basis without interruption.

Baffle

A partition or plate that changes the direction or restricts the cross section of a fluid, thus increasing the velocity or turbulence.

Base

Alkaline substances (pH >7.0) that yield hydroxyl ions (OH–) in solution. As a general rule, as the pH value increases, the corrosive ability of the solution increases.

Benchmarking

A comparison or scale of product, function, practice, or strategy between identical industry segments. There are four types of benchmarking:

— Product benchmarking, which evaluates the current and future strengths and weaknesses of internal and external competitive products or packages.

— Functional benchmarking, which can be a comparison of the functional process or manufacturing technique relating to product development, packaging-line design, machinery setup, packaging-line control, and logistics of inputs in and packages out. When set up correctly, utilization can be a form of functional benchmarking.

— Best-practices benchmarking, which goes beyond the functional benchmarking by focusing on management practices.

— Strategic benchmarking, which compares the goals, direction, and key performance measure of a company within an industry sector against their internal or external competitors.

The performance index is a benchmark of functional and best practices.

Biodegradability
Susceptibility of a chemical compound to depolymerization by the action of biological agents.

Blanching
Heating by direct contact with hot water or live steam. It softens the tissues, eliminates air from the tissues, destroys enzymes, and washes away raw flavors.

Blow Molding
When something is formed from a molten plastic tube inflated with air expanding to the shape of a mold cavity.

Breakdown Maintenance
Breakdown maintenance and emergency maintenance are basically the same, when the predominant method of maintenance is breakdown maintenance. Breakdown maintenance is doing no maintenance other than lubrication between breakdowns. Repairs and adjustments are done as a result of reduced or no production occurring. Emergency maintenance is when a technical person is called to perform a repair at any time of day without being forewarned. With most other types of maintenance, emergency maintenance should be the exception, not the rule, as in breakdown maintenance.

British Thermal Unit (Btu)
The British engineering unit of heat quantity. It is approximately the quantity of heat that will raise the temperature of 1 pound of water 1 degree Fahrenheit. 1 Btu = 0.252 calories = 1054 joules.

Buffer
The definition of a buffer is to shield or cushion (via conveyor length or off-load areas to let the inputs gather) an upstream machine from a downstream machine that stops or slows down. Generally, a buffer is a technique used to maintain uptime and effect utilization. It should not be confused with accumulation. The definition of accumulation is a device that deliberately amasses inputs or products into one place for the next required process. The two definitions are similar but different.

Bulk Density
Weight per unit volume of a quantity of solid particles that depends on the packing density.

Bursting Strength
The strength of material in pounds per square inch, measured by the Cady or Mullen tester.

CAD
Computer-aided design is a term that implies the use of a computer and drafting software such as AutoCAD,™ to produce and store prints for layout, installation, machining, assembly, and fabrication. Another definition is the use of computers in interactive engineering drawings and the storage and retrieval of designs.

Caliper
The thickness, as related to paperboard, of a sheet measured under specified procedures expressed in thousandths of an inch, which are sometimes termed "points." The precision instrument used in the paperboard industry to measure thickness. To measure with a caliper.

Calorie

A unit of heat or the amount of heat necessary to raise the temperature of a gram of water 1 degree Celsius. Nutritionists use the large Calorie or kilo-Calorie (spelled with a capital C), which is 1000 calories. 1 Calorie (kilo-calorie) = 4,184 joules or 3.968 Btu.

CAM

Computer-aided manufacturing. This term implies the use of a computer and postprocessing or linking software (such as Smartcam or Mastercam) to manipulate and compile data into a machine language for a machine(s) to execute the desired function. Another definition is the use of computers to program, direct, and control production equipment.

Can, cylinder

A can whose height is relatively large compared to its diameter. Generally called a "tall can."

Can, flat

A can whose height is equal to or smaller than its diameter.

Can, key-opening

A can opened by tearing off a second strip of metal around the body by means of a key, or any can opened by means of a key.

Cap

See also Closure. Any form or device used to seal off the opening of the container so as to prevent loss of its contents.

Cap, lug

A cap closure for glass containers in which impressions in the side of the cap engage appropriately formed members on the neck finish to provide a grip when the cap is given a quarter turn, as compared to the full turn necessary with a screw cap.

Cap, screw

A cylindrical closure having a thread on the internal surface of the cylinder capable of engaging a comparable external thread on the finish or neck of a container, such as a glass bottle or collapsible tube.

Cap, snap-on

A type of closure for rigid containers. The sealing action of a snap-on cap is effected by a gasket in the top of the cap that is held to the neck or spout of the container by means of a friction fit on a circumferential bead. Construction material is either metal or semirigid plastic.

Cap, two-piece vacuum

Standard CT (continuous-thread) or DS (deep-screw) caps, equipped with a separate disk or lid that is lined with sealing for vacuum-packing processes.

Capacity

Capacity for a given packaging line and product is the upper possible sustainable limit of packages passing a point just before warehousing or shipping in a given amount of time (usually one minute or one hour or one shift). Sustainable refers to the ability to maintain consistent production of quality packages at a given speed. One could argue that it is the speed at which the percentage of rejects and/or jams begins to rise in a nonlinear manner. Capacity is usually expressed as a rate (packages/minute, and so on). Typically, a line will operate at a somewhat lower speed, called the actual set run speed. For just-in-time (JIT) processing, all machines and systems in the packaging process as well as making must have excess capacity.

Capacity Requirements Planning (CRP)

The process of reconciling the master production schedule to the labor and machine capacities of the production departments over the planning horizon.

This process is generally used in conjunction with MRP systems.

Cardboard

Cardboard is a generic, nonspecific, lay term used to refer to any heavy paper-pulp based board.

Carton/Container

Generally refers to a shipping/transport box made of corrugated board. The *regular slotted carton (or container) (RSC)* is the most commonly used style of carton. One side is glued, taped, or stapled at time of manufacture, making the final unit easy to set up, fill, and close. Other types include *center special slotted container (CSSC)*, *full overlap slotted container (FOL)*, *book wrap*, *bliss box*, and *slide box*.

Carton, double-wall

A corrugated fiberboard carton made of three sheets of linerboard interleaved with two sheets of fluted corrugate.

Carton, single-wall

A corrugated fiberboard carton made by gluing a sheet of fluted corrugate between two flat sheets of linerboard.

Carton Dimensions

Dimensions for packaging refer to the interior, measured in millimeters of Length x Width x Height. Length (L) is the longer side of the opening and Width (W) is the shorter. Height (H) is the length between the openings on either end.

Case

A nonspecific term for a shipping container. In domestic commerce, "case" usually refers to a box made from corrugated or solid fiberboard. In maritime or export usage, "case" refers to a wooden or metal box.

Catalyst

A substance that alters the rate of chemical change and remains unchanged at the end of a reaction.

Cellulose

The main fibrous material in paper.

Celsius (°C)

The temperature on a scale of 100° between the freezing point (0°) and the boiling point (100°) of water.

Centimeter (cm)

One-hundredth of a meter. Equivalent to 0.3937 in. One inch equals 2.54 cm.

Centipoise (cP)

Unit of viscosity equal to dyd/s2.cm2).

Changeover Time (or Period)

The time to complete the following items:

1. Exchange of changeover parts or tooling for all line elements.

2. Recalibration and/or adjustment of all line elements.

3. Run the first 1,000 packages or 15 minutes of production, whichever comes first.

At the end of this procedure, the line and all machine elements are expected to perform the desired functions to produce quality packages at the required output rate.

Clean in Place (CIP)

A machine's (such as a filler's) ability to be cleaned and sanitized in place on the packaging line without dismantling any components and minimizing time, product loss, cleaning solutions, cleaning procedures, and volume of water required.

Cleanup Time or (Period)

The time required to (1) remove change parts from

the previous package run cycle and (2) clean and/or flush out and inspect areas of the machine and line.

Closures

Closures are caps or lids used to seal bottle, jars, and cans. Closures are made from plastic, steel or aluminium and can be screw, twist or pop-up style. Closures can also include plastic seal types used to reseal a metal can after opening.

Commissioning

Commissioning is the act of sequentially and systemically starting up and testing machines or systems to ensure that they function as specified and that they can meet the needs of production. All components are tested and evaluated as to fit, function, vibration, alignment, integration, control, ergonomics, input flow, installation, and safety.

Commissioning, Qualifying, and Verifying (CQV)

Commissioning, qualifying, and verifying (CQV), or, more simply, "get up and stay up" (GUSU), is basically a management structure to ensure that a new or modified packaging line and all its machinery and systems are tested properly, the operators and maintenance personnel are adequately trained, and the results of the testing and training are verified or observed in the production runs without special assistance of any kind. Some companies restrict CQV to the machinery and systems and keep people and training separate.

Commissioning is the act of sequentially and systemically starting up and testing machines or systems to ensure that they function as specified. All components are tested and evaluated as to fit, function, vibration, alignment, integration, control, ergonomics, input flow, installation, and safety.

Qualifying is the act of setting up and administering a training program that ensures the people who will be interfacing with the packaging line are given a thorough overview of the packaging line and a detailed program on what they need to know to complete their tasks without hesitation or guessing. All training must address the following questions:

— When should training be done?

— What training should be done?

— How should we do training?

— Where should we do training?

— How much is enough training?

— Manuals and other self-help tools?

— Performance reviews and continuing improvement?

— Company standards and policy?

Verifying is the act of being able to determine without hesitation that the machine testing and training of personnel is not only thorough but also effective in the day-to-day production of the packaging line without senior staff, consultants, and/or machinery service personnel being involved in any manner.

Training of all line and maintenance personnel is critical to the performance of any packaging line. Training must be thorough, to the extent that all personnel working on the line are knowledgeable in the overall operation and the technical expert in their specific task(s). Management people must be experts in the overall operations of the line, and knowledgeable about the tasks and performance of each person working on the line.

Complete Kit (CK)

The complete kit (CK) is a managerial method or concept. It suggests that no work should start until all the items required for the completion of the job are available. Items such as components, tools, drawings information, and samples constitute the kit.

Computer-Integrated Manufacturing (CIM)

The integration of the total manufacturing enterprise through the use of integrated systems and data communications coupled with new managerial philosophies that improve organizational and personnel efficiency. In other words, the business enterprise is dependent on human knowledge and information flow in order to operate efficiently. Companies that have implemented CIM successfully tend to say that they get the right information to the right people or devices in the right places at the right times to make the right decisions (SME Blue Book series, 1990). CIM uses such a broad spectrum of technologies that it is best to think of CIM as a goal or strategy or philosophy as outlined by the company's needs and direction.

Components

Components can be either input items or product items. Examples of components are labels, caps, containers, seals, cartons, and cases; examples of products are liquids, pastes, pills, hardware, and powders.

Composite Cans

Cans made from paperboard. These include a variety of barrier materials and fittings enabling composite cans to be used for packaging: food, powdered beverages, wine, spirits and perfume.

Consistency

Resistance of a fluid to deformation. For sample (Newtonian) fluids, the consistency is identical with viscosity; for complex (non-Newtonian) fluids, the consistency is identical with apparent viscosity.

Control

The authority or ability to regulate, direct, or dominate a situation or series of events. For any packaging line, whether manual, semiautomatic, or automatic, control is critical.

Converter

A company that takes base materials, and turns them into finished packaging.

Cop

Clean-out-of-place.

Corrugation (Corrugate, Corrugated)

Wave shaped medium sandwiched between flat sheets of liner to form corrugated fiberboard. Flutes act as protective cushioning, as well as structural strengtheners, and offer distinctive performance advantages depending on the flute size. Depending on desired traits for stacking strength, puncture resistance , crush strength, corrugated cartons feature either of the types below.

A-Flute: Flute thickness of 4.7 mm
 Excellent stacking strength.

B-Flute: Flute thickness of 2.5 mm
 Good puncture resistance.

C-Flute: Flute thickness of 3.6 mm
 Optimum combination of A and B.

E-Flute: Flute thickness of 1.5 mm
 Generally used for light applications such as pizza boxes, mailers, shoe boxes, and warehouse club primary packaging.

AC Flute
 A double-wall combination of single wall sheets of one A-flute and one C-flute, to create a strong

final sheet when extra thickness or strength is needed.

BC Flute

A double-wall combination of single wall sheets of one B-flute and one C-flute, to create a strong final sheet when extra thickness or stacking strength is needed.

Customer

The individuals, companies, or their representative that receive a company's product, use a company's services, or purchase a company's product for resale (trade).

Cycle Rate

The cycle rate is the number of machine cycles per minute. We denote the number of cycles as N, so the cycle rate is dN / dt. It is not necessarily equal to the run speed of the Over an 8-hour period, the cycle rate of any machine in the packaging line is always higher than any set run speed. Most OEMs specify their machine speeds based on cycle rates, not output, and therefore the OEM's speeds are the theoretical or design speeds that are possible.

Deliverable

A product that satisfies one or more objectives and that must be delivered to meet contractual obligations

Design

Design is a catch-all word that refers to front end concepting, graphics, and user interface experience creation. Design can be used to describe any part of the nonword related (copywriting or strategic marketing) creative process.

Design Basis

A document defining the project scope for designers and communicating how the engineering packages must be structured to fit construction requirements.

Design Engineering

The application of process engineering, machine design engineering, or power and controls engineering and the production of detailed engineering documentation, such as drawings and specifications, that explain how the technology defined in the design basis will be embodied in equipment and how the equipment will be constructed, assembled, and installed.

Design for Manufacture (DFM)

A general approach to designing products that can be more effectively manufactured. Often used in conjunction with databases, it includes such concepts as design for assembly, design for serviceability, or design for test.

Design Speed

The theoretical capacity obtained in a perfect operating environment. All adverse operating conditions are neglected, and all machinery is assumed to be in optimum operating condition. The design speed usually does not take into consideration the natural handling difficulties or stability of the inputs (K value), environmental concerns, or training. This is usually the machinery builders' advertised maximum functioning cycle speed for a given range of optimum inputs under ideal conditions. The concept of line speeds is not well understood in the packaging industry; thus there is a lot of confusion and disappointment over the actual results achieved. The following is a summary of the speed hierarchy from highest to lowest:

1. Design speed (usually the OEM's maximum cycle rate)

2. Capacity (highest sustainable cycle rate — about 80 to 90 percent of design speed)

3. Achievable run speed (target set speed or required steady-state condition)

4. Actual set run speed (actual packaging line set speed or dial speed)

5. Output rate (what goes to the warehouse or shipping per time period)

The actual run speed will be set and its result will equal the output rate plus losses from rework, wastage, and stoppages.

Detergent
Surface-active material or combination of surfactants designed for removal of unwanted contamination from the surface of an article.

Dew Point
The temperature at which air or other gases become saturated with vapor, causing the vapor to deposit as a liquid. The temperature at which 100 percent RH is reached.

Die Cutting
The process of cutting substrates into a shape to converting it to the final desired size and form. Die cutters can use cylindrical or flatbed types depending on the application.

Direct Labor
The labor expended in directly adding value to the package. For simplicity, it could be looked at as "touch" labor since direct-labor employees usually physically touch the product or inputs.

Disturbance
Any anomaly in the flow of product, inputs, or packages in the packaging process that may or may not cause production to cease or slow down.

Disturbance Frequency
The number of disturbances for a specific output (quantitative amount) as determined by the set or actual run speed of the line.

Disturbance-Frequency Analysis (DFA)
A production process tool that tracks and eliminates disturbances and their source(s). It is an excellent troubleshooting method for the analysis of small or large sections of the packaging process. DFA states that when the causes of disturbances are eliminated the downtime disappears, so why worry about time?

Disturbance-Frequency Period
The minimum number of outputs allowed for one disturbance. The minimum number of outputs is determined mathematically from the actual set speed of the packaging process. As the actual set speed increases, the minimum number of outputs required increases exponentially.

Double-facer
Part of a corrugator which bonds single-face board to another liner to produce a double-faced corrugated sheet.

Downtime
The amount of time a machine or system is not functioning due to stoppages in a given shift or time period. Downtime should not include idle time or time the machine or system is waiting for inputs. Therefore downtime is made up stoppages and company policies.

Downtime Analysis (DA)
A production process tool that tracks the amount of time a given machine or system ceases production. Since it is time-based and monitors symptoms, not causes, its effectiveness is limited to specific applications. Historically, downtime analysis has been applied in an ineffective manner.

Drawings and Specifications

Engineering details for projects, packages, equipment, systems, and facilities.

Drop Test

A test for measuring the properties of a container by subjecting the packaged product to a free fall from predetermined heights onto a surface with prescribed characteristics.

Duration

A unit measure of time for the time interval of a given stoppage.

Efficiency (n)

A fundamental engineering term that is broadly defined as the ratio of benefits/penalties or, for packaging, the ratio of output/input. In keeping with this engineering definition, we define it as the average ratio of packaged output multiplied by the number of components over the sum of input components. Unfortunately, in the packaging industry, efficiency has become a generic catchall term whose definition varies depending on the political needs of the organization, not its real needs.

Elemendorf Test

A test for measuring the tearing resistance of paper, paperboard, tape, and other sheet materials.

Element Utilization

The fraction of time a given machine or element is actually producing output at a set run speed divided by the total time available for production. Changeover, cleanup, and prep work are not included. This definition usually relates to machinery and/or components.

Elements

Any machines, equipment, conveyors, or mechanical components by which the product and/or inputs are manipulated, assembled, transferred, collated, or brought into contact with each other. Examples of elements are fillers, cappers (with sortation), labelers, unscramblers, case packers soap presses, calenders, meat grinders, wrappers, packers, banders, and conveyors. For the purpose of clarification, all elements are considered or designated as machines. For example, we assume that all types of conveyors, collators, or buffers are elements.

Excess Capacity (EC)

A managerial concept or approach advocating that a system's or process's capacity or limit should exceed the average demand (throughput or output). This position has been developed by Dr. Abraham Grosfeld-Nir from the University of Waterloo. The author agrees strongly with this concept. This concept is in contrast to the "lean and mean" approach, where any attempt to have a capacity that exceeds the demand is viewed as wasteful ("fat") and any system or process having a capacity equal to the demand is perceived as ideal. Added to this is the traditional accountants' advice to cut extra capacity, in particular the work force, to force a balance between capacity and demand. In other words, the packaging process capacity is equal to the customer's demand and no more. It is very likely that, at times, EC will recommend buying more capacity under given conditions, while an accountant would recommend a cut. The need for excess capacity arises from the presence of randomness in demand, processing time, quality, and the like. (In a deterministic world, EC would indeed be wasteful.) Benefits of operating with EC are small WIP (work in process), quick response time, and increased quality. In observing JIT multistage systems it is clear that each stage is utilized only to a fraction of its capacity as it relates to the speed potential. Each stage is idle some of the time as a result of stoppages. Thus stages of a properly designed JIT system operate with excess capacity. Experience indicates that in the automotive industry, stages are typically utilized 60 to 80 percent of their capacity. To use JIT in packaging, it can be argued (because of the speeds involved) that "speed utilization" or the set run speed of 50 to 70 percent of the capacity speed are proper for JIT to be effective.

Extrusion
The process of forcing a material in plastic condition through an orifice.

Factory End
Bottom or can manufacturer's end.

Failure Rate
The ratio of the total number of failures to the cumulative operating time for a stated period of time.

Feasibility Studies
Experimental studies on a process or equipment to access what results are achievable and/or what will be required to produce a desired result.

Flexible Packaging
The lay term is "bag" but in the industry side this term refers to a wide variety of packaging that can be single and multi-layered and is supplied in semi-formed reels, as sheet, or ready-to-use bags. It can be paper, polyethylene, foil, or nylon, or a combination of materials to provide a variety of characteristics.

Flexographic Printing/Flexography
Flexography is the major process used to print packaging materials. Flexography is used to print corrugated containers, folding cartons, multiwall sacks, paper sacks, plastic bags, milk and beverage cartons, disposable cups and containers, labels, adhesive tapes, envelopes, newspapers, and wrappers (candy and food). Flexographic presses are capable of producing good quality images on many different materials and is the least expensive of the printing processes used for package printing. Flexographic plates are made of a flexible material, such as plastic, rubber or UV sensitive polymer. Flexography is enjoying an increase in interest due to: its relatively simple operation; and the fact that it can be easily adapted for water-based ink use. Moving toward water-based ink use makes large reductions in VOC emissions possible, especially when compared to heatset web or gravure printing processes.

Fluidity
Reciprocal of viscosity.

Folding Cartons
Paperboard cartons with preapplied creases to enable the carton to be formed at the time of fulfillment for packaging product.

Freight on Board (FOB)
The term used to signify that the seller is required to bear all costs required to place the goods aboard equipment of the transporting carrier. The stated FOB point is usually the location where title to the goods passes to the buyer. The buyer is liable for all charges and risks after passing of title.

Frequency
The number of occurrences in a given period of time.

Functional Coatings
Polyethylene and/or plastic or foil films laminated to paper, providing a water or oil barrier, typically used for meat, seafood, pet food, fruit, and produce.

Gelometer
Instrument used to measure the time required for a fluid to gel. Also instrument used to determine the firmness of a gel.

Good Manufacturing Practices (GMP)

A document that describes agreed-to best or optimal procedures for manufacturing.

Gram (g)

Metric unit of weight equal to 0.035 oz. One kilogram is equivalent to1000 g, and one pound equals 453.6 gs.

Gravure Printing

This printing technique uses the transfer of ink from an etched cylinder to the paper/film/foil. The presses are can be multi station, allowing for a variety of color applications plus coating.

Headspace, gross

The vertical distance between the level of the product (generally the liquid surface) and the inside surface of the lid in an upright rigid container (the top of the double seam of a can or the top edge of a glass jar).

Headspace, net

The vertical distance between the level of the product (generally the liquid surface) and the inside surface of the lid in an upright, rigid container having a double seam, such as a can.

Hermetically Sealed Container

A container designed and intended to be secure against the entry of microorganisms and to maintain the commercial sterility of its contents after processing.

High-Performance Products

Products with clearly superior attributes such as taste, styling, speed, smell, comfort, and effectiveness, which results in the packager's receiving a premium price and/or dominating market share more than the perceived normal product.

Hydrometer Densimeter

Device used for the measurement of specific gravity or density.

Injection Molding

The process of converting plastic pellets by applying heat and pressure to inject molten material into a mold cavity.

Institute of Food Technologies (IFT)

The professional society of food scientists and technologists in the United States.

Impact Strength

The ability of a material to withstand mechanical shock.

Indirect Labor

Any labor, including supervision and management, that is not direct labor or directly connected to the production or manufacturing process. Overhead activities such as material handling, stockroom, inspection, all engineering functions, maintenance, supervision, cost, accounting, and personnel are usually included.

Input (X,x)

Input for a given packaging line is the specific item or part required for the package assembly operation or packaging process to form part of the complete package. Examples of input items are bottles, cartons, caps, labels, cases, pallets, tubes, and so on. Inputs are not product entities, but product entities can be classed as inputs. In general, inputs are discard items that are trashed or recycled after product use. Since we use the symbol X for systems input, we will use xi, for the ith machine as the input for a machine. Several types of inputs may be required by a machine (and certainly by a line), but in general, only one output is produced. Minimizing input losses reduces cost, increases the performance index, and reduces the waste headed to landfills. From the economic point of view, reducing input item losses as well as the number of different types of inputs makes business sense. Minimizing the types of inputs maximizes performance and quality

Input Rate

The input rate for a given packaging line is the amount of a specific item or part (required to form part of the complete package) processed or consumed in a given amount of time.

Integration

Integration as it relates to the packaging process is defined as the mechanical, pneumatic, hydraulic, and/or electrical method of physically (mechanically or electronically) connecting machinery and input handling systems to ensure a smooth, harmonized throughput operation. It should not be confused with automation and control. Usually control or automation cannot solve or correct poor or faulty integration. Integration principles for input and product handling

1. Once you have it, don't let go. Having it means complete physical or electronic engagement so that the mechanism motion and the input motion are identical or within a tolerance range that is smaller than the functional requirements.

2. Eliminate or minimize input and package manipulations or change of direction, velocity, and/or inertia.

3. Always interface using complete integration or handshaking pass off within a defined boundary, not at a point. The interface position tolerance must be smaller than the operational functional window.

4. If manipulations are required because of overall design constraints, always match motions (intermittent to intermittent, continuous to continuous). Incompatible motions (continuous to intermittent

and intermittent to continuous) always yield the highest unreliability.

5. For cycles >60 minutes^{-1}, continuous is superior to intermittent.

Islands of Automation

Pieces of equipment or systems that are not integrated with the packaging line. They can be considered independent and not controlled by the packaging process directly. The output from each island of automation does not affect the other directly.

ISO 9000 Series Protocol

ISO (International Standards Organization) is an international set of documents written by members of a worldwide delegation. Its primary purpose is to harmonize the large number of national and international standards adopted by many countries. This series is also intended to be driven by market and customer needs. The ISO series consists of five main documents:

— Three core quality system documents that are models of quality assurance: ISO 9001, ISO 9002, and ISO 9003.

— Two supporting guideline documents: ISO 9000 and ISO 9004.

ISO 9000 (ANSI/ASQC Q90-1987)

Quality Management and Quality Assurance Standards: Guidelines for Selection and Use.

ISO 9001 (ANSI/ASQC Q91-1987)

Quality Systems — Model for Quality Assurance in Design/Development, Production, Installation and Servicing, Applicable to contractual arrangements, requiring that design effort and the product requirements are stated principally in performance terms or they need to be established. Confidence in product conformance can be attained by adequate demonstration of certain supplier's capabilities in design, development, production, installation, and servicing.

ISO 9002 (ANSI/ASQC Q92-1987)

Quality Systems — Model for Quality Assurance in Production and Installation. The specific requirements for the product are stated in terms of an established design or specification. Confidence in product conformance can be attained by adequate demonstration of a certain supplier's capabilities in production and installation.

ISO 9003 (ANSI/ASQC Q93-1989)

Quality Systems — Model for Quality Assurance in Final Inspection and Test. The conformance of the product to specified requirements can be shown with adequate confidence, provided certain supplier's capabilities for inspection and test conducted on the product supplied can be satisfactorily demonstrated on completion.

ISO 9004 (ANSI/ASQC Q94-1987)

Quality Management and Quality System Elements Guidelines.

ISO 14000

Just as many companies joined the quality revolution by embracing ISO 9000 as a quality system, many have now embraced sustainability by becoming ISO 14000 certified.

ISO 14000 encompasses a range of quality activities, but at its heart is the requirement to do life cycle assessment on company products. While the detailed impacts of each material are beyond the standard, the requirements are clear: Define the product system, identify the product functions, and perform life cycle assessment continuously as an improvement practice. Record the results of the LCA and make them available to auditors.

A requirement of ISO 14000 is that a company has an environmental management system with the following characteristics:

An Environmental Management System (EMS) for ISO 14001:2004 is required to:

— Document and manage the environmental impact of activities, products, or services

— Continually improve environmental performance

— Establish a system to set environmental goals, to accomplish them, and to document the performance."

Levels of environmental performance are specific for each business and type of activity so they are not specified in the standard. The intent of the standard is to enable a consistent framework for reporting and managing environmental issues.

There are many other ISO standards for environmental issues, but ISO 14001:2004 is intended to provide a comprehensive and consistent approach on environmental issues, with generic requirements as effective EMSs are the same regardless of business type or activity.

Given a consistent approach to environmental management systems, there is now a consistent approach to the communication of environmental issues.

Since the levels of environmental performance are not specified, organizations in a variety of fields and stages of development can use the standard. As with other quality standards, organizations must commit to comply with all applicable environmental legislation and regulations. In addition, the standard requires continuous improvement as a practice.

As the reader can see, the standards require that each company adopt continuous monitoring and improvement policies with regard to the environment.

Justification

For most industries a justification is a written request for action that consists of

1. Acquisition of valid data

2. Presentation of the problem, need and data

3. A logical course of action with options and alternatives

4. Cost profiles

5. Benefits of undertaking a specific course of action

Just-In-Time (JIT)

First used by Toyota in Japan as the "Kanban system," it has been successful in reducing inventory while maintaining high throughput and increased quality. Kanbans are cards authorizing production or shipment of material. In 1981, Mondem defined JIT as a production system to produce a kind of unit needed, at the time needed and in the quantities needed. In 1982, Schonberger defined JIT as goods produced just in time to be sold and only purchase materials just in time to be transformed into the product. In 1988, Sohal defined JIT as more of a philosophy than a series of techniques, the basic tenet of which is to minimize cost by restricting commitment to expenditure until the last possible moment. In 1991, Groenvelt defined JIT as a management philosophy that fosters change and improvement through inventory reduction, to have the ideal situation of exactly the necessary amount of material available where it is needed and when it is needed. From the book *Benchmarking Global Manufacturing*, 1992, just-in-time is both a philosophy of eliminating waste and a toolset for pacing and controlling production and vendor deliveries on time, with short notice and with little or no inventory. According to JIT, multistage systems as found in packaging lines should be pull (produce only in response to demand) and not push (produce as long as there is raw material to be processed). In simple terms, JIT means that regardless of what disasters happen in my packaging process, you have the excess capacity to guarantee the highest probability of attaining the exact delivery window required by the customer with quality packages.

Kilogram (kg)

A unit weight in the metric system equivalent to 1000 g or 2.2046 lb.

Kilopascal (kPa)

Unit of pressure. One kilopascal equals 1000 pascals (Pa); 1 atmosphere (atm) equals 1.01325×105 pascals.

Kraft

A term derived from a German word meaning "strength," applied to pulp, paper, or paperboard produced from virgin wood fibers by the sulfate process. Kraft paper is also commonly used for grocery bags and commercial wrapping paper.

Label

Any display of written, printed, or graphic matter on the container of any consumer commodity, affixed to any package containing a consumer commodity.

Lag

Specified time increment between the start or completion of an activity and the start or completion of a successor activity.

Latent Heat

The quantity of heat, measured in Btus or calories, necessary to change the physical state of a substance without changing its temperature, such as in distillation. A definite quantity of heat, the latent heat, must be removed from water at 0°C (32°F) to change it to ice at 0°C.

Lid

Can end applied to open end of can in a cannery. Also known as top, cap, or packer's end.

Liner

Generally, any liner material that separates a product within a container from the basic walls of the container.

Linerboards

Linerboards form the inner and outer facings of corrugated boxes. They are selected for their structural and/or decorative properties, and can be made from white or brown, kraft or recycled pulps, or a blend of fibers.

Logic Diagram

Drawings using logic symbols that tell how a piece of equipment or system is to operate.

Lug

A type of thread configuration, usually thread segments disposed equidistantly around a bottle neck (finish). The matching closure has matching portions that engage each of the thread segments.

Machine

A system of components arranged to transmit motion and energy in a predetermined fashion. Another definition is that a machine typically contains mechanisms designed to provide significant forces and transmit significant power.

Machine Downtime

Machine (or element) downtime is the total amount of time a given machine in the packaging line stopped or ceased production during the run period.

Maintainability or mean time to repair (MTTR). The average time required to repair a device or system. This includes preparation time, active maintenance time, and delay time associated with the repair. It is quantified as the mean time to repair (MTTR).

Maintenance

The physical act of ensuring that all machinery and systems are in operable condition at all times, especially during scheduled periods of demand. Maintenance can also be defined as the ability to keep all mechanisms and machines required for optimum production available not only to produce but also maintain a steady flow of quality packages without interruption. Types of maintenance programs to maximize operational readiness and sustainability: (1) breakdown, (2) preventive, and (3) predictive.

Manufacturing Costs

Raw and packing materials, manufacturing expenses, processing costs, and variations.

Manufacturing Lead Time (MLT)

The cumulative time from the beginning of the production cycle until an item is finally finished. Time spent in inventory as work in process, setup times, move times, inspection, and order preparation time are included.

Manufacturing Overhead Costs (MOC)

Costs allocated to unit product costs, including the cost of indirect labor as well as indirect purchased services and supplies but excluding unallocated period costs such as sales and marketing and R&D.

Master Production Schedule (MPS)

The main or overriding schedule of the number and timing of all end items to be produced in a manufacturing plant over a specific planning horizon. An important input to the MRP computer program.

Material Requirements Planning (MRP)

MRP is more of a computerized information system than a managerial philosophy that determines how much of each material, any inventory item with a unique part number, should be purchased or produced in each future time period to support the master production schedule (MPS). It is designed to contain information required for efficient decision making. MRP is mainly used by large industrial organizations but as more improved computer software and hardware emerge, smaller organizations will find MRP advantageous in their operations. Input to MRP is information from the "master production schedule" (MPS) and the "bill of materials" (BOM). The MPS determines starting times for future jobs, while the BOM is a detailed description of all inputs (material and work) required for each job. MRP also monitors all in-stock inventory and outstanding purchase orders. On the basis of information about jobs in progress and waiting jobs, MRP regulates the purchase of material from internal and external suppliers. It also provides information about jobs behind schedule for potential expediting, Methods such as the "economic order quantity" (EOQ) and "reorder point" (ROP) control material requirements, without taking into account information about job scheduling from the MPS. In contrast, MRP recognizes that handling material is more efficient when the information from the MPS is incorporated. MRP also aggregates requirements from different sources and sets timing for arrivals considering overall system performance, rather than aiming at local satisfaction. In other words, unlike EOQ and ROP, MRP takes advantage of dependent demand. MRP assumes all operations to be deterministic, which is unrealistic. One consequence of this assumption is the frequent need for expediting jobs. MRP requires dealing with an enormous amount of information that needs continuous update. It turns out that when details are required,

MRP is unreliable. Maybe this will be taken care of as technology and advanced software are developed.

Meantime Between Failures (MTBF)

The cumulative operating time divided by the number of failures. This is the reciprocal of the failure rate.

Meantime to Failure (MTTF)

The average life of nonrepairable items. This does not apply to most machinery in the packaging industry, but it does apply to certain components (e.g., seals, bearings).

Meantime to Repair (MTTR)

Mean time to repair (or maintainability) is the average time required to repair a device or system. This includes preparation time, active maintenance time, and delay time associated with the repair. It is quantified as the mean time to repair (MTTR).

Mechanical Pulp

Pulp produced by reducing logs and chips into their fiber components by the use of mechanical energy.

Mechanism

A system of components arranged to transmit motion in a predetermined fashion. Another definition is that a mechanism is a device that transforms motion to some desirable pattern and typically develops very low forces and transmits little power.

Melting

The change from the solid to the liquid state. Also the softening of harder compounds.

Metallizing

A vacuum process used to apply a thin metal layer onto flexible plastic film.

Model

A model consists of one or more mathematical equations that describe some idealized from of a system. The idealized form is rendered from the real form by making one or more simplifying assumptions. It is an attempt to explain or predict a portion of reality using mathematics.

Molecular Weight

Sum of the weights of all the atoms in a molecule.

Molecule

The smallest theoretical quantity of a material that retains the properties exhibited by the material.

Monitoring

Following the progress of the project. This phase follows the preparation of the CPM plan and schedule.

Mylar

A synthetic polyester fiber or film.

Neck

The part of a container where the bottle cross section decreases to form the finish.

NLEA

The law behind the use of the *Nutrition Facts* label, the Nutrition Labeling and Education Act of 1990 (NLEA) provides the US Food and Drug Administration (FDA) with specific authority to require nutrition labeling of most foods regulated by the Agency, and to require that all nutrient content claims (i.e., "high fiber," "low fat," etc.) and health claims be consistent with agency regulations.

Occupational Safety and Health Administration (OSHA)

Federal organization responsible for health and safety on construction sites and in plants.

Occurrence

Any anomaly or action in the packaging process that actually stops that process. A stoppage and an occurrence are the same.

OEM

OEM (Original equipment manufacturer) is a term used to describe the manufacturing and marketing of products where one company uses a component made by another company in its own product, or sells the product of the second company under its own brand.

Offset/Lithographic Printing

This printing technique uses the transfer of ink from a sensitized plate, offset to a rubber blanket then transferred to the final surface to be decorated. The presses are can be multi-station, allowing for a variety of color applications plus coating.

Optimized Production Technology (OPT)

A philosophical approach that maximizes throughput by the modification or elimination of bottlenecks. Claiming that (only) throughput or output translates into sales, OPT aims at maximizing throughput. Improvements that do not render increased output are viewed as negligible. OPT concentrates on "bottlenecks" or critical resources. A bottleneck is a resource that is utilized to its full capacity. This aged manufacturing concept is still quite common in many packaging plants. Typically OPT can lead to extremely large inventory levels, which is contrary to JIT. OPT can give substantial gains in short time periods of three to six months.

Output (Y,y)

Output for a given packaging line and product is the exact quantity of quality packages produced in a package run cycle as required by the customer and shipped to the customer. It is denoted by the symbol Y. Similarly, we define the output for a machine or output rate as the number of items (of acceptable quality) leaving a machine in a given amount of time. We denote this by yi, for the ith machine. The word throughput has the same definition as output, but we use the word output, which is the more correct term.

Output Rate

The output rate for a machine or system is the number of items (of acceptable assembled quality) leaving a machine or system in a given amount of time. We denote this by yi for the ith machine. It is always less than the machine cycle rate and/or the actual set run speed, due to the effects of wastage, rework, and stoppages.

Package/Packaging

A quality assembly of two or more quality input items and product items. In some cases, the package becomes the product (e.g., consider a synthetic fire log — the consumer burns the package [both the product and the input: log and wrapper]). A good marketing view of a package is one presented by Robert E. Smith, senior vice president of research and development at Nabisco Foods Group. He says, "The package is also a facilitator of new manufacturing systems, adds convenience far consumers, and is beneficial to the environment. The package must play all of these roles to perfection." Therefore a package is a product that is wrapped in a protective shroud, identified through a label, informs the consumer of its use, and uses color, shape, and name to establish consumer recognition.

Packaging made of any substrate is broken down into function layers:

> **Primary packaging** is the material that first envelops the product and holds it. Sometimes this will be the only packaging the product needs. Warehouse Club packages will often be sold directly off of the pallet used to get the product from manufacturer to store, with no shipping box needed.

> **Secondary packaging** is outside the primary packaging, and is used to group primary packages together (shipper), or to create a display facing or multi-pack the consumer sees. For example: Aspirin will often come in a bottle packed inside of a paperboard box vs. just the bottle alone, beer in bottles often comes in a six-pack. Both examples are in turn packed with others in a shipper box.

> **Tertiary packaging** is used for bulk shipping.

Packaging Changeout (tpc)

Packaging changeout is the sum of the changeover time, cleanup time, and prep work time. The package changeout is the total interval between finishing one run of a given package and starting another run with a different package.

Package-changeout Utilization (Uc)

The fraction of the package run cycle time the packaging line has available for producing output at a set run speed after changeover, cleanup, and prep time have been completed.

Package Run Cycle (PRC)

The duration of specific events needed to produce a given amount of quality packages. It consists of the total end of the first production run to the end of the next production run period, which involves changeout and the entire run or producing period.

Packaging Line

An assemblage of specialty-function machinery or systems and/or manual workstations from depalletizing to palletizing integrated together to carry out a process in which a given product is combined, inspected, and transported with inputs or media. The inputs themselves protect, control, and identify the product: (1) bottling lines for liquid products such as beverages; (2) canning lines for products such as precooked cooked foods, or (3) box-packaging lines for materials such as powdered detergents.

Packaging Process

The combined execution of specialty-function machinery or systems and/or manual workstations in order to carry out a process in which a given product is combined an/or assembled with inputs or media. Basically the packaging process has the same definition as a packaging line but is more encompassing since it makes people part of the packaging line. Some companies, by nature of their operations, may include the making as part of the packaging process.

Paneling

Distortion (sidewall collapses) of a container caused by development of a reduced pressure (too high to vacuum) inside the container.

Paper, water-resistant

Paper that is treated by the addition of materials to provide a degree of resistance to damage or deterioration by water in liquid form.

Paper, wet-strength

Paper that has been treated with chemical additives to aid in the retention of bursting, tearing, or rupturing resistance when wet.

Parallel Elements

Parallel elements (i.e., machines) perform the same type of operation in a system. The main line is split into two to feed each machine with consistent product and/or inputs. The elements need not be identical, and the speeds of each can be a factor of the total main-line output. Parallel machines provide system redundancy; the failure of any one of them will not stop the line, but only reduce output by a factor. Usually, the combined capacity of the two parallel elements should equal over 125 percent of the total output plus wastage, rework, and stoppage losses.

Pasting

Multiple paper and paperboard plies glued together to form a solid board.

Pasteurization

A heat treatment of food usually below 212°F intended to destroy all organisms dangerous to health, or a heat treatment that destroys some but not all microorganisms that cause food spoilage or that interfere with a desirable fermentation.

Performance

Performance can be defined as the level or effectiveness of carrying out an action or execution of a sequence of events according to a prescribed functional description.

Performance in the packaging industry is a widely used term such as efficiency that means different things to many people. Therefore the word *performance* is relative and qualitative. The only understanding that may be common to all is that it is a reflection of productivity, output, or effectiveness of time. Unless it is rigorously defined and understood, the word performance has limited value to decision makers other than projecting a sense of being or desire. For many people, performance is the best bang for the buck based on up-front costs or capital costs only, not on the best value, which is based on capital and ongoing operational costs. If one buys a system based on up-front costs or lowest costs to get in without working out operational costs over a one-, three-, or five-year period, then their anticipated profits (based on marketing targets) will rarely materialize. Too many people are hooked on this false sense of performance that only contributes to the long-term uncompetitiveness of the company. Short-term or no planning leads to long-term disasters.

Performance Index (PI)

A method of evaluating, benchmarking, tracking, and verifying a company's packaging processes. It gets rid of the old confusing notion of line efficiency and establishes a new framework that establishes a level playing field, especially among multiple corporate plants running the same or similar products. The performance index can also be used to evaluate dissimilar types of packaging lines that are internal or external to the organization. The effectiveness of a packaging operation that relates directly to the profit of the product is the objective of the performance index. PI also utilizes the most effective ideas an/or techniques used in OPT, JIT, TQM, TPM, and MRP and applies them to the packaging process. As such, the PI can be considered an operation's tool, but only a tool in the benchmarking sense, because it is the tip of the pyramid from which everything else expands out to explain the PI value. As a benchmark, it can evaluate functional and best practices of a company against itself or competitors. The performance index is a mathematical model that projects the overall rating of a packaging line. Technically PI is a composite measurement of the productivity of a given packaging line.

Permeability

The passage or diffusion of a gas, vapor liquid, or solid through a barrier without physically or chemically affecting it.

pH

The effective acidity or alkalinity of a solution; not to be confused with the total acidity or alkalinity. The pH scale is:

Acid solutions	Neutral	Alkaline solutions
0 1 2 3 4 5 6	7	8 9 10 11 12 13 14

pH 7 is the neutral point (pure water). Decreasing values below 7 indicate increasing activity, while increasing values above 7 indicate increasing acidity, while increasing values above 7 to indicate alkalinity.

Planned Maintenance

A type of maintenance in which a company has a given period or periods of production idle times each month in which maintenance activities can be undertaken. In periods of heavy production demands, this type of maintenance breaks down into simple breakdown maintenance.

Predictive Maintenance

A type of maintenance that utilizes an array of sensors and/or monitoring equipment to determine the status and condition of critical wear components in machinery and systems so that proactive procedures or replacement can be undertaken at a convenient time period before the failure of the component could cause any unscheduled downtime.

Preventive Maintenance

A type of maintenance determined by historical data and life cycle testing to determine the optimum time of part life and therefore by extension lead to a program of part changeout prior to the anticipated part failure. Carried to its extreme, it can be a costly venture to a company, and therefore most preventive programs are tempered by budgets and other constraints.

Primary Spoilage
Spoilage due to bacterial or chemical action of product packed within the can. *See also* Secondary Spoilage.

Procurement Leadtime
The cumulative time from the beginning of the procurement order cycle (order commitment) until the procured item is delivered. It includes vendor lead time, transportation, receiving, and inspection time.

Product
Those items used or consumed by the customer. They are usually items made or modified by human industry. Take shampoo as an example; the consumer uses the shampoo and throws away its container, cap, and labels. The product is the shampoo and the input items are the container, cap, and labels. (The term product as a collective noun can have a plural sense.)

Product Amenities
The extra product features that enhance the basic product and make it easier to use or more enjoyable. For example, a finger pump spray on a bottle versus a pull-and-squeeze cap.

Product Run Cycle (PRC)
The duration of time needed to produce a given amount of quality packages based on the designed or historical output. It is the same as the package run cycle. The word package is more applicable than product in most industries.

Product Specifications
The written description of the products to be manufactured.

Product Stability (K value)
The ability of the product to be handled in a stable and consistent manner, A beer bottle, for example,

has all the features necessary to make it a stable and consistent product:

— Cylindrical parallel shape

— Relatively low center of gravity

— Heavy, smooth base for stability and low friction

— Relatively hard to break

— A shape that remains stable throughout the packaging cycle

Generally, a stable product is a product that gives a packaging line the least amount of handling problems. This stability can be defined as a value K. A more rigorous definition of K value is left for future development. As a packaging line increases its level of automation, the K value becomes very critical.

Product Support
Those activities that support the customer in the use of a product, such as customer education, information about related products, or services and information hotlines.

Productivity
The level of ability or effectiveness in marketing, manufacturing, distributing, and servicing a package.

Psychrometer
An instrument for measuring the humidity (water-vapor) content of air by means of two thermometers, one dry and one wet.

Pulp
The raw material from which paper is made. A fibrous product produced by mechanical or chemical processes. Pulp for paper can be made from wide variety of plants grown specifically for their fiber properties, or even from agricultural waste.

QA

Acronym for quality assurance.

Qualifying

The act of setting up and administering a training program that ensures that the people who will be interfacing with the packaging line are given a thorough overview of the packaging line and a detailed program on what they need to know to complete their tasks without hesitation or guessing. All training must address the following questions:

— Who should be trained?

— When should training be done?

— What training should be done?

— How should we do training?

— Where should we do training?

— How much is enough training?

— Manuals and other self-help tools?

— Performance reviews and continuing improvement?

— Company standards and policy?

Quality circles

Teams of employees used to diagnose and solve quality problems relating to fulfilling the needs of the customer. It also includes the use of the work team concept for solving other problems related to productivity improvement, safety, and so on.

Quality Control (QC)

A system for assuring that commercial products meet certain standards of identity, fill of container, and quality sanitation and adequate plant procedures.

Quality Function Deployment (QFD)

A set of techniques for determining and communicating customer needs and translating them into product and service design specifications and manufacturing methods.

Quality Package

A package that meets all design specifications and is manufactured in compliance is ISO 9001 or ISO 9002. Take a bottle of shampoo as an example of a quality package:

— The content must comply with internal and governmental weight and/or volume regulations.

— The print documentation must be clear, readable, accurate, and acceptable to the end customer and comply with governmental regulations at point of manufacture to point of end use.

— The container must be clearly coded and identified using industry-standard codes such as UPC and comply with customer and governmental regulations at point of manufacture to point of end use.

— The seal on the package must be seated correctly to a specified torque and/or form a protective seal against leakage, spoilage, contamination, and/or tampering.

In short, a quality package is the end product envisioned by the marketing group that will fulfill all the design criteria and packaging standards, either internal, governmental, or required by the customer.

Quick-change Process (QCP)

A common phrase to describe the techniques used to design and operate a packaging line that is always prepared to change from one product to another within a minute's notice. This encompasses quick changeover (QCO), clean-in-place (CIP), eradication of all possible adjustments, matchmark position settings for remaining adjustments, flexible crewing, tooling readiness, and a streamlined results-oriented management. A similar phrase is "quick changeout."

Quick Changeout

The total downtime between production runs of different packages or the end of the first production run to the end of the next production run time. It encompasses the same time-period definition as the quick-change process involving preparation time, cleanup time, and changeover time.

Quick Changeover (QCO)

A common phrase to describe the technique of effective tooling used to change a packaging line over from one product to another using no tools and that can be done in minutes or less.

Radio-Frequency Identification (RFID)

An automatic identification method remotely retrieving data using tags or transponders. Chipless RFID does not require an integrated circuit, and can be printed directly onto items at a lower cost than their chip-based counterparts.

Retort

A process and packaging type where food filled into the final selling unit is cooked to a temperature sufficient to kill off toxic micro-organisms. The temperature is generally around 121° C.

Relative Humidity

The ratio of actual humidity to the maximum humidity that air can retain without precipitation at a given temperature and pressure. Expressed as percent of saturation at a specified temperature. *See also* Absolute Humidity.

Reliability

The probability that a device or system will not fail within a given time frame under given conditions.

Quantitatively, this is expressed as a true mathematical probability.

Rework (Q)

Components or packages produced that are of unacceptable quality but are acceptable for reprocessing (denoted by Q and qi). Furthermore, the product is reclaimable and some input items are reusable. If the product cannot be restored to an acceptable quality, it becomes wastage.

Rigid Plastic Packaging

Freestanding plastic packaging. The main raw materials used are PET, HDPE, and PP.

Risk

A perceived probability of failure or not achieving the target(s) or goal(s) as originally established at the start of the project as well as its consequences. No project or decision is risk-free. It is understood that all efforts can include several types of risk, but most can be boiled down to two main types: Political and technical risks.

Risk, political

Political risk is a perceived probability of management's ability of not understanding the basic technical and marketing techniques and philosophies in order to make clear timely and profitable decisions and to accept their consequences in the marketplace. It is also related to management's ability to admit mistakes quickly, change direction, and learn from the experience. Finally, it relates to ego and power, elements of which make up humanity and the complexity of life. In some cases where the consequences are death, a low probability is of little comfort and must not be traded off.

Risk, technical

Risk strictly related to a new process, machine, or

component used in packaging a known product or a new untried product or package design. Since technical risk is a probability of failure and its consequences, it is logical to assume that additional money and time will be expended in a direct relationship to the shortfalls that occurs in the first attempt. Sometimes management will deem a project that is partly successful to be satisfactory since the costs and time to correct the shortfall are not economical. In this case, although the project is technically a failure, politically it was approved. As a guideline, more than 70 percent of all projects fail to reach the original technical targets or goals and less than half of all projects that have shortfalls are completely corrected. In some cases where the consequences are death, a low probability is of little comfort and must not be traded off.

Run Speed

The run speed of a machine is the instantaneous operating rate at some point in time. It is derived in terms of the output rate at that time. For example, if a machine is outputting at a rate of 300 (not necessarily quality) containers per minute (cpm) at a given point in time, then that is the run speed. As the time interval increases, the output rate is always lower than the run speed, due to stoppages, wastage, rework, and so on. When the output approaches the run speed for any given time period, then the line is approaching the steady-state condition. In a perfect world, the output and the run speed would be equal.

Run Utilization

The fraction of time the packaging line is producing output at a set run speed divided by the total time available for production. Changeover, cleanup, and prep work are not included. This factor can be considered the uptime during the producing time period.

Run Up Period

The time required after the package changeout has been completed to get the given interval actual run speed (or output rate) to exceed the 80 percent of achievable run speed. The more correct term is transient period. If the packaging process cannot move out of the run up period quick enough, the loss in potential production can be staggering.

Sanitize

To reduce the microbial flora in or on articles such as food-plant equipment or eating utensils to levels judged safe by public health authorities.

Sanitizer

A chemical agent that reduces the number of microbial contaminants on food-contact surfaces to safe levels from the standpoint of public health requirements. Sanitizing can also be done by heating.

Schedule Capability (Cp)

In simple terms, the schedule capability is the relative measure of how capable or effective the actual packaging process is in producing the appropriate volume of needed packages within the planned plant operational time period or schedule. The schedule capability relates to the ratio of the scheduled run cycle time available divided by the actual package run cycle time used. This definition is valid only if the actual time taken is greater than the scheduled time. If the actual time is less than the scheduled time, the capability is the actual package run cycle time divided by the scheduled run cycle time. The schedule capability is always equal to or less than 1. The term schedule capability is sometimes shortened to just capability.

Scheduled Package Run Cycle (SPRC)

The scheduled package (or product) run cycle refers to the time that management allots the packaging line to yield a required quantity of quality packages.

It can also be defined as the total plant asset available time based on a 24-hour clock. If this definition is used, it should be defined as the asset package run cycle (APRC). In an ideal system, the scheduled package run cycle and the package run cycle are equal. Normally, the scheduled product run cycle is far longer than the product run cycle, based on the designed or historical output. For an optimized packaging process, PRC is usually more than 90 percent of the SPRC.

Secondary Spoilage

Consists of those cans rusted or corroded as a result of bursting or leaking cans. May occur during warehousing.

Setup

This is basically the same as the changeover but relates only to a given machine, not the packaging line. It is defined as the completion of the following items:

1. The exchange of changeover parts or tooling

2. The recalibration and/or adjustment of the machine

3. The preliminary test with samples

At the end of the procedure, the machine is expected to perform the desired function to produce a quality package at the achievable run speed.

Sheet Feeder

A corrugating plant with no converting equipment and producing only corrugated sheet. The term "sheet feeder" can also mean the device at the front of converting machinery.

Shelf Life

The length of time a container will maintain market acceptability under specified conditions of storage. Also known as merchantable life.

Shipper/Transport Container

The container/carton used to transport primary packaging.

Simulation

The modeling or effect by computer, scale models, or mathematics to play out a scenario or sequence of events that would give the appearance or outcome approximating the real world as closely as possible. A computer simulation is a means of representing the behavior of real-life systems over time, using some combination of models, initial conditions, and discrete time steps. Real-time computer simulation is always the optimal condition.

Single-facer

The section of a corrugator which forms the corrugated shape in the medium, applies adhesive to it and then bonds it to the flat linerboard creating a single-face board.

Solvent

A substance that dissolves or holds another substance in solution such as common salt in water. Solvents are used in some foods as carriers for flavors, colors, stabilizers, emulsifiers, antioxidants, and other ingredients.

Speed Factor (Sf)

The actual average output rate or actual run speed of a packaging line divided by the achievable run speed of the packaging line for a given package run cycle and time period. It does not include changeover, prep time, and cleanup already in utilization.

Standard Practice

A written description of the minimum necessary to meet the intent of policy and standards. To the extent possible, standards should describe the "what" and not the "how."

Statistical Control

The state of predictable stability.

Statistical Process Control (SPC)

A statistical method of using control charts to monitor whether a process is in or out of control. It is a method that requires planning teamwork, methodology of measurement, knowledge of measurement techniques, and acute knowledge of the process. In most causes, the packaging process must be improved first before control charts can be used effectively.

Statistical Quality Control (SQC)

The use of statistical techniques for process control or product and package inspection. It also includes the use of experimental design techniques for process improvement.

Steel, 3P

Steel cans are generally three-piece cans (3P) made of a top and a body, and an end or base. The cylinder of the body is formed from a sheet of pre-printed or plain tin-coated steel and the end is seamed to it prior to delivery to the filler. The customer will add the top (second piece), and label, after filling.

Stockkeeping Unit (SKU)

An industry term that details the assortment or variety of items shipped in one physical case.

Stoppage

A short time occurrence that causes the packaging line or any portion of the packaging line to cease production of a quality package. A stoppage is made up of frequency and duration.

Surfactant

Surface-active agent.

System Downtime

The total amount of time the packaging line stopped or ceased production during the run period. System downtime is generally less than the total sum of all machine and conveyor downtimes, due to buffers and idle machine factors. It is best measured after the last operation in the packaging process, which usually is palletizing. System downtime normally should not include changeover, cleanup, and prep time periods, which should be documented separately.

Temper

A measure of the ductility and hardness of steel plate.

Thermocouple

A bimetallic device used to measure temperatures electrically.

Thermoforming

The process of shaping a plastic sheet of styrene or PVC under heat and pressure.

Tolerance

A specified allowance for deviations in weighing, measuring, and so on from the standard dimensions or weight.

Total Productive Maintenance (TPM)

A philosophy or management tool that views maintenance not as a necessary evil but a vital operation that contributes to the productivity and profitability of the company. For JIT to work, one of the keys is to ensure the process availability to produce is maximized. A coordinated maintenance program which integrates QCP, TQM, preventive maintenance, predictive maintenance, and DFA is needed to have a successful TPM program.

Throughput

Throughput for a given packaging line and product is the exact quantity of quality packages produced in a package run cycle required by the customer and shipped to the customer. It is denoted by the symbol Y. Similarly, we define the throughput for a machine or throughput rate as the number of items (of acceptable quality) leaving a machine in a given amount of time. We denote this by yi, for the ith machine. The word throughput has the same definition as output.

Translucent

Descriptive of a material or substance capable of transmitting some light but not clear enough to be seen through.

Transparent

Descriptive of a material or substance capable of a high degree of light transmission (e.g., glass).

Uptime

The time a machine or process is available to produce a quality product during the run period of the package run cycle.

USDA

United States Department of Agriculture. The USDA Labeling and Consumer Protection Staff (LCPS) develops policies and inspection methods, and administers programs to protect consumers from misbranded and economically adulterated meat, poultry, and egg products.

Utilization (U)

The fraction of a defined time period that is actually used to produce quality packages. There are many definitions of utilization, but there are five main types of utilization:

1. System utilization

2. Run utilization

3. Package changeout utilization

4. Element or machine utilization

5. Asset utilization

System utilization is the fraction of the total package run cycle actually used to produce a needed quantity of quality packages at a set run speed. Run utilization is the fraction of time the packaging line is producing output at a set run speed divided by the total time available for production. Changeover, cleanup, and prep work are not included. This factor can be considered the uptime during the producing time period. Package changeout utilization is the fraction of the package run cycle time the packaging line has available for producing output at a set run speed after changeover, cleanup, and prep time have been completed. Element utilization is the fraction of time a given machine or element is actually producing output at a set run speed divided by the total time available for production. Changeover, cleanup, and prep work are not included. This definition usually relates to machinery and/or components. Asset utilization is the fraction of a 24-hour-per-day clock that is actually used in producing quality packages until the package run cycle is completed. If the package run cycle takes exactly 3 days, then the total asset utilization time is $24 \times 3 = 72$ hours, even though only one shift per day is being used. When calculating PI, only the system utilization is used that considers the entire package run cycle with changeover, cleanup, prep work, and run utilization. Run utilization is used to get an overview of the integration, control, and elements that make up the total packaging line. Element utilization is used to get an overview of a given machine, conveyor, or equipment. It can be used as a general guideline for acceptance of a vendor's machine. But for a specific specification for acceptance of a vendor's machine, the disturbance frequency (DF) should be used with the element utilization. The word *utilization* refers to system utilization.

Vacuum Packaging

Packaging in rigid or flexible containers from which substantially all gases have been removed prior to final sealing of the container.

Value Analysis

A systematic approach to simplification and standardization of products so that they provide needed value at minimum cost. Usually applied to existing products to reduce input counts or amount of packaging.

Variables

Quantities that describe the current operating state of a machine or system. Output rate, wastage rate, and cycle rates are examples of variables.

Verifying

The act of being able to determine without hesitation that the machine testing and training of personnel is not only thorough but also effective in the day-to-day production of the packaging line without senior staff, consultants, and/or machinery service personnel being involved in any shape or form.

Viscometer

An instrument to measure viscosity.

Viscosity

Internal friction or resistance to flow of a liquid. The constant ratio of shearing stress to rate of shear. In liquids for which this ratio is a function of stress, the term apparent viscosity is defined as this ratio.

Wastage (W)

Components or packages produced that are of unacceptable quality. The quantity of such items is denoted by the symbol W for a system and w_i for the ith machine. Items of unacceptable quality cannot be reused or recycled back into the system. As a general policy, food and pharmaceutical products that fall onto the production floor are discarded and are therefore wastage. In other industries, wastage may be reworked. Usually employees use their discretion to decide on wastage items, unless company policy or government regulations clearly define wastage. Wastage increases manufacturing costs. Some basic costs relating to wastage are:

1. Initial cost for the product and/or inputs

2. Overhead cost

3. Opportunity cost

4. Disposal cost

5. Recycling cost

A decrease in wastage will in turn lower production costs and increase output. In general, wastage is an indicator of a process out of control.

Select Bibliography

Knowledge Is Power

List provided by o2-USA/Upper Midwest (o2umw.org).

By educating ourselves, we can in turn educate our clients, suppliers, and the consumer, the driving force behind it all. Green design simply becomes good design, and suddenly the whole landscape has changed — quite a lot to demand of a little lunchtime reading, but every journey starts with a single step. This one doesn't even require special shoes.

The Big Picture

Biomimicry: Innovation Inspired by Nature
Janine M. Benyus

Cradle to Cradle: Remaking the Way We Make Things
William McDonough and Michael Braungart

Design for the Real World: Human Ecology and Social Change
Victor Papanek

Earth in Mind: On Education, Environment, and the Human Prospect
David W. Orr

Ecodesign: The Sourcebook
Alastair Fuad-Luke

Eco-Economy: Building an Economy for the Earth
Lester R. Brown
www.earth-policy.org

Ecological Design
Sim van der Ryn and Stuart Cowan
www.serve.com/ecobooks/ecodesig.htm

Eternally Yours: Visions on Product Endurance
Edited by Ed van Hinte, Liesbeth Bonekamp, Henk Muis, and Arnout Odding
www.eternally-yours.org

Green Marketing: Opportunity for Innovation
Jacquelyn A. Ottman
www.GreenMarketing.com

The Landscape of Man: Shaping the Environment from Prehistory to the Present Day
Geoffrey Jellicoe and Susan Jellicoe

Natural Capitalism: Creating the Next Industrial Revolution
Paul Hawken, Amory Lovins, and L. Hunter Lovins

The Nature of Design: Ecology, Culture, and Human Intention
David W. Orr

The Natural Step for Business
Natural Step Publications

Trespassers: Inspirations for Eco-Efficient Design
Conny Bakker and Ed van Hinte
www.010publishers.nl

Architecture and Community Development

Building With Vision: Optimizing and Finding Alternatives to Wood
Dan Imhoff
www.watershedmedia.org

Dimensions of Sustainability: Architecture, Form, Technology, Environment and Culture
Edited by Andrew Scott

From Eco-Cities to Living Machines: Principles of Ecological Design
Nancy Todd, John Todd, and Jeffrey Parkin, illustrator

Sustainable Ecosystems and the Built Environment
Christopher McCarthy and Guy Battle

Packaging and Print Design

The Complete Guide to Eco-Friendly Design
Poppy Evans
www.poppyevans.com/books.htm

Design Guidelines for Sustainable Packaging
www.sustainablepackaging.org

The Guide to Tree-Free, Recycled and Certified Papers
Dan Imhoff
www.watershedmedia.org

Packaging, Policy and the Environment
Edited by Geoffrey M. Levy
http://www.iopp.org/store

Paper or Plastic: Searching for Solutions to an Overpackaged World
Dan Imhoff
www.watershedmedia.org

Package Design Magazine: Sustainablity Update
www.packagedesignmag.com/sustainableresource

Product Design

Design + Environment: A Global Guide to Designing Greener Goods
Helen Lewis and John Gertsakis with Tim Grant, Nicola Morelli, and Andrew Sweatman
www.greenleaf-publishing.com

Sustainable Solutions: Developing Products and Services for the Future
Edited by Matin Charter and Ursula Tischner
www.greenleaf-publishing.com

The Total Beauty of Sustainable Products
Edwin Datschefski
www.biothinking.com

Paperboard tubes were used to craft a functioning, vertical, urban eco-farm. The 2008 installation in the courtyard of MoMA's P.S.1 museum in Queens, New York, yielded fresh produce all that summer and was the creation of WORK Architecture. (publicfarm1.org)

Notes by Chapter

Chapter 1: Taking the First Step

Endnotes

1. *Wikipedia,* "Tylenol," http://en.wikipedia.org/wiki/Tylenol.

2. "Sustainable Consumption: Why Consumption Matters," Dave Tilford, Sierra Club Sustainable Consumption Committee Web site, 2000, http://www.sierraclub.org/sustainable_consumption/tilford.asp.

3. Data from http://www.footprintnetwork.org.

4. *The Story of Stuff,* Annie Leonard (Free Range Studios), 2005, http://storyofstuff.com.

5. "Sustainable Consumption: Why Consumption Matters," Dave Tilford, Sierra Club Sustainable Consumption Committee Web site, 2000.

6. ibid

7. http://www.calvert-henderson.com/update-globalboom.htm.

8. "Sustainable Consumption: Why Consumption Matters," Dave Tilford, Sierra Club Sustainable Consumption Committee Web site, 2000

9. Neva Goodwin, "Economic Vitality in a Transition to Sustainability," Civil Society Institute, 2008.

10. *2007 Cause Evolution & Environmental Survey,* Cone LLC, http://www.coneinc.com/files/2007ConeSurveyReport.pdf.

11. UN NGO Committee on Sustainable Development, http://www.unngocsd.org/CSD_Definitions%20SD.htm.

12. Ron Romanik, "The Wal-Mart Sustainability Scorecard Becomes Interactive, Competitive Reality," *Package Design Magazine,* Nov. 2006.

13. GreenBiz.com. "Wal-Mart's Newest Green Goal: Cleaner Supply Chains," September 2007, http://www.greenbizleaders.com/NewsDetail.cfm?NewsID=35966.

14. "Sustainable Consumption: Why Consumption Matters," Dave Tilford, Sierra Club Sustainable Consumption Committee Web site, 2000

15. Ceres Annual Report, "2006 & Beyond," foreword letter by Mindy S. Lubber, president of Ceres, August 2007.

16. "Playing games with the planet," *The Economist,* September 27, 2007.

17. Robert Axelrod and William D. Hamilton, "The Evolution of Cooperation," *Science,* 1981, http://www.cscs.umich.edu/Software/ComplexCoop.html.

18. *Wikipedia,* "Code of Hammurabi," http://en.wikipedia.org/wiki/Code_of_Hammurabi.

19. Science and Environmental Health Network, http://www.sehn.org/precaution.html.

20. Tim O'Riordan and James Cameron editors, *Interpreting The Precautionary Principle,* (London: Earthscan Publications Ltd., 1994), http://dieoff.org/page31.htm.

21. World Charter for Nature, 48th plenary meeting, 28 October 1982, http://www.un.org/documents/ga/res/37/a37r007.htm

22. Science and Environmental Health Network, http://www.sehn.org/precaution.html.

23. "The Precautionary Principle in Action," Bay Area Working Group on the Precautionary Principle, http://www.takingprecaution.org.

24. City and County of San Francisco Environment Code, Ord. No. 279-07, File No. 070678, approved Dec. 12, 2007 (added by Ord. 171-03, File No. 030422, App. 7/3/2003), http://www.municode.com/Resources/gateway.asp?pid=14134&sid=5.

25. The Body Shop International, Chemicals Strategy, August 2006, http://www.thebodyshopinternational.com/NR/rdonlyres/D7F2A9D1-416A-47B8-8BC3-1E858A37F81C/0/BSI_Chemicals_Strategy.pdf.

26. Blue Planet Village, http://www.blueplanetvillage.com/articles.php?a=read&aid=22.

27. "Japan's Sustainable Society in the Edo Period (1603–1867)," *Japan for Sustainability Newsletter* #007, March, 2003.

28. "The Confucian Roots of Business Kyosei," C.M. Boardman and H. K. Kato, (*Journal of Business Ethics*, V48, no.4, December 2003) 317–33.

29. The Caux Round Table, excerpts reprinted with permission, http://www.cauxroundtable.org/history.html, /about.htm, /principles.html.

30. Canon Global, Environmental Activities, http://www.canon.com/environment, http://www.usa.canon.com/html/templatedata/pressrelease/20071022_iso14001.html.

31. *Wikipedia*, "Overview of Triple Bottom Line", http://en.wikipedia.org/wiki/Triple_bottom_line.

32. John A. Luke, Jr., MeadWestvaco Stewardship & Sustainability statement, http://www.meadwestvaco.com/sustainability.ns.

33. Ceres, http://www.ceres.org.

34. *Carbon Beta™ and Equity Performance: An Empirical Analysis, Innovest Strategic Value Advisors*, October 2007, http://www.innovestgroup.com.

35. John Kalkowski, "State of 'green packaging,'" *Packaging Digest*, December 1, 2007, http://www.packagingdigest.com/article/CA6505215.html?q=state+of+green+packaging.

36. "Playing games with the planet," *The Economist*, September 2, 2007.

37. http://walmartstores.com/GlobalWMStoresWeb/navigate.do?catg=345.

38. Nichola Groom, "Wal-Mart to pay more for 'greener' goods," *Reuters*, February 7, 2008 http://www.reuters.com/article/ousiv/idUSN0741043320080208?sp=true.

Chapter 2: Mechanics of Human Behavior

Resources

J. S. Adams, "Inequity in social exchange." *Advances in Experimental and Social Psychology*, no. 62 (1965): 335-43.

Amel, E. L. and Manning, C. M. 2007. "What are they thinking? Sustainability and the American psyche." *Package Design Magazine*, http://www.packagedesignmag.com.

Cialdini, R. B., *Influence: Science and practice*, 4th ed., Boston, MA: Allyn & Bacon, (2001).

Corbett, J. B., *Communicating Nature: How We Create and Understand Environmental Messages*, Washington, DC: Island Press, 2006.

Cornell, T., *A Brief Introduction to the Catholic Worker Movement*, http://www.catholicworker.com/cwo010.htm, September 25, 2007.

Farrell, J., "The Nature of American Life." Unpublished manuscript, 2007.

Gander, P., "Refill and reuse to reduce cost." *Packaging News.* http://www.packagingnews.co.uk/ thisIssue/PackagingNews/ September 25, 2007.

Gross, D., "Pocket more green with 'green' hype." Newsweek September 24, 2007.

Hongkong and Shanghai Banking Corporation. "HSBC launches international survey of public attitudes towards climate change." September 25, 2007. http://www.hsbc.com/1/2/newsroom/news/news-archive-2007/hsbc-launches-international-survey-of-public-attitudes-towards-climate-change.

Hunt, R. R. and Ellis, H. C., *Fundamentals of Cognitive Psychology*, 7th ed., New York: McGraw-Hill, 2004.

Kasser, T., *The High Price of Materialism.* Cambridge, MA: MIT Press, 2002.

Lakoff. G., *Moral politics: How Liberals and Conservatives think,* 2nd ed.. Chicago, IL: The University of Chicago Press, 2002.

Langer, E. J., *Mindfulness.* Reading, MA: Addison-Wesley, 1989.

Litwin, M. S., *How to Assess and Interpret Survey Psychometrics,* 2nd ed., Thousand Oaks, CA: Sage, 2003.

McDonough, W. and Braungart, M., *Cradle to cradle: Remaking The Way We Make Things.* New York: North Point Press, 2002.

McKenzie-Mohr, D. and Smith, W. *Fostering Sustainable Behavior: An Introduction to Community Based Social Marketing.* British Columbia: New Society Publishers, 1999.

Morgan, D. L., *The Focus Group Guidebook.* Thousand Oaks, CA: Sage, 1998.

Norman, D., *The Design of Everyday Things.* New York: Basic Books, 2002.

Schultz, P. W. and Zelezny, L., "Reframing environmental messages to be congruent with American values." *Human Ecology Review* 10, no. 2 2003:126–36.

Shaw, D., Newholm, T., Dickinson, R., "Consumption as voting: An exploration of consumer empowerment." *European Journal of Marketing. Special Issue: Consumer Empowerment* 40 no. 9–10:1049–67.

Vroom, V. H., *Work and Motivation.* New York: Wiley, 1964.

Weiten, W., *Psychology: Themes and variations,* 7th ed. Belmont, CA: Thomson, 2007.

Yale Center for Environmental Law and Policy. *Sea change in public attitudes toward global warming.* http://www.yale.edu/envirocenter/, Sept. 25, 2007.

Chapter 3: Marketing and Truth

Endnotes

1. Wendy Jedlička, "Consumers: The Best Force for Change," *Twin Cities Green Guide,* 2000. http://www.thegreenguide.org/article/goods/ environmental

2. Aveda Web site, http://aveda.aveda.com/ aboutaveda/mission.asp.

3. Jim Carlton, "Retailer Leans on Suppliers to Protect Forests Abroad; Playing Mediator in Chile Indonesian Loggers Resist" *The Wall Street Journal,* August 6, 2004.

4. Press release, Nike, April 13, 2005, http://www. ceres.org/news/news_item.php?nid=113.

5. Center for Biodiversity and Conservation, "Biodiversity in Crisis? Losses of Species and Habitats An Introduction to the Issues and Comparison of Opinions from Scientists and the Public," American Museum of Natural History, http://cbc.amnh.org/crisis/resconpercap.html.

6. Rich Pirog, "Food, Fuel, and Freeways: An Iowa Perspective On How Far Food Travels, Fuel Usage, And Greenhouse Gas Emissions," Leopold Center for Sustainable Agriculture, June 2001, http://www.leopold.iastate.edu/pubs/staff/ppp/

7. http://www.guardian.co.uk/environment/2007/may/31/greenpolitics.retail/print http://www.greenbiz.com/news/news_third.cfm?NewsID=36271

8. Heather Green, "How Green Is That Gizmo?" *Business Week,* December 20, 2007, http://www.businessweek.com/magazine/content/07_53/b4065036215848.htm?chan=innovation_innovation+%2B+design_green+design

9. "FTC Announces Workshop on 'Green Guides' and Packaging," February 25, 2008, http://www.ftc.gov/opa/2008/02/greenguides.shtm

10. Actual comments made to author in innumerable meetings.

11. GreenBiz.com, "Most Green Marketing Claims Aren't True, Says New Report," http://www.greenbiz.com/news/news_third.cfm?NewsID=36271

12. TerraChoice Environmental Marketing "Six Sins of Greenwashing," http://www.terrachoice.com

13. "Guides for the Use of Environmental Marketing claims" http://www.ftc.gov/bcp/grnrule/guides 980427.htm, presented here with FTC acknowledgment and permission through the Freedom of Information Act.

14. Laura Everage, "Understanding the LOHAS Lifestyle," *The Gourmet Retailer,* October 01, 2002, http://www.gourmetretailer.com/gourmetretailer/magazine/article_display.jsp?vnu_content_id=1738479

15. Paul H. Ray, Ph.D. and Sherry Ruth Anderson, Ph.D., *The Cultural Creatives: How 50 Million People Are Changing the World,* (New York: Harmony Books, 2000), http://www.culturalcreatives.org

16. Are you a Cultural Creative? http://www.culturalcreatives.org/questionnaire.html.

17. Steve Myers and Somlynn Rorie comp., "Organic and Natural News, Facts and Stats — The Year in Review," http://www.organicandnaturalnews.com/articles/0c1feat1.html

18. "Lund Food's careful plan for two-chain natural and organic program pays off," *Natural Grocery Buyer,* Jan./Feb. 2003. http://www.newhope.com/naturalcategorybuyer/ncb_backs/Jan-Feb_03/retailsuccess.cfm

Chapter 4: Laws and Economics

Regulations — Endnotes

1. Thomas Lindhqvist, "Extended producer responsibility in cleaner production: policy principle to promote environmental improvements of product systems." (IIEEE, 2000).

2. OECD, *Extended Producer Responsibility: A Guidance Manual for Governments*, OECD, Paris: 2001.

3. National Carpet Recycling Agreement http://www.pca.state.mn.us/oea/carpet/index.cfm.

4. The National Vehicle Mercury Switch Recovery Program http://www.epa.gov/mercury/switch.htm.

5. Oregon Department of Environmental Quality, "International Packaging Regulations," 2005.

6. Charles Fishman, "Message in a Bottle." *FastCompany.com,* July 2007.

7. Directive 2002/96/EC and Directive 2000/53/EC., http://eur-lex.europa.eu/LexUriServ/LexUriServ.do?uri=CELEX:32002L0096:EN:HTML.

8. *See* Directive 94/62/EC. http://eur-lex.europa.eu.

9. The National Beverage Producer Responsibility Act of 2003 was introduced by Senator Jim Jeffords on November 14, 2003.

10. http://www.ciwmb.ca.gov/Plastic/RPPC/ and http://www.deq.state.or.us/lq/sw/recovery/rpc.htm.

11. http://www.meti.go.jp/policy/recycle/main/english/law/contain.html.

12. http://law.epa.gov.tw/en/laws/962396701.html.

13. http://law.epa.gov.tw/en/laws/648849199.html.

14. http://www.ccme.ca/ourwork/waste.html?category_id=18.

15. http://www.ene.gov.on.ca/envision/land/wda/index.htm.

16. http://www.mddep.gouv.qc.ca/matieres/mat_res-en/parts-1-4.htm.

17. http://www.packagingcovenant.org.au.

Economics — Endnotes and Resources

18. World Packaging Organization, http://www.wpo.org.

19. The trade data used to generate the figures reported in this article are from the Comtrade dataset published by the United Nations. http://comtrade.un.org.

20. Packaging is defined to include the following standard international trade classifications (SITC): wood packaging containers and pallets (6351), paper and paperboard containers (6421), glass containers (6651), metal storage and transport containers (692), and plastic containers (8931). http://comtrade.un.org.

21. The gross domestic product (GDP) data used to generate the reported figures are from the World Development Indicators published by the World Bank. http://www.worldbank.org.

22. The trade sensitivity measure is calculated as exports minus importer as a percent of gross domestic product. This measure is calculated for each country in each market.

23. The value of net exports of waste materials as a percent of GDP is 0.3 percent or less for all countries.

24. International Trade Center, http://www.intracen.org.

Chapter 5: Systems Thinking

Notes on Chapter Material

This section includes more detail and references on information in this chapter.

Exploring Buckminster Fuller's ideas:

Many resources are available at the Buckminster Fuller Institute, http://www.bfi.org.

The World of Buckminster Fuller, dir. Robert Snyder, DVD, Mystic Fire Video, 1995.

Amy Edmondson, *A Fuller Explanation* (Boston: Birkhauser, 1985) Online at: May 2008, http://www.angelfire.com/mt/marksomers/40.html.

R. Buckminster Fuller, *Synergetics and Synergetics II* (New York: MacMillan, 1975, 1979) Online at: Summer 1997, May 2008, http://www.rwgrayprojects.com/synergetics/toc/toc.html.

Designers influenced by Fuller's ideas:

Paul MacReady: August 2007, May 2008, http://www.achievement.org/autodoc/page/mac0pro-1.

Stewart Brand: Sept. 2006, May 2008, http://sb.longnow.org/Home.html.

Medard Gabel: 2008, May 2008, http://www.bigpicturesmallworld.com/index.shtml.

Harold Brown: 2007, May 2008, http://www.osearth.com.

Lovins and Lovins: 2008, May 2008, http://www.rmi.org.

William McDonough: April 2008, May 2008, http://en.wikipedia.org/wiki/William_McDonough.

Understanding systems properties:

Christopher Alexander, *The Timeless Way of Building and A Pattern Language* (New York: Oxford, 1979, 1977). These teach the basics of building multilayer systems in a way which connects the user and designer. In addition, the pattern language form allows design information to be shared as open source.

Mark Buchanan, *Nexus* (New York: Norton, 2002). This book summarizes the latest topics on network theory and emergence.

These next books are at a higher systems level, yet the principles are clear:

Sim Van Der Ryn, *Ecological Design* (Washington: Island Press, 2007).

Edward Goldsmith, *The Way* (Athens: University of Georgia Press, 1998).

John Todd, *From Eco-Cities to Living Machines* (Berkeley: North Atlantic, 1994), May 2008, http://www.toddecological.com/ecomachineprincipals.html.

Life Cycle Assessment:

Dr Heinz Stichnothe of The University of Manchester School of Chemical Engineering and Analytical Science for review comments, http://www.earthshift.com.

Commercial LCA software:

Simapro, May 2008, http://www.pre.nl/simapro.

Gabi, May 2008, http://www.gabi-software.com.

Noncommercial LCA:

Eco-Indicator 99 and Eco-Indicator 95. May 2008, http://www.pre.nl/eco-indicator99/default.htm.

Examples on how to conduct LCA:

Design for Sustainability at Delft: May 2008 http://www.io.tudelft.nl/research/dfs.

Jensen et al., *Overview of Life Cycle Assessment (LCA): A guide to approaches, experiences and information sources*, 2008, http://reports.eea.europa.eu/GH-07-97-595-EN-C/en.

Cradle to Cradle:

McDonough, W. and Braungart, M., *Cradle to Cradle: Remaking The Way We Make Things* (New York: North Point Press, 2002), May 2008, http://www.mcdonough.com/cradle_to_cradle.htm.

Design examples: 2007, May 2008,
http://www.mbdc.com/c2c.

Biomimicry Consulting:

The Biomimicry Guild: May 2008,
http://www.biomimicryguild.com/indexguild.html.

Biomimicry Education:

The Biomimicry Institute 2008, May 2008,
http://www.biomimicryinstitute.org.

Permaculture:

Ross Mars, *The Basics of Permaculture Design* (White River Jct: Chelsea Green, 2005).

Change Management:

Manns and Rising, *Fearless Change* (Indianapolis: Addison Wesley, 2004) May 2008, http://www.cs.unca.edu/~manns/intropatterns.html.

Endnotes

1. Jay Baldwin, *Buckyworks: Buckminster Fuller's Ideas for Today* (New York: Wiley, 1997).

2. *Wikipedia,* "Dymaxion map," May 2008, May 2008, http://en.wikipedia.org/w/index.php?title=Dymaxion_map&oldid=213706482.

3. Mahlon Hoagland and Bert Dodson, *The Way Life Works* (New York: Three Rivers, 1998).

4. William McDonough and Michael Braugart, "Design for Triple Top Line," 2002, May 2008, http://www.mcdonough.com/writings/design_for_triple.htm.

5. "United Nations Environment Programme Division of Technology, Industry and Economics" May 2008, http://www.unep.fr/pc/sustain/design/pss.htm.

6. Spencer Johnson, *Who Moved My Cheese* (New York: Putnam, 1998).

7. The Engineer, "3M-inent thinking," May 2005, May 2008, http://www.theengineer.co.uk/Articles/290942/3M-inent+thinking.htm.

8. Technical nutrients are from William McDonough and Michael Braungart, *Cradle to Cradle* (New York: North Point, 2002).

9. *Wikipedia,* "Competitive exclusion principle," April 2008, May 2008, http://en.wikipedia.org/w/index.php?title=Competitive_exclusion_principle&oldid=205650952.

10. Edward de Bono, *Sur/petition* (New York: HarperCollins, 1992).

11. David G. Ullman, *Making Robust Decisions* (Victoria, BC: Trafford, 2006).

12. J. Lagerstedt, "Functional and environmental factors in early phases of product development — Eco functional matrix," KTH PhD thesis, 2003.

13. CTQ Media LLC, "Triz Journal" 2006, May 2008, http://www.triz-journal.com.

14. Darrell Mann, "Hands-On Systematic Innovation," Presentation, 2003, http://www.osaka.gu.ac.jp/php/nakagawa/TRIZ/eTRIZ/epapers/e2004Papers/eMann0409/eMannForum040930.pdf.

15. Alan Van Pelt and Jonathan Hay, "Using Triz and Human-Centered Design for Consumer Product Development," (Berkley: Berkley Institute of Design, 2006), http://best.berkeley.edu/~jhey03/files/Publications/TRIZ%20and%20Human-Centered%20design%20TF2006%20Van%20Pelt%20Hey.pdf.

16. Environmental Protection Agency, "Energy Star," May 2008, http://www.energystar.gov.

17. Christopher Alexander, *The Timeless Way of Building* (Oxford: Oxford University Press, 1979).

18. "Bio Signal" May 2008, http://www.biosignal. com.au/main.htm.

19. *Wikipedia*, "Lotus effect," May 2008, http://en. wikipedia.org/w/index.php?title=Lotus_effect& oldid=211937920.

20. David Holmgren, "The Essence of Permaculture" 2002, May 2008, http://www.holmgren. com.au/html/Writings/essence.html.

21. Bill Mollison. "Permaculture: Design for Living." In Context. no. 28 (Spring 1991): pp. 50. May 2008, http://www.context.org/ICLIB/IC28/ Mollison.htm.

22. Ray Jardine, *Beyond Backpacking, A guide to Lightweight Hiking* (LaPine, Ore.: Adventurelore Press, 1999).

23. Bill Mollison, *Permaculture: A Designers' Manual* (Tasmania: Tagari, 1997).

24. *Wikipedia*, "Change Management" June 2008, http://en.wikipedia.org/wiki/Change_ management_%28people%29.

25. *Wikipedia*, "Everett Rogers" June 2008 http://en.wikipedia.org/wiki/Everett_Rogers.

26. Mary Lynn Manns and Linda Rising, *Fearless Change* (Indianapolis: Addison-Wesley 2004) May 2008, http://www.cs.unca.edu/ ~manns/intropatterns.html.

27. Fred Nickols, "Change Management 101: A Primer," 2006, May 2008, http://home.att.net/ ~nickols/change.htm.

28. *Wikipedia*, "Twelve leverage points," April 2008, May 2008, http://en.wikipedia.org/w/

index.php?title=Twelve_leverage_points &oldid=206754218.

29. *Journal of Industrial Ecology*, Yale University, Blackwell Publishing, Inc., http://www.mitpress journals.org/jie.

30. Industrial Ecology Academic departments, May 2008, http://en.wikipedia.org/ wiki/Industrial_ecology#External_links.

31. Paraphrased from Keoleian et al., "Life Cycle Design Framework and Demonstration Projects," (Washington, DC: Risk Reduction Engineering Laboratory, Office of Research and Development, U.S. Environmental Protection Agency, July 1995) EPA 600/R-95/107. *See also*: Keoleian, G.A., and D. Menerey. "Sustainable Development by Design: Review of Life Cycle Design and Related Approaches." *Journal of the Air and Waste Management Association* (1994) 44: 644–668.

32. Summary of product service systems, May 2008, http://www.unep.fr/pc/sustain/design/pss.htm.

33. *Wikipedia*, "Analytic Hierarchy Process," May 2008, May 2008, http://en.wikipedia.org/w/ index.php?title=Analytic_Hierarchy_Process&ol did=211638724.

34. Wendy Jedlička, "The Times They Are a-Changin'," *Package Design Magazine*, May 2008 http://www.packagedesignmag.com/issues/200 6.06/sustainable.shtml.

35. International Organization for Standardization, "ISO – ISO 9000 / ISO 14000 – ISO 14000 essen-tials," May 2008, http://www.iso.org/iso/iso_ catalogue/management_standards/iso_9000_ iso_14000/iso_14000_essentials.htm.

36. European Food Transport System, May 2008, http://www.europoolsystem.com.

37. *Wikipedia*, "Environmental impact assessment," May 2008, May 2008, http://en.wikipedia.org/w/index.php?title=Environmental_impact_assessment&oldid=213415820.

38. "SimaPro LCA software," May 2008 http://www.pre.nl/simapro.

39. The EcoCost approach. May 2008 http://www.ecocostsvalue.com.

40. "World Business Council for Sustainable Development," 2008, http://www.wbcsd.org/templates/TemplateWBCSD5/layout.asp?MenuID=1.

41. Ir Joost G. Vogtländer, "The Model of the Eco-costs / Value Ratio (EVR)," TUDelft: Delft University of Technology, May 2008, http://www.ecocostsvalue.com.

42. GreenBlue,[SM] "Sustainable Packaging Coalition," 2007, http://www.sustainablepackaging.org.

43. Sustainable Packaging Coalition,[SM] "Definition of Sustainable Packaging," October 2005, http://sustainablepackaging.org/about_sustainable_packaging.asp.

44. ibid

45. GreenBlue,[SM] "The Design Guidelines for Sustainable Packaging," 2006, May 2008 http://www.greenblue.org/resources_documents.html.

46. ibid

47. Sustainable Packaging Coalition, "What is Sustainable Packaging?" May 2008, http://sustainablepackaging.org/about_sustainable_packaging.asp.

48. Remigijus Ciegis and Rokas Grunda, "Sustainable Business: The Natural Step Framework" May 2008, http://www1.apini.lt/includes/getfile.php?id=115.

49. Architecture for Humanity May 2008 http://www.architectureforhumanity.org.

50. Universal Design. May 2008, http://www.design.ncsu.edu/cud/about_ud/udprinciples htmlformat.html#top.

51. McDonough, W. and Braungart, M., *Cradle to Cradle: Remaking the Way We Make Things.* (New York: North Point Press, 2002).

52. ibid

53. Designtex. May 2008, http://cti.itc.virginia.edu/~meg3c/ethics/cases/dtex/dtex_1.html.

54. Solar Power. July 2007, May 2008 http://www.nytimes.com/2007/07/16/business/16solar.html?_r=1&oref=slogin.

55. *Wikipedia,* "Process Diagram," Feb. 2008, May 2008, http://en.wikipedia.org/wiki/Process_Diagram.

56. Shaw Contract Group — Processes Web page. http://www.shawcontractgroup.com.

57. Carbohydrate Economy. May 2008 http://www.carbohydrateeconomy.org.

58. Cradle to Cradle Design Protocol. 2008, May 2008, http://www.mbdc.com/c2c_mbdp.htm.

59. Design for Triple Top Line. 2002, May 2008. http://www.mcdonough.com/writings/design_for_triple.htm.

60. Design for Environment: Feb. 2008, May 2008 http://www.pca.state.mn.us/oea/p2/design.cfm.

61. Hannover Principles. 1992, May 2008. http://www.mcdonough.com/principles.pdf.

62. Sim van der Ryn, *Ecological Design Principles* (Washington: Island Press, 1996).

63. Nancy Todd and John Todd, *From Eco-Cities to Living Machines* (Berkeley: North Atlantic 1993).

64. Eric Von Hipple, *Democratizing Innovation* (Cambridge: MIT, 2006).

65. Wikipedia, "Innovation" May 2008, May 2008 http://en.wikipedia.org/wiki/Innovation#Techn ological_concepts_of_innovation.

66. John Thackara, *In The Bubble* (Cambridge: MIT, 2005).

67. "What is Triz?" May 2008, http://www.triz-journal.com/archives/what_is_triz/.

68. Universals of Culture. 2005, May 2008, http://everything2.com/index.pl?node_id=1744457.

Chapter 6: Materials and Processes
Endnotes

1. Facts and figures regarding the true cost of plastic bags, http://reusablebags.com/facts.php.

2. Planet Ark, "In US, Plastic Shopping Bag Still Rules," January 25, 2008, http://www.planetark.com/dailynewsstory.cfm/newsid/46606/story.htm.

3. FRIDGE: Socio-economic impact assessment of the proposed plastic bag regulations, Life cycle assessment of paper and plastic checkout carrier bags, http://www.nedlac.org.za/research/fridge/plastics/life.pdf.

4. Six-Month Report of Beverage Container Recycling & Significant Carbon Reductions, California Department of Conservation, 2007.

5. Lars J. Nilsson, Eric D. Larson, Kenneth Gilbreath, and Ashok Gupta, Energy Efficiency and the Pulp and Paper Industry, American Council for an Energy Efficient Economy, 1996.

6. International Institute for Environment and Development, *Toward a Sustainable Paper Cycle Executive Summary*, November 2000.

7. Dan Imhoff, *The Guide to Tree-free Recycled and Certified Paper*, (Healdsburg, CA: Watershed Media, 1999).

8. "Greener Choices, Plastics Recycling Tips," *Consumer Reports*, http://www.greenerchoices.org/products.cfm?product=plastic&pcat=homegarden.

9. E. S. Stevens, *Green Plastics: An Introduction to the New Science of Biodegradable Plastics* (Princeton, NJ: Princeton University Press, 2002), http://greenplastics.com.

10. ibid

11. Planet Ark, "Brazil Beaches: Streets Recycle Aluminum," May 10, 2006, http://www.planetark.com/dailynewsstory.cfm/newsid/36292/story.htm.

12. Jacob Sørensen, "Ecological rucksack for materials used in everyday products, NOAH — Friends of the Earth Denmark," http://www.noah.dk/baeredygtig/rucksack/rucksack.pdf.

13. "Rice University's Chemical 'Scissors' Yield Short Carbon Nanotubes; New Process Yields Nanotubes Small Enough to Migrate Through Cells," *ScienceDaily*, July 23, 2003, http://www.

sciencedaily.com/releases/2003/07/
030723083644.htm.

14. Lorie A. Wagner, *Materials in the Economy —
Material Flows, Scarcity, and the Environment,*
US Geological Survey Circular 1221,
http://pubs.usgs.gov/circ/2002/c1221.

15. "How long does litter last?" http://www.donttras
nevada.org/facts_figures.htm.

16. Ugo Bardi, "The Oil Drum: Europe,"
http://europe.theoildrum.com/node/3086.

17. David Cohen, "Earth's natural wealth: an audit,"
NewScientist.com, May 23, 2007.

18. Frank T. Manheim, "A New Look at Mining and
the Environment: Finding Common Ground,"
Geotimes, April 2006, http://www.agiweb.org/
geotimes/apr06/feature_MiningCommonGround.
html.

19. 2000 TRI Data Release, http://www.epa.gov/
tri/tridata/tri00/index.htm

20. *Encyclopedia of Earth,* http://www.eoearth.org
/article/Computer_recycling.

21. Rich Pirog, "Checking the food odometer:
Comparing food miles for local versus conven-
tional produce sales to Iowa institutions,"
Leopold Center for Sustainable Agriculture,
July 2003.

22. John G. Mitchell, "When Mountains Move,"
National Geographic, March 2006,
http://science.nationalgeographic.com/science
/earth/surface-of-the-earth/when-mountains-
move.html.

23. *Stern Review on the Economics of Climate
Change,* Report to UK Chancellor of the
Exchequer, 2006, Executive Summary, vii.

24. Jeremy Wheatland, *L.E.K. Consulting Carbon
Footprint Report 2007: Carbon Footprints and
the Evolution of Brand-Consumer Relationships,*
L.E.K. London.

25. Team Treehugger, "How to Green Your Carbon
Offsets," July 13, 2007, http://www.treehugger.com/
files/2007/07/how-to-green-your-carbon-offsets.php.

26. ODO Project Work Sheet 2006,
http://www.themightyodo.com.

27. *Life Cycle of Waste Image and Description,* US
Environmental Protection Agency (EPA),
December 2007, http://www.epa.gov/climate-
change/wycd/waste/lifecycle.html.

28. Landfill Methane Outreach Program (LMOP),
US Environmental Protection Agency, August
2007, http://www.epa.gov/lmop/overview.htm

29. Mary Crane, "Making Green from Garbage,"
Forbes, December 19, 2006.

Packaging takes on a new life from RePlayGround.com.

RePlayGround grew from the imagination of Tiffany
Threadgould. While doing graduate studies at Pratt Institute
in Brooklyn, New York, she wrote her thesis titled "Trash
Nouveau — reincarnating garbage into usable products."
She's been a design junkie ever since.

Index

A

Abalone, 138, 161

ABC (activity-based costing), 288

Abrasion resistance, 162

Acceptability, zone of, 42, 44, 47

Adachi, Joe, 24

Adaptation to environment, 142–149
 and boundary, 143–145
 by designers, 143
 ethical reasons for, 142
 and feedback/interchange, 148–149
 and function, 146–147

Advertising, 62–63, 157

Aerospace industry, 160

Aesthetics, as design driver, 172

AFF (ancient forest friendly), 278

Affordance, 56

Agents, change, 177–181

Agriculture, self-sustaining systems in, see Permaculture principles

Agripulp, 63, 232

Aizoaceae (plant family), 161

Alloys, 136

Alpine strawberries, 172

Alternative papers, 232–233, 278

Aluminum, 243

Aluminum cans, 93, 145

Amazon rainforest, 255

Amel, Elise L., xii, 58
 Chapter 2, 41–60

American Council for an Energy Efficient Economy, 229

Ancient forest friendly (AFF), 278

Anderson, Sherry Ruth, 99, 101

Animal testing, 82

Annie Chun's (company), 152–153

Anthocyanin, 166

Antibiotics, 163

Antimony, 247

Aracruz Cellulose, 231

Aseptic packaging, 110

Asia, producer responsibility in, 112–113

Assumptions, making, 42

Attachment, package as, 157

Attention, paying, 42, 48–49

Attractant, package as, 157

Attractiveness, 51

Australia, 113–115

Authority, 51

Auto industry, 78

Automatic behaviors, 48–49

Automotive parts, 95

Availability, 49

Aveda, 30–31, 46, 65–66

Axelrod, Robert, 16

B

Babylon, ancient, 17

Background Stories, 73–74

Backpacking, 173

Bacteria, 163–164, 167

Bald eagle, 134

Baldwin, Jay, 135

Bananas, 165

Bangladesh, 5

Bank of America, 28–29

Bardi, Ugo, 246

Bark, tree, 162

Barnes, David, 224

Barriers to action, 55–56

Barter economy, 62

Base maps, 173

Basements, wet, 174

Basic needs, 43–45

Baumeister, Dayna, xii
 "Biomimicry" 158

Beans, 176

Bees, 136, 157

The Beer Store, 252

Beetles, 164

Behavior, see Human behavior

Belgium, 120, 121, 123

Belize, 122

Bender, Walter, 36

Benefits, 50, 140

Ben & Jerry's, 65

Benyus, Janine, 145

Berkeley, California, 19

Best practices, 154, 194

Beyond Backpacking (Ray Jardine), 173

Big Box retailers, 10, 102

Billboards, 164

Billiard balls, 239

Biocides, 229

Biodegradability, 56, 278

"Biodegradable," 88–89

Biodiesel, 245

Biofilms, 163

Biomimicry, 158–168
 in communication, 164–166
 for containment, 158–161
 for protection, 161–164
 of working principles of life, 166–168

Biomimicry Guild, 166–167

Biomineralization, 161

Bioplastics, 117, 237–240

Biosignal, 164

Birds, 150, 157

Birt, Arlene, xii, 74
 "Communicating a Product's Story," 72

Blindness, inattentional, 45–46

Bloomberg, Michael, 263

Blue Angel, 278

Blue Planet 2020, 20

The Body Shop International, 20, 55

Bottles:
 "recyclable," 91
 soft drink, 86
 water, 56

Bottle Whimsy (Eric Edelman), xviii

Boundary, 140, 143–145, 157, 186

Brand, Stewart, 135

Brand loyalty, 65

Brand names, deceptive, 87

Braungart, M., 44, 46, 248

Brazil, 145, 231

Bridges, 136, 157

Britain, 77

Brown, Howard, 135

Brown-paper packaging, 46

Brundtland Commission, *see* World Commission on Environment and Development

BSI British Standards, 77

Buckyballs, 138

Buffers, 179–180

Burdock, 157

Burrs, 166

Busyness, 49

C

C2C, *see* Cradle to Cradle

CA (cellulose acetate), 237

Cables, 136

Cadmium, 246

California, 78, 112, 226–227

Cameras, one-time, 92

Canada, 230, 231
producer responsibility in, 113–114
and trade in packaging and waste, 119, 120, 122, 124

Canadian Council of Environmental Ministers (CCME), 113

Cannibals with Forks (John Elkington), 26

Canon, 23–24

Cans,
aluminum, 93, 145

Capital, 6, 26–27, 173

Capsules, hygrochastic, 161

Carbon accounting, 255–257

Carbon Beta and Equity Performance study, 32

Carbonfund.org, 256

Carbon labeling, 77–78, 278

Carbon Trust, 77

Cardboard, 167

Cause Evolution & Environmental Survey, 9

Caux Round Table (CRT), 22–24

Cbsm.com, 55, 57

CCME (Canadian Council of Environmental Ministers), 113

Celery Design, 46

Cell, as system, 144–145

Cellophane, 239, 240–241

Cell phone networks, 136

Cellular manufacturing, 215–216

Celluloid, 239

Cellulose acetate (CA), 237

Center for Resource Solutions, 256

Centrists, 100

Cereal boxes, commemorative, 157

Cereplast Compostables™, 238

Cereplast Hybrid Resins™, 238

Ceres, 28–30

Ceres Principles, 29–30

Certifiers, third-party, 82

CFCs, *see* Chlorofluorocarbons

"CFC-free," 82

CFL, *see* Compact fluorescent lightbulb

CFPA (Chlorine Free Products Association), 82

Chains, 137

Change, 14, 16–17, 269
responding to, 176–177
and sustainability, 178

Change agents, 177–181

Change management, 177–181
with change agent as peer, 178–179
with change agent in authority, 179–180
by individuals in changing environment, 180

Chasing arrow logo, 279

Cheek pouches, 158

"Chemical-free," 82

Chemistry, green, 194

Chile, 67

China, 129
ecological footprint of, 5
and trade in packaging and waste, 119, 120, 122–125

Chlorine free, 279–280

Chlorine Free Products Association (CFPA), 82

Chlorofluorocarbons (CFCs), 96, 278

Choice, encouraging consumer, 72–74

Cholesteric crystals, 164

Churchman, C. West, 133

Cialdini, R. B., 51

Circular consumption, 2

Citizens of our world, 168

Clamshell packaging, 39, 157

Clarity, 56

Clear glass, 251–252

Clear instructions, creating, 54

Cliffdale Associates, Inc., 97

Climate change, 16, 134, 230, 255, 263

Closed loop systems, 182

"Closing the loop," 147

Clueless, the, 54

Coconuts, 161

Codes of ethics, 17

Code of Hammurabi, 17

Coffee, 53

Coffee filters, 86, 90

Cognitive closure, 48

Cognitive dissonance, 50

Cohen, Rich, 69

Cold calling, 99

Collagen, 162

Collection, decay vs., 145

Colombia, 128

Color, without use of dye, 164

Combining, of functions, 146

Comfort:
  desire for, 44
  as value, 50

Commemorative cereal boxes, 157

Commercial ecology, 141

Common sense:
  collective, 17
  using, 64

Communication, 47, 54–55. *See also* Marketing and biomimicry, 164–166
  truthful, 78–79, 82–83

Communities, creating, 157

Community investment, 70

Community Waste Strategy, 111

Compact fluorescent light-bulb (CFL), 80, 81

Comparative claims, 86–87

Comparisons, social, 50

Compartmentalization, of resources, 174

Competition, 138, 154

Competitor focus, consumer focus vs., 151

Complexity, and perception, 45

Complex packaging, 110

Composites, 136

Compostability, claims of, 89–90, 278

Composting, 172, 196

Computer viruses, 157

CONEG (Council of Northeastern Governors), 112

Cone LLC, 9

Cone snail, 161

Conformity, 50

Confucian philosophy, 21

Congo, 245

Conseil, Dominique, 66

Consistency, 46, 51

Consumer behavior, *see* Human behavior

Consumer choice, encouraging, 72–74

Consumer empowerment, 62–63

Consumer focus, competitor focus vs., 151

Consumer relationship, 62–65

Consumer Reports, 235

Consumption, 171

Container deposit, 112

Containers and Packaging Recycling Law (Japan), 113

Containment, and biomimicry, 158–161

Continuous source reduction, 193

Convenience, 50, 55–56

Converted, the, 55

Converting magazine, 34, 39

Co-op America, 70–71

Cooperative Coffees, 53

Copper, 247

Corbett, J. B., 48

Core values, 50

"Corn" economy, 240

Cornell, T., 50

Corn ethanol, 173

Corporate culture, 173–174

Corporate Equality Index, 76

"Corporate immune response," 178–179

Corrugated cardboard, 167

Cost(s):
  eco-, 187–189
  ecological, of renewable resources, 173
  life cycle, 189
  true, 64–65, 140
  virtual, 189
  whole life, 189

Costa Rica, 123

Council of Economic Advisors, 6

Council of Northeastern Governors (CONEG), 112

Council on Environmental Quality, 97

Crabs, 157

Cradle to Cradle^{SM} (C2C^{SM}), 27, 39, 64, 81, 145, 167, 205–212

Craftsmanship, 12

Credibility, building, 51

Cross-fertilization, 145

Crown Holdings, Inc., 248

CRT, *see* Caux Round Table

Crystals, cholesteric, 164–165

Cultural Creatives, 24, 99, 101–102

Culture, corporate, 173–174

Curbside recycling, 56

Currency, 62

Current state, desired vs., 180–181

Cycles, 138, 167, 185–187

Czech Republic, 120

D

Databases, 57

DeBeers Group, 248

Decay, 138

Deceptive practices, 84–85. *See also* Greenwashing

Decisions (product), 189

Decision making:
  in-store, 71
  styles of, 151

Defensive measures, to change, 176–177

Degradability, claims of, 88–89

Dehiscence, 161

Dehydration resistance, 163

Delays, in systems, 180

Delicia pulchra, 163–164

Dell Computer, 28

Demographics, 99–101

Deposit, container, 112

Description, in systems view, 140, 141

Desertification, 175

Design checklists, 154

Designers, adaptation by, 143

Designers Accord, 81

Design language, 154–155

Design mindfulness, 219

Desired state, current vs., 180–181

Dimensions, design, 152, 154

Dioxins, 229

Dispersal, 161, 166

Disposable diaper liners, 90

Distance, 254

Distant Village, 69, 98, 104–105

Diversity, and sustainability, 174, 175

Domes, 161

Dominica, 122

Dow Jones Sustainability World Index, 27

Downspouts, 174

Driving, 48–49

Duals System Deutschland (DSD), 111

E

Early adopters, 178

Early majority, 178

Earth Charter, 20

Easter Islanders, 2

Eco-advocates, 63

Eco-costs approach, 187–189

Eco-costs to value ratio (EVR), 188, 189

Eco Enterprises Quebec, 114

Eco-labeling, 72, 74–78

Ecological economics, 11

Ecological footprint, 5

EcoLogo™, 82, 280

Ecology, commercial and industrial, 141

Eco-marketing, 74–78

Eco Mark program, 280

Eco-materials, vii–viii, 223

Eco-ness, 78

Economics, 184

Economic system, 139

Economist, 16, 25, 66–67

Economy, market-based, 63

Economy of scale, 149

Eco-packaging, viii, 104, 268

Ecopackaging.net, viii

Eco-products, 102–103

Eco-resources, 284–287

Edelman, Eric, xviii

Edge areas, environmental, 157

Efficiency, 50, 254

Eggs, 163

Eggplants, 160

Egg sacs, insect, 161

Eggshells, 158

Elimination, of functions, 146

Elkington, John, 26

Elm, Tyler, 35

Empowerment:
consumer, 62–63
stakeholder, 71
of women, 71

Encyclopedia of Earth, 248

End of life, 184

Energy, 237, 252, 254–257
dissipation of, 162
free, 170
regulating, 148

Energy Star rating, 154

Environment, adaptation to, 142–149

Environmental Achievement Award, 152

Environmental best practices, 194

Environmental Facts label, 75–76

Environmental impact, of packaging, 126–128

Environmental Management Systems, 184

Environmental Marketing Guidelines (FTC), 83

Environmental Paper Network, xvi, 231
"Why What's In Your Paper Matters," 230

Environmental Protection Agency (EPA), 79, 96, 110, 131, 152, 214, 226, 247, 262, 263

Environmental Working Group, 247

EnviroShell®, 39

EPA, *see* Environmental Protection Agency

The Essence of Permaculture (David Holmgren), 173

Ethanol, 173

Ethics-based marketing, 65–67

Ethnographics, 101–102

EU, *see* European Union

Eureka Recycling, xvi

European Commission, 76

European Union (EU), 19, 34, 76, 111

Evolution, 157

EVR, *see* Eco-costs to value ratio

Existing systems, enhancing, 174

Experimentation, 219, 273

Externalities, environmental, 126

Extinction, 142

Eye-catching design, 49

F

Failure, product, 142

Fair Trade, 26, 70–71, 275–276

Fair Trade Certified™ products, 70, 71, 276, 280

Fair Trade Labeling Organization, 70

Faludi, Jeremy, xii–xiii, 77
"Nutrition Facts Panel for a Healthier Planet," 75
"If It Can't Be Grown, It Must Be Mined," 244

Familiarity, 49, 51

Farrell, J., 50

Fast food industry, 176

Federal Trade Commission (FTC), 78, 278. *See also* FTC Green Guides

Feedback, 140, 148, 157, 171

Fibbing, 82, 277

Filter, package as, 148

Finland, 227, 231

Fish, 163

Fitzgerald, Patrick, 263–264 215

"Flat earth" thinking, 135

Flat earth worldview, 135–136

Flexibility, 160

Foam, in nature, 162, 163

Foamed starch, 238

Foam nester frogs, 163

Foam polystyrene cups, 92

Focus groups, 57, 99

Folding strategies, 160

Force, distribution of, 161

Ford, Henry, 239

Ford teamwork principle, 138

Forests and forest management, 4–5, 10, 67, 157, 175, 230

Forest fires, 163

Forest Stewardship Council (FSC), 82, 231, 280–281

Fortune 500 companies, 29

Fractals, 136

Framing, message, 54–55

France, 119–122

Free energy, 170

Free fuel, 170

Friction, reduction, 162

Frito-Lay, 256

Frogs, 163

Frozen dinners, 94

Fruit, 160, 163, 166

FSC, *see* Forest Stewardship Council

FTC, *see* Federal Trade Commission

FTC Green Guides, 78–79, 83–98
    environmental assessment, 97
    environmental marketing claims, 87–98
    general principles, 85–87
    interpretation and substantiation of claims, 84–85
    review procedure, 84
    scope of guides, 83–84
    statement of purpose, 83
    structure of guides, 84

Fuel, free, 170

Fuller, R. Buckminster, xi, 134–136, 138, 142

Full life cycle label, 76–77

Fun, 50

Function, 140, 146–147
    in LCA, 186
    in permaculture, 172

Functional Relationships, 169

Funding, and producer responsibility, 109

Furanone, 164

G

Gabel, Medard, 135

Gallium, 246

Game theory, 16–17

Gander, P., 55

Gas exchanges, 163

GATT, 23

GDP, *see* Gross Domestic Product

Genuine Progress Index (GPI), 6

Geodesic dome, 134–135, 138

Germany, 72, 111, 119–124

Ghana, 123

GHG emissions, *see* Greenhouse gas emissions

Gips, Terry, xiii
    "Natural Step Framework (NSF)," 197

Giscard d'Estaing, Olivier, 22

Glass, 250–252

Glass packaging, 63, 64, 119

Glass Plus, 14-15

Global issues, 116–125, 129. *See also* Producer

responsibility
    materials markets, 117
    purposes of packaging, 117–118
    supply chain, 117
    trade, 119–125

Global Reporting Initiative (GRI), 26, 28

Gold, 245

Gonen, Ron, 264

Good Practice, 248

Goodwin, Neva, 7

Gore, Al, 77, 255

Government policy, 126–128

GPI (Genuine Progress Index), 6

Grand Canyon, 247

Graphics, 149

Grass, 174

"Green," 47, 48, 82–83, 281

Green chemistry, 194

Green Dot, *see* Grüne Punkt

Green-e, 281

Green glass, 252

Green Guard, 82

Greenhouse gas (GHG) emissions, 226, 227, 230, 262–263

Green Seal, 82, 281

Greenwashing, 47, 48, 79, 82–83, 276–277

Greeting cards, 94

GRI, *see* Global Reporting Initiative

Grocery sacks, 86

Groom, Nichola, 35

Gross, D., 48

Gross Domestic Product (GDP), 6, 7, 11, 122

Gross National Happiness, 6

Ground cover (plants), 172

Growth potential, 184

Grüne Punkt (Green Dot), 111, 281

The Guide to Tree-free Recycled and Certified Papers (Dan Imhoff), 232

Guyana, 122

H

Haberman, Fred, xiii, 74
    "Communicating a Product's Story," 72

Habit, 49

Hagfish, 165

Halsey, Dan, xiii, 169
    "Permaculture Principles in Design," 169

Hanover Principles, 20–21

Hawken, Paul, 26

Hayden, Thomas, 224

HCFCs (hydrochlorofluorocarbons), 96

HDPE, *see* High density polyethylene

Heritage Flakes, 2–4

Heuristics, 51

Hickle, Garth, xiii–xiv
    Chapter 4, 108–115

Hidden trade-off, 82, 276

High density polyethylene (HDPE), 235–236

Hiking, 173

Hippocratic Oath, 17

Holistic view, 100, 134. *See also* Systems thinking (systems view)

Holmberg, John, 197

Holmgren, David, 169

Home Depot, 67

Honduras, 123

Honesty, 28

Hong Kong, 124, 125

Hook and loop tape, 157

Horse, 163

House sparrow, 150

Housing, 135

HP, 76

Human behavior, 41–58
  and attention, 48–49
  and awareness of others' behavior, 50–51
  and barriers to action, 55–56
  and basic needs, 43–45
  case study, 53
  and communication, 54–55
  and knowledge, 46–48
  and motivation, 49–50
  and perception, 45–46
  researching, 42, 57–58

Human capital, 26

Human centered design, 154

Human factors, 56

Human Rights Campaign, 76

Humidity, absolute, 288

Hyatt, John Wesley, Jr., 239

Hydrochlorofluorocarbons (HCFCs), 96

Hygrochastic capsules, 161

I

ICLEI (International Council for Local Environmental Initiatives), 26

Icosahedral symmetry, 161

IDSA, *see* Industrial Designers Society of America

IKEA, 48

Image, 50

Imhoff, Dan, 232

Impact resistance, 161–162

Impacts, material, 186, 187

Improvement processes, 215–217

Inattentional blindness, 45–46

Income, renewable resources as, 173

An Inconvenient Truth (film), 255

India, 124, 128

Indifferents, 100

Indigenous peoples, 231

Indium, 247

Individuality, expression of, 42

Indonesia, 124

Industrial Arts, age of, 12

Industrial Design, age of, 12

Industrial Designers Society of America (IDSA), 13, 214

Industrial ecology, 141, 181–183

Industrial metabolism, 181, 182

Industrial Revolution, 12

Informal reviews, 151

Information:
  as design requirement, 143
  organization with, 138
  presenting, 47
  processing of, 48

Information flow, 180

Initiative for Responsible Mining Assurance (IRMA), 248

Ink, toxic, 149

Innovation, 217–221, 269–275

Innovators, 178, 180

Innovest Strategic Value Advisors, 32–33

In-store decision making, 71

Interaction, in permaculture, 170

Interchange, 148–149

Interconnections, 136, 151

Interface(s):
  active, 165
  environmental, 143

International Council for Local Environmental Initiatives (ICLEI), 26

International Institute for Environment and Development, 232

International Trade Center (ITC), 128

Intertidal zones, 161

Iowa State University, 77

IRMA (Initiative for Responsible Mining Assurance), 248

Irrelevance, 82, 277

ISO 14000, 154, 184–185

Italy, 120–122, 124

ITC (International Trade Center), 128

J

Jamaica, 122, 128

Japan, 21, 78, 113, 124, 160, 164

Jedlička, Wendy, xi
  Chapter 1, 1–34
  Chapter 3, 61–106
  Chapter 6, 233–266

Jedlička Design Ltd., 270

Jeffords, Jim, 112

JIT, *see* Just-in-time

Johnson Foundation, 17

Johnson & Johnson, 4, 177

Jones, Hannah, 70

Jordan, 123

Just-in-time protection, 162

K

Kaku, Ryuzaburo, 22

Kalkowski, John, 34

Kangaroo's pouch, 160

Kasser, T., 45

Keratin, 162

Kiernan, Matthew, 33

Kiribati, 122

Kjelleberg, Staffan, 163–164

Knoend, 81

Knowledge, 46–48, 55

Korea, 113, 123

Kuznets, Simon, 7

Kyosei, 21, 23–24

Kyoto Protocol, 17, 67

L

Landfill Methane Outreach Program (LMOP), 263

Landscape design, 174

Language, design, 154–155

Lao-tzu, 1

Late majority, 178

Lawn and leaf bags, 90

Lawn-care pesticides, 88

Laws, 118. *See also* Producer responsibility

LCA, *see* Life Cycle Analysis; Life cycle assessment

LCC (life cycle costs), 189

LCM (life cycle management) approach, 185

LDPE (low-density polyethylene), 236

Lead, 246

Lead paint, 141–142, 151

Lean enterprise, 216

Leatherman, 39

Leaves, 160, 164

Lebow, Victor, 6

L.E.K. Consulting, 256

Lesser of two evils, 82–83, 277

Lettuce, 160

Levelling down, 146

Levelling up, 146

LG Electronics, 39

Liebreich, Michael, 16, 17

Life, working principles of, 166–168

Life cycle:
package, 157
product, 140, 141

Life Cycle Analysis (LCA), 73, 76

Life cycle assessment (LCA), 26–27, 146, 183–186, 205
eco-costs approach vs., 185–189
steps in, 185–187

Life cycle costs (LCC), 189

Life cycle inventory, 186

Life cycle management (LCM) approach, 185

Life cycle thinking, 183

Life spans, of products, 166

Lifetime, physical, 152

Light, reflection of, 164

Lightening, package, 146

Liking, 51

Lindqvist, Thomas, 108

Linear consumption, 2

Lite2go, 80, 81

Literature reviews, 42, 57

Litwin, M. S., 58

Livingry, 135

LMOP (Landfill Methane Outreach Program), 263

Locality, 219, 273

Local sourcing, 170

Logging practices, 67

LOHAS group, 99–101

Loops, 140, 141, 157, 180

Lost resources, 170

Lotus-Effect™ 164

Lovins, Amory, 26, 135

Lovins, Hunter, 26, 135

Low-density polyethylene (LDPE), 236

Lubber, Mindy S., 14

Lubricating oil, 170

Luke, John A., Jr., 27–28

Lund University, 108

Luttenberger, David, 32

Lyons, Susan, 206

M

Macaskie, Lynne, 247

McCormick Distilling, 194–195, 283

McDonough, William, 8, 44, 46, 107, 135, 206, 248

McGee, Tim, xiv, "Biomimicry"158

McKenzie-Mohr, Doug, 55

McNamara, Amelia, xvii

McNamara, Curt, xiv Chapter 5, 133-222

MacReady, Paul, 135

Majority, early vs. late, 178

Malawi, 123, 128

Malnutrition, 4

Malta, 123

Manitoba, 114

Manitoba Product Stewardship Council (MPSC), 114

Manning, Christie, xiv, 58 Chapter 2, 41–60

Marginal areas, of resources, 175–176

Marketability, 184

Market-based economy, 63

Market-based mechanisms, 11

Market capitalism, 7

Marketing, 61–104
case studies, 68–69,
80–81
and consumer relationship, 62–65
and Co-op America's Guide to Fair Trade, 70–71
and customer "need," 99–104
eco-, 74–78
ethics-based, 65–67
and FTC Green Guides, 83–98
with packaging, 71–74
social, 55–56
and social justice, 66–67, 70
of thing vs. service, 74
and truthful communication, 78–79, 82–83

Marketing claims, environmental, 87–98
compostability claims, 89–90
degradability claims, 88–89
general claims, 87–88
ozone-related claims, 96
recyclability claims, 90–93
recycled content, 93–95
refillability claims, 96
source reduction, 95

Martin, Joshua "Why What's In Your Paper Matters," 230

Marty Metro, 131

Mass production, 62

Materials, local, 166–167

Material health, 192

Material impacts, 186, 187

Materialism, 45

Material self-interest, 51

Matrices:
for containment, 160
for protection, 162
sustainability, 187

Maximization, optimization vs., 138

MeadWestvaco, 27–28

Meaning, discovering, 45

MEMS display™ (Qualcomm), 164

Mercury, 110, 246

Mercury-Containing and Rechargeable Battery Management Act, 97–98

Message framing, 54–55

Metabolix, 238

Metal, 242–249
aluminum, 243
and mining, 244–248
steel, 243–244

Metal packaging, 63, 64, 119

Methane, 230

Mexico, 119, 121, 124

Microbes, protection from, 163–164

Micro Electronic Memory Systems (MEMS) display™ (Qualcomm), 164

Micropatterning, 164

Micro-replication, 145

Microsoft, 39

Milk cartons, 116

Mindless behavior, 49

Mineral Information Institute, 245

Mining, 244–248

The Minnesota Principles, 22

Minnovation, 53

Mobility, 219, 273

Moes, John, xvii–xviii

Moldova, 122, 123

Mollison, Bill, 169

Monetary capital, 27

Money, 6

Monocrops, 175

Morgan, D. L., 57

Morpho butterfly, 164

Mother-of-pearl, 161

Motivation(s), 42, 49–50

MPSC (Manitoba Product Stewardship Council), 114

Mulch film, 89

Multitasking, 42, 49

Mussels, 161, 162

N

Namibia, 122

NaPP (National Packaging Protocol), 113

National Beverage Producer Responsibility Act of 2003, 112

National Carpet Recycling Agreement, 110

National Environmental Policy Act, 97

National Marketing Institute, 100

National Mercury Auto Switch Agreement, 110

National Packaging Covenant (NPC), 114–115

National Packaging Protocol (NaPP), 113

National Recycling Coalition (NRC), 261, 262

National Starch & Chemical, 238

"Natural," 281

Natural capital, 26–27

Natural Capitalism (Hawken, Lovins & Lovins), 26

Natural Step Framework (NSF), 197–200

Natural Step method, 66, 244

Nature, distribution model of, 42

Nature's Path, 2–4

NatureWorks, 238

Nautilus, 161

Need(s):
basic, 43–45
customer, 99–104
wants vs., 99

Negative feedback, 171

Negative feedback loops, 180

Nelson, Tom, xvii

Netherlands, 123, 124

New Energy Finance, 16

New products, failure of, 8–9

The New Science of Biodegradable Plastics (E. S. Stevens), 239, 240

New Scientist, 246, 247

New World, 6

New York City, 261, 263

New York Times Magazine, 19

New Zealand, 231

Niche, in marketplace, 150–151

Niger, 174

Nike, 28, 67, 70

NOAH, 245

Nomadics, 100

Nonrenewable resources, 173

"Nontoxic," 281

No proof, sin of, 82, 276

Noranda, Inc., 248

Norman, D., 56

Novelty, 50

NPC, *see* National Packaging Covenant

NRC, *see* National Recycling Coalition

NSF, *see* Natural Step Framework

Nuclear power plants, 134

Nutrients, technical, 147

Nutrition facts panel, 75, 76

O

O2 International Network for Sustainable Design, 81, 201–203

Objectives, technical, 143

Observation, 57, 170

OECD, *see* Organization for Economic Cooperation and Development

Office, reducing waste in, 172

Oil, 64, 170, 227

Okala Design Guide, 214

OLPC, *see* "One Laptop per Child"

1Bowl Campaign, 152

100% Recycled Paper Alliance (RPA-100%), 232

"One Laptop per Child" (OLPC), 36–37

One-time photographic cameras, 92

Ontario, 113–114, 252

Open-minded, the, 54–55

Open systems, 179

Opportunism, 138

Optimization, 160
maximization vs., 138
of resources, 192
of single attribute, 139

Oregon, 112

Organic Trade Association (OTA), 69

Organisms, products as, 150

Organization for Economic Cooperation and Development (OECD), 108, 110

Origami, 160

Orr, David, xv

OTA (Organic Trade Association), 69

Ottman, Jacquelyn, xiv–xv
Chapter 3, 61–106

Overconsumption, 5–6

Overdesigning, 146

Overengineering, 193

Overgrazing, 4

Overpopulation, 4

Overstatement of environmental attribute, 86

Oxfam America, 248

Oxygen, passage of, 163

Ozone-related claims, 96

P

Package, systems definition of, 141–142

Packagedesignmag.com, viii

Package Design Mazagine, xvi

Package innovation, 218, 272

Packaging:
as customer attractant, 140
defined, 307
encouraging consumer choice with, 72–74
"good" vs. "great," 71–72
as percentage of waste, 226
trade in manufactured, 119–123

Packaging Digest, 34–35

Packaging Directive (European Union), 111, 112

Packaging materials, trade in, 123

Packaging Strategies, xvi, 32

Pagani, Marco, 246

Paint, lead, 141–142, 151

Paper(s), 82, 229–233
alternative, 232–233, 278
benefits of, 229
choices involving, 230–231
and printing, 259
recycling of, 229
waste of, 172
wood based, 229

Paperboard, 94, 119

Paper packaging, 119

Papilio butterfly, 164

Paradigms, 177

Passive permaculture principles, 170–172

Patterns, 154–155
and change, 177–178
in permaculture, 173–174

PCR (post-consumer recycled), 282

PCW (post consumer waste), 282

Peace Coffee, 52–53

Peacock, 164

Peak minerals, 246

Pearson, Ian, 77–78

Pelican, 160

"People + Planet + Profit," 26–27

Perception, 45–46

Perennial plants, 172

Permaculture (David Holmgren), 169

Permaculture principles, 169–177
observing and interacting as, 170–172
obtaining a yield from, 172–174
passive, 170–172
proactive, 172–174
progressive, 174–176
using small and slow solutions with, 174–176

Personal care products, 82

Perspective(s):
changes in, 140
continuum of, 142
diversity in, 182

Pesticides, lawn-care, 88

PETE (polyethylene terephthalate), 235

Pet Rock, 64, 104

PHA, 238

Pharmaceutical industry, 4

PHB, 237–238

PHBV, 238

Phillips, Frederick, 22

Phosphate rock, 246

Phospholipids, as boundary, 144

"Photodegradable," 88–89

Photographic cameras, one-time, 92

Physical lifetime, 152

Physiological needs, 43

Pi, 135

Pink, Daniel, 134

PLA (polylactide acid), 238

Plants, 157, 160, 165, 172

Plastics, 234–240
biobased (renewable), 237–240
nonrenewable, 235–236
recycling of, 235–236

Plastic bags, 224

Plastic packaging, 119

Plastic water bottles, 56

Platform design, 149

"Playing Games with the Planet" (*Economist* article), 16

Pleasure, desire for, 44

Point solutions, 141

Poland, 120, 122

Policy Statement on the Advertising Substantiation Doctrine (FTC), 85

Pollination, 136, 157

Polyethylene terephthalate (PETE, PET), 235

Polylactide acid (PLA), 238

Polypropylene (PP), 236

Polystyrene (PS), 236

Polystyrene cups, 92

Polyvinyl chloride (PVC), 39, 236

Ponderosa pine, 163

Positive feedback, 171 loops, 180

Post-consumer materials, 93

Post-consumer recycled (PCR), 282

Post consumer waste (PCW), 282

Potash, 246

Potatoes, 162

Poverty, 12–13

PP (polypropylene), 236

Pragmatists, 178

Precautionary principle, 17–19

Pre-consumer materials, 93

Pre-consumer waste, 282

Predators, 157

Pre-production planning (3P), 216

Preservatives, 163

Preserve™ Tableware (Recycline), 58–59

Price, 12
and Fair Trade, 70
selling, 63, 64

PricewaterhouseCoopers LLP, 9

Prichard, Hazel, 247

Printing, 257–260

Prioritization, 152

"Prisoner's dilemma," 16

PROs, see Producer Responsibility Organizations

Proactive permaculture principles, 172–174

Process innovation, 218, 272

Producer responsibility, 108–115
in Asia, 112–113
in Australia, 114–115
in Canada, 113–114
in European Union, 111
and funding, 109
implementation mechanisms for, 109–110
individual vs. collective, 109
and level playing field, 109
need for, 110
in United States, 109–110, 112

Producer responsibility laws, 71–72

Producer Responsibility Organizations (PROs), 109, 111

Products, 150

Product failure, 142

Productivity, 49

Product life cycle, 140, 141

Product stewardship, 108. See also Producer responsibility

Profit, 27

Progressive permaculture principles, 174–176

Propaganda, 54

Protection:
and biomimicry, 161–164
as design requirement, 143
just-in-time, 162
long-term vs. short-term, 176–177

PS (polystyrene), 236

Psychological needs, 43–44

PVC, see Polyvinyl chloride

Q

Quality, 192–193, 254

Quantity, as value, 50

Quebec, 114

R

Radio-frequency identification (RFID), 144

Rainforest, 255

Ray, Paul H., 24, 99, 101, 102

REACH, 19, 76

Reciprocation, 51

Reconditioned components, 93

Recovery, resource, 192

Recyclability, claims of, 90–93, 282

"Recyclable," 85, 86

RecycleBank, 264

Recycled (term), 86, 282

Recycled content:
claims of, 93–95
disclosure of, 66
expanding use of, 193–194
laws, 112

Recycline, 58–59

Recycling:
benefits of, 261–262
and carbon accounting, 256
curbside, 56
designing for, 196
encouraging, 263–264
of glass, 251–252

by living systems, 134, 138
of metals, 243, 246
of paper, 229
of plastics, 235–236
rates of, 226–227

Recycling Economic Information Project, 261

RECYC-Quebec, 114

Reductionism, 133–134, 138, 139

Redwood trees, 167

"Refillable," 96

Refill pouches, 221

Reflection, color display via, 164

Relations, in systems view, 140–141

Relationship, consumer, 62–65

Remanufactured components, 93

Renewable resources, 173

Replication, 145

Requirements engineering, 181–182

Research, 42, 57–58

Resources:
compartmentalization of, 174
lost, 171
renewable vs. non-renewable, 173

Resource recovery, 192

Resources Recycling and Reuse Act (Taiwan), 113

Resource use, 76

Responsibility, producer, see Producer responsibility

Responsible sourcing, 192

Responsive packaging, 165–166

Restorative consumption, 6–8

Restorative economy, 201

Restore Products, 74

"Reusable," 86

Reusable bags, 224–226

Reusable containers, 24–25, 167

Reuse:
designing for, 196
in permaculture, 172

Reusing waste, 145

Review procedure (FTC Green Guides), 84

Reviews, informal, 151

RFID, *see* Radio-frequency identification

Rhenium, 246

Rhino horns, 162

Rivers, 175

Robbins, Holly, xvii

Robert, Karl Henrik, 197

Robinson Mine (Nevada), 244

RockTenn, 227–228

Rohner, 206

RPA-100% (100% Recycled Paper Alliance), 232

Rudders, 136

Russia, 230, 231

S

Sacrificial material, 163

Safety and security, need for, 44

St. Lucia, 122

Salazar, Dennis, xv, 14

Sam's Club, 39

Samsung, 39

Sandfish lizard, 162

San Francisco, California, 19

Saudi Arabia, 123

Scarcity, 51

Schultz, P. W., 42

Sea cucumber, 162

Security, 157

Seeds, 152, 157, 161

Seed pods, 42

Seiko, 39

Selenium, 246

Self-assembly, 145

Self-cleaning surfaces, 164

Self-fulfillment, 45

Self-interest, material, 51

Self-regulation, 171

Self-repair, 162

Selling environment, 8–9

Selling price, 63, 64

Senge, Peter, xix

Service, thing vs., 74

Seychelles, 122

SFI (Sustainable Forestry Initiative), 282

Shampoos, 82, 89

Shape, optimal, 160

Shelf life, 166

Shells, 157

Shield, 157

Shopping, 49

Shortcuts, 51

Shuchu kiyaku, 21

Side-by-side planting, 174

Sierra Club, 7, 11

Silver, 247

SimaPro (modeling software), 187, 188

Simplicity, and perception, 45

Singapore, 123

Six-pack ring carriers, 89

Six Sigma, 216

Six Sins of Greenwashing, 82–83

Size, 254

Skin:
human, 162, 165
as packaging, 146

Smith, Pamela, xv
Chapter 4, 116–132

Snails, 161, 163

Snakeskin, 158

Soap, 89

Social acceptability, 45, 47, 48

Social comparisons, 50

Social connections, need for, 44

Social influence, 54

Social justice, and marketing, 66–67, 70

Social marketing, 55–56

Social needs, 43–44

Social norms, creating, 56

Social proof, 51

Society of Plastics Industry (SPI), 90

Soft drink bottles, 86

Soil, as asset, 173

Soil saturation, reducing, 174

Solar energy, 170

Solution space, 219, 273

Source, 254–255

Source reduction:
claims of, 95
continuous, 193

Sourcing:
local, 170
responsible, 192

Soy-based ink, 282

Spain, 120

Spam, 157

SPC, *see* Sustainable Packaging Coalition[SM]

Speedo, 38, 39

SPI (Society of Plastics Industry), 90

SPI code, 90

Splitting, of functions, 146

SRI World Group, 33

Stakeholders, design evaluation by, 152

Stakeholder connections, 141

Stakeholder empowerment, 71

"Standard of living," 245

Standard work, 215

Starch-based polymers, 238

Starch foam, 264-265

StarchTech, 238

Steel, 243–244

Steffen, Alex, 77

Steinberg, Peter, 163–164

Sterling, Bruce, 77

Stern Review, 255

Stevens, E. S., 239, 240

Stewardship Ontario, 114

Stocks (stockpiles), 180

Stomata, 165

Stored energy, 171

Strawberries, 160

Structure, package as, 157

Subsidies, 179

Sudman, Sharon, xvii

Sugar, 162

Sunflowers, 160

Sunoco, 29

SuperEnd® can, 248–249

Supply chain, 117

Support, 157

Suriname, 122

Surveys, 57–58

Sustainability, 139
  barriers to, 55
  checklist for design
    strategies for, 193–
    194, 196
  defining, 10
  and Fair Trade, 70
  and interchange, 148–
    149
  misconceptions about,
    10–11
  and packaging, 42
  in product decisions,
    189

Sustainability Survey
  Report, 9

Sustainable Forestry Initiative (SFI), 282

Sustainable packaging, 268

Sustainable Packaging
  Coalition℠ (SPC), xvi,
  9–10, 34–35, 268
  definition of sustainable

packaging, 166–167,
  191–192
  design guidelines, 192–
    196

Sustainable Packaging Fo-
  rum, 32, 35, 39

Swales, 170

Swartz, Jeffrey, 29

Swim bladders, 163

Switzerland, 227

Syria, 123

Systems:
  closed loop, 182
  open, 179

Systems analysis, 181–182

Systems thinking (systems
  view), 103–104, 133–221
  and adaptation to envi-
    ronment, 142–149
  and biomimicry,
    158–168
  boundary in, 143–145
  and change manage-
    ment, 177–181
  cycles in, 185–187
  in design, 139–142, 151,
    152, 154–155, 157–
    158, 183–184
  and eco-costs approach,
    187–189
  feedback and inter-
    change in, 148–149
  Buckminster Fuller as
    pioneer of, 134–135
  function in, 146–147
  as holistic view, 134
  and improvement
    processes, 215–217
  in industrial ecology,
    181–183
  and innovation, 217–221
  and ISO 14000, 184–185
  levels in, 149
  and Natural Step Frame-
    work, 197–200
  and package/product
    team, 151–152, 154–

155
  and permaculture
    principles, 169–177
  and prescriptive
    approaches, 200–214
  and reductionism, 133–
    134, 139
  and Sustainable Packag-
    ing Coalition guide-
    lines, 189–196
  taking advantage of,
    150–158
  technical approaches in,
    181–189
  universal principles of,
    135–139

T

Taiwan, 113

"Tamper-proof" packag-
  ing, 44

Tantalum, 245

Tanzania, 123

Tasmania, 230

Taxes, 179

Tazo Tea Infuser, 74

Teams:
  integration of, 174
  package/product, 151–
    152, 154–155, 157

Team learning, 141, 151

Team TreeHugger, 257

Technical nutrients, 147

Technology, 62, 181–189

Telemarketing, 99

Tellurium, 246

Tension, 136

TerraChoice Environ-
  mental Marketing, 79,
  82, 276

Tesco, 77, 256

Thackara, 219, 273

Thailand, 123

Thallium, 246

Thermostats, 148

Thing, service vs., 74

Third-party certifiers, 82

3M, 76, 145

3P (pre-production plan-
  ning), 216

Three part accounting
  method, 139

Ticks (animals), 160

Tiffany & Co., 248

Tilford, Dave, 5, 7, 11

The Timberland Com-
  pany, 29, 256

Timing factors, 103

Todd, John, 135, 218, 272

Togo, 122

Toll-free phone numbers, 82

Toner cartridges, 92–93, 95

Toshiba, 39

Total productive mainte-
  nance (TPM), 216

Total Quality Management
  (TQM), 215

Toucan, 161–162

"Toward a Sustainable Pa-
  per Cycle" (report), 232

Toxics in Packaging Clearinghouse, 112

Toxins:
  in metals, 243–244
  in plastics, 235, 237

Toyota, 76

TQM (Total Quality
  Management), 215

Trade:
  in manufactured pack-
    aging, 119–123

in packaging materials, 123

in waste materials, 123–125

Trader Joe's, 240–241

TransFair USA, 280

Transparency, 28

Transport, designing for, 194

Trash, 226

Trash bags, 86, 89

Tree bark, 162

Tree plantings, 175

Trees, 63, 151, 167, 173, 230

Trendiness, 50

Trimtabs, 136

Triple Bottom Line, 24–27

Triple Top Line, 139

Triz (creativity technique), 154

True cost, 64, 65

Trust, 47

Truthful communication, 78–79, 82–83

Turkey, 123

Twinkie, 166

Tylenol murders, 4, 177

U

UCB (UsedCardboard-Boxes.com), 131

Underconsumption, 4–5

United Kingdom:
coastline of, 135–136
recycling rates in, 227
and trade in packaging and waste, 119, 121, 122, 124

United Nations, 17, 18, 22, 29, 119, 152, 263

United States:
ecological footprint of, 5
eco-marketing in, 78, 79
producer responsibility in, 109–110, 112
and trade in packaging and waste, 119–125

United States Department of Agriculture (USDA), 178

United States Geological Survey (USGS), 245, 246

Universal principles, 135–139

University of the Arts, 145

Uruku lipstick (Aveda), 30–31

U.S. News & World Report, 224

U.S. Postal Service, 115

USDA (United States Department of Agriculture), 178

User Pays, 108

Users, learning from, 219, 273

USGS, *see* United States Geological Survey

V

Vagueness, 82, 276–277

Value:
for collection, 145
of renewable resources, 173

Value systems, 50

Van der Ryn, Sim, 218, 272

Variety, 138

VCRs (video cassette recorders), 95

Vegetables, as containers, 160

Vegetable-based ink, 282

Video cassette recorders (VCRs), 95

Viewpoints, multiple, 151

Vineyards, 177

Virtual costs, 189

Viruses:
biological, 161
computer, 157

Visual controls, 215

Volatile organic compounds (VOCs), 88, 96

W

Wants, needs vs., 99

Waste:
manufacturer, 145
in permaculture, 172

Waste Diversion Act (Ontario), 113–114

Waste Diversion Ontario, 114

Waste materials, trade in, 123–125

Water, collection of, 170

Water bottles, plastic, 56

Watermelons, 160

Web sites, 57, 82

Weeds, 177

Weight, 254

Weiten, W., 46, 50

Whole Foods Market, 224–225

Whole life costs (WLC), 189

A Whole New Mind (Daniel Pink), 134

Wiley Encyclopedia of Packaging Technology, x

Willow tree, 174

Winterborne, 39

WLC (whole life costs), 189

Women, empowerment of, 71

Wood based paper, 229

Wood packaging, 119

Workflow, 174

World Charter for Nature, 18–20

World Commission on Environment and Development (Brundtland Commission), 10

World Summit on Social Development, 22

World Wildlife Fund, 248

Worst case, designing for, 145, 146

Wrong environment, design for, 143

Y

Yale University, 47

Yellowstone National Park, 167

Z

Zelezny, L., 42

Zimbabwe, 128

Zirconium, 246

Zone of acceptability, 42, 44, 47

Zuess, Dion, xv

**Man is not apart from Nature,
but a part of Nature.**

Unknown